"The Kensingtons"
13TH LONDON REGIMENT

HER ROYAL HIGHNESS
PRINCESS LOUISE, DUCHESS OF ARGYLL, G.B.E., C.I., R.R.C.

[*Frontispiece.*

"The Kensingtons"
13TH LONDON REGIMENT

By
SERGEANT O. F. BAILEY
and
SERGEANT H. M. HOLLIER

Published by the
REGIMENTAL OLD COMRADES' ASSOCIATION

13TH LONDON REGIMENT
(PRINCESS LOUISE'S KENSINGTON REGIMENT)

(*Forms part of the Corps of the King's Royal Rifle Corps*)

The Arms of the Royal Borough of Kensington
Quid nobis ardui.

"South Africa, 1900–02."

The Great War—3 *Battalions.*—" **Neuve Chapelle,**" " **Aubers,**" " **Somme, 1916, '18,**" " Albert, 1916, '18," " Guillemont," " Ginchy," " Flers-Courcelette," " Morval," " Le Transloy," " **Arras, 1917, '18,**" " Scarpe, 1917, '18," " **Ypres, 1917,**" " Langemarck, 1917," " **Cambrai, 1917, '18,**" " Hindenburg Line," " Canal du Nord," " Valenciennes," " Sambre," " France and Flanders, 1914–18. " **Doiran, 1917,**" " Macedonia, 1916–17," " **Gaza,**" " El Mughar," " Nebi Samwil," " **Jerusalem,**" " Jericho," " Jordan," " Megiddo," " **Sharon,**" " Palestine, 1917–18."

N.B.—*Those in heavy type are borne on the Regimental Colour.*

FOREWORD

BY

H.R.H. THE PRINCESS LOUISE, DUCHESS OF ARGYLL, G.B.E., C.I., R.R.C.

I HAVE been requested to add a short foreword to an interesting compilation which is about to appear and gives an account of the Thirteenth London Regiment, now called Princess Louise's Kensington Regiment.

There has been a desire to know how it was that my name became associated with the Regiment.

It was thus: I received a communication one day from His Majesty the King, saying that he had been approached by the 13th London Regiment with the request to obtain His Majesty's permission to associate my name with them, and that His Majesty had given his full consent.

I naturally was infinitely touched and proud on receiving this intimation that those with whom I had long lived should have wished to associate my name with themselves. From that day I have been able to watch their career with much interest and satisfaction.

FOREWORD

As the volume is already with the printers, I do not, therefore, like personally to touch on any particular point which is sure to be ably recorded.

But I feel I may add that when the orders were given that my Kensington Regiment was to prepare immediately to go to the Front I was often informed of their progress. Even their Chaplain (our Kensington Vicar, the Rev. Prebendary Pennefather) came and expounded his equal keenness and interest. He fully expected that he would follow with the Regiment he was so devoted to, but when told that age and health debarred him from doing so, he was a very sorry man and came to pour out his disappointment to me ; he even wept.

The Regiment went first to Abbots Langley, where they trained for active service. I visited them there, and attended their Church Parade.

On the day of the departure of the Regiment I well remember how they all came in full marching order to bid me farewell. A very affecting moment for all of us. Colonel Lewis (then in Command), when leaving their Headquarters, seized a tea-spoon from the mess table and pressed it in my hand as a remembrance of that day.

FOREWORD

It is interesting to note that the 2nd Battalion was on active service in France, the Balkans, Egypt, Palestine and Macedonia, both Battalions being heavily engaged on various occasions and frequently in very severe fighting.

It was very gratifying to learn that they received congratulations from the Generals Commanding the Divisions and Army Corps for the brilliant manner they carried out their duties.

All who were left behind watched with keen anxiety for news of them, and when news did come it was often sad indeed to learn of the many heavy casualties in dead and wounded. How sad I and all felt in those days for the many losses and the suffering the Regiment sustained it is difficult to express.

The record that the 13th London Regiment hold is one indeed to be proud of, and the many honours both Battalions have received are an ample proof of its recognition. We can but ever mourn for those fine fellows who gave their lives for their King, Home and Country, and are full of the deepest sympathy with those who have suffered, and still suffer, from effects of wounds, hardships and sickness. Yet we must be glad to feel

FOREWORD

that there are many who came home still amongst us, who went through the dangers in the front line, and who in their own way are able to tell the younger ones of the value of discipline, fellowship and loyalty, proving themselves an example of all that is best, and to be treasured and respected.

Louise

Kensington Palace

November 1935.

AUTHORS' PREFACE

IN this book the Old Comrades' Association of the 13th London Regiment (Princess Louise's Kensington Regiment) have attempted to record the early history of the " Kensingtons," the part they played in the Great War, and their post-war activities. The work has been rendered difficult owing to the lack of relevant material and the scarcity of official records: the authors acknowledge with sincere thanks the loan of certain diaries and other matter by fellow members of the O.C.A., without which the book could not have been completed. They are grateful to those who rendered invaluable assistance in many ways. Every effort has been made to ensure accuracy and a complete record, particularly of the years 1914–1919, but for errors and omissions the authors crave the reader's forbearance—one's memory is apt to play tricks after a lapse of twenty years.

The book is dedicated to the spirit of comradeship permeating the whole seventy-six years under review, and to the memory of the gallant Kensingtons whose supreme sacrifice we are proud to honour in these pages.

OLIVER F. BAILEY, 1st Battalion.
HAROLD M. HOLLIER, 2nd Battalion.

CONTENTS

CHAPTER		PAGE
I.	SEMPER PARATUS—QUID NOBIS ARDUI	1

THE 1st BATTALION

II.	MOBILISATION AND TRAINING	11
III.	A WINTER IN THE LINE	20
IV.	THE BATTLE OF NEUVE CHAPELLE	31
V.	AUBERS RIDGE—MAY 9TH, 1915	42
VI.	LINES OF COMMUNICATION	53
VII.	WITH THE 56TH DIVISION	60
VIII.	THE BATTLE OF JULY 1ST, 1916	72
IX.	THE SOMME	80
X.	LAVENTIE AGAIN	101
XI.	ON THE ARRAS FRONT	107
XII.	THE THIRD BATTLE OF YPRES	120
XIII.	THE CAMBRAI FRONT	131
XIV.	THE OPPY FRONT; AND THE GERMAN OFFENSIVE, 1918	143
XV.	THE FINAL BRITISH OFFENSIVE—BOYELLES AND BULLECOURT	167
XVI.	THE CANAL DU NORD	179
XVII.	OPEN WARFARE AND THE END	190

CONTENTS

THE 2ND BATTALION

CHAPTER		PAGE
XVIII.	ENGLAND—FORMATION AND TRAINING.	209
XIX.	FRANCE	225
XX.	SALONIKA	240
XXI.	PALESTINE	261
XXII.	KAUWUKAH—SHERIA—HUJ	288
XXIII.	THE BATTLE OF JERUSALEM	310
XXIV.	THE DEFENCE OF JERUSALEM	320
XXV.	JEBEL EKTEIF—JERICHO	330
XXVI.	THE SECOND RAID ACROSS THE JORDAN.	350
XXVII.	THE SUMMER LULL—1918	357
XXVIII.	THE SEPTEMBER OFFENSIVE—ARMISTICE	365
XXIX.	FINALE—EPILOGUE	373
XXX.	POST WAR	379
XXXI.	THE OLD COMRADES' ASSOCIATION	401
	ROLL OF HONOUR	407
	LIST OF HONOURS AND AWARDS	425
	INDEX	431

LIST OF MAPS

1st BATTALION

		PAGE
1.	NEUVE CHAPELLE, MARCH 1915	36
2.	AUBERS RIDGE, MAY 1915	45
3.	GOMMECOURT, JULY 1916	75
4.	THE SOMME, SEPTEMBER–OCTOBER 1916	87
5.	NEUVILLE VITASSE, APRIL 1917	111
6.	GENERAL MAP—ARRAS FRONT	113
7.	CAMBRAI, NOVEMBER 1917	137
8.	OPPY, WINTER 1917–18	154
9.	BOYELLES, AUGUST 1918	170
10.	BULLECOURT, AUGUST 1918	174
11.	CANAL DU NORD, SEPTEMBER–OCTOBER 1918	183
12.	THE ADVANCE ON MONS, NOVEMBER 1918	195

2nd BATTALION

13.	NEUVILLE ST. VAAST, 1916	229
14.	MACEDONIA, 1916–17	244
15.	ATTACK ON BEERSHEBA DEFENCES, 1917	278
16.	BATTLE OF KAUWUKAH, 1917	292
17.	AIN KARIM (JERUSALEM), 1917	311
18.	JORDAN AND ES SALT, 1917	340

LIST OF ILLUSTRATIONS

H.R.H. PRINCESS LOUISE, DUCHESS OF ARGYLL, G.B.E., C.I., R.R.C. . . . . . . *Frontispiece*

	FACING PAGE
GROUP OF 1ST BATTALION OFFICERS	16
FRONT LINE TRENCH, LAVENTIE, 1915	24
GENERAL VIEW OF THE BATTLEFIELD, GUILLEMONT, SEPTEMBER 1916	88
BATTLE OF ARRAS, APRIL 9TH, 1917. MOVING FORWARD FROM ASSEMBLY TRENCH	108
BATTLE OF ARRAS, APRIL 1917; 9·2 HOWITZERS, NEUVILLE VITASSE	114
GROUP OF 3RD BATTALION OFFICERS	207
GROUP OF 2ND BATTALION OFFICERS	219
2ND BATTALION BRIDGE-BUILDING AT KATERINA, JANUARY 1917	249
TURKISH POSITIONS TO THE WEST OF JERUSALEM	306
THE RAID ON AMMAN, MARCH 1918	344
PONTOON BRIDGE ACROSS THE RIVER JORDAN AT EL GHORANIYEH	356
GUARD OF HONOUR TO HIS MAJESTY THE KING, MAY 21ST, 1928	390
HER ROYAL HIGHNESS PRINCESS LOUISE AT THE KENSINGTON WAR MEMORIAL, NOVEMBER 4TH, 1928	390
WAR MEMORIAL AT HEADQUARTERS, KENSINGTON	407

CHAPTER I

SEMPER PARATUS—QUID NOBIS ARDUI

(Pre-war Chapter of Collaborated Notes Edited by
O. F. BAILEY)

IN order to trace the growth of the 13th London Regiment (Princess Louise's Kensington Regiment) as it is now known, it is necessary to turn back to the Volunteer movement of 1859. In that year the warlike policy of France under the Emperor Napoleon III aroused a distrust and anxiety in England which found its expression in the formation of a large number of Volunteer corps designed to ensure an adequate defence force in the event of invasion. The young men of London came forward prepared to enrol and train as soldiers, and the public generally were equally enthusiastic in subscribing to funds to defray in some measure the cost of arming the Volunteers. Some indication of the vigour of the movement is shown by the fact that over 100,000 men enrolled during the first year following the inception of the movement. Men of rank and position devoted their time and energy to the task of forming Volunteer corps, and among the most active of these were Lord Truro and Lord Ranelagh. The former founded the 4th Middlesex Volunteer Corps in Islington in 1859, and also a light horse cavalry known as the Middlesex Cavalry, and an artillery brigade, the 3rd Middlesex Artillery. In similar fashion the "Victorias," or 1st Middlesex, and the "South," or 2nd Middlesex, owed their existence to the zeal and enthusiasm of Lord Ranelagh. The 4th Middlesex V.R.C. and the 2nd (South) Middlesex V.R.C. were destined to become the present Kensingtons.

Although the war scare was of short duration, the newly formed Volunteer units had come to stay. The enthusiasm of these early volunteers was of no mean order; spurred by the highest motives of self-sacrifice and devotion to their country, they bore the expense of their equipment and training apart from such assistance as was provided by public voluntary subscription. They trained themselves as well as circumstances allowed and then offered their services to the Government. All the official encouragement they received was a grudging acknowledgment of their existence and an acceptance of their offer, but, nothing daunted, they continued training with muzzle-loading rifles, enjoying an occasional field day on Streatham Common.

The question of uniform was at first a vexed one. Something different from the scarlet of the regular line regiments and the green of the Rifles was felt to be required. Until the matter was ultimately settled, the diversity of uniforms, occasioned by the zeal of the commanders, produced some startling effects. One such incident is recounted in a book entitled *The Volunteers from Wimbledon to Bisley*, by William Trounce, published in 1899. Trounce narrates how the 4th and 7th Middlesex V.R.C. were united under one command and the Commandant desired a change of uniform from the sombre hues then worn. The 7th Middlesex was formed of men of superior rank paying their own expenses, and it was not felt that they could be put to the cost of new uniforms, so the experiment was tried with the band of the 4th Middlesex V.R.C., enjoying no doubt some financial assistance in the purchase of the new attire. The dress selected was a Zouave costume modelled after the style of Louis Napoleon's famous (or infamous) Algerians. The colour scheme when the complete unit marched through the streets of London was, however, so unfortunate, that the gallant Volunteers had to endure a fire of ridicule more devastating than any enemy fusillade could have been. It was more than the superior 7th Middlesex could stand, and they preferred to be disbanded rather than suffer the laughter that greeted their many-coloured Battalion during its public appearances.

The London Volunteer Corps received public recognition in June 1860, when the whole force was reviewed in Hyde Park by Queen Victoria.

Time went on, bringing with it some falling off in the enthusiasms of the early days of the force. Some units dropped out, amongst them the Middlesex Cavalry, but most managed to survive, thanks to the untiring efforts of individuals who embarked on recruiting campaigns, and thus again brought the strength of units up to the required standard. Recruits had to be men of some standing, able to devote both time and money to the task of becoming efficient soldiers. In the case of the 4th Middlesex the men were expected to purchase their own uniforms and pay an annual subscription of 5s. There were no annual camps, but, in addition to the frequent Saturday-afternoon training on the open spaces in or about London, there were occasional field days at Brighton, Dover, or Portsmouth, each man providing his own food and paying his expenses. Both the 4th Middlesex V.R.C. and the 2nd (South) Middlesex V.R.C. enjoyed a continuity of leadership, for Lord Truro retained his command of the former for twenty years and Lord Ranelagh of the latter for twenty-six years. The 2nd (South) Middlesex had always been centred about the south-west of London, and the 4th Middlesex now had a move of Headquarters to Swallow Street, Piccadilly, and training was carried out in cellars under the Theistic Church near-by. The question of uniform was now settled as grey with red facings, with a shako having a glazed peak. The belts were black, and the trimming of the uniform was of buff laces with silver appointments. As volunteer battalions of the 60th King's Royal Rifles, the 4th and 2nd Middlesex V.R.C. were rifle corps and trained as such. The regimental motto of the 4th Middlesex was " Semper Paratus," meaning " Always Ready," the words surrounding the Maltese cross of the K.R.R.C. on the badge. The move of Headquarters to West London occasioned the use of the name " West London Rifles " as a sub-title.

In 1885 there came another move of the Headquarters of the 4th Middlesex V.R.C., this time to Adam and Eve

Mews, Kensington. The land where the drill-hall now stands was a builder's yard, and it was entirely due to the energetic efforts of Colonel Somers Lewis, C.B., V.D., who took command in 1879, following Lord Truro, that the hall was built. Colonel A. J. Hopkins, V.D., who later commanded from 1905 to 1907, was professionally an architect, and he acted in that capacity for the new building. Subsequently two houses were bought in Abingdon Villas and added to Headquarters, and they in turn were exchanged for the modern wing containing the officers' and sergeants' messes and the men's recreation rooms.

There were now about thirty Volunteer corps in London, and an effort towards organisation was made, the corps being brigaded roughly according to the colour of the uniform, the Volunteer Force going for training at Easter in these groups. The temporary command and the staff work were provided voluntarily by officers of H.M. Brigade of Guards, and the volunteers gained much experience from this contact with the regular army.

These groups were very unhandy, and the next stage in organisation was the formation of four brigades, north, south, east, and west, each commanded by a colonel of the Guards. As the colour scheme was still popular, the word " Grey " was allotted to the South London Volunteer Infantry Brigade, of which the West London Rifles formed part. The Easter training was each year taken more seriously, and all ranks vied with each other to become proficient in the art of soldiering. By 1899, when the Prince of Wales reviewed the London Volunteers, the parade revealed a discipline and martial bearing that won for the Force the well-merited approval of the public.

Then came the South African War. At first there was no thought of the inadequacy of the regular army to deal with the situation and offers of service made by the volunteers to the Government received scant attention. The situation changed, however, after the receipt of the news of the disasters of December 1899, and the latent possibilities of the Volunteers received serious consideration for the first time. The City Imperial Volunteers was the first volunteer unit to be formed, and, composed of contingents of selected men from the various London units, was speedily up to establishment, in spite of the severe conditions imposed upon recruits. These had to be between the ages of twenty-five and thirty-five, unmarried, and men of three years' training. They had, of course, to be physically fit. The completion of this unit, to which the West London Rifles sent a detachment, still left numbers of Volunteers eager to serve overseas, and for these men the last hope was the Imperial Yeomanry, which was still recruiting. As few were horsemen, some difficulty was found in passing the riding test in the limited time available. This obstacle was surmounted somehow or other and a large proportion contrived to gain admittance and with their fellows in the C.I.V. rendered invaluable service in South Africa. As is well known, the C.I.V., landing in Cape Town in February 1900, took their share in the ardours of the campaign and saw plenty of fighting. They remained overseas until October of the same year, when the war was considered to be virtually over. The campaign, however, dragged on until May 1902. For their share in the war, the battle honour (South Africa 1900–1902) was awarded to the West London Rifles.

During the war, Volunteer units were allowed to train for a week in brigade camps at military stations, and after the cessation of hostilities a distinct improvement in military usefulness became apparent each year, chiefly owing to the enthusiasm of individuals rather than the support of authority.

The following account from the pen of Brig.-General F. G. Lewis, C.B., C.M.G., T.D., who commanded the Battalion from 1910 to 1915, describes graphically the work of the Volunteers:

In Volunteer days, although the work was magnificent, things were very amateurish, the so-called training being a glorified picnic with a dash of formal soldiering and inevitably ending with a set piece battle from which the troops hurried, all sticky and hungry, to the home-bound train.

The organisation beyond the Battalion did not exist except on paper; equipment was lacking and very much antiquated.

It may be of interest to acquaint soldiers of to-day with a description of the most important function of the Volunteer year, the Annual Inspection. This took place usually on the Guards' ground in Hyde Park on a Saturday evening in summer, and most of the friends of the serving soldiers came to it as spectators. A very lengthy dress parade preceded it in the privacy of Knightsbridge Barracks. This lasted upwards of an hour, as the intricacies of the Slade Wallace equipment were many and a considerable proportion of the men wore it only on this one occasion. Every buckle and strap had to be adjusted correctly, an immaculate white haversack, often starched, had to be slung at a fixed level with sling passing between the third and fourth buttons, over certain straps and under others; all this was in those days regarded as of the utmost importance.

Preceded by band and drums, the Regiment marched out and formed up in line at open order, after elaborate dressing, to receive the inspecting officer, usually a Guards colonel. After marching past in column and returning in quarter column, the firing exercise (a stereotyped display of volley firing) was carried out under the senior major.

The junior major then manœuvred four companies to prove his fitness to command a battalion, being followed in turn by the four senior captains, whilst simultaneously a staff officer tested the capacity of the four senior subalterns to handle a company in the very precise close order drill of the period. Parrot-like accuracy in the details of the "Red Book" was insisted on.

Finally "Line" was reformed and, after advancing in review order, the inspecting officer addressed the unit and so brought the ceremony to a close. Any individual, officer or man, absent without leave could not be classed as "efficient," and failed to earn the annual grant of 35s., which was the only public money available to a Commanding Officer out of which to maintain the unit.

The ties binding the West London Rifles to the Royal Borough of Kensington, already formed by the location of their Headquarters within the Borough, were further strengthened when in 1905, following a meeting of the Borough Council, it was decided to accord to the Battalion the right to adopt and use the Arms of the Royal Borough. This implied a change from the old motto of " Semper Paratus " to the present one of " Quid Nobis Ardui," meaning " Nothing is too hard for us." During the same year permission was received for the substitution of the sub-title " Kensington " for the old name of West London Rifles.

The year 1908 saw a great change. The nation as a whole awoke to the potentialities of the Volunteers and the Territorial Force was formed by Viscount Haldane. The 13th Battalion, the London Regiment, came into being as a Territorial unit on April 1st of that year. It was formed by the amalgamation of the 4th Middlesex V.R.C. (Kensington Rifles) and the 2nd (South) Middlesex V.R.C. These two Volunteer corps had experienced almost parallel histories, and their Headquarters were comparatively close, the 2nd South at Fulham, and the 4th Middlesex at Iverna Gardens, Kensington. The 2nd (South) Middlesex had earned for itself a most distinguished name in the shooting world, and few Volunteer corps could boast a larger record of trophies. It included in its ranks the premier shots of these pre-Bisley days.

The County of London Territorial Force Association decided that the Headquarters of the new Battalion should be the Headquarters of the late 4th Middlesex V.R.C. in Kensington, and that the uniform of the late 4th Middlesex should be adopted for the new Battalion. The title " Kensington " and the Arms of the Royal Borough were retained by the new unit. It is seen that the 2nd (South) Middlesex had its identity merged with that of the Kensington Rifles, losing Headquarters, name, and uniform. This was not entirely popular with the slightly senior Corps; a large proportion, however, including Captains McLean and Parnell and Lieutenants Thompson and Chance, came over and gave their enthusiastic support to the new unit, the dissentients ultimately joining the 10th Battalion Middlesex Regiment.

The conversion of the Volunteer Force to the Territorial

Force carried with it sweeping changes in the conditions. Formation and organisation on the lines of the regular army came into existence, with senior leaders and a staff on a permanent basis. County Associations were responsible for recruiting, the War Office supplied equipment and arms, and pay on similar scales to the regular army was introduced.

Annual training took place at the seaside and a large military station, on alternate years. The units were usually brigaded, though a Divisional Camp was formed once every four years.

Two such trainings are worthy of special note, as they were each much more like the real thing and, carried out under service conditions, were of exceptional interest and benefit.

In 1912, at the Minster Camp, an invasion of England executed in conjunction with the Royal Navy and regular troops was of a very interesting and exacting nature. The Brigade was carrying out the ordinary training near its standing camp when on " Declaration of War " two hours were given in which to pack up and move out into the " blue " for four days. During this period the Battalion bivouacked in the open, crossed the Medway in picquet boats of the Royal Navy, lived on bully beef, and incidentally covered a good deal of ground on foot.

Again in 1913 the Brigade was in camp under Colonel G. J. Cuthbert, C.B., commanding the Scots Guards, at Abergavenny and went on " trek " into the Black Mountains. The first night was spent in bivouacs in Lord Glanusk's park near Crickhowell; on the following day a climb of about 3,000 feet took the troops to a wild rocky hollow in the mountains, where, bivouacking and working under active-service conditions, a programme of very real and useful, if strenuous, training was carried out in brilliant weather amidst glorious and unusual surroundings.

An honour was conferred upon the Battalion at this time by H.R.H. Princess Louise, Duchess of Argyll, who, at the express wish of His Majesty the King, allowed her name to be borne by the Battalion, thereby more closely than ever associating herself with the Kensington Territorials. This Royal Lady has never lost a single opportunity of helping the Battalion either before, during, or since the Great War, and her unflagging interest and gracious support have always been a great encouragement to all ranks.

When the Army Council on January 6th, 1909, gave permission for the new Battalion to be a " line " Battalion, it was made a condition that all rifle appointments should be discarded, and as a corollary it was authorised to carry colours. The Mayor of Kensington, Major-General Cavaye, convened a meeting of residents in the Borough, and under the enthusiastic lead of H.R.H. Princess Louise, it was unanimously decided that the ladies of the Royal Borough should provide the colours. A committee was formed to deal with the matter, and Her Royal Highness consented to be president. The design for the colours having been prepared by the Royal College of Heralds, they were worked and put together under the direct supervision of Her Royal Highness, who invited all those who had subscribed to the fund to call and work a stitch in them. The colours were presented by His Late Majesty, King Edward VII, at Windsor on June 19th, 1909.

It is of interest to note that in 1799 the Duchess of Gloucester, with her daughter Princess Sophia Matilda, supervised the working of the colours for the Volunteer Regiment belonging to Kensington at that date. These colours were presented on Palace Green by the Duchess of Gloucester on May 20th, 1799, and they are now hanging in St. Mary Abbots Church, Kensington.

On July 22nd, 1911, H.R.H. Princess Louise inspected the Battalion in Holland Park and presented silver plates for the colour belts and drum major's staff.

"THE KENSINGTONS"

Pre-war Commanding Officers

2nd Middlesex V.R.C.

Honorary Colonels
Lord Abinger.

Earl Cadogan, K.G., P.C.

Lord Wolverton, D.L.

Commanding Officers
Colonel Lord Ranelagh, 1859–85.
Colonel Wylde, C.M.G., V.D.
Colonel Horace Gray, V.D.
Colonel C. B. Dimond, V.D.

4th Middlesex V.R.C.

Honorary Colonels
General Lord Chelmsford, 1887–1906.
Major-General Sir Alfred Turner, K.C.B., 1906–08.

Commanding Officers
Colonel Lord Truro, 1859–79.
Colonel A. Somers Lewis, C.B., V.D., 1879–98.
Colonel A. S. Daniell, 1898–1905.
Colonel A. J. Hopkins, V.D., 1905–1907.
Lieut.-Colonel A. Sutherland-Harris, 1907–8.

13th Battalion the London Regiment.

Honorary Colonel
Major-General Sir Alfred Turner, K.C.B., 1908.

Commanding Officers
Lieut.-Colonel A. Sutherland-Harris, 1908–10.
Lieut.-Colonel F. G. Lewis, 1910–15.

The foregoing traces the growth of the Kensingtons from a Volunteer Rifle Corps to a well-organised and efficient Territorial infantry battalion. When war clouds gathered over Europe in the summer of 1914, the Battalion was ready for any call which might be made upon it in the service of King and country.

THE 1st BATTALION

By O. F. BAILEY

CHAPTER II

MOBILISATION AND TRAINING

THE declaration of war with Germany on August 4th, 1914, came at a time when the Territorial Army normally does its annual training, and the Kensingtons had entrained at Addison Road Station on August 2nd for Salisbury Plain, where, with other units of the 4th London Infantry Brigade, the first day was spent in the usual routine of settling down in camp in spite of rumours of war which even then were current. However, after the troops had retired for the night orders were received at about 10 p.m. to pack up and move, one of the first of the sudden orders that became a feature of the war. Rumour now had something to get on with, and various were the reasons suggested for the sudden emergency which had recalled the Kensingtons to their Headquarters at the Drill Hall within twenty-four hours of leaving.

On arrival, the Battalion was dismissed with instructions to be ready for mobilisation if and when it came. The fateful declaration of war was made on Tuesday, August 4th, and mobilisation ordered for the following day. The days following saw the convergence on the Drill Hall of hundreds of men, not only serving members of the Regiment, but large numbers of recruits, all needing equipment of one kind or another. What might easily have been a time of great confusion proved, thanks to the intelligent planning of the Commanding Officer, Lieut.-Colonel F. G. Lewis, T.D., and his staff, to be a period of well-organised activity, so that in a very short space of time the Battalion was ready to move to the training area.

During this busy fortnight the Battalion was brought up to strength and equipped, in spite of the serious deficiency of war equipment which existed at this time. The men were billeted in Headquarters, the Town Hall, and neighbouring schools, and fed from the day of mobilisation. It is believed that no other London unit did this. Recruits were sworn in, medically examined, and equipped, and issues were made to all ranks of those items required only for active service—identity discs, ball ammunition, field dressing, iron ration, and housewife, in addition to which all the multitudinous stores and equipment required to maintain a unit in the field had to be procured and issued. It is interesting to note that a practice mobilisation had been carried out on March 8th, 1914, and there is no doubt that the experience gained on this and similar occasions proved of immense value now that the real thing had come.

The civilian vehicles, which normally comprised the transport for the Territorial Army in peace-time, were, in the case of the Kensingtons, Idris Mineral Water delivery vans, and many of their regular drivers belonged to the transport section.

In spite of all this activity, time was found for physical training and drill in the grounds of Holland House, and in the intervals the men were proud to show themselves in their uniforms in the highways and by-ways of Kensington. No one now questioned the importance of the Territorial Army, and popular appreciation was as evident as previously it had been lacking. It was felt an honour to be seen abroad in uniform in those days of August 1914, and those who had sacrificed their time and given of their enthusiasm in the past were now reaping a belated reward. The war began to be real when route marches were made along the hot and tiring streets of London, and when additional rifles were fetched from the Tower.

During the month the colours were handed over by the Commanding Officer, in the presence of H.R.H. Princess Louise, to Sir William Davison, K.B.E., in his capacity as Mayor of the Royal Borough, for safe keeping in the

Town Hall. In undertaking this responsibility Sir William said: " I will keep the silken fabric, but its honour goes with you."

How well this trust was carried out these pages will show.

The Kensingtons were the first of the 4th London Brigade to report their mobilisation complete, and by the 15th all units had similarly reported. On the following day the march to the war station near Watford began, and on this fine Sunday morning crowds of Londoners turned out to witness the departure of the 4th London Territorial Infantry Brigade from the rendezvous at Marble Arch. The march along the Edgware Road to the vicinity of Watford taxed the marching powers of the men, as yet unseasoned, but enthusiasm ran high, and after a night's bivouac at Canons Park the Battalion reached Abbots Langley on the 17th and entered on the training period with zest. The eight companies were billeted in barns, outbuildings, and schoolrooms, and were soon on the happiest of terms with the inhabitants of the village. The other units of the 4th London Infantry Brigade, the London Scottish (14th London), Civil Service Rifles (15th London), and the Queen's Westminsters (16th London), were billeted in the vicinity, and in the route marches which formed a regular feature of the training, encounters with these other London Territorials were frequent. At the beginning of their service overseas, these fine battalions were separated, each going to different regular divisions, but on the re-formation of the London Territorial Divisions later in the war, the 13th, 14th, and 16th went to the 56th Division, and the 15th to the 47th Division.

When the Battalion left for Hertfordshire a working body of Kensington women, mostly relatives of the officers, was organised by Mrs. A. C. Lewis, O.B.E., wife of the Commanding Officer, who completed the " papers " of the men so successfully that pay allotments were made three weeks earlier than any other unit of the county of London.

Thus the narrow Hertfordshire lanes, gay with autumn

tints, echoed to the marching songs of the Kensingtons as, preceded by either the brass band or the drum-and-fife band, they swung along through the English country-side. The rhythmic crunch of army boots on the gritty surface and the swing of the khaki-clad limbs formed, with the martial music, associations in the mind that time cannot efface.

Training was vigorous and, in the short time that was actually available, effective. Physical training was predominant, and properly so, but tactical exercises were also undertaken both by companies and by the Battalion as a whole. Short sharp rushes over the stubble in extended-order drill, followed by the sudden fall to the prone position, probably did more in the way of improving the stamina of the men than in preparing them for the kind of fighting that came their way. The open-air life reacted with surprising speed on the physique of men whose normal occupation kept them largely indoors. A cross-country race in full order with rifles, carried out by one picked section per company, showed the marked increase in staying power that had been achieved. There was so little to choose between the competing teams that the deciding factor was often such a minor fault as the safety catch of the rifle being in the wrong position.

In the meantime the 2nd Battalion of the Kensingtons was forming, and a number of men who had volunteered for foreign service were drafted to the 1st Battalion. These for the most part had received previous military training and their absorption presented no difficulty.

During September H.R.H. Princess Louise visited the Battalion, and attended Church Parade, and inspected billets.

That the Territorials were needed was soon proved by the disappearance from the quiet Hertfordshire countryside on September 15th of the London Scottish and their replacement by the Artists' Rifles (28th London). The Queen's Westminsters were the next to go, and the Kensingtons knew that their turn might come at any time. In fact, one night when the troops were comfortably settled,

MOBILISATION AND TRAINING

a sudden order was received to march to King's Langley Station. Good-bye post cards by the dozen were given to the disturbed villagers to post, and the station was reached in record time. To the disappointment of all, however, the alarm proved to be a false one, merely intended as a test of the time required for such a move.

The real call came on October 28th, 1914, when orders were received to prepare for foreign service. Short leave was granted on the 29th and 30th, and on November 3rd the Battalion, preceded by the band, marched in the early morning to Watford and entrained at 11 a.m. for Southampton. A long wait ensued here at the docks, but embarkation was completed and the Battalion set off for the great adventure aboard S.S. *Matheran* by 1 a.m. on the 4th. The night was spent in the bare quarters aboard or on deck watching the last of the lightships slipping astern as the troopship, with dimmed lights, met the smooth swell of the open sea.

Although the actual departure from England had been quiet and apparently unnoticed, the Battalion had received many messages of Godspeed from its numerous friends. Chief amongst these was the following telegram from H.R.H. Princess Louise:

ROSEMEATH.   *October* 30th, 1914
To—COLONEL LEWIS, OFFICERS, AND MEN OF KENSINGTON BATTALION, ABBOTS LANGLEY.

Just received telegram. Proud my Battalion selected for service abroad. Disappointed business here prevents seeing you before embarkation. My thoughts and wishes will ever be with you. I know from your efficiency you will do honour to your calling. Remember Lord Kitchener's beautiful words to the Army and hold God in your hearts.

                                       LOUISE.

Le Havre was reached at noon on the 4th, and the Kensingtons, their civilian transport now exchanged for army G.S. wagons, soon found themselves marching through the town and breasting the long hill to Rest Camp No. 1.

"THE KENSINGTONS"

The streets were thronged with people, who showed their enthusiasm at the arrival of more English troops by presenting cigarettes to the men and crying "Vive les Anglais." The rest camp proved to be a dreary and comfortless spot for which the magnificent view over the harbour was poor compensation, and the Kensingtons were not sorry when, after a cold and blanketless night under canvas, they descended the hill again at 3 p.m. on the 5th and entrained, thirty men to a truck, for St. Omer.

The Battalion, thus on its way to the line, had a strength of 29 officers and 835 other ranks. The senior officers were: Commanding Officer, Lieut.-Colonel F. G. Lewis, T.D.; Senior Major, H. J. Stafford, T.D.; Junior Major, H. Campbell; officers commanding companies (eight company basis): A Company, Captain H. L. Cabuche; B Company, Captain C. C. Dickens; C Company, Captain H. W. Barnett; D Company, Captain A. Prismall; E Company, Captain E. L. Parnell; F Company, Captain A. C. Herne; G Company, Captain E. G. Kimber; H Company, Captain J. E. L. Higgins.

The equipment of the rank and file at this period is of some interest, as certain modifications were made at later dates. The long rifle (Lee-Enfield) and bayonet had been issued and 120 rounds of S.A.A. were carried in the pouches of the Web equipment, which also consisted of pack, haversack, entrenching-tool carrier, and water-bottle. Waterproof ground-sheets were carried in the pack with the great-coat and the mess tin. Iron ration, knife, fork, spoon, razor, jack-knife, and housewife were carried in the haversack. Each man had also his Army pay-book, First Field Dressing, and identity disc, the latter hung about the neck on a string. In addition to this official outfit all men carried "mossings"—spare socks, body belts, Balaclava helmets, etc., presented by anxious relatives, so it is realised that the burden of the infantryman, or "footslogger" as he was popularly called, was no light one. His financial reward was meagre in the extreme. The pay of the rank-and-file amounted to 1*s.* per day, from which many men

1ST BATTALION OFFICERS

Back Row (Left to Right).—2nd-Lieut. F. J. Robertson, 2nd-Lieut. N. O. Sewell, Lieut. H. N. Whitty, 2nd-Lieut. K. Bamber.
Second Row (Left to Right).—2nd-Lieut. R. M. Macgregor, 2nd-Lieut. C. C. Strong, Lieut. C. J. Fox, 2nd-Lieut. E. V. Field, 2nd-Lieut. T. E. G. Leigh-Pemberton, Capt. C. C. Dickens, Lieut. C. Howard, Lieut. E. B. Keen, M.O., Capt. A. C. Herne, Capt. H. W. Barnett, Capt. J. E. L. Higgins, 2nd-Lieut. O. Hall, 2nd-Lieut. L. L. Cohen, 2nd-Lieut. W. E. Burn, 2nd-Lieut. H. Holland.
Front Row (Left to Right).—Capt. E. L. Parnell, Capt. E. G. Kimber, Lieut. and Quartermaster A. G. Ridley, Major H. H. Campbell, Major H. J. Stafford, Lieut.-Col. F. G. Lewis, Capt. and Adj. Gilbert Thompson, Rev. S. E. Pennefather, C.F., Capt. A. Prismall, Capt. H. L. Cabuche.
Inset.—Lieut.-Col. R. E. F. Shaw, M.C.

161

made an allotment of 6d., thus leaving very little for the purchase of such luxuries as were available.

The troop train pursued its way in the leisurely manner of such, via Abbeville, Boulogne, and Calais, to St. Omer, while the Kensingtons endeavoured to keep warm by avoiding the wide cracks between the floor-boards of the bare wagons, until, after a twenty-three-hour journey, St. Omer was reached at 8.30 p.m. on the 6th. Detrainment was completed by 11 p.m., half the Battalion staying in barracks in the town for the night, while the remainder trudged through the dark streets and out into the country to the village of Blendecques, about five miles distant, where what was left of the night was spent in barns and farm buildings. B Company was quartered in close vicinity to an enormous pile of cider apples in the store barn of a cider distillery. M. le Proprietaire, by allowing the men to eat as many apples as they desired, soon cured them of a taste for cider apples. The villagers were very friendly, and the men soon began to acquire that version of the French language so useful to the British soldier throughout the war. Those with a knowledge of French were in great demand, particularly after a long-awaited pay day materialised.

The village preserved its pre-war characteristics and furnished to those abroad for the first time a typical specimen of the Flanders village. Whitewashed houses, neat and clean, fronted the cobbled street with estaminets every few paces. Here warmth and cheer prevailed, and red and white wine was to be had at a very modest price. Many Kensingtons sampled the varied assortment of liqueurs and colourful syrupy liquids that adorned the bar.

The hand of the censor now lay heavy upon all correspondence. It was thrilling to be able to head the letter "British Expeditionary Force," but rather a shock to realise that no mention of essential details could be given, and that the letter must be handed unsealed to an officer to scrutinise.

During the few days spent at Blendecques, trench

digging was done in the vicinity, and some training was also carried out. This period served as a breathing space, during which the men could get used to the new conditions. The guns were plainly to be heard, and various rumours were current as to the progress of the war.

The weather had become cold and wet, and it was under uncertain skies that the Battalion began the march on November 12th towards the line. Orders had been received overnight, unexpectedly, at the conclusion of a day's training over the sodden sugar-beet fields surrounding the village. All felt that this was business at last as kilometre after kilometre was covered on the cobbled surface. During the morning stage of the journey a car stopped at the head of the column and a staff officer descended and took the salute as the Battalion marched past. It was the veteran Field-Marshal Lord Roberts. With a smile and a salute he passed towards St. Omer, and none realised that within a few days the whole nation would be mourning his passing. One cannot do better than quote from the poem entitled "Lord Roberts," by Rudyard Kipling, copies of which were printed in the field and issued to the troops:

> He passed in the very battle smoke
>   Of the war that he had descried,
> Three hundred miles of cannon spoke
>   When the master gunner died.
>
> He passed to the very sound of the guns,
>   But before his eye grew dim
> He had seen the faces of the sons
>   Whose sires had served with him.
>
> He had touched their sword hilts and greeted each
>   With the old sure word of praise,
> And there was virtue in touch and speech
>   As it had been in olden days.

It was fitting that the man whose enthusiasm had done so much to foster the growth of the Territorial Army should have greeted the fine body of men that marched to their duty on that November morning.

MOBILISATION AND TRAINING

The night was spent at Boesghem, and on the following day the Kensingtons marched in the rain to the Merville district, where signs of bombardment became apparent. A battered church or a ruined farm-house, and occasionally the spatter of rifle fire on walls, told a tale of recent fighting. It is worth noting how, in the absence of authoritative news, rumour spreads among the troops. As the men lay in their sodden clothes in the straw-strewn barns at Vieux Berquin that night, the inevitable rumour came round, official, of course, that America had declared war, the Russians were within one day's march of Berlin, and the Germans were retreating rapidly all along the Front. This no doubt arose from a lively fear that had been at the back of everyone's mind all along, that the war would be over before the Battalion got to the Front. Such rumours had the effect of breeding a scepticism that became so strong that the old soldier refused to believe good news when it came at last four weary years later.

On the 14th the Kensingtons marched to Estaires, a small town on the banks of the Lys, and were billeted in a cotton mill on the river bank close to the bridge. The district here, to become so familiar to the Battalion, is a low-lying one, the Lys valley being very wide and rising to the Aubers Ridge with the villages of Aubers and Fromelles in the foreground, the great town of Lille being screened by this high ground. Cobbled roads, bordered by deep drainage ditches and avenues of poplars in places, link the neat villages. The land is fertile, but apt to become water-logged, so the fields are divided by ditches marked by pollarded willows, the water thus draining towards the river. Mills for the manufacture of a tough kind of fabric are common in Estaires and the adjoining village of La Gorgue. It was in such a mill, abandoned since the arrival of the Germans five weeks before, but with its machinery intact and rolls of fabric lying about indicating the hurried departure of the occupants, that the Kensingtons were billeted.

CHAPTER III

A WINTER IN THE LINE

WHILE the Kensingtons had been training at Abbots Langley, the 8th Division, under the command of Major-General F. J. Davies, C.B., had been in process of formation at Hursley Park, near Winchester. The three infantry brigades, the 23rd, 24th, and 25th, and the Royal Engineers, were composed entirely of regular troops who had been withdrawn from foreign service at Malta, Singapore, and India since the outbreak of war. The urgency of the situation denied these troops the period required for acclimatisation, and after a short training they landed in France between November 5th and November 7th and were concentrated in the Estaires–La Gorgue area preparatory to taking over the sector held by the Lahore Division. Reliefs were completed by the 16th and the 8th Division became responsible for a front some 8,000 yards in length, extending from the La Bassée–Estaires Road to the Rue Tilleloy, near Laventie. Two Territorial battalions were attached to the Division, the Kensingtons going to the 25th Infantry Brigade, and the 5th Black Watch to the 24th Infantry Brigade. The Kensingtons thus found themselves brigaded with the 2nd Lincolnshires, 2nd Royal Berkshires, 1st Royal Irish Rifles, and the 2nd Rifle Brigade, with Brig.-General A. W. G. Lowry-Cole, C.B., D.S.O., commanding the Brigade.

The general situation on the Western Front at this period is worth consideration. Following the victory of the Marne which finally stemmed the German influx and saved Paris, the Allies began a forward movement which, dying out for lack of men and material, ended in the stage of trench warfare on a limited front. Attempts by both sides to turn the western flank of the line culminated in its rapid extension northwards until by the beginning of October 1914 the trench system stretched to Lens. The gap that remained, which included the Estaires area, was unoccupied save for German cavalry, and every effort was made to close up this gap as the necessary troops became available. This was partly accomplished by the withdrawal of the British Expeditionary Force from the Aisne, and by the end of October the British line was extended to Ypres, clearing the area of enemy cavalry. At this stage the enemy resistance stiffened, and not only was further advance checked, but the Germans began the first of the many assaults on the Ypres front in an endeavour to penetrate the thin British line and turn its flank. This attack, fortunately, was successfully resisted, and thereupon offensive operations on both sides flagged, so that by the time the Kensingtons arrived in the field the combatants had embarked on the trench warfare which was to become a feature of the Great War. The British front now extended from Ypres to La Bassée.

Sunday, November 15th, found the Kensingtons settled in the mill. A church parade was held during the morning, necessarily short, for the men were assembled in the field beside the mill, and snow was falling heavily. During the afternoon the Battalion was inspected by Major-General Davies, commanding the Division, and General Sir Henry Rawlinson, commanding IVth Corps. Addressing the Battalion, the latter explained the duties and aims of the Allies in this particular theatre of the war. He said that the Division was holding quite twice its number of enemy troops in the hope that the Russians would be able to advance.

During the march from Blendecques the Battalion had been reorganised on a four-company basis, A and B Companies forming the new A Company, C and D Companies the new B Company, and so on, the Company Commanders being: A Company, Captain H. L. Cabuche; B Company, Captain A. Prismall; C Company, Captain E. L. Parnell; D Company, Captain E. G. Kimber. After a few days spent in trench digging and general training, orders came on November 18th for the right half Battalion to take over a portion of the trenches from the 2nd Royal Berkshires that night, and accordingly A and B Companies under the command of Major H. J. Stafford, took over 600 yards of trench south-east of Fauquissart, the relief being complete by 8 p.m. C and D Companies remained in the mill at Estaires, and were occupied, under the command of Major H. Campbell, in digging a system of second-line trenches.

This first tour in the line was a memorable one and tested the physical endurance of all ranks to the utmost. The weather was bitterly cold and wet, and the fields near the trench system, with their ditches choked as a result of shell fire, were morasses of mud. A Kensington describes the events of that night and the appalling conditions in the line in graphic words:

"While passing along Rue Tilleloy, the Battalion had its baptism of fire—machine-gun bullets whizzed overhead and shells churned up the mud in the fields beside the road. Although unpleasant, all felt exhilarated, though this exhilaration was soon modified when the actual trenches were seen. These were little more than ditches about six feet deep and three to four feet wide. They were full of mud, and in parts the water was rising. Duckboards or dugouts and other luxuries of trench warfare were unknown in these days. The men of the Berkshires were already out of the trench when our fellows entered it, standing on top waiting to move off. Their officers explained roughly the limits of the company lines, the whereabouts of ammunition and Verey lights, and departed into the night to dry themselves before braziers and fires in Laventie. The Kensingtons were alone for the first time with the enemy, whose trenches lay some 300 yards away across a No-man's-land which in parts was knee-deep in mud. Headquarters was, for a time, in the front line in a shelter made out of sandbags, while Company Headquarters was no more than holes in the ground covered with short lengths of corrugated iron. The men had no shelters at all. They dug themselves cubby-holes in the sides of the trench and crept in to rest with knees doubled up to their chins. The cold was so intense that, after lying in these cubby-holes for a time they were unable to move and had to be pulled out and massaged back into 'life' again. This, together with the fact that the cubby-holes tended to undermine the trench, produced an order forbidding them altogether. There was then nothing to do when not on sentry duty but stamp about to keep warm, or lie down in the mud and water to snatch a few moments of sleep, only to wake with limbs that refused to move, and aching pains from head to feet."

This unnatural state of affairs led to the complaint known as "trench feet," which reduced the strength of some units by 150 men in the course of a single tour in the line during the worst of the winter months. The men so affected were disabled for long periods, and many were compelled to undergo amputation of a more or less serious character. Various remedies were tried during this first winter, including wrapping the feet in sandbags stuffed with straw. Later in the war gum-boots, frequent foot inspections, and regular rubbing of the feet with whale oil reduced the casualties from trench feet to negligible proportions, so that it became a matter for official enquiry when a case arose. The obvious remedy was some improvement in the trenches themselves, but in spite of all efforts the water continued to rise and the sides fell in from the top. A breastwork line constructed of sandbags above ground level appeared to be the only solution, and the building of this became a nightly activity for the men in the line, and when completed provided a most welcome change from the old deep ditch.

As regards actual operations, the area at this time would be designated as "quiet." Neither side could make an attack across the thick mud of No-man's-land, and in places the proximity of the two lines made systematic shelling hazardous. However, the lack of energy in attack or artillery manifestations was more than made up for by the assiduity of the snipers on both sides. Loopholes were marked with deadly accuracy, and an instant's exposure was a risk too often attended with fatal result. On November 19th the Kensingtons sustained their first casualties, Privates Webster and Mooring being wounded, and on the following day Private Perry was killed.

The first half-Battalion relief took place on November 21st, and from then onwards until more active operations in March 1915, half the Battalion was in the line and half out, for three-day periods. A and B Companies, due to hold the line, would exchange friendly greetings in the dark with C and D Companies on taking over. Casualties continued to mount up. Major H. Campbell was wounded on the 27th, and by Christmas 1914, 15 had been killed, 29 wounded, and a large number evacuated to hospital suffering from exposure.

During the long hours in the line the men watched the enemy through periscopes, did what they could to drain the water away, slept when they could, tried to maintain a little fire, and waited patiently for relief. The brief rest period was spent in an endeavour to get dry and clean, and anxious enquiries were made for letters and parcels from home. As frequent reference will be made during the course of this history to long periods in the line, a description of a typical day in the trenches at Picantin, written by a member of the Battalion, follows:

"The day began with 'stand to,' an hour before dawn. Stiff with cold and half dazed from lack of sleep, the men stood in the trenches peering across the waste of No-man's-land with the grey outline of the German trenches beyond. A line of stunted willows ran along a ditch full of water; pools of muddy water filled the shell-holes, and our own twisted barbed wire and the barbed wire in front of the enemy's trenches looked like heaps of rusty rubbish on a dust heap in some abandoned slum.

"As the hour of 'stand to' passed, thin wisps of smoke began to rise from both English and German trenches, betraying rough attempts at cooking breakfast. Never in

Front Line Trench, Laventie, 1915.
Imperial War Museum photograph. Copyright reserved.

all one's life was the thought of bacon and eggs and that rare homely smell of breakfast in England so vivid and poignant. The day began with attempts to tidy up the trench. Bully-beef tins had to be collected and buried, mud had to be cleared from the fairway of the trench, water had to be drained away as far as was possible, rifles (sometimes so caked with mud that they would not fire) cleaned, and some feeble attempts made to scrape the mud from tunic, trousers, puttees, and boots. The routine of sentry duty went forward—even an hour or more peering through the end of the periscope was relief from the monotony. Occasionally one saw a man move past a gap in the enemy line, and a shot or two (with, of course, a certain hit, in the opinion of the marksman) provided a mild excitement. The morning dragged away, neither side showing their heads above the parapet. The afternoon was much the same, but as night began to cover up No-man's-land and the fields behind the line, more activity was manifest. Evening tea came in dixies and gave some temporary warmth and comfort. Patrols, wiring parties, and sentry duties were arranged, all of which, disagreeable though they were, helped to make the dark hours pass more quickly. The patrols were poor unexciting affairs, the mud and water of No-man's-land making them into stumbling, tiring walks along the line of the wire, while wiring parties found that the heavy coils of wire stuck in the mud and could not be unravelled. The mud and water conspired to frustrate all human efforts."

When the open warfare of the early autumn stagnated into the holding of trenches, little damage had been done to the villages near the line. As the enemy artillery was brought up, however, systematic shelling started, and the quiet village of Laventie was the first to suffer, situated, as it was, very close to the line. Pitiful processions of refugees were to be seen carrying bundles and wheeling trucks containing some cherished possessions to less dangerous areas. The village itself was a sorry spectacle. The church, a fine old structure dominating the village square, showed the destructive effects of shell fire. A huge shell had burst just in front of the west door and the top of the tower had fallen in, the mechanism of the clock blocking the entrance. Inside, venerable cane-seated chairs were tumbled hither and thither, sprinkled with fragments of the stained-glass windows. In the village a street appeared as though a giant hand had swept all the houses on one side into ruins, while the other side was untouched. In a humble cottage which a shell had penetrated from wall to wall, a loaf of bread on the table and coffee cups half full of coffee testified to the hurried departure of the inhabitants. Nor were buildings the only things destroyed. Families were scattered. A poor woman wandering towards the line stopped a Kensington to enquire if she might be allowed to go to a farm near-by. Her six children were there with her father, she said, her husband being with the French Army. She had been separated from them when the enemy overran the district and wanted to find them again. She said that she had no anxiety as regards food, for were there not eight cows at the farm and a large store of potatoes in the barn? From her description it was patent that the farm was one quite near the front line, ruined and desolate, the starved cows having been shot out of compassion by the troops, and the potatoes requisitioned, long since, for military consumption.

This is but one instance of what these people in the invaded territory suffered.

Winter fell early in 1914 with frost and snow a month before Christmas, adding to the sufferings of both the military and the civil population, the latter deprived to a large extent of their normal supplies. The troops in the area were cheered on December 1st by a visit from His Majesty the King. The route was lined by representatives of all units in the Division, including C and D Companies of the Kensingtons, while aeroplanes patrolled above. Preceded by the guard of honour, the Divisional band, and the Kensington drums, the Royal Party drove slowly along the Merville–La Gorgue Road. The Prince of Wales came first, followed by the King, President Poincaré, General

Joffre, and General French. At Divisional Headquarters at La Gorgue His Majesty inspected the guard of honour and also a party of men attired in fur coats and wearing sandbag footwear, of which the Staff were inordinately proud.

As Christmas approached, heralded by very severe weather, gifts began to arrive in large numbers for the men in the trenches. Special gifts were made by the Royal Family, the most appreciated being the Princess Mary gift box, containing chocolate and cigarettes. The box itself was a thing of beauty much prized by the troops. The rations were supplemented also by special issues of Christmas pudding, tobacco, and cigarettes.

Christmas Day came and found A and B Companies of the Kensingtons in the line at Picantin. The amazing events of that day are reported verbatim from an account of an eye-witness.

"It was the first Christmas of the war and the enemy, no less than ourselves, felt very homesick. The Germans gave the first sign. A tired sentry in the Battalion, looking out over the waste towards their lines, spread the exciting news that the enemy's trenches were 'all alight.' He had hardly uttered the words before other sentries took up the cry and we all looked at the enemy's line, which was dotted here and there with clusters of lights. From behind the lights came voices crying 'English soldiers, English soldiers, Happy Christmas. Where are your Christmas trees?' and faint but clear, the songs of the season. We were a little embarrassed by this sudden comradeship and, as a lasting joke against us, let it be said that the order was given to stand to arms. But we did not fire, for the battalion on our right, the Royal Irish Rifles, with their national sense of humour, answered the enemy's salutations with songs and jokes and made appointments in No-man's-land for Christmas Day. We felt small and subdued and spent the remainder of Christmas Eve in watching the lights flicker and fade on the 'Christmas Trees' in their trenches and hearing the voices grow fainter and eventually cease.

"The early morning of Christmas Day was a revelation

of the friendship of enemies. At 'stand to' the Germans were singing and wishing us a Happy Christmas, and a few bold ones were standing outside their trenches inviting us to 'come over and talk.' Many of us wanted to respond to this friendly invitation, but the officers were cautious and doubted the safety of such friendship, even on Christmas Day. Men of the Battalion on our right were, however, already responding to a similar invitation, and we saw them greeting the enemy in the friendliest manner. This seemed a sufficient guarantee of friendship, and over we went into No-man's-land. Apart from the officers, the Germans we saw were strangely old. We took with us bits of Christmas pudding, tobacco, cigarettes, and other oddments, but were ordered to preserve the identity of our regiment by giving away no badges or buttons. The 'enemies' shook hands cordially and gifts were exchanged (and occasionally conversations, chiefly relating to hotels in the West End of London). We seemed to be better supplied with rations than the Germans, for all they could give us were their regimental badges and buttons and a few odd bottles of Schnapps. We agreed that the weather was abominable and thought that on this day, at least, the war was absurd, and agreed that the truce should be ended at midnight by the simultaneous firing, very high, of all rifles, so that there might be no casualties. Although ordered to say no more than 'a Happy Christmas,' it has to be admitted that many were guilty of talking quite a lot. The Germans were amazed at our youthfulness as we were at their advanced years. We talked about this, the enemy being of the opinion that we were England's last hope—all the other soldiers having been killed, wounded, or captured. They were ignorant of the fact that thousands were training in England, but they had a very good idea about our reserves in Flanders; that is to say, they knew that we had practically none. We spoke, of course, of thousands and thousands of men ready to support us at any time.

"The officers began to be apprehensive of too much conversation and we were ordered to return to our trenches.

A WINTER IN THE LINE

In the most cordial manner farewells were taken and the enemy and ourselves returned like rabbits to our respective burrows. It was agreed that, for the moment at any rate, it was a most amusing war. No shots were fired during the day, and it was not until the 28th that normal hostilities recommenced and even then there was not much firing."

What occurred on the Battalion front was not an isolated instance, for fraternising with the enemy, in some form or another, was a feature of this first Christmas Day of the war. It was, of course, frowned on by the Staff and never occurred again. On the whole, however, it served to show that the British Tommy had no quarrel with the individual German as a man. It was his race as a whole that had violated the neutrality of Belgium and was thereby responsible for the war. The same attitude was apparent towards prisoners, who were frequently astounded at the friendly reception given to them by our men, who always managed somehow to find a cigarette for a captured foe.

During the months of January and February the situation on the front remained quiet, though enemy snipers and occasional shell fire took their toll. On January 11th the Battalion lost its first officer, 2nd Lieut. Leigh Pemberton, a popular officer in A Company, who was killed by a sniper's bullet. Captain C. C. Dickens, commanding A Company, Major H. Campbell, and Lieut. E. V. Field were wounded, Lieut. Field seriously, and on February 24th Captain and Adjutant G. Thompson was killed by an enemy sniper while making a tour of the trenches with the Brigadier-General. Captain Thompson was a regular officer of the Connaught Rangers and had done much to make the Battalion the efficient fighting unit it was. His death cast a gloom over the Kensingtons, for he was a very gallant officer and one of the most lovable and humane of men. By the beginning of March the Battalions' casualties were 96, of these 2 officers and 25 other ranks being the first of the long roll of those who died for King and country.

The spirit of the men remained undaunted in spite of the

severe climatic conditions. Two Kensingtons were honoured at this period by the award of the Distinguished Conduct Medal for gallantry in the field—Drummer Emery and Lance-Corporal Shepherd. Frost and snow came in the early weeks of January, followed by a thaw which flooded the Lys valley and made the trenches more water-logged than ever. A daily entry in the records was the words " trenches flooded and water rising." All this served to encourage work on the new breastwork line, which not only offered the prospect of an escape from the all-pervading water, but gave the men in the line an interest to relieve the tedium of trench warfare. Rest billets had been moved from Estaires to Laventie on December 26th, and the old racing stables which formed the billets came to be the nearest approach to a home that the tortured land of France could offer to her weather-worn defenders.

So the weeks wore on without relief until the end of February, when a certain activity on the part of the Staff spoke in no uncertain manner of the imminence of active operations.

CHAPTER IV

THE BATTLE OF NEUVE CHAPELLE

SINCE the opening of the prolonged stage of trench warfare at the end of October 1914, the enemy had held, on the front occupied by the 8th Division, a strong trench system with the front line running north and south about 400 yards to the west of the village of Neuve Chapelle. To the north of the village the almost parallel lines of the combatants stretched away to the north-east, and the village thus formed a strong point which was a constant source of irritation to the British troops holding the line. The buildings, as yet largely intact, made ideal posts for enemy snipers, who not only had good observation on the immediate front, but were also able to enfilade the sector of our line beyond the La Bassée Road. Any divisional offensive would naturally aim at this village as the first objective. In December an attack, subsidiary to French operations against enemy positions to the south of the La Bassée Road, was carried out by the 23rd Brigade, in the course of which some of the enemy's trenches near the village were captured. The ground taken was, however, not retained, for not only were the trenches water-logged, but the enemy showed great superiority in the ensuing bomb fight. This was not surprising, for the British bombs were crude affairs improvised from jam tins, and had to be lit before being thrown, whereas the German bombs were of a more modern pattern.

Planned initially as a purely local operation, the battle of Neuve Chapelle became an offensive of wider significance, involving an attack by the 7th and 8th Divisions and Indian Corps, with the IVth Corps to the north, the ultimate objective being the Aubers Ridge and the ground beyond to Herlies. The comparative inaction of the enemy had undoubtedly deluded the Staff into an optimistic expectation of a break-through on a wide front in a single day's fighting. On the 8th Division front the 23rd and 25th Brigades were to attack with the 24th Brigade in support, and accordingly the attacking brigades were relieved from the line and moved to the La Gorgue area for rest and training.

The right half-battalion of the Kensingtons was relieved on March 1st, and for the first time since entering the line in November, the four companies were united in billets in La Francas Mill. While here, apart from furnishing working parties, the time was spent in physical training and instruction in attack formation. On the 7th surplus kit was handed in and the Battalion moved to Lestrem, where training was continued until the eve of the battle. This had been fixed for March 10th, and preparations on the front were hurried forward, ladders for climbing over the breastworks were made, supplies of ammunition, food, and water carried forward, extra communication trenches and artillery emplacements dug. What was at that time considered a large number of guns was concentrated in the area and registration carried out. Unfortunately the general shortage of ammunition prevented the efficient performance of this vital preparation. The importance of the occasion was stressed by the issue to every man of the following note:

> The attack which we are about to undertake is of the first importance to the Allied Cause. The Army and the Nation are watching the results, and Sir John French is confident that every individual in the IVth Corps will do his duty and inflict a crushing defeat on the German VIIth Corps which is opposed to us.
>
> (Signed) H. RAWLINSON, Lieut.-General Commanding IVth Corps.

HEADQUARTERS IVTH CORPS,
9-3-15.

The 25th Brigade was to attack at 8.5 a.m., with the Royal Berkshires, supported by the Rifle Brigade, on the right and the Lincolns, supported by the Royal Irish Rifles, on the left, the Kensingtons to be in Brigade Reserve. The front-line troops were to carry the assault to the third line of the enemy trench system, and the supporting battalions were then to pass through them and capture the village. In accordance with this programme the Kensingtons marched from Lestrem on March 9th, each man carrying two extra bandoliers of ammunition and wearing greatcoats fastened back in the French style. Packs were left behind. Rations were carried in a sandbag, two spare sandbags also being taken for the erection of breastworks if required.

In common with other units of the 25th Brigade, a hot meal was taken at Rouge Croix and water-bottles filled with tea, and the Battalion then moved into the support trenches, all ranks imbued with a high spirit of adventure and an expectation of making a decisive step towards the winning of the war.

The artillery bombardment by 500 guns opened at 7.30 a.m. on the 10th and made a great impression on the British infantry at any rate, for it was the first concentrated bombardment of any length of the Great War. The men had been issued with cotton-wool to deaden the sound, and for half an hour the roar of the guns provided the overture for the drama in which the infantry, crouching keyed up in their assembly trenches, were now to play the principal part. At 8.5 a.m. the assaulting troops clambered over the ladders to the assault, marked at the outset by enemy machine guns and rifles, but nevertheless surging onwards and gaining the trenches which were the first objective. The casualties were unduly heavy in this first assault, for the bombardment seemed to have made very little impression on the enemy machine-gun posts, and our men made easy targets as they surmounted the breastworks. Our artillery fire was now concentrated on the village itself for half an hour, following which the supporting battalions passed through and continued the advance to the crossroads in the village. Thus, despite the volume of enemy fire, which increased rapidly and took a heavy toll of the advancing troops, the second objectives of the 25th Brigade were gained.

In the meantime the Kensingtons moved forward at 8.15 a.m. and occupied the breastwork vacated by the Rifle Brigade, who had advanced to a forward position preparatory to attacking the second objective. Here the first prisoners passed through on their way to the rear, tall well-built men, their officers moving with the swagger commonly associated with the German officer. They had many wounded with them. Up to now the battle seemed to be going well. C Company was detailed as a working party with the Lincolns and the Royal Berks, and at 9 a.m. moved forward into the thick of the battle. On reaching the village, they were ordered to take cover in the village cemetery while awaiting instructions. As the shell fire had been heavy on this spot, it was a gruesome ordeal lying amongst churned-up graves amid the wreckage of the tombstones and artificial flowers. Later, at 10 a.m., B Company was the next to be called upon, and it moved forward to the support of the Royal Irish Rifles, while D Company was attached to the Royal Engineers for carrying barbed wire to the foremost battalions. A Kensington in B Company describes the scene that met their gaze as, under the command of Captain A. Prismall, they moved forward to their allotted task: " Passing quickly over the old No-man's-land, swept by an intermittent machine-gun fire, but as yet free from shell fire, we saw the first horrors of the attack, officers and men lying dead in every kind of attitude just as they had fallen. Pushing on, we came to the village, battered considerably by the bombardment, but with one large crucifix still standing intact at the cross-roads. The task set us was to dig furiously and to put what was left of the houses into a state of defence." If the preliminary bombardment had been ineffective in quelling the enemy opposition in the village itself, it at least had battered the front-line trenches considerably, and the whole zone forward of the old British front line bore witness to the severity of the fighting in the initial assault.

THE BATTLE OF NEUVE CHAPELLE

The 23rd Brigade on the left of the Divisional front had not been so fortunate as the 25th Brigade, and support from the 24th Brigade and further artillery assistance had to be called for before the satisfactory completion of the first stage in the 8th Divisional operations could be reported. By 1 p.m., however, these objectives had been obtained, and the next stage in the battle began with an attack during the afternoon by the 24th Brigade. The enemy resistance had, however, stiffened, and further advance was found to be impossible and, rain falling in the early evening, the troops were compelled to dig in on the line gained. Two platoons of B Company were put in support to the Lincolns and were disposed in odd lengths of trenches or in the ruined houses, the remainder of the Battalion being by this time back in the old British front line. The night passed fairly quietly save for desultory shell fire, but over everything there was an air of expectancy mingled with doubt—no one knew what would happen next.

Further attempts were made on the following day by the 24th Brigade to drive the enemy from the village, but advance was found to be utterly impossible, so intense now was the machine-gun fire from the ruined houses in the village. The enemy artillery bombardment was increasing hourly as new guns came into action, and with the consequent destruction of communications, co-operation became increasingly difficult. With the utmost gallantry the regular battalions advanced to the assault, only to be mown down by the intense fire.

B Company of the Kensingtons rejoined the Battalion during the morning. They had considerable difficulty in getting back, for they had several wounded with them and they came under heavy shell fire as soon as they started. Lance-Corporal J. Jones volunteered to remain with the wounded, and later in the day stretcher bearers made five journeys under fire in order to bring them in. For this courageous action Lance-Corporal Jones was awarded the Military Medal.

During the morning the Battalion remained in the old front line, but in the early afternoon it moved into the

"THE KENSINGTONS"

Neuve Chapelle cemetery under orders to attack on the left of the Rifle Brigade, the 25th Brigade being in support to the proposed attack by the 24th Brigade. As has been stated, this attack failed and the Battalion was not called on.

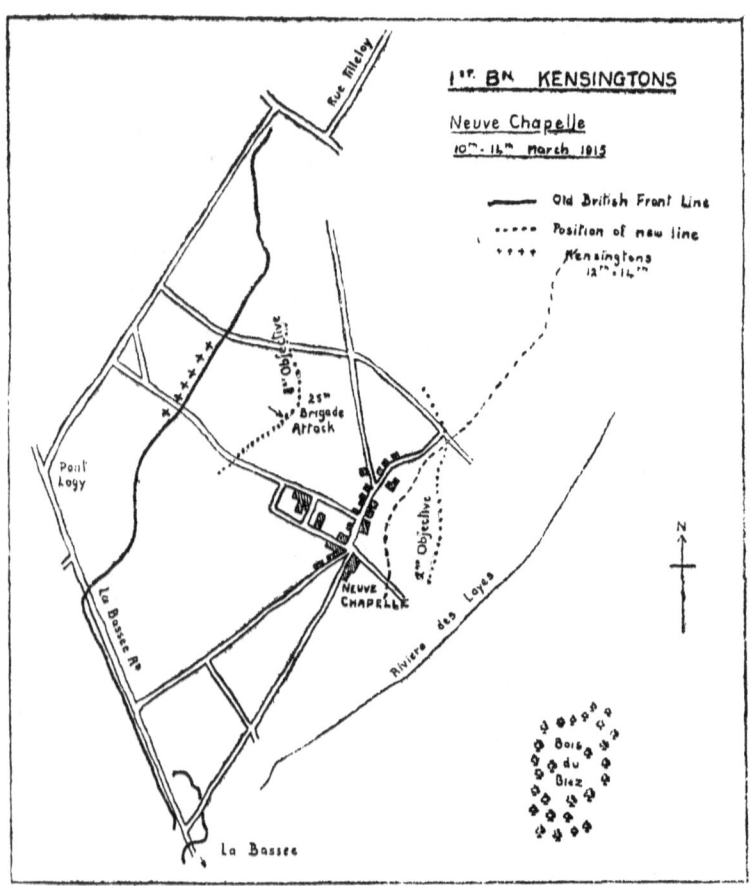

On this day the 7th Division on the right reached the Bois de Biez, but failed to hold the position, for the enemy shelled the wood heavily, and expected support from the Indian Corps failed to materialise, owing to the breakdown of communications. Runners found the greatest difficulty in getting through with messages; flares, rockets, and other means of signalling had not then been devised. This second day of the battle closed with the position unaltered as regards the front, but the volume of the enemy artillery bombardment showed a steady increase. A platoon of the Kensingtons, under Lieuts. Shaw and Cohen, was working with the Royal Engineers when a large shell burst amongst them, killing and wounding 15 men, both officers having very narrow escapes. A draft had arrived during that day consisting of 2 officers, Captain E. O. Taggart and Lieut. M. A. Prismall (son of Captain A. Prismall commanding B Company), and 131 men. They came in the thick of the battle and received their baptism of fire without delay, so that by the end of the battle they could be regarded as seasoned troops. At 11 p.m. orders were received to attack on the following morning, but cancellation came in the early hours of the 12th. The enemy bombardment had now intensified to a degree hitherto without parallel, and throughout the day both front-line troops and those in support were subjected to continuous shell fire. Attacks were ordered later in the day in an endeavour to carry on the advance, but the Staff had no real knowledge of the situation. All efforts to push forward found an enemy on the alert in well-prepared positions, amply supplied with ammunition and well supported by artillery. The attacking troops were cut down by machine-gun fire as soon as they emerged from their trenches and the attack was perforce abandoned. The men, too, were exhausted after three days without sleep, three days of stupendous exertions and continuous strain from shell fire. The Kensingtons spent the day in the old front line under a sustained bombardment. The report of the Commanding Officer, Lieut.-Colonel F. G. Lewis, T.D., on the events of this day provides a telling picture of what the Battalion endured:

March 12th, 1915.

5.15 a.m.   Orders for attack cancelled.
5.30 a.m.   German artillery begin to shell our trenches, apparently with a lot of guns.

"THE KENSINGTONS"

6.0 a.m.	German bombardment increases in intensity, about 100 guns at work.
7.35 a.m.	Bombardment on our trenches continues.
8.35 a.m.	Still continues with same intensity.
10.15 a.m.	Continued intense bombardment without a moment's cessation, every sort of gun and shell, working backwards and forwards up and down each line of trenches. Bombardment has now lasted 4¾ hours. Men calm and collected.
11.30 a.m.	Still continues. More Jack Johnsons. G.O.C. wounded and rest of his Staff killed or wounded. Sent Higgins to help on Staff. Orders to send fifty boxes ammunition to R.B. Headquarters. Lieut. Gates and most of his platoon knocked out by a Jack Johnson. Nearly all the signallers and Lieut. Lukis dangerously wounded. Awful holocaust.
12.25 p.m.	German shelling increases in intensity. "Perfect Hell." A semi-official report that La Bassée is taken. Probable invention to keep up spirit of the troops.
12.45 p.m.	Bombardment continues. G.O.C. moves to point 49. Higgins follows him and is brought back wounded in thigh. Casualties very heavy.
2.0 p.m.	Attack by R.B. and R.I.R. in progress.
2.15 p.m.	Attack not successful owing to machine-gun fire.
2.20 p.m.	Jack Johnsons again in profusion.
2.30 p.m.	Ninth hour of intense bombardment. Can it go on for ever? Men calm and collected.
3.0 p.m.	7th Division attempting to take Aubers. Day very dark and grey.
3.20 p.m.	Airman flew over German lines at height of about 1,000 feet, heavily fired on, but continued reconnaissance. Very plucky incident.
4.30 p.m.	R.B. and R.I.R. order to take German trenches at all costs. Kensingtons ordered to support this attack and move into Neuve Chapelle. The R.B. and R.I.R. were enfiladed by a murderous fire from the Bois de Biez, where there were machine guns. An advance utterly impossible. Our casualties terrible. Attack stopped and Kensingtons ordered back to former positions.

8.45 p.m.   G.O.C. returns to B lines. All telephone communication stopped and all wires and telephone instruments broken by shell fire and most of operators out of action. Awful sights to be seen as the result of Jack Johnson shells.

So ended a day calling for all the powers of endurance of the men. They had remained steadily at their posts under a sustained nerve-racking bombardment, during which very heavy casualties were incurred. The shells described at that time as Jack Johnsons, because they burst with a discharge of dense black smoke, were particularly destructive, falling as they did amongst troops devoid of all protection. The shell mentioned by Lieut.-Colonel Lewis as falling amongst the Signal Section was a case in point, all the section except one being killed or wounded. It was this same shell-burst that caused the casualties amongst the Brigade Staff.

The battle of Neuve Chapelle was virtually at an end by the 13th and the line gained in the initial assault was consolidated. On the 14th the Battalion was attached to the 23rd Infantry Brigade and took over from the 2nd Middlesex a series of disconnected fire trenches north of Neuve Chapelle. Desultory shell fire still persisted, and just as the companies were about to move off, the Battalion sustained a further loss in the person of Captain A. Prismall, commanding B Company. This officer was very popular, not only in his own company, but with the whole Battalion. The senior officer in age, he had nevertheless endured the long and arduous months of trench warfare, ever ready to encourage with a cheery word the men under his command. The sympathy of all ranks went out to his son, Lieut. Prismall, who had joined the Battalion but two days previously.

The situation quietened down, and on the 16th C and D Companies relieved A and B in the front line. Opportunity now occurred to look around. Hundreds of dead, both friend and foe, lay in all directions, and burial became an urgent matter. The men were too exhausted by lack of sleep and weakened by exposure to do much, and special parties were brought up for the purpose. Relief came at last in the shape of a Gurkha battalion of the Dehra Dun Brigade, and on the 24th the Battalion assembled as a complete unit at La Gorgue and marched to Croix Barbée, and thence to Bac St. Maur.

This battle, which was carried out by the 8th Division without support or reserves, was a costly one, for nearly 5,000 men were either killed or wounded. The primary objectives had been gained under the impetus of the initial assault, but further attempts to advance were foiled by the superior organisation of the enemy defence, which was found to be much stronger than anticipated. With strong fortified positions behind the front line, ample supply of artillery and machine guns, and uninterrupted communications, he was able not only to stem the first advance, but, by bringing up artillery, to shell effectively the supporting troops in their open trenches.

However, it cannot be denied that the German line had been broken for the first time. *The Times* reported:

> For the first time the British Army had broken the German line and struck the enemy a blow he will remember. The importance of the success does not lie so much in the capture of the German trenches along a front of two miles, the killing and capturing of some thousands of Germans, as the revelation of the fact that the much-vaunted German Army Machine, on which the whole attention of a mighty Nation had been lavished for four decades, is not invincible.

The Kensingtons had lost 6 officers and about 150 N.C.O.s and men, killed or wounded, in the engagement. Captain A. Prismall and Lieut. Gates had been killed, and Major H. Campbell, Lieuts. Lukis, Higgins, and Bamber wounded. Lieut. Lukis afterwards died of wounds. The steadiness of the men under the appalling shell fire had confirmed the opinion that the Territorials were second to none in warlike qualities. From now on they were to share fully all the hazards of war with the regular troops. The

THE BATTLE OF NEUVE CHAPELLE

following message was received from the General Officer Commanding the 25th Brigade, Brig.-General A. Lowry-Cole, C.B.

The G.O.C. the Division desires me to convey to you and all ranks under your command his deep appreciation of the splendid work performed by your battalion during the last few days' hard fighting. For my own part I find it difficult to express adequately my admiration for the way in which you have fought. I mourn with you for our gallant comrades who have fallen, but the splendid cause for which they have fought, and the noble way in which they have died, must always be the greatest comfort to those whom they have left behind, and stimulate them to fresh efforts.

CHAPTER V

AUBERS RIDGE—MAY 9TH, 1915

THE period of rest at Bac St. Maur was of brief duration. Reserves in those days were insufficient for a Divisional relief, and, despite the severity of the winter in the trenches and the recent ordeal of Neuve Chapelle, the line had still to be held by the same troops. In consequence the Kensingtons were again in the trenches on April 1st, having relieved the East Lancs. However, the sector, which was on the left of the old front, was quiet, and the improvement in the weather made the period tolerable. When out of the line the Battalion occupied billets at Bac St. Maur or Fleurbaix, and training was the order of the day. On the 17th of this month the Battalion was inspected by the Commander-in-Chief, Sir John French, who congratulated all ranks on the good work done at Neuve Chapelle and the patriotism displayed in volunteering for service abroad. During this inspection, one of the Battalion billets was burned to the ground, but the presence of the whole Battalion at a general inspection was adjudged a sufficient alibi.

Other Territorial battalions were by this time appearing in France, and served to relieve to some degree the pressure on the troops holding the line. The 1st London Regiment was attached to the 25th Infantry Brigade, which had thus six battalions. Changes occurred in the Battalion. Captain H. E. Huntriss (2nd Beds), who had been acting as Adjutant, left the Battalion, and Lieut. C. N. C. Howard was appointed in his place. Drafts of officers and men arrived from the 2nd Battalion in England and the strength of the Kensingtons grew to normal figures again.

On the 28th the Battalion went into Divisional reserve and marched to billets at Laventie, where a hearty reception was accorded by the Maison Leclerq, where most of the time when out of the line during the early months of the year had been spent. Curiously enough, the arrival of the Battalion was the occasion for a display of hostile shell fire on the village, which had been quiet for some time. Nothing daunted, a Battalion concert was held that evening in the convent of the Sacré Cœur, at which the customary good-fellowship prevailed.

A tour in the trenches at Picantin on the 30th brought the Kensingtons once more into familiar surroundings under vastly different weather conditions. Gone were the water-logged trenches where men had shivered and floundered in the mud. Instead, under sunny skies, the usual trench routine was carried out in the warm air of spring, on firm dry ground. It was realised how much the climatic conditions had been responsible for the sufferings of the winter.

To the discerning, however, this quiet was but the prelude to the storm. News had come to the Battalion on April 28th of the heavy fighting at Ypres, but the true nature of events in that district was not realised until later. Actually on the 22nd the Germans had made their first gas attack of the war against the French and Canadians at Ypres, an act which, while it contravened the accepted usages of war, was destined to introduce a factor into future operations which had not been anticipated and which had far-reaching consequences. Fortunately the enemy did not exploit to the full the opportunity thus created and the line held, but for a considerable time the enemy pressure was severe.

Quite apart from the necessity for relieving this pressure by operations elsewhere, however, an attack on the Aubers Ridge had been planned since the beginning of April to coincide with French operations against the Vimy Ridge; the whole to comprise a great offensive, breaking, if possible, the German line south of Lille and leading to decisive results. Moreover, it was hoped thereby to relieve to some extent the enemy pressure on the Russians. Optimism was again rife, for there had been no substantial increase in either the number of Divisions in the field or the weight of artillery for effective support to the infantry.

The attack was planned originally for May 8th, but was ultimately carried out on the 9th. On the 8th Divisional sector, the main attack was to be delivered on a three-battalion front by the 24th and 25th Brigades, the frontal attack being followed three minutes later by attacks on either flank. On the extreme left, where were the Kensingtons, tunnelling companies of the Royal Engineers had penetrated under the German front line and had placed in position two mines in close proximity. The explosion of these mines was to be the signal for this flank attack. The responsibility for seizing and occupying the crater formed by the explosion, and the formation of a defensive flank at 45 degrees, was allotted to the Kensingtons. The choice of this Battalion for such an important share in the operations was a tribute to the steadiness and courage demonstrated at Neuve Chapelle, and it was the first occasion on which Territorials were employed as an assaulting unit in a major operation. General Lowry-Cole, when asked why he had selected the Kensingtons for the left-flank attack, had stated emphatically, " The Kensingtons will not fail."

In accordance with this project the Battalion was relieved on May 1st and marched to Bac St. Maur, where training for the proposed attack was undertaken. Every detail of the operation was explained to the N.C.O.s and men by the Commanding Officer, and it was with a very full sense of responsibility that all ranks prepared for the coming offensive. It was hoped that, profiting by the experience gained at Neuve Chapelle, definite results would be obtained this time.

As already stated, the rising ground, known as the Aubers Ridge, with Fromelles in the foreground, dominates the flat ground where lay the trench system. No one at the time knew to what extent the ridge was fortified, though in post-war visits to this area members of the Battalion have seen the concrete emplacements in this much-disputed zone, many of them concealed in farm outbuildings and all commanding a perfect field of fire over the low-lying ground

AUBERS RIDGE—MAY 9TH, 1915

towards the Lys. The Division, however, had a definite task to perform, and preparations were hurried forward, every possible contingency being provided for. Profiting by the gas casualties at Ypres, a primitive respirator was issued, consisting of a pad to affix to the mouth and nose.

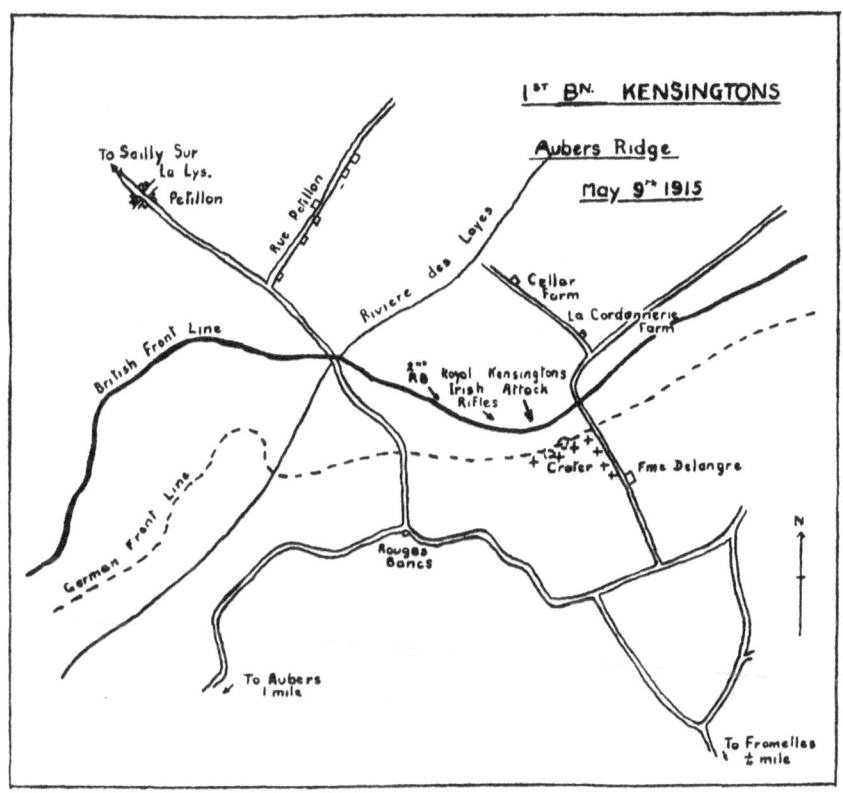

Fortunately this crude device was not required, for it is doubtful if it would have proved efficient. The preparations on the front, though carried out with secrecy, seemed to have been perceived by the enemy, and there is little doubt that he knew the whereabouts of the coming attack and even its date.

The Kensingtons moved up to the trenches on the evening

of the 8th, the attack, as stated, having been postponed for twenty-four hours. At 5 p.m. C Company went forward to complete preparations and furnish a party for wire cutting; the remainder of the Battalion, after halting at Cordonnerie Farm, occupied the assault trenches in preparation for the morrow, the leading company taking up a position in front of the British parapet. By 2 a.m. the wire on the Battalion front was reported to be cut, and at 5 a.m. the bombardment commenced. This was intended first to cut the wire and then, lifting, destroy the enemy trenches. It failed lamentably in both objects, not through any fault of the gunners, but through general insufficiency of artillery. It is recorded that ancient brass mortars dating from 1840 were used to supplement the volume of fire, but at its height it was insufficient even to keep the enemy under cover, and in the time available its destructive effect was negligible. On the Kensingtons' front 4·7 howitzers were supposed to bombard Delangre Farm, but actually not a single shell touched it and a battalion on the right of the Divisional front, which had to occupy forward assault trenches under cover of the bombardment, came under a murderous rifle and machine-gun fire as soon as they left their trenches. It was revealed afterwards that the batteries had had insufficient rounds for registration on their targets.

At 5.40 a.m. the mines were exploded and C and D Companies advanced to the assault across No-man's-land. They were at once subjected to a withering fire, but in spite of heavy losses, advanced on a fifty-yards front to the enemy line and occupied the right-hand crater and a portion of the trenches on either side. A party of bombers worked along the trench a distance of 100 yards, clearing it of the enemy, and, A and B Companies following in support, by 6.30 a.m. they had secured their objectives, occupying a line from the crater back to the track leading to Delangre Farm. There had been some stiff fighting. About 30 prisoners were taken, the Commanding Officer capturing four in a dugout, but so intense had the fire now become in No-man's-land that only 10 of these reached the British lines. By

6.45 a.m. the line was extended to the south of Delangre Farm by the remains of the two leading companies, C and D, but the supply of bombs began to fail, and there was no sign of British troops either on the right or behind. No-man's-land was by now a bullet-swept zone in which it was impossible for men to move, for the enemy had numbers of machine guns in Delangre Farm which, free from molestation from artillery fire, had opened on the attack from its inception. The casualties, which had been heavy in the initial assault, began to mount up. Captain Barnett and Lieut. Sewell had been killed, and at 8.30 a.m. the Commanding Officer reported to Brigade that the Battalion objectives had been gained, but that he had exhausted every available reinforcement. The reply received later was, " 2nd Scottish Rifles moving to support you. You have done splendidly."

B Company had the difficult task of forming a defensive flank by swinging to the left, for it will be remembered that the Kensingtons occupied the extreme left of the attacking front. The narrow frontage of the assault made this difficult, as D Company had received a severe check, and Captain Whitty, O.C. B Company, had great difficulty in getting his men in position. Though wounded, he succeeded in carrying out the operation, and later the defensive flank was held by Major H. Stafford. Although during the morning their numbers were reduced to 24 men, and the machine guns were put out of action, they stood their ground with the enemy only thirty yards away.

As the morning wore on, the position became desperate. The promised support never materialised, for only 1 officer and 2 bombers of the Scottish Rifles got over, and it became evident that, deficient of ammunition and reduced in numbers, the Kensingtons could not long withstand the enemy counter-attacks, which now began to be felt. Indeed, at 11.30 a.m. the enemy broke through a block and began bombing up the trench, and trench mortars opened fire on B Company in their precarious position on the left.

By making use of the ammunition collected from the belt of the disabled machine gun, the attacks were held.

Elsewhere things were going badly. The main idea of the Divisional attack on such a narrow front had been that fresh troops were to follow on as the leading waves moved forward. The enemy fire was, however, so intense from the outset that the foremost lines were checked and the succeeding troops found their advance impeded. There was great confusion, of which the enemy took the fullest advantage, and concentrated a deadly fire on the comparatively limited area. The attack of the East Lancs on the right had been held up from the start. The wire was found to be uncut, and attempts to advance under the intense machine-gun fire were immediately frustrated. The leading waves were mown down as soon as they moved. The Royal Irish Rifles and Royal Berks were more fortunate, and parties succeeded in reaching the outskirts of Rouge Bancs, behind the German trenches, under the impetus of the initial assault. It was found, however, utterly impossible to exploit these gains, for by this time the enemy had found that no real danger to his trenches, with their twenty-foot-thick breastworks and bullet-proof shelters, existed, and he was therefore free to concentrate his fire on No-man's-land with a view to preventing the arrival of reinforcements or ammunition to the hard-pressed attacking troops.

Superhuman efforts had been directed to this end, but such supporting troops that did succeed in getting across were so reduced in numbers that by the time they reached their objective the support they could give was negligible. General Lowry-Cole, realising that failure was inevitable unless substantial support could be got to his men in the German front line, leapt on the parapet and shouted encouragement to the supporting troops. While so doing he was wounded and died shortly afterwards.

Noon came, and found the Kensingtons and some other small sections of the attacking battalions holding on precariously to isolated sections of the German trenches, short of ammunition and without hope of reinforcement, for they saw their supports start out and saw them fade away. The trench was full of dead and wounded, the last grenade had been fired, and slowly the thin line of Kensingtons towards Delangre Farm was forced back. At 2.45 p.m. orders were received from General Pinney, now commanding 25th Brigade, to retire to the British breastwork.

This proved to be the most costly operation of the day, for an almost impregnable barrier of fire existed in No-man's-land, an inferno of bursting shell and whining bullets, in which any movement was attended by the certain chance of being hit. By worming their way along, taking advantage of any protection that existed, the survivors got out into the open. The plight of the wounded was terrible. Many had lain all day without attention, for the fighting had been too severe for the handful of survivors to give them much assistance, and evacuation was impossible. Such as were able dragged themselves out into the open waiting for nightfall. The men in the trench towards Delangre Farm had to fight their way out, floundering through the slime of disused enemy trenches with the enemy bombing towards them.

How many were lost in this terrible withdrawal will never be known. The following account serves to show what it was like:

Then we got the order to retire. There was nothing else to do, and it was bitter. Moreover, we had to fight our way through the German lines in order to regain our men. For hours we were above our waists in the mud and foul water of the German communicating trenches, isolated and cut off by an enemy we could not see, but who was steadily reducing our numbers by excellent sniping. We decided to wait until darkness and then try to get through the German lines to our own. We made the venture and got back to our trenches by about 8.15 p.m. How I got through without being hit I shall never know. We crawled about 120 to 150 yards through German barbed wire and across ground raked by a withering cross-fire. It was a hailstorm of lead, bullets splitting up the ground and filling the air with the buzz as of angry bees, and bursting shells. For a moment I was caught on the barbed wire, but managed somehow to wrench clear, my nose almost burrowing the ground. Men were being hit all about me. Somehow we got across to the foot of our parapet. There was a slight ridge there and, lying absolutely flat, it gave cover. It was still light, and I told the men to wait until dark before the last dash over the sandbags into our lines. To my surprise, lying there flat under the cover of the ridge with shells bursting and whistling overhead and bullets throwing up earth behind and before and around me and striking against the parapet which was our haven only twenty yards away, I fell asleep from sheer exhaustion. It must have been nearly half an hour later when, awaking in the darkness, I scrambled up the parapet and threw myself down amongst our own men, to find that I had been reported killed.

As much bravery was shown in this retreat to our line as in the initial assault; the day had been lost, but there was no " Sauve qui peut " in the Kensingtons' retirement. As many of the wounded as could be found were got in, and the officers were confronted with a difficult task in collecting their men and getting them back to safety. Captain Kimber, who was awarded the D.S.O. for his gallantry in the fighting at the crater and the subsequent withdrawal, was but one case of heroism. Indeed, all men were heroes that day.

The attempt to capture the Aubers Ridge had been a failure in spite of the heroic bravery of the attacking troops and the supporting battalions, for the latter had again and again made the most determined efforts to furnish help and ammunition to their comrades in the German trenches. The enemy position was found to be much stronger than anticipated, and the preparatory bombardment had made no impression on it at all. With superior weight of machine guns and artillery, directed from the commanding slopes of the Ridge, he had been able to place a devastating fire on No-man's-land and our assembly positions and effectively bring our attack to a standstill.

By nightfall about 50 survivors of the Kensingtons had reached a rendezvous near Cellar Farm, where, under continuous shell fire, they remained until the early hours of May 10th, when the Battalion was ordered to Croix

Blanche. Other survivors had come in during the night, but it was soon learnt that the battle had occasioned the loss of 13 officers and 423 other ranks. As a fighting unit the Kensington Battalion was temporarily non-existent, for the strength was thus reduced to 30 per cent., and no reinforcements were immediately available.

In the next few days the Kensingtons received recognition for the valiant part that they had played in the battle. They could justly claim to be the only battalion that had gained all its objectives, and the regular soldiers were not slow in showing their appreciation of men who had endured so much beside them. General Davies went personally to the Battalion on the 13th to congratulate the men on their achievement. But the losses occasioned by the battle meant that some time must elapse before they could again take their share in active operations. It was good-bye to the 8th Division just at a time when the Kensingtons had won their spurs with them, and within the next few days the remnants of the Battalion, now transferred to General Headquarters as Line of Communication troops, took the road to St. Omer. At Le Sart on the line of march on May 20th, Sir H. Rawlinson, commanding the IVth Corps, met the Battalion and congratulated the men for their excellent work on the 9th, and pointed out that it had not been in vain. At the very first onset the terrible pressure at Ypres had been relieved and the French had been enabled to gain the victory round Arras. " By your splendid attack and dogged endurance, you and your fallen comrades won imperishable glory for the 13th London Battalion. It was a feat of arms surpassed by no battalion in the Great War. Though no accounts of your work on that day have been published in the press, do not think that it is not known and fully appreciated. It is known fully and valued in the highest degree by myself and the Staff of the IVth Corps, by General Sir John French and the H.Q. Staff, and by the authorities at home, the War Office."

The march was continued via Thiennes, Wittes, Wardreques to Racquinghem, where thirteen buses of the Royal

Naval Division transported the Battalion to Tatenghem, near St. Omer, where some delay and amusement were caused by the discovery of the motor-cycle orderly under arrest as a spy. This difficulty cleared up, the unit marched to billets in barracks in the town.

This marks the conclusion of an epoch in the life of the Kensington Battalion during the Great War. A large and gallant company was left behind. The Kensington Cemetery in the Rue Bacquerot, next to the old Aid Post, and the Neuve Chapelle Cemetery, are the last resting-places of many who fell before the end of March 1915, but the bodies of those who fell on May 9th were in many cases never recovered. Their names, however, are engraved on the walls of the noble Ploegsteert memorial under the inscription:

To the Glory of God and to the memory of officers and men of the British Empire who fell fighting in the years 1914–1915 between the River Douve and the towns of Estaires and Furnes, whose names are here recorded, but to whom the fortunes of war denied the known and honoured burial given to their comrades in death.

CHAPTER VI

LINES OF COMMUNICATION

In the early days of the war, before the true nature of the long grim struggle that lay before the nation was realised, it was commonly stated that the Territorial Army might be required for duty on lines of communication, but their services in the firing line would certainly not be called for. As has been seen, the urgency of the situation compelled their entry into the trenches almost immediately after landing in France, and they had subsequently shared the full rigours of the campaign with the regular army. As the result of the severity of the losses sustained in the campaign the Kensingtons were now to learn the meaning of the term "lines of communication," a term often used, but not hitherto appreciated in its full significance by men who had been continuously at the Front.

On arrival at St. Omer, the Battalion found the London Rifle Brigade and the Rangers, both Territorial units, already there. These units as well as the Kensingtons had suffered heavy losses, and the three regiments were temporarily combined into a single composite battalion under the command of Major H. J. Stafford, Lieut.-Colonel Lewis being in hospital. On May 29th relief of the 6th Welch Regiment, which was serving on the lines of communication, commenced, the London Rifle Brigade taking over southern railheads, the Rangers, Calais and Etaples, and the Kensingtons the northern railheads. Until the end of the month parties from the Battalion departed daily to take over duties at Steenwerck, Bailleul, Strazeele, Caestre, Godewaersvelde, Abeele, Steenbecque, Arneke, Ebblinghem, and Hazebrouck. Some of these parties were under the command of an officer, others were in the charge of a senior N.C.O., and the duties, which were very varied in character, resolved themselves chiefly into the furnishing of guards, the offloading of wagons, and other miscellaneous tasks as required by the Railway Transport Officer of the railhead concerned. New Divisions, reinforcements, and quantities of war material were constantly arriving during the summer of 1915, and the railhead detachments found strenuous employment in detraining these units. G.S. wagons and limbers had to be slid cautiously down the wooden ramps from the trucks to the ground, horses and mules persuaded to trust themselves to the same primitive means of descent, and kit of all sorts to be unloaded. As the railheads were frequently at insignificant stations, raised platforms were uncommon, and the expeditious detraining of a unit meant skill and forethought. In this the detraining parties came to be expert.

It was a novelty also for the men to be stationed thus quietly out of the sound of the guns in many cases, and it gave an opportunity to see a side of French life hitherto unsuspected, accustomed as they were to the dreary shell-scarred wastes of Flanders. Some of these railheads lay beside quiet rivers or near great woods. Civilian trains ran into them and the war seemed remote. A diarist, describing the journey to his railhead, which involved changing at Amiens, says:

We went into the town and found a new world. There was the thrill at the sight of the great cathedral, as yet untouched by shell fire, and inside a wonderful peace with quiet groups of people coming in to offer up prayer. The streets were thronged with people, a medley of soldiers and civilians, with here and there inviting little cafés and American bars. In the train again on the way to Ribemont, we found the country-side changing. Great fields in which groups of peasants bent to their tasks stretched away into the far distance. Little streams wound among the trees, and here and there one saw men fishing, as though there was nothing in the world but the peace of spring, and fish to be caught. Yet the trains passed through this quiet countryside carrying munitions of war in one direction, and others, slow-moving, bore a burden of tortured humanity in the other.

LINES OF COMMUNICATION

After the horrors through which we had passed it seemed incredible that the world could thus quietly carry on its ordinary business and pleasures, and so near to the scene of those horrors.

The troops on these railheads were comfortably billeted. Some of the officers occupied first-class railway carriages cunningly converted into living-rooms and bedrooms, while the men, wherever they were, soon displayed the invariable ingenuity of the British soldier in making himself comfortable, given the time and the opportunity to do so.

Quite apart from the interest aroused by the close-up view of French country life thus afforded, the period had its military lessons too. The men began to realise the complex organisation of the army machine and the co-operation between other branches of the service that was required in order that supplies of ammunition, rations, reinforcements, mails, and medical services could be regularly maintained for the troops in the line. The infantryman is all too prone to take this for granted, and it is not until things go wrong that he begins to realise the complexity of the business. In the maintenance of these services, in addition to the usual English troops, men of various nationalities were employed—Chinese coolies and Indians. Labour battalions of unfit or over-age men were busy on roads, reserve trenches, and in general acted as navvies for the Army.

In the meantime, the Headquarters of the Battalion, with a small nucleus of N.C.O.s and men, remained at St. Omer. Three guards were regularly furnished during the whole period—a station guard, Railhead Commandant guard, and the guard at Battalion Headquarters—and from time to time parties were called on to escort prisoners to the base or detrain a Division near at hand. Otherwise the time was spent in training, mostly squad drill and exercises for newly made N.C.O.s. The numbers present at any one time were rarely sufficient for training of a more serious character. Drafts arrived from time to time from the 3rd Battalion, and many men rejoined from hospital, so that, little by little, the Battalion strength began to approach normal figures.

At the end of June a camp near the infantry barracks was completed and the Headquarters moved under canvas for what turned out to be an exceptionally wet summer. The ground was soon churned into mud, and by the winter conditions became very uncomfortable, all efforts at drainage proving futile. The tents were each provided with a boarded floor, but on stepping off this the men were at once ankle deep in mud, and, as a smart appearance at all times was expected, a great deal of time was spent in cleaning up.

At the beginning of August the composite battalion was broken up, to the satisfaction of all concerned, for there had been some fear that the units involved might lose their identity. Certain duties were taken over by the Kensingtons from the London Rifle Brigade and the Rangers, who left for other areas. On the 13th of this month Lieut.-Colonel Lewis, who had rejoined eleven days previously to assume command of the composite battalion, was promoted Brig.-General commanding 142nd Infantry Brigade, and left the Regiment to take up his new duties. Major Stafford was promoted Lieut.-Colonel and assumed the command. Although regretting the loss of Colonel Lewis, all felt that an honour had been conferred upon the Battalion by his promotion. He had brought the Kensingtons overseas, and had been their pilot through dark and difficult days. All ranks knew him to be a courageous, just, and efficient Commanding Officer, with a full appreciation of the points of view of the men under his command. Battalion orders dated August 14th, 1915, contained the following farewell letter:

> After over twenty-two years of service in it, I cannot hand over the Battalion without a deep feeling of regret at leaving it. I take the opportunity of thanking most sincerely all ranks for the magnificent response they have made to my demands. Words fail me in which to

express my feelings. I can only hope in the future the Battalion will add to its laurels, as I feel sure it will so long as it adheres to the traditions it has made for itself.

(Signed) F. G. LEWIS, Brig.-General.

At the end of the month the Battalion strength had increased to 733 all ranks, and the officers present were: A Company, Captain C. C. Dickens (O.C.), Lieuts. Robertson, Lewin, and Venables. B Company, Captain H. N. Whitty (O.C.), Capt. Harris, Lieuts. Roseveare and Penn. C Company, Captain Ware (O.C.), Lieuts. Cohen and Heath, 2nd Lieut. Mason. D Company, Captain Longuet Higgins (O.C.), Lieuts. Parton and Barnes, 2nd Lieut. Beggs. Major Mackenzie was second-in-command, Lieut. Holland Transport Officer, Lieut. Keen Medical Officer, and Lieut. Ridley Quartermaster. Shortly afterwards Lieut. Barnes was posted to the Ordnance Corps, and Lieuts. Vincent, Leggett, and Williams joined from England.

During the summer strict orders were issued that cameras were not to be carried or used. Some interesting snapshots of a personal nature had been taken during the winter months, but now treasured vest-pocket Kodaks were despatched to England and the opportunity of acquiring some records of scenes and incidents vanished.

Correspondence with home became easier with the issue, very sparingly at first, of the green envelope. This could be sealed, provided the writer signed an undertaking on the envelope that nothing of military importance was mentioned within. It was a privilege much appreciated, and permitted the discussion of private and personal matters.

The remainder of the year proved uneventful. There was occasional bombing at St. Omer by enemy aeroplanes, but fortunately no bombs fell in the camp. The days were spent in drill or the performance of the necessary camp fatigues. In the evening the men off duty cleaned up and spent the few hours of liberty at the Y.M.C.A. or a favourite estaminet in the town. At the former some excellent concerts were arranged, the Artists' Rifles, who also furnished guards at St. Omer, providing some accomplished performers. Musical comedies were staged in an admirable manner considering the difficulties, and the "ladies" carried out their parts with surprising skill. In the estaminet the entertainment was less formal, presided over by a good-tempered hostess with a lively fear of the military police, assisted by an attractive daughter who, by this time, had acquired a considerable fluency in English. When funds permitted, the men patronised a little restaurant where appetising dishes could be had for the modest sum of one franc. The *pièce de résistance* was reputed to be horseflesh, but, nevertheless, was eaten with relish as a variant to the monotony of the army rations.

Christmas, the second in France, came, and the Kensingtons, wherever they were stationed, entered into the spirit of the festivities with their customary zeal. At Headquarters a dining-hut had recently been erected at the camp, and a real Christmas dinner, the rations supplemented by pudding and other seasonable dishes, was enjoyed. A cinema had been fitted up in the town by the Y.M.C.A. and was packed to overflowing by the troops at the afternoon performance. Although breakdowns were frequent and the crazy piano was in much demand to accompany popular songs of the day, the interrupted performances of Charlie Chaplin, then in his zenith, made a welcome break in the routine. The camp by this time was a quagmire, and many were the rescues from the drainage ditches that intersected the lines as homecoming wanderers sought vainly to find their damp and dismal tents in the mud and darkness.

However, although the amenities of life in town or railhead made up to some extent for the dreariness of winter, a feeling grew that this was not the sort of life for which the Battalion came overseas, and that some definite action towards winning the war was imperative. It was therefore with a feeling of some relief that news was received that the Kensingtons were to form part of the 56th London Division and that the associations formed at St. Omer or on the railheads were soon to be severed.

LINES OF COMMUNICATION

The beginning of February 1916 saw the Battalion in the throes of preparation for assembly as a complete unit once more. Railhead detachments returned as they were relieved by the 9th Highland Light Infantry (Territorials), and the same battalion took over the duties at the camp at St. Omer, all reliefs being completed by the 7th. On the 11th the Kensingtons bade good-bye to the pleasant town of St. Omer and, escorted by the pipes of the H.L.I. and the band of the Artists' Rifles, marched to the station and entrained for Pont Remy to join the 56th Division.

CHAPTER VII

WITH THE 56TH DIVISION

THE railhead at Pont Remy was reached at 5 p.m. on February 11th, and a long march ensued through a chilling downpour of rain to Citerne. The training area thus reached proved to be undulating country, thinly populated by a peasantry gaining a sparse living by agriculture and the weaving of a coarse sacking. The weather became cold, and heavy snowfalls made training difficult.

The Kensingtons were now definitely part of the 56th Division, commanded by Major-General C. P. A. Hull. This Division, with which the Battalion was destined to serve for the remainder of the war, was composed entirely of first battalions of London regiments. The three infantry brigades were made up as follows:

167th Brigade	1/1 London Regiment (Royal Fusiliers).
	1/3 London Regiment (Royal Fusiliers).
	1/8 Middlesex.
	1/7 Middlesex.
168th Brigade	1/4 London Regiment (Royal Fusiliers).
	1/12 London Regiment (Rangers).
	1/13 London Regiment (Kensingtons).
	1/14 London Regiment (London Scottish).
169th Brigade	1/2 London Regiment (Royal Fusiliers).
	1/5 London Regiment (London Rifle Brigade).

169th Brigade—*cont.*
            1/9 London Regiment (Queen Victoria Rifles).
            1/16 London Regiment (Queen's Westminsters).

Pioneer Battalion   The 5th Cheshires.

It is thus seen that the Kensingtons were now with old friends. The 1/1st Londons and the 1/8th Middlesex had seen service with the 8th Division and the L.R.B., and the Rangers had been associated with the Battalion at St. Omer.

The 168th Infantry Brigade was commanded by Brig.-General G. C. Loch, with Captain P. Neame, V.C., as Brigade Major and Major L. C. Wheatley as Staff Captain. Captain Neame had won his V.C. in the 8th Division trenches in the winter of 1914, when serving with the Royal Engineers during the December attack on the Neuve Chapelle trenches. The artillery and field ambulances were also London units, so that the Division was truly a London Division. During the months of February, March, and April 1916, the Division thus newly formed was busily perfecting its organisation, until by easy stages the troops came forward to the Hebuterne sector on the extreme left of the Somme front.

During these months the Kensingtons were similarly occupied in training and organisation. The separation of the last few months had tended to destroy that unity which is a *sine qua non* of a battalion no less than of a Division. Men had been in isolated groups on railheads with no opportunity for training, and newly promoted N.C.O.s and officers, fresh from England, needed time to become acquainted with their duties. The methods of attack were also being modified to suit the changing character of the operations. However, within a short space of time the Battalion became once more a unified whole, with the same spirit of determination as predominant as ever. By this time protective measures against gas attack became part of the training. The new respirators, now issued to the troops, completely covered the head, and instruction was given in the use of them, fifteen seconds being allowed in which to put them on. As a part of the training, the men, while wearing them, passed in parties through a gas-filled room, thus providing a test of each individual respirator and giving the wearer some confidence in its efficiency.

The billets at Citerne were indifferent and offered a poor protection against the snow which fell heavily from time to time during the month of February. The Kensingtons were glad to partake of such hospitality as the village offered, and, following the day's training, they sought out the cottages where eggs and chips could be bought. These were plentiful in this rural area, and the poorest of linguists was able to demand, "Deux œufs avec pommes de terre frites," and no matter how atrocious the accent was certain to be understood. For a modest sum the hungry soldier sat in a warm room and watched with anticipation the expert efforts of madame to coax the charcoal stove into a blaze and cook the appetising dish. It was common ground between French cooking and English tastes—the men enjoyed it, and every French woman seemed able to do the required cooking. Soups and other poor country fare with which they graced their own tables aroused no enthusiasm amongst the troops. Coffee followed and, if the meagre pay allowed, coffee cognac, there being no licence required for the selling of spirits. No doubt they entertained the troops partly for profit, but one prefers to think that these humble women did this service for the English soldiers also because they were but boys, and, as such, reminded them of their own sons serving as poilus away on the French front. Until actually ordered to leave the village, these simple peasants would remain in a semi-ruined village with shells falling in the garden, and dispense cheer and good fare to all and sundry. Probably they did more to keep up the spirit of the men than has ever been realised.

The snow lingered and it was over roads eighteen inches

deep in places that the Battalion marched from Citerne on February 27th and joined the rest of the Brigade at Hallencourt, where the transport was brigaded under Lieut. Holland. The going was very difficult, and the men were utterly exhausted by the time the billeting areas around Longpré were reached. The transport, in fact, failed to reach the area until the following day. Several wagons stuck on the hills, and it was only by the greatest exertions on the part of the horses that they were got up at all. The Kensingtons reached Surcamps, their allotted area, in the late afternoon and, due to the non-arrival of the transport, had neither rations nor blankets. Fortunately the field kitchens had kept up with the troops, and tea and stew were served on arrival, following which an attempt was made to sleep in the barns and stables provided, without blankets or further food. The odoriferous fur coat carried by all received some appreciation on this occasion. Some pride was felt that in this long and arduous march, only seven men fell out, and these all joined during the evening.

The morning revealed an undulating country-side now white with snow, with pine woods here and there standing out stark against the white background. The preceding day's march had not been without its scenic effects as the column of marching men and transport, two miles in length, wound in snakelike fashion through the snow-covered country. The original intention had been to stay but one night at Surcamps, but the congestion on the roads due to French troops and transport moving south to Verdun, where a battle had been raging for a week, and to some degree the difficulty of moving the Divisional transport, caused a postponement of the move for some days. The period was usefully spent in company training and, the baggage wagons now having turned up, the men enjoyed some degree of comfort. On March 12th the Battalion left Surcamps and marched via Domart, Bien Fienvillers, and Candas to Doullens sixteen miles distant, which was reached at 4 p.m. The G.O.C. 56th Division, General Hull, watched the various units *en route*, and, reporting later, mentioned the Kensingtons favourably for march discipline, general turn-out, and transport. No other unit in the Division was reported as " good " in all three items.

After two days' rest, much appreciated, for Doullens is an attractive little town, the Battalion marched via Grand Rullecourt and Ambrines to Magnicourt sur Canche, a small village on a steep hillside. A demonstration was given here with a captured flammenwerfer, an enemy offensive weapon designed to project a long jet of flame. It was shown to be ineffective on troops in trenches, as the flame could not be directed downwards. A reshuffling of billets within the Brigade caused a move to Lignereuil on the 21st, where the Battalion stayed for some weeks, the men being accommodated in barns, nearly all of which were infested with rats. Rations were consumed during the night by these pests, and men frequently found that a much-prized parcel from home had been eaten right through for the sake of the food within.

Serious training in attack was now begun, and instruction in bombing was given in schools organised by the Division. The Battalion was selected to carry out a demonstration of trench-mortar and grenade attack before the Commander-in-Chief and the G.O.C. VIth Corps. This demonstration commenced at noon on March 30th and was realistic in all respects except that the enemy was imaginary. The Stokes mortars opened on the " enemy trenches " with good accuracy, and the assaulting platoon, under Lieut. Penn, advanced from the assembly trench and took the first-line enemy trench at the point of the bayonet. One hundred yards in rear, the grenade, Lewis-gun, and signalling detachments, under Capts. Cohen and Harris, advanced to the first-line enemy trench, where the signallers established two stations, while the grenade and Lewis-gun parties worked to the flanks and up the communication trenches. Live grenades No. 5 were thrown and the trenches blocked. The support platoon, under 2nd Lieut. R. E. F. Shaw, advanced to the first-line " enemy trench " and proceeded to reverse the parapet and fire step, thus consolidating the position. In the rear of the support platoon, and after all live grenades had been thrown, a Stokes mortar was advanced to an emplacement on the left flank of the " enemy trench " and four rounds were fired towards the left into a support enemy position. This demonstration, which was a complete success, is here described in detail in order to show how things were supposed to go in an actual attack, but frequently did not owing to enemy opposition or unforeseen circumstances. At the conclusion of the event the Commanding Officer, Lieut.-Colonel H. Stafford, was congratulated by the Commander-in-Chief.

The equipment carried by the men had recently been increased by the addition of the steel helmet, an uncomfortable headgear which was difficult to keep on. They, however, proved to be splinter proof and undoubtedly prevented many casualties. Respirators were, of course, carried, and for marching order the mess tin was now slung under the pack in a cover and the water-proof sheet folded and carried on the top of the pack. In the demonstration attack the haversack was carried on the back and steel helmets worn, the respirator being carried on the chest in the " alert " position.

Other activities during this period included shooting matches, in addition to the courses at the grenade school, until on April 10th the Battalion marched to Dainville, near Arras, for trench digging under the Royal Engineers, relieving the Rangers, who had been similarly employed. The work involved was the construction of a reserve system of trenches in extension of the existing system, which was of French origin. The men had thus their first view of a front which was to become very familiar later on in the war. Dainville was at the time under observation from enemy observation balloons, or " sausages " as they were popularly called, and movement during daylight was strictly limited and rations had to be brought in under cover of darkness. The digging was done at night when the weather permitted and proved to be heavy work, for, although the subsoil was chalk, the top surface was very heavy and sticky after rain. When constructed, however, the trenches were, naturally, more solid and dry than those constructed in the Lys valley. Dugouts were also made, though not in any way approaching the well-constructed type afterwards found in the German trench system. In the village of Dainville there was a whole labyrinth of underground passages cut in the chalk and approached from several points. Many Kensingtons took the opportunity to explore these workings with the aid of candles. Their utility from a military point of view was obvious, and in this particular case they had been used by the French during their occupation of this front.

After a fortnight of these nocturnal working parties, the Battalion returned to Lignereuil by route march, arriving at 4 a.m. on the 25th. The training period was nearing its completion, but before its conclusion Brigade sports were held on May 1st, the Kensingtons winning the parade competition and the limber turn-out and driving, though in the other events they were not so successful. Just prior to leaving the area a demonstration of attack under cover of a smoke cloud was carried out by A Company, under Capt. Robertson.

On May 6th the whole Division moved to the Pas area, the Kensingtons marching to Souastre near the Hebuterne front. Training continued, and time was found for two interesting football matches with the 4th Londons and the Scottish, respectively, the former being a draw and the latter a clear victory. On the 7th (Sunday) a service in commemoration of May 9th, 1915, was conducted by the chaplain, Brig.-General Loch being present, and on the 21st the Battalion took over trenches at Hebuterne in relief of the 8th Middlesex. The sector was approached via Bayencourt and Sailly au Bois, and after leaving the latter village the road passed over the crest of a low hill, whence the Verey lights and the dark silhouette of Gommecourt Wood against the night sky could be seen.

This sector, which had originally been held by the

French, consisted of trenches constructed in orchards and gardens fringing the eastern side of the village, with a strong point, known as the " Keep," to the left. Advance lines had been subsequently pushed out when the British took over, linked up with, in many cases, very poor communication trenches, well marked by enemy snipers in Gommecourt Wood. Cellars under the ruined buildings in the village had been fortified with sandbag breastworks and fitted with wire beds. Battalion Headquarters was established in cellars under the ruins of Hebuterne mill, and the breastwork afforded some protection against the long-range machine-gun fire that was a feature of the enemy activities, particularly during the night. In this first tour in the W sector A Company occupied the front line, which could only be approached at night, for the communication trench was under constant observation by the enemy. Apart from occasional enemy trench-mortar fire and the nightly " hymn of hate " from Gommecourt, the situation was quiet.

During this period a draft of 200 men of the 2/4th London Regiment arrived for the Kensingtons. Something like dismay was occasioned by this reinforcement of battalions by men from other units, especially when it was learnt that a Kensington draft had been posted elsewhere. The Fusiliers continued to wear their regimental badges and were considered as attached only. Actually at this period men of the Kensingtons who had served overseas and had been wounded might, on rearrival in France, find themselves included in a draft for any battalion. The position was regularised later by an order permitting the return to their own unit of men who had already served overseas with it, and the attached men who had not hitherto seen service in France, were definitely transferred to the unit with which they were then serving. One can understand the necessity for some such transference of men from one battalion to another while deploring it. In active operations the losses varied considerably, so that one unit might impose a heavy tax on the source of reinforcements in England. However, in this case no such active operations were yet in progress, and the fact that a draft despatched from the 3rd Battalion of the Kensingtons in England should go elsewhere, while an equivalent number of another unit was received, looked on the face of it as sheer muddling. Perhaps some adequate reasons existed, but a move more calculated to destroy *esprit de corps* and nullify the co-operation between the training battalion at home and the 1st or 2nd Battalions in the fighting line cannot be imagined.

It also had its amusing aspects, for, later, a draft arrived containing men from the so-called " Bantam " Battalion. These men, however, in spite of their diminutive height, after a short time settled down and became good soldiers. In fact, it was remarkable that all such drafts were very soon assimilated into the Battalion and came to be regarded in all respects as men of " ours."

By this time all ranks knew that a great offensive was imminent, for preparations on an unprecedented scale were being made. Dumps of ammunition appeared dotted about the landscape, and new camouflaged gun positions could be discerned among the neglected fields behind Hebuterne. The British Army was, in fact, committed to operations on a large scale in conjunction with the French, the aim being to relieve the situation at Verdun and, if possible, break through the enemy line on a wide front. The offensive was to open as soon as the now rapidly growing British Expeditionary Force in France had reached the required proportions, and initially the French were to take the major share in the operations. Such, however, had been the French losses at Verdun that a considerable revision of plans became necessary, and actually the major share of the offensive fell to the British. Sir Douglas Haig, speaking of the situation says:

> The heroic defence of our French Allies had already gained many weeks of inestimable value and had caused the enemy very heavy losses, but the strain continued to increase. In view, therefore, of the situation in the various theatres of war, it was eventually agreed between General Joffre and myself that the combined French and

British offensive should not be postponed beyond the end of June. The object of that offensive was threefold:

(1) To relieve the pressure on Verdun.

(2) To assist our Allies in the other theatres of war by stopping any further transfer of German troops from the Western Front.

(3) To wear down the strength of the forces opposed to us.

The first step in the preparation of the Hebuterne front for the battle was taken on the night of May 25th–26th. The front line of the sector held by the 56th Division was about 700 yards from the enemy, a distance too great for the jumping-off point of an assault, and to remedy this without incurring heavy casualties, it was decided to dig a new trench 400 yards in front of the existing front line in one night. As this meant that about 3,000 yards of trench required constructing in the few hours of darkness available at this time of the year, it was realised that a great many men would be required. Actually the whole of the 167th Brigade carried out the work on the night of May 26th, following careful preparations beforehand, and the trench was dug to a depth of four feet and wired by 2.30 a.m., 3,000 men being out at work in No-man's-land without being perceived by the enemy.

Every precaution had been taken and provision made for every contingency that might arise. Eight hundred guns were standing by to put down a barrage on the German lines, covering parties were in position, gaps in the wire had been cut by the Kensingtons and other units then holding the front line. The digging party carried specially sharpened shovels and picks wrapped in sandbags to prevent noise, and wagons loaded with empty biscuit tins were galloped up and down the roads behind the lines to cover any incidental noise. No casualties directly attributable to this well-organised operation were incurred, and it was a feat of which the 56th Division could justly be proud, for a usually alert enemy was completely hoodwinked for once.

Posts in the completed trench were occupied by volunteers from the 167th Brigade, and on the following night the depth of the new trench was increased to six feet and support lines and communication trenches constructed to the same depth linking up the new trench to the existing system, the Kensingtons doing their share in this work and manning that night the new line on their front. The enemy showed that he had observed the advanced trench by bombarding it with high-explosive shell, but without doing any damage or causing any casualties. It was undoubtedly a registering shoot.

The Battalion was relieved on the 28th by the 1/4th London Regiment and marched to billets at Sailly au Bois, which was at that time receiving a good deal of unwelcome attention from enemy artillery. In fact, the men felt less protected in the poor ruins in which they were housed than in the line. Plans for the attack on the Gommecourt salient were now maturing, and when on June 2nd the Kensingtons marched to Halloy, they found that preparations had been made for intensive training in trenches modelled on the enemy system on the Hebuterne front. On this march, for the first time since the winter of 1914, the Battalion was escorted by its own drum-and-fife band playing the favourite tunes reminiscent of pre-war days. Soon after arrival in France the instruments had been returned to England and the drummers had since acted as stretcher bearers. Since the beginning of May, however, the instruments having arrived from England, the band had been re-formed under Drum-Major Skinner and martial music became a feature of marches when out of the line, helping the overloaded infantryman over many a weary mile. No music was ever so sweet as the Battalion march played by the drums on arrival at the journey's end with the prospect of " packs off " at last.

The training at Halloy was intensive, and every detail of the proposed attack was rehearsed. As the advance of the infantry was to be covered by a smoke cloud, the necessity for careful practice in order that direction should not be lost is apparent The map* shows the lie of the land, and it will be seen that the enemy lines formed a

* See page 75

salient with Gommecourt Wood and Park as the foremost points. It was known that both of these positions were strong and well fortified—in fact, veritable nests of machine guns. The general scheme, therefore, consisted in attempting to drive through the enemy trench system to the Quadrilateral and then, linking up with the 46th Division, which was to attack on the north, cut off the strong points from the rear and establish a new line—Nameless Farm–Quadrilateral–Little Z. It is to be noted that, for identification purposes, enemy trenches were given English names, communication-trench names beginning with the initial letter E, and F in the case of the fire trenches. The nearest attack on the right of the 56th Division was that to be carried out at Serre by the 10th Division.

On June 8th the Kensingtons returned to Sailly au Bois, and on the 13th took over the trenches again, relieving the Rangers. This tour ended on the 21st, when they marched to Souastre and final preparations for the battle, now fixed for the 29th, were completed. Packs were handed in and a selection made of officers, N.C.O.s, and men to stay out of the battle to form a nucleus should necessity arise. This practice now became general prior to major operations and caused some heart-burning, for the men selected were usually among the most valuable to the Battalion, and therefore the keenest to accompany it into action.

The Kensingtons had a change of Commanding Officer on the 28th, when Lieut.-Colonel W. H. Young of the Leicester Regiment took over command, Lieut.-Colonel H. Stafford returning to England.

CHAPTER VIII

THE BATTLE OF JULY 1ST, 1916

THE homeric conflict of the Somme was opened by the artillery, which, five days before the proposed attack by the infantry, burst into a roar of sound as the massed guns poured a torrent of shells on the enemy trench system, gun positions, and back areas. On the three days prior to the attack, a discharge of smoke was made, accompanying an intensification of the bombardment in an attempt to cry " wolf." The roar of our guns was continuous, and the din was further increased as the enemy artillery retaliated both on the trenches and the billeting areas. Souastre received its share of shells during this period. The weather, however, turned very wet and caused a postponement of the battle by forty-eight hours to July 1st, so that there was some slackening of the bombardment as the fateful day approached.

In the meantime the Kensingtons had little to do but await the appointed day. The country-side was in its prime, and the fields and orchards surrounding the village were deep in rich grass and the hedges gay with the wild rose, while the wild birds sang as gaily as at home in England. This may seem strange, but the birds appeared as loath to leave their accustomed haunts as the peasants, in spite of the ever-present din of battle and occasional shell fire.

The scheme of the Divisional attack was roughly that the 168th Brigade on the right in the W. Sector and the 169th Brigade on the left in the Y sector should each advance to the German front line and then swing outwards, establishing themselves in the captured trenches. The Queen's Westminsters were then to go straight forward into the gap so created and capture the Quadrilateral, thus linking up

THE BATTLE OF JULY 1ST, 1916

with the 46th Division. The 168th Brigade attack was to be carried out by the London Scottish, supported by the Kensingtons on the right flank, and the Rangers, supported by the 4th Londons, on the left. The Scottish were thus on the extreme right of the Divisional attack, and in order to link up with them, A Company of the Kensingtons, strengthened for the purpose by the trench pioneers and 30 men from C and D Companies, was to dig a trench across No-man's-land facing south to form a defensive flank. Snipers and observers were to act as a covering party during the digging, and a platoon of the 5th Cheshires was to be attached for wiring the trench when completed. Major C. C. Dickens was to be in command of the whole of this trench-digging operation. The Battalion was also to find a cleaning-up party for the trenches taken by the Scottish, and two platoons of B Company, with two squads of Headquarters bombers, were detailed for this duty under Lieut. Penn and 2nd Lieut. Pike. This party was to follow 100 yards in rear of the last wave of the Scottish, and would then come under their orders. B Company was also to provide Brigade carrying parties, the Lewis-gun sections remaining in a trench near Battalion Headquarters. C and D Companies (Captains Ware and Taggart) were to be in reserve in the English front line.

Final arrangements were completed on the last day of June, the men being issued with two hot meals, and arrangements were made for carrying hot soup into the assembly area. At 8.25 p.m. the platoons, in fighting order, moved off from Souastre at two-minute intervals. At the Brigade dump at Bayencourt extra ammunition was picked up, the digging party having picks, shovels, and sandbags as an additional load, and thus burdened the Battalion reached the assembly positions in the early hours of July 1st.

The day dawned bright and clear with every promise of a glorious summer day as the men waited tense for the opening of the conflict. The clamour of the guns shattered the quiet of the summer morning at 6.25 a.m., and bursting shells rent the earth all along the line of the enemy trenches. Fountains of soil leapt into the air, and gashes of flame marked the destruction wrought by high-explosive shells of all calibres now being concentrated on the German trenches. The enemy artillery was not slow in answering and shells began to fall in our assembly trenches and some units suffered heavy casualties right at the outset. The roar of the guns and the crash of bursting shell rose to a fury as at 7.26 a.m. the smoke cloud was released, and at 7.30 a.m., " zero " hour, the infantry attack was launched. The assaulting waves left their trenches and, crossing over the open, disappeared into the enveloping smoke. Devastating as had been our bombardment, the enemy was by no means subdued, and an intense machine-gun fire swept the zone between the opposing lines and exacted a heavy toll from the men advancing in the open. The Scottish, closely followed by the cleaning-up party of B Company, had vanished into the obscurity ahead, and C and D Companies of the Kensingtons moved forward and occupied the trenches thus vacated. A Company was anxiously awaiting news of the Scottish in order to make a start on the trench, for strict orders had been given that no digging was to be done until the Scottish had reached and secured their objective. That battalion, however, was fighting hard. Great difficulty had been experienced in keeping direction, as the smoke cloud obscured everything right from the start. Designed to protect the infantry during the assault, it merely added to their difficulties, for it was much thicker than it had been in the practice attacks, and, combined with the fact that the bombardment had so destroyed the enemy's trenches as to make them unrecognisable, the attacking troops were frequently at a loss to know where they really were. The Scottish had got into the enemy system without much difficulty, only to encounter an increasing resistance as they neared their objective. The enemy had, it appeared, withdrawn his troops to a large extent from the front line, thus escaping much of the bombardment, and was able to concentrate his counter-attack on our men

THE BATTLE OF JULY 1ST, 1916

when they had reached the support trenches, and were thus as remote as possible from reinforcements and to some extent disorganised.

In the meantime, the position of the Kensingtons was none too healthy. Very heavy shell fire began to fall on No-man's-land and our front-line trenches, and as

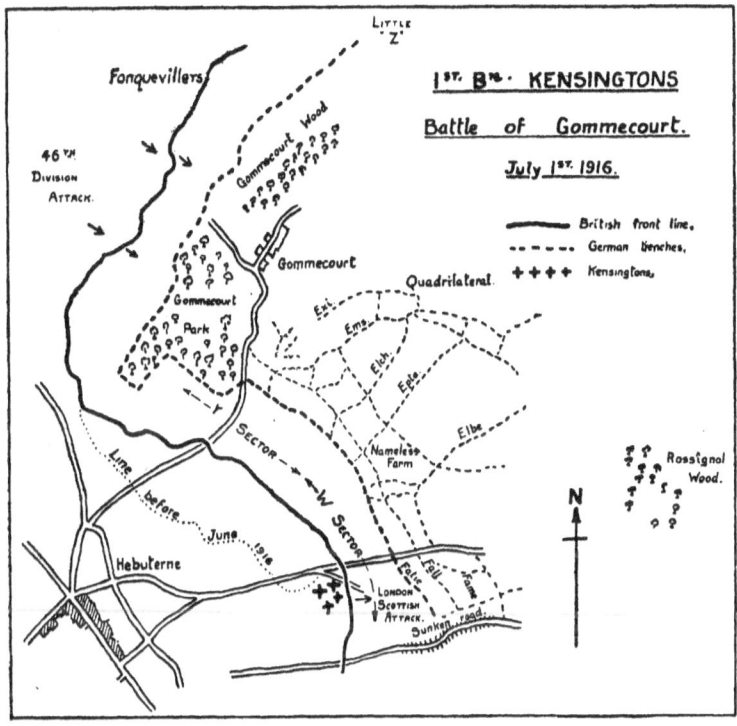

these had been hastily constructed and were devoid of dugouts or bomb-proof shelters, heavy casualties were incurred.

Although the initial assault on the 168th Brigade front carried the German front-line trenches, further progress was hampered by happenings on the left. The 169th Brigade found much uncut wire, and this unforeseen obstruction, coupled with the smoke difficulty, occasioned much loss of direction. Progress was made ultimately, and after gallant fighting some troops actually reached the Quadrilateral. It was, however, the failure of the 46th Division to the north of the Gommecourt salient that decided the issue on the 56th Divisional front. The attack of the former Division was held at the outset, the assaulting platoons being simply mown down by machine-gun fire as soon as they advanced. Progress was utterly impossible, and the enemy was soon free to concentrate his attention on the 56th Divisional attack. Gommecourt Park swarmed with men who had safely endured the bombardment in deep dugouts, none of which had been affected in the least, and a heavy machine-gun fire from well-sited emplacements was soon sweeping the 56th Divisional front. This, combined with an increasing shell fire and determined counter-attacks, rendered the position of the Scottish precarious, and the first news received from that battalion by the Kensingtons consisted of urgent appeals for bombs. As it was impossible to dig the trench, A Company concentrated on keeping the Scottish supplied with bombs, but as the time went on the enemy shell fire increased to such a degree that this became more and more difficult. Other companies were called upon for this duty, and Captain Ware, commanding C Company, was killed while endeavouring to get across with a party to the Scottish.

The position of that battalion had become obscure, and 2nd-Lieut. Beggs was sent forward with a patrol to ascertain how they were faring. The patrol got separated, and 2nd-Lieut. Beggs went on alone to find the Scottish in the German front line, weakened by the losses they had sustained, yet still holding at bay determined enemy counter-attacks. It was also discovered that a gap existed between the Scottish and the Rangers, and orders were sent to D Company of the Kensingtons to go forward and link up these two battalions. This company was, however, almost non-existent. They had suffered terribly, the company commander had been wounded and, the enemy bombardment having destroyed the front line, they were

THE BATTLE OF JULY 1ST, 1916

in scattered sections of trench. It is very doubtful if the message ever reached them. At 11.30 a.m. Captain Harris (B Company) went forward to collect all available men of D Company and take them across to fill the gap. He returned with the news that only 20 men of that company were left, and that the shell fire in No-man's-land was so intense that it was impossible to get over. At the same time a message was got through to Battalion Headquarters from Major Dickens reporting that 50 men only of A and C Companies were left.

The situation was becoming desperate. The Scottish were isolated in the German front line without hope of reinforcement or supplies of ammunition, and our own lines were held by a mere handful of men; dead and wounded men lay in all the trenches, both in the front-line and the communication trenches.

The terrible state of affairs on the front is plainly revealed by the messages received at Battalion Headquarters from Major Dickens.

1.10 p.m. Shelling fearful. Mackenzie killed. Trench practically untenable, full of dead and wounded. Very few men indeed left. Must have instructions and assistance.

1.48 p.m. Sap absolutely impassable owing to shell fire. Every party that enters it knocked out at once. Captain Ware has been wounded somewhere there. I have just crawled to the end of it with Scottish machine-gun party. Could not find him. One of Scottish had his hand blown off. Our front line in an awful state. Two more men killed and 1 wounded. Estimate casualties to A and C Companies at least 25 killed and 50 wounded. Impossible to man large lengths of our front line. Digging quite out of the question and position of the Scottish serious.

2.4 p.m. I have as far as I can find only 13 left besides myself. Trenches unrecognisable. Quite impossible to hold. Bombardment fearful for last two hours. I am the only officer left. Please send instructions.

The need for a garrison for our own system became urgent during the afternoon, and Captain Harris was sent forward with a mixed party of signallers, Headquarter details, and B Company Lewis gunners to man the front line, thus relieving Major Dickens, who, with 13 men, the survivors of two companies, reported to Battalion Headquarters. There had been hopes during the day that the attack on the 46th Division front might be resumed and thus relieve the situation, but as the afternoon wore on these hopes dwindled and died, for no progress whatever was made on the north of the salient.

By 4 p.m. the Scottish found their position untenable. With their left flank in the air, devoid of ammunition, and seriously reduced in numbers, they were unable to cope with the increasing ferocity of the enemy counter-attacks, and, fighting their way out, they got into the open and across to our lines. The battle was at an end, and at 5.30 p.m. a slackening in the enemy bombardment was noticed, and within a few minutes it had died down and ceased, bringing a wonderful sense of peace to the exhausted and strained remnants of the Brigade. As night fell survivors came in and the wounded were carried painfully through the havoc of the communication trenches out into the road and along to the dressing-station in Hebuterne. During the hours of darkness parties were out burying the dead or getting in badly wounded men, both British and German, a brief truce being observed by both sides.

The Kensingtons were relieved by the 8th Middlesex during the night and marched back to old French trenches near Sailly au Bois, where, crowded together in the open, some much-needed rest was obtained. The battle of Gommecourt had been in many ways a parallel case to May 9th at Fromelles, but in one respect it differed, for the Division could claim to have assisted materially in the British gains that were made in the present instance, for our front was advanced a distance of one mile over a six-mile front to the south on the Somme. A fierce resistance was encountered by all Divisions attacking on the left

THE BATTLE OF JULY 1ST, 1916

of the great battle front on that day, for not only had no attempt been made to disguise the intention to attack, but the enemy was holding the line in force, his men sheltered in deep dugouts with many exits. The postponement of the attack by forty-eight hours meant that our bombardment was necessarily slackened to some degree during the last two days, thus giving the enemy opportunity for reliefs, which he was not slow to seize. It is interesting to note that the 8th Division was attacking on the northern front of the battle, and met with no better success than the 56th Division.

The Kensingtons had lost 16 officers and 300 other ranks out of a fighting strength of 23 officers and 592 other ranks. Two company commanders became casualties, Captain Ware was killed and Captain Taggart wounded. 2nd Lieuts. Mager and Sach were also killed. Both rest and reinforcement were urgently needed, but, although a draft of 100 men from the Civil Service Rifles provided some reinforcement, rest was denied, for the 56th Division took over, in addition to the existing front, the sector occupied by the 46th Division, thus freeing the latter for operations farther south. The Kensingtons were ordered on the 2nd to relieve the 4th Lincolns in trenches near Fonquevillers on the north of the Gommecourt salient.

CHAPTER IX

THE SOMME

THE Fonquevillers front was fortunately quiet, and, save for the fact that heavy rain fell during the four days that the Kensingtons were in the trenches, making conditions most uncomfortable, the period provided some relief after the ordeal of battle. On the 6th the Battalion was relieved, and enjoyed a brief rest of four days in Souastre before taking over the Y sector of the Hebuterne front. During this period at Souastre the General Officers commanding both VIIth Corps and Third Army congratulated the Kensingtons on the part they had played in the recent fighting.

In the quiet that had now descended on the Hebuterne sector it was possible to look round and take stock of the havoc wrought by the enemy bombardment of the 1st. The line then held was the old French front line near the village, and the trenches forward of this, dug at such cost of time and effort, were deep in mud and so smashed by shell fire as to bear no resemblance to their original appearance. From now on until the 56th Division left the area, all efforts were directed towards putting the system once more into a state of defence. It was at this period that the Battalion had its first experience of raids. It should be explained that a raid is a minor operation carried out by a comparatively small party, usually with the view to securing identification—that is to say, capturing a prisoner and thus finding out the regiment holding that particular front. Sometimes the object was to unsettle the enemy and weaken his morale. Raids later came to be the subject of much attention, every detail being planned with great thoroughness, artillery support arranged for, and covering fire from troops on either flank. The Kensingtons came to acquire a name for successful raids, as will be seen later.

The raid carried out on this occasion was aimed primarily at securing identification, for it was of importance to know if the enemy had moved his troops into the Somme area. It came too soon after July 1st, however, to inspire much enthusiasm at first, but as the time approached, the spirit of adventure, which was not quelled for long, infused the selected party, who had been practising for the event back at Halloy. In the early hours of July 17th, a dark night with a fine rain falling, they moved forward stealthily in front of the enemy barbed wire and lay flat on the ground, awaiting the signal to dash forward. The wire had been well cut, and a surprise attack, an essential in a raid, might have been delivered had not an alert sentry, perceiving in the darkness a suspected movement, hurled a bomb at a venture. It fell at the feet of Lieut. R. E. F. Shaw, who was with the party, but with great presence of mind he threw it farther on, where it burst with a crash. The explosion appeared to satisfy the sentry, but not those on his left, who probably spotted the party in the flash of the bomb. Immediately a bombardment with "minnies" was opened on the raiders, whiz-bangs and Verey lights joining in to heighten the effect. It was now clearly impossible to effect a surprise attack, which was the essence of the raid, and the party returned to our trenches, bringing in 6 wounded with them. The raid was unsuccessful, but valuable experience had been gained for use in similar enterprises in the future.

Until the end of August the Kensingtons spent fairly uneventful tours in the Hebuterne line, interspersed with brief rests in billets in the village of Sailly au Bois, which was by this time deserted by its inhabitants and to a large extent in ruins. Now and again shells of a heavy calibre fell on the trench system, and one such shell fell in a dugout at Hebuterne occupied by a number of Headquarters details, killing 5 and wounding 4 others. Sergeant Perris, an old pre-war Territorial who had been continuously with the Battalion since November 1914, was killed.

Drafts continued to arrive during July and August

from various London regiments, and some sorting out took place to enable those who had served with a first-line battalion overseas to rejoin their units. The new men were the first to be received of those who had joined the army under the Derby scheme. Their training had been very brief, in many cases not more than three months.

At the end of August 1916, the 56th Division was relieved and moved to the St. Riquier area, near Abbeville, for rest and training. The Kensingtons were relieved by the 7th Yorkshires, and on the 20th marched to Bayencourt for the night. On the following day the march was resumed to Halloy, which was reached at 11 p.m., and in the morning they entrained for St. Riquier. Following a five-mile march from the rail-head, the Battalion arrived at the quiet village of Millancourt, near Abbeville, where all ranks settled down happily in billets, anticipating a quiet period of rest and comfort for at least a few weeks. Such hopes were always aroused by a move into back areas, for, seeing the immense amount of trouble that such a move entailed, all felt certain that a substantial period of rest was coming. Old soldiers, however, were always sceptical and never surprised by a sudden order to move after only a few days' rest.

It must not be imagined that the term "rest" implies idleness, for such periods invariably saw considerable activity in section and company training, route marches, practice attacks, inspections, and the like, the days proving more exhausting physically than a normal day in the line. Trench warfare, while developing certain qualities in the men, in no sense tended to maintain physical fitness, and on relief after a spell of trenches it was invariably found that men were unfit for marching, or indeed for any activity demanding much physical exertion.

While in this area, the 168th Brigade had its first view of the tanks, freshly imported, and some instruction was given in co-operation with this new offensive weapon. As these early tanks were slow and very prone to breakdown, they aroused more amusement than respect, though all welcomed them as an attempt to grapple with the problem of enemy wire. As has been seen, the most intense bombardment had failed to deal efficiently with the ever-present wire entanglement protecting the enemy trenches. A direct hit merely scattered the wire and left fragments here and there to trip the unwary, while a sustained bombardment churned up the ground to such an extent that a new obstacle was thereby created. One of the most obvious possibilities of the tanks was to flatten out the wire and permit the passage of the infantry.

After but ten days at peaceful Millancourt, during which the opportunity was taken to visit Abbeville, a town offering many amenities approved by men who had not been near a town for many months, orders came to prepare to move on September 3rd. With the usual optimism, anticipating a stay of some weeks, Battalion sports had been arranged for the 2nd, but the activities necessitated by the move compelled cancellation. Entraining at St. Riquier on this day, the Kensingtons reached Corbie and marched towards Daours, which had been allotted as a billeting area. When a mile and a half out of Corbie, however, sudden orders were received changing the billets to Sailly le Sec, and the Battalion had therefore to turn about and plod on to the new area, which was reached at 5 p.m. This village was quite close to the River Somme, which could be seen gleaming amongst the trees in its wide valley, peaceful enough to outward appearance in the September sunshine. On the following day the road was again taken towards Citadel Camp, near Bray. On this march the touch of the hand of war on the country-side became increasingly evident as the moving column neared Bray. The roads were congested with French troops and transport, and on either hand the undulating country was pitted with shell-holes. At Citadel Camp, where the Kensingtons bivouacked for the night, getting what shelter they could, the effects of the recent fighting were still more noticeable, for it was on the site of the old British front line of July 1st. The rolling country was featureless, for all landmarks had disappeared under the shell fire of that battle, the ground was churned up and littered with débris, and the slopes were dotted with the horse lines and transports of the units farther forward in the fighting zone.

Orders came on the following day, September 5th, to move forward into the line and, *en route*, the Commanding Officer was informed that the Battalion would temporarily be attached to the 15th Brigade. The position of this Brigade Headquarters was given, and the Battalion continued the march over tracks which a heavy shower of rain had made slippery and treacherous, to Maricourt siding, where packs were dumped and extra ammunition, bombs, rockets, and flares, picked up. It was now learnt that the 7th Royal Irish Fusiliers were to be relieved in trenches near Falfemont Farm and, conducted by guides from this Battalion, the Kensingtons set off in the dusk over ground which became increasingly difficult to the burdened men. It was a memorable journey, for it provided the first acquaintance with conditions on the Somme battlefield. The tracks led over the remains of trenches and amongst barbed wire, skirting the larger shell-holes. The litter of battle lay on all sides, abandoned guns, British, French, and German, all axle deep in mud. Broken rifles, ammunition, and equipment were beaten into the soft ground by the never-ceasing traffic. A detour was frequently necessary in order to avoid an overturned limber, the horses lying mangled and torn beside it. Halts were frequent, for strings of pack animals and limbers were travelling in both directions. To add to the confusion, the guides, who had but recently come to the area, were uncertain of the way. Thus stumbling and halting, the exhausted Battalion at length reached the trenches, the relief being completed by 6.15 a.m. The journey from Citadel Camp had taken fifteen hours, though as the crow flies the distance was but seven miles.

The situation on this front must now be considered. Following the preliminary success of July 1st when, as has been already stated, our attack had penetrated a depth of one mile into the enemy system over a front of six miles, a succession of hammer-like blows had been delivered on the enemy in order to follow up the initial gains, but with varying success. While gaining ground at some points, at others a stubborn resistance was encountered, with the result that the line was irregular, with numerous salients about these strong points. Consequently, prior to any general attack on a wide front, localised operations were carried out, aimed at capturing these positions and straightening out the line. At the time the 56th Division was assembling in the arena, one such attack was made, and, by the combined efforts of British and French Divisions, Guillemont was finally carried on September 6th. Following this success, the British line was again advanced, and by the time the first units of the Division came into the line, Falfemont Farm and a part of Leuze Wood were in our hands. The situation was, however, very vague, and the fact that the enemy were holding the front here in force was not appreciated by the Staff at Brigade Headquarters. Orders had been given to the Kensingtons by the 15th Brigade that on relieving the 7th Royal Irish Fusiliers they were to endeavour to extend the line from the southern corner of Leuze Wood in an easterly direction, and dig in as close to the enemy trench, known as Combles trench, as possible. Active patrolling was to be carried out to ascertain whether this trench was held or not, it being considered that Combles was not strongly held by the enemy. This, however, was not in accordance with the report of the Commanding Officer of the Royal Irish Fusiliers, for on the preceding day this battalion, which was, like the Kensingtons, only temporarily attached to the 15th Brigade, had attacked this enemy trench and, coming under heavy machine-gun fire from Bouleaux Wood, had lost 350 men in a vain endeavour to obtain a foothold in it. The trench was found to be protected by a strong uncut wire entanglement, which was hidden by standing corn and weeds, and the survivors had fallen back and taken up a position in shell-holes. The Kensingtons took over this position and proceeded to link the shell-holes by means of a trench. It was gruesome work, for there had been no opportunity for burying the dead, and the most hardened were affected by the ordeal. In pursuance of orders, a patrol of B Company, under Captain Cohen, went out in daylight immediately after relief, in order to ascertain whether Combles trench was occupied by the enemy. They found this trench was constructed as a fire trench and was heavily wired, and also came under heavy enemy fire, one man being killed.

During the afternoon orders were received to occupy Combles trench, as a contact aeroplane had reported it unoccupied. In view of the results of the patrolling this seemed unlikely, but in obedience to orders D Company was moved forward towards the wood with the intention of bombing down the trench in a south-easterly direction. This drew heavy shell fire on the company, and as the ground was quite open and under direct observation, it was decided to postpone the operation until dark. Just before dark D Company began to move across to Leuze Wood in small parties, but the enemy evidently suspected an organised attack, and a heavy barrage fell on the wood and its approaches. At the same time he counter-attacked strongly in the wood, and for some time the situation was very obscure. The bombers and other men of D Company went forward into the fighting and became mixed up with the Scottish in the wood. The remainder of the company withdrew to Falfemont Farm. Later C Company went forward and occupied positions in the wood.

The French had attacked Combles that day and had encountered a stubborn resistance, against which all efforts to capture the town by frontal assault were in vain. The opposition encountered on the Kensingtons' front was undoubtedly part of the enemy counter-attack. On the 7th A and B Companies came under very heavy shell fire between 11 a.m. and 2 p.m., but otherwise the day was quiet. It was now quite clear that Combles trench could not be taken by a minor operation without artillery support, and that evening the Battalion was relieved and moved back to Casement trenches, once more under the orders of the 168th Brigade.

This preliminary bout gives some idea of the state of

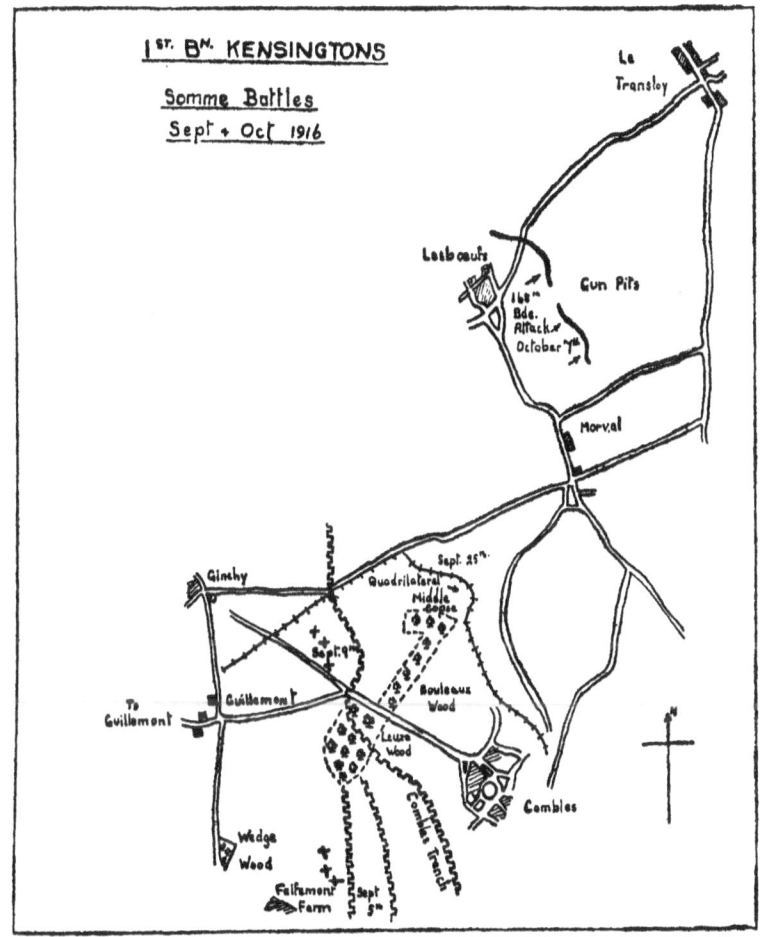

affairs on this front. The situation was vague, not only as regards the position of the enemy, but frequently as regards our own position as well. Map references of trenches were given, but the almost entire absence of landmarks caused them to be meaningless. Frequently a battalion reported itself in a certain position when in reality it was a hundred or more yards from it, and a distance such as that was important when artillery co-operation was sought or reinforcement needed. In short, the situation that had prevailed during the battle of July 1st was the state of affairs here on taking over the line. Then again the fighting was continuous; trenches were wrested from the enemy, only to be lost again, for during the month of September a fierce enemy resistance was encountered. The Staff, too, were often misinformed as to the true nature of the situation, which was not to be wondered at when the troops themselves were ignorant of their true position on the map. Messages went astray, for it took a runner an hour to reach Brigade Headquarters, and many became casualties in the shell fire that swept the whole zone. The task of the signal sections was a nightmare, the telephone cables constantly being destroyed by shell fire. The difficulty of maintaining communication, and the conflicting nature of the reports received by the Headquarters Staffs of Brigades and Divisions, were responsible for the vague and often inaccurate instructions which were given to the infantry during this difficult period.

The 56th Division had taken over the line on the 7th, and plans were now maturing for an attack on the front in conjunction with other neighbouring Divisions, as a preliminary to a general advance. The unsatisfactory nature of the line held rendered such an operation imperative. Ginchy was in the hands of the enemy, as was most of the country between that village and Leuze Wood. We held the southern portion of the wood, Guillemont, and the road between Guillemont and the wood. The intention of this attack was to capture Ginchy and, by building up defensive flanks round Combles, compel the evacuation of the town, frontal attacks having failed. The task allotted to the 168th Brigade was to make a half-right form and advance the line to a position giving direct observation on the Morval–Les Bœufs line. This involved subduing the

General View of the Battlefield, Guillemont, September 1916.
Imperial War Museum photograph. Copyright reserved.

Quadrilateral, a suspected strong point, the impregnable character of which was not at this time appreciated. In the meantime, the 16th Division was to attack Ginchy and, having carried this position, move forward and establish contact with the 168th Brigade.

The Kensingtons had spent what remained of the night after relief in the discomfort of Casement trenches, intense shell fire on the morning of the 8th causing a number of casualties. At 3 p.m. details of the operations for the morrow came through from Brigade, and at 1 a.m. on the 9th they moved off to the assembly trenches, A and C Companies occupying a trench along the Wedge Wood—Ginchy Road, the right of A Company being in the wood, and B and D Companies in an old German trench behind. Working parties which had been out rejoined the Battalion in the assembly position.

The attack opened at 4.45 p.m. on the 9th with the Rangers on the left and the Fusiliers on the right of the Brigade front, the Kensingtons being in support. The right battalion, following close upon the " creeping barrage," a recent development in artillery co-operation with infantry, soon obtained their objectives, but on the left the Rangers came under heavy machine-gun fire from the Quadrilateral. The situation became grave, for the attack by the 16th Division was also held up. At zero hour A and C Companies of the Kensingtons had moved forward to the trenches vacated by the assaulting battalions, while B and D Companies, following, took up the position previously occupied by A and C. The forward companies now advanced through the enemy barrage which had been falling on No-man's-land since the opening of the attack to the support of the Rangers and the Fusiliers in the second objective. They found the trench full of dead and wounded, with the enemy counter-attacking vigorously from behind a bombing-block. A section of the trench was cleared and determined efforts made to push forward and link up with the Irish Division, who were supposed to be on the left. While leading his men in this endeavour,

Major C. C. Dickens, commanding A Company, was killed. This company had suffered severely during the passage of No-man's-land, one platoon being annihilated by the bursting of one huge shell. In the failing light the situation became very obscure on the left of the front, and all efforts to link up were doomed to fail, for the Irish were nowhere near that point, Ginchy still being in German hands.

B Company had also advanced to the second objective, and a party went to the right into Bouleaux Wood, where the Queen Victoria Rifles were hard pressed. This party bombed up the trench and, having cleared it, established a block and held on.

It was now dark and the attack came to a standstill. The situation was obscure in the extreme; no one knew how the day had gone elsewhere, and there was nothing to do but hang on until morning. The losses had been out of all proportion to the gains.

The morning brought no clearer view of the situation, though it was discovered that the trench was too full of troops, and the Kensingtons were accordingly withdrawn to their old positions prior to the attack, where the opportunity was taken to reorganise. The attack was resumed during the day by the Scottish, who had been in reserve during the preceding day, in an endeavour to fill the gap between the Rangers and the 16th Irish Division, for it was thought that the Quadrilateral had been taken and Ginchy occupied. The fog which hung about all day rendered the situation still more obscure, and efforts at establishing contact on the left met with failure, as neither of these parties were where they had reported themselves to be.

On the following day, September 11th, the Kensingtons were relieved in their assembly trenches by the 7th Middlesex, and at 3 a.m., worn out by lack of sleep and the physical and mental strain of the preceding days, struggled to bivouacs near Billon Farm. As supporting Battalion the Kensingtons had had no spectacular share in the battle on the 9th, but, nevertheless, in the fighting in which they had been involved they had lost 15 officers and 282 other ranks. The loss in senior officers and N.C.O.s, both on this occasion and on July 1st, had been exceptionally severe, and it was a loss that could not readily be made good. The men who had been wounded had suffered terribly, for the state of the country was now appalling. The tracks were becoming impassable, and the roads were deep in mud. The walking wounded dragged their way to the nearest aid post, sinking frequently into the water-filled shell-holes in their exhaustion. Some, more fortunate, contrived a lift on passing transport. The regimental stretcher bearers did heroic deeds in their efforts to cope with the worst cases. So heavy was the going that it frequently took eight men to carry a stretcher.

The rest, such as it was, proved of short duration, for the great attack, to which the battle on the 9th had been but a preliminary, was in preparation. On the 13th all officers reconnoitred the approaches to Combles and the valley south of Leuze Wood, and on the following day operation orders for the attack on the 16th came to hand. The stubborn defence on the left had revealed that the Quadrilateral was strongly held, and it became clear that this strong point, which had withstood onslaughts from both artillery and infantry, would have to be dealt with seriously. Contact had by this time been established between the 56th Division and the Guards Division, which was now on the left, though not on the line originally hoped for, and Ginchy was in our hands. The operation now contemplated was to be an attack on a wide front against Les Bœufs, Morval, Combles, and Flers, and was to be preceded by a three-day bombardment. Nine Divisions in line were to assault the German third-line trenches, tanks co-operating with the infantry for the first time. The 56th Division was again to be associated with the formation of the defensive flank round Combles, this time by means of an attack on Bouleaux Wood. The French were attacking to the east of Combles, and the Guards Division on the left was directed against the Quadrilateral. The 168th Brigade was allotted the task of protecting the flank of that Division in its attack on Morval by an assault on the enemy third line to the north-east of Bouleaux Wood, though this operation was not to be carried out until the capture of Morval was definitely assured.

The Kensingtons marched from their bivouacs during the night of the 14th and, after spending the night in the back assembly area near Crucifix Hardicourt, moved forward in the morning in artillery formation towards the advanced assembly area near Bouleaux Wood. On the way they received orders from the 168th Brigade to halt at Angle Wood valley and dig in, and here they remained throughout the day.

The battle had opened at 6.20 a.m., when the roar of the guns, which had been firing continuously day and night for three days, reached a crescendo as the infantry advanced, following close upon the creeping barrage. The tanks proved a failure on the 56th Divisional front, in spite of the utmost gallantry on the part of their crews. Only one got away, and this was quickly put out of action by a direct hit from a field gun. The progress made during the day on this front was disappointing, for the Quadrilateral, in spite of the most determined efforts of the Guards Division, still held out and rendered such ground as was captured by the 56th Division in Bouleaux Wood untenable. The failure of the attempt to carry this strong point meant that Morval remained out of reach and the 168th Brigade was not called upon to enter the battle, so the Kensingtons remained in Angle Wood valley. There was occasional shell fire, Major H. Campbell was wounded, but he remained on duty; otherwise there were no casualties.

The state of the ground continued to deteriorate, and it became increasingly difficult for men to get about in the deep mud. Progress became so slow and exhausting that it was impossible to take full advantage of opportunities that occurred to improve the position of affairs on this part of the front. The Quadrilateral remained the key to the situation, and efforts in the succeeding days were directed towards subduing this formidable obstacle. This was finally accomplished by the Guards Division, thus clearing up the situation considerably at this point. It was found, when once occupied, to be ideally situated for defence, and was heavily wired and well furnished with deep dugouts, which had enabled the defenders to maintain such a stout opposition to the most determined onslaughts.

The successes on the 56th Divisional front had been small, but elsewhere the attack had been crowned with success. Flers, Martinpuich, and Courcelette were taken, and Morval, Les Bœufs, and Geudecourt brought within striking distance. Sir Douglas Haig reported of these operations:

The result of the fighting on the 15th September and the following days was a gain more considerable than any which had attended our arms in the course of a single operation since the commencement of the offensive. In the course of one day's fighting we had broken through two of the enemy's main defensive systems and had advanced on a front of over six miles to an average depth of one mile. In the course of this advance we had taken three villages, each powerfully organised for prolonged resistance. The total number of prisoners taken by us in these operations amounted to over 4,000, including 127 officers.

But Combles still held out. Now the Quadrilateral was taken, however, the defensive flank movement on the left of the town could be developed with more chance of success. As a preliminary to this, the 168th Brigade on taking over the line at Middle Copse was occupied in constructing a trench facing Bouleaux Wood to provide assault positions for a new attack on that stronghold. The Kensingtons, who had been in and about Angle Wood valley since the 15th, engaged in various duties, moved up into the line in Leuze Wood and the trench immediately in front on the evening of the 20th. The weather had been so bad on the 17th and 18th that the ground had become a morass, and it was felt that any change of position would be preferable to enduring the mud of Angle Wood valley. A Company now occupied a position in the wood amongst the splintered boles of the trees, with C Company in front, while B and

D Companies took over a trench facing Bouleaux Wood. The tour was comparatively uneventful, and on the 22nd the Battalion was relieved, the relief taking such a long time in the darkness among that confused maze of sodden earthworks, that the reserve trenches at Maltz Horn Farm were not reached until 6 a.m. on the following day.

Preparations were again afoot for a renewed attack on Combles, the policy being to maintain pressure on the enemy and wear down his resistance. Planned initially for September 23rd, the heavy rains of this very wet autumn delayed the attack until the 25th. This time the 168th Brigade was to attack with the 4th Londons on the right and the Scottish on the left and, working round the northeast end of Bouleaux Wood, establish contact with the French, who were again attacking to the east of Combles. The Kensingtons, who were in reserve, left Maltz Horn Farm, where they had provided large working parties to prepare for the coming battle and incidentally had endured a good deal of shell fire, and arrived in the allotted assembly area in the Falfemont Farm–Wedge Wood line at 10 p.m. on the 24th.

The attack this time was very successful. Patrols were pushed out by the assaulting battalions, and by midday the 168th Brigade had established posts east of Combles and contact had been made with the French. The enemy had evacuated the town. The Kensingtons were not called upon in this engagement and, apart from furnishing carrying parties for rations and water for the assaulting battalions, and stores for the Royal Engineers, remained in the assembly trenches. The advance was continued on the following day, and the Battalion moved ahead and at nightfall relieved the 4th Londons and the Scottish in their advanced positions to the north and east of Leuze Wood. No enemy activity developed, and except for intermittent shell fire, which occasioned the loss of about 50 men, the day was regarded under the circumstances as being fairly uneventful.

The following night the 56th Division was relieved, and

the Kensingtons, after handing over to the 1st Battalion 33rd Regiment d'Infanterie, proceeded once more to Maltz Horn Farm, and thence by stages to Morlancourt, thankful, in spite of their utter exhaustion, to feel a firm road underfoot leaving behind the Somme battlefield with all its associations. For more than three weeks they had not slept under a roof, rations had been uncertain, and the water, carried up in petrol tins with the greatest difficulty by carrying parties, had been tainted with petrol. When the brief reliefs from the front line had permitted an attempt to get clean, a shortage of water prevented it. The Battalion had sustained severe losses at the outset, and the only draft arriving at the transport lines during the period consisted of but 2 officers and 50 men, and neither of the officers reached the Battalion in the line. During the greater part of the time there had been only 6 officers with the whole of the four companies and some of these were inexperienced.

Morlancourt offered dry, comfortable barns, and at 7.30 p.m. the Kensingtons, at the limit of their endurance, thankfully took advantage of the opportunity to indulge in a real night's sleep. All felt that a difficult task had been well done and material gains made, and the chance of getting clean once more, with possibly the prospect of a speedy move to a back area, added a deep joy to the blessing of undisturbed sleep. The 29th saw an orgy of washing and polishing, followed by the appearance in the village streets of revived men trying to forget the mud and horror of the battlefield.

Such were the fortunes of war, however, that the Somme had yet one more grim call to make on the London Division. As the result of a sudden order on the 30th, the Battalion was on parade at 11.25 a.m. with the head of the column once more pointing to the battlefield. There had been time neither for rest, reinforcement, nor reorganisation. It took all their philosophy to endure this final straw, and it says much for the loyal spirit of the Division that this last call received a ready response from the weary troops.

A halt of two days was spent under canvas at Citadel

Camp, where a draft of 6 officers and 200 men arrived, none of whom, unfortunately, had seen active service before, and on October 3rd the Battalion marched towards the line, leaving the Citadel at midday. The 168th Brigade had been ordered to relieve the 169th Brigade in the right sector of the Divisional front, and the Kensingtons were to relieve the Queen's Westminsters, who were in support in the old third German line. There now began the first of a series of indecisions, uncertainties, and changes in the orders given, that proved exasperating in the extreme. The going was very bad, the heavy rains having reduced the ground to a quagmire, and the leading company of the Kensingtons had just reached Billon Farm after ploughing through the mud, when orders were received to the effect that the move was postponed for twenty-four hours and the Battalion was to return to Citadel Camp. On once more reaching the camp, further orders came that the relief would take place as originally ordered, so the muddy track was pursued once more, this time to the required position. The Battalion marched by companies at five-minute intervals, and some indication of the extreme difficulty of moving on the sodden ground may be seen from the fact that while the leading company reached the trenches at 10 p.m., the last company did not arrive until 3 a.m. on the following day. Orders were received during the relief that, in preparation for an attack on the 5th, assault trenches between 25 Trench and Fusilier Post, and between Foggy and Burnaby trenches, were to be dug on the night of the 4th, the Brigade expecting to attack on a three-battalion front in an endeavour to advance to a position commanding the Le Transloy system of enemy defences. The weather had deteriorated rapidly, making the area even worse, so that movement was exhausting to a degree, and news came during the day that the attack was postponed for forty-eight hours. The assault trenches, however, had still to be dug as arranged, and this task was allotted to A and C Companies. These companies moved off in the evening, accompanied by a covering party from D Company, piloted by guides from the battalions in the front line. Application had been made for tape for laying out the trench, but none was available, so some difficulty was anticipated in carrying out the work in the rain and darkness. However, the guides lost their way and, leaving the parties while they endeavoured to locate themselves, disappeared into the night and were not seen again. The officers, on unfamiliar ground, tried all night to locate their position, and as dawn approached the task was perforce abandoned, the parties returning to the Battalion in the early morning. That night the Kensingtons relieved the Scottish in the front line and an officer patrol went out at once to reconnoitre the German trenches and gun pits opposite the Battalion front. These trenches were found to be occupied by the enemy and the gun pits were well wired.

Confirmatory orders were received in the early hours of the 6th relating to the attack on the morrow, the general aim of which was, as has been stated, to establish a line from which the Le Transloy system could be attacked at a later date. This implied the capture of Dewdrop and Hazy trenches, to be followed by an assault on the isolated trenches behind.

In the meantime A and C Companies had again gone out to dig the assault trenches which had been attempted on the preceding night. Tape was supplied this time, but bad luck once more attended their efforts. A Company was to dig between 25 Trench and Fusilier Post, and C Company between Foggy and Burnaby trenches. In the former case Fusilier Post promised some definite point from which to locate the position, and the A Company Commander left his Company to search for it, being joined by the Commanding Officer four hours later. Their joint efforts failed to locate it, and it is doubtful whether the Post ever existed except in someone's imagination. C Company was found waiting for its Company Commander, who had gone out some time before to locate the position and tape out the trench. He had not returned, and it afterwards transpired that he had been wounded. As he was the only officer with that company, and no one else had the faintest idea of what was required, the trench remained undug.

During the day efforts were made to find out the exact position for the required trenches. The non-existent Fusilier Post was abandoned as a landmark, and that night the assembly trenches, slightly modified in position, were completed and the Kensingtons moved back to the 3rd German line, their previous reserve position.

The battle on the 7th opened at 1.45 p.m., the 167th and 168th Brigades attacking in conjunction with the French on the right. From the first things went badly. The atrocious state of the ground impeded all movement, but, in spite of this handicap and the stubborn enemy resistance, some advance was made, and the Scottish occupied the gun pits and parts of Hazy Trench. The situation was, however, very vague, an inevitable accompaniment of hard fighting. B and D Companies of the Kensingtons were sent forward at 5 p.m. to the support of the Rangers in Rainy Trench and the 4th Londons in 25 Trench. These battalions had met a devastating machine-gun fire from Dewdrop Trench, and a heavy barrage had also fallen upon them. The leading companies in the attack were practically annihilated.

Heavy German counter-attacks developed as the night came on, and by 9 p.m. the men of the 168th Brigade were all back in their original positions. The French attack on the right had failed, and the enemy was thus free to concentrate his efforts against the 56th Divisional front.

The attack was renewed on the following day in order to exploit the small gains that had been made elsewhere on the Divisional front, but, in the case of the 168th Brigade, was aimed at the first objective only. The Kensingtons, who were in support to these operations, were disposed in positions in Shamrock trench to enable them to deal with any enemy counter-attack which might develop. During the night the attacking troops were again driven back to their original line and the operation as a whole had failed, defeated as much by the weather as by the enemy. Artillery support had been poor, largely due to the uncertainty of the position of the infantry.

This last difficult and disappointing operation was the final effort of the wearied troops of the 56th Division in the prolonged offensive of the Somme, for on the 8th the Division was relieved and the Kensingtons, in their turn being relieved on the 9th, partly by the 1st Royal Warwicks and partly by the 1st Royal Irish Rifles, arrived at Mansell Camp on the following day. On the 12th the Battalion marched to Ville sur Ancre, where a convoy of French motor-buses transported them to Vaux en Amienois.

A rest was needed by all. It was amazing that men could endure as much as had the infantry in this prolonged spell of dogged fighting. They fought not only the enemy, but the weather. Indeed, it was the latter that caused the slowing down and final cessation of hostilities on this front. Other auxiliaries, while not exposed to the same hardship and suffering as the fighting men, nevertheless had their share of the rigours of those never-to-be-forgotten weeks. Transport men had laboured incessantly to bring rations up over the atrocious tracks. So long did the journeys take that they were hardly back from one expedition before another was due to start. The machine failed where it was most needed, for lorries sank axle deep in mud, and the provisioning of the troops was only accomplished by the joint efforts of sweating and struggling men and horses.

This last spell had been particularly trying. The Kensingtons had lost 4 officers and 179 other ranks between the 3rd and 9th October, and there was nothing to show for it. Most of the time there had been but 6 officers with the whole of the companies. Battle-worn, and needing time for reorganisation, the Battalion had been unable to do justice to a fine reputation gained over a long period of warfare in France.

"THE KENSINGTONS"

Sir Douglas Haig had hoped for better results in this battle for the Le Transloy ridges. He says:

> Here the enemy still possessed a strong system of trenches covering the villages of Le Transloy and Beaulencourt, and the town of Bapaume; but although he was digging with feverish haste he had not been able to create any very formidable defences behind this line. In this direction, in fact, we had at last reached a stage at which a successful attack might reasonably be expected to yield much greater results than anything we had as yet attained.

The unfavourable weather, however, turned the trenches into channels of mud, and the roads, now almost impassable, hampered the supplies to the infantry and artillery, so that the favourable moment passed. The 8th Division attacked over almost the same ground on October 23rd and made only trifling gains as the results of prodigious efforts and at the cost of heavy losses.

The quiet days at Vaux gave some opportunity for reorganisation and that sorrowful task that followed all active operations—the collection and despatch of the effects of the men who had fallen. The Battalion rested and cleaned up, and by the 20th when they moved to Wanel and Sorel, a distance of about 19 miles, the remarkable recuperative powers of the British soldier became manifest. Here comfortable billets had been arranged in the empty houses which abounded in the two villages, and the men were able to defy the cold and frosty nights which now heralded the approach of winter. Such comfort was felt to be too good to last, however; it was already known that a spell of trench warfare was to be expected, and no surprise was occasioned by orders to move after but three days at Wanel and Sorel. On the 23rd the Kensingtons were again on the move and, entraining at Longpré, reached Merville at 4 p.m., the 56th Division having taken over the very sector in which the Battalion had first seen the realities of war in 1914.

CHAPTER X

LAVENTIE AGAIN

It was with mixed feelings that the old members of the Kensingtons, after detraining at Merville, marched along the familiar cobbled road to Estaires—joy to find the town more active than ever, apparently quite unchanged by all that had happened since 1914, blended with sorrow at the thought of the comrades who had marched along this road in those early days and who now lay at Neuve Chapelle, Fromelles, Gommecourt, or the Somme.

Fully appreciative, however, of the joys of the moment, six happy days were spent in the town. The drums marched bravely through the streets, playing familiar tunes, and in the evenings the little town was alive with men seeking such diversion as was offered. The estaminets, bright and warm, were well patronised during the brief hours permitted by the vigilant Military Police. When, on the 29th, the Battalion moved to Laventie, it was almost a homecoming. New-comers who knew not Laventie were speedily informed of all it meant to the Kensingtons. The inhabitants were as hospitable as ever. Good billets were readily obtained, most of the officers even getting the luxury of a bed. Bathing parades were a regular feature, and it was soon a very different Battalion from the muddy, haggard survivors who had dragged themselves out of the Somme battlefield but three weeks before.

The Kensingtons now had a change of Commanding Officer, Lieut.-Colonel J. C. R. King assuming the command on the 27th in succession to Lieut.-Colonel W. H. Young, who had been in command since June 28th. On November 19th Captain R. E. F. Shaw rejoined and was appointed Adjutant, a position which he held until he became Commanding Officer in August 1917.

"THE KENSINGTONS"

On November 1st the Battalion took over the Fauquissart sector, and there ensued a quiet period of trench warfare, at first with four days in the line and four days in support at Laventie, later extended to six-day periods. The line was exceptionally quiet, save for occasional raids, and the time was largely spent in repairing the trenches and making good the damage caused by the weather. The improved state of the trench system was commented on by all who had known it during the winter of 1914–15. The ground was as water-logged as ever, but the trenches were well drained and provided with duck-boards so that the footway was raised well above the water level. Deep dugouts were, of course, impossible, but, as the next best thing, elephant-iron bomb-proof shelters had been erected, packed in with sandbags and well camouflaged overhead. Many of these in the support lines possessed primitive stoves, so that quite a degree of comfort was attainable. The breastworks were sufficiently high to permit daylight reliefs being carried out. During this period the Battalion returned to the same billets at Laventie on relief, and this certainty of tenure led to the establishment of messes, canteens, and other amenities in the town.

As regards the front line, it was suspected that the enemy occupied his posts only in the daytime. In fact, it was commonly stated that a few aged German reservists were employed merely to pass from post to post and loose off a few rounds to indicate some activity. In order to ascertain the truth of this conjecture a raid was carried out by the Kensingtons on December 2nd, the party consisting of one officer and his platoon. The raid provided an amusing adventure for the party, and it is described in racy style by the platoon sergeant:

"The object of this raid was to put an end to the nightly peregrinations of a certain bearded old 'dugout' whose special job (so the legend ran) was to go to certain points along the enemy front line in order to fire a Verey light and pull a string, which was connected to all the machine guns on his front. The party set out for its task with one Lewis-gun section as a covering party in case of sudden retirement. These unfortunate fellows were deposited in a swamp with their gun well in the shelter of a ruined house in front of our line. They did not appear to enjoy the business at all. The approach to the enemy line was made by paths, all in bad condition and running through acres of old barbed wire. One N.C.O. got lost and was abandoned to his fate. His plaintive cries were heard till the small hours of the morning, when, by an accident, he fell out of the grip of the wire and was able to get back. When asked why he had been running, he explained that the vision of the raiders' rum, which he was afraid of losing, had urged him on. The enemy machine guns had nothing to do with his hurry.

"The remainder of the party reached the objective, known as the Devil's Jump, unobserved, and crept up to the parapet of the trench. On receiving the order to jump, they did so, only to land on a beautiful mat of wire. That was all they disturbed. They searched the trenches and shelters and, finding nothing, decided to return. A machine-gun emplacement was 'salted' and a fuse run out into the open. With great caution the party retired and the fuse was lighted. It was then discovered that one member of the party was missing, the only man in the Battalion taking a size-12 Army boot. Just as his friends were beginning to worry, he came rushing towards them with an excited whisper, 'There he comes!' and at the same time his foot landed on the burning fuse, thus effectively putting an end to the blowing-up business. After this incident the raiders stayed long enough to throw a couple of bombs in the direction of the approaching 'he,' and then withdrew from the possible consequences of their action."

The raiders had spent one hour and three-quarters in the enemy front line without coming across any enemy garrison, thereby establishing the fact that, on this front at least, the Germans withdrew their troops during the night to drier and warmer quarters in the support lines.

Christmas approached and, calculating ahead, the Kensingtons anticipated passing this, their third Christmas, in the line. However, an unexpected change of routine intervened and the festive season was spent in billets at Le Grand Pacaut, near Merville. The quarters occupied were Nissen huts and barns, and, as the cobbled roads were bordered by deep water-filled ditches, narrow plank bridges gave access to the billets from the road. Needless to say, more than one roysterer fell therein on attempting to regain his billet following a convivial evening. On Christmas Day the Kensingtons beat the Rangers at football, and on the last day of the year, following the defeat of the Royal Fusiliers by 5 goals to 1, gained the Brigade Cup.

After twelve days in Divisional reserve, the Battalion took over the Moated Grange sector to the right of the one held before Christmas and north of Neuve Chapelle, and there ensued a further period of trench warfare, most of the time in frost-bound trenches. The periods of relief were spent at La Fosse, Croix Barbée or Vieille Chapelle, considered by all to be a poor exchange for the comforts of Laventie. The situation on the front now became more active. The Corps Commander insisted on an aggressive attitude being maintained, and the quiet of the area was again disturbed by a series of raids on the enemy posts, some of these actually being occupied for a time. The enemy was, however, on the alert, and the raids, while achieving nothing, caused heavy casualties among the raiding parties. The first of these carried out by the Kensingtons took place on January 19th. The whole of A Company, under Captain Clarke, was detailed for the operation, and very thorough arrangements were made, including the provision of white suits for the raiders, as No-man's-land was at the time covered with snow. The company advanced to the objective at 3.30 a.m., following the lifting of the barrage, but were immediately perceived by a thoroughly awakened enemy. They were met by heavy machine-gun and rifle fire, and all efforts to get into the enemy trench failed. Sergeant Oborn made no less than three gallant attempts to enter the German trench, and was killed on the parapet. On the way back the raiders

LAVENTIE AGAIN

were heavily shelled, and the enemy also sent out strong counter-attacking parties. The raid was a costly one, for 21 men were either killed or wounded.

Another raid was carried out by the Kensingtons on February 17th in daylight in the Neuve Chapelle sector, by a party numbering about 150. The details were carefully rehearsed, and full information about the front (about 200 yards) obtained from aeroplane photographs. A misty morning favoured the operation, and the men took up their positions in front of our line at 7.15 a.m. unperceived by the enemy. The barrage was so arranged that it played on the objective while the party worked up to that point, and then lifted on to the enemy support lines and flanks of the front to be raided. As soon as the barrage lifted, the whole party entered the enemy trench and the work of clearing the trench proceeded. Only one party of the enemy was discovered, and they had evidently just "stood down," as their equipment was hanging outside their concrete shelters. They were easily persuaded to come out, and 5 prisoners of the 1st Battalion 13th Bavarian Infantry Regiment were secured. By this time the second party, detailed to carry on to the support lines, was on its way as arranged. They found nothing but derelict trenches, and returned on hearing the recall signal blown by a bugler with the support party in the enemy front line. The whole party returned to our support lines "over the top," thus avoiding casualties which would undoubtedly have occurred from the shells which were now falling on the communication trenches. As it was, the 37 casualties of the Kensingtons nearly all happened after getting back to our own system. In addition to the 5 prisoners, it was estimated that 40 of the enemy were accounted for. The success attending this raid brought congratulatory messages to the Battalion from the Higher Command.

During the period on this front the strength of the Battalion, under the steady flow of reinforcements, had grown to 38 officers and 1,043 other ranks, and it was realised that a move into more active areas was inevitable.

Frost and snow yielded to rain and wind, and as the days lengthened the peasants began their ploughing and sowing in the neighbourhood of Vieille Chapelle. Times were difficult for them. In a small holding near the Kensingtons' billets a woman steered a plough drawn by an emaciated "mulet." Her farm labourers comprised her son, aged twelve, and her brother, discharged from the French Army as the result of wounds, their efforts united in an endeavour to keep the farm going while the head of the family was away at the front.

CHAPTER XI

ON THE ARRAS FRONT

THE move to the new front began on March 9th, when the Kensingtons, having been relieved by the 7th Battalion West Riding Regiment, 49th Division, marched to La Fosse, where they spent the night. On the following day they entrained at Merville for Doullens, and thence marched to Ivergny. This proved to be quite a small village with a normal population of about 300, but now its accommodation was taxed to the utmost by the presence of at least 5,000 troops, with numbers of horses in addition. Here vigorous training, very necessary after a winter in the trenches and the absorption of large reinforcements, was carried out in the sodden fields surrounding the village.

The general situation must now be considered in order that the operations in which the Kensingtons were involved may be understood in relation to the wider issues at stake. The expenditure of men and munitions on the Somme in the previous autumn began to yield more results, as, following further British successes to the north of that area at Gommecourt, Beaumont Hamel, and Grandcourt, in January the enemy began a systematic retreat to the Hindenburg Line, a well-planned defence system branching off the original line near Arras and continuing towards St. Quentin. True, by this retreat, the German transferred the shattered territory to our side of the line, while he was able to establish his communications in country as yet untouched by shell fire; nevertheless, many square miles of French territory were thus regained.

However, this retreat but modified plans already made by which the British were to carry out an offensive on the Arras front as a supporting effort to a great French offensive under General Nivelle against the Chemin des Dames on the Aisne front in Champagne. The 56th Division, now in the Third Army, was definitely committed to operations on the Arras front. Indeed, from now on until the end of the war, save for two periods in other areas, the Division was continuously associated with the fighting on the front round about this historic town.

The 169th Brigade took over the front opposite Beaurains on March 14th, and plans were at once initiated for an attack by the 56th Division in conjunction with other Divisions on the front. However, on the 18th, it was discovered by patrols of this brigade that the enemy had withdrawn from Beaurains, and, when contact was again established, it was found that he was now occupying a line—Tilloy, the Harp, Telegraph Hill, and in front of Neuville Vitasse. This was the final stage in the retirement. No evacuation took place north of Arras, but further south, where the retreat was to a depth of several miles, some days passed before it was completed, our troops pressing forward in a constant endeavour to maintain contact.

Plans were at once modified to include as the objective of the 56th Division the capture of Neuville Vitasse and the advancing of the line towards Wancourt, the Kensingtons and the Rangers to be the front assaulting battalions on the 168th Brigade front, immediately opposite the village.

In the meantime the Battalion continued training at Ivergny, and on Sunday, March 18th, the day that the evacuation of Beaurains took place, Battalion sports were held. The event was a great success, the transport section as usual providing the humorous element by producing a mock General, complete with red tabs, accompanied by two "ladies." On the 23rd there was a move to Gouy en Artois, a ten-mile march over roads that, under the abnormal traffic consequent upon the enormous concentration of troops and artillery in the area, were almost impassable. As at Ivergny, the accommodation here was overtaxed, even though Nissen huts had been erected in fields adjoining the village. By this time news of the forthcoming operations was generally known, and the weather, as usual, appeared

BATTLE OF ARRAS, 9TH APRIL, 1917. MOVING FORWARD FROM ASSEMBLY TRENCH.
Imperial War Museum photograph. Copyright reserved.

to be on the side of the enemy, for the nights were frosty and snow or rain fell almost daily. The news of the enemy evacuation caused general rejoicing and the circulation of a multitude of stories, some doubtless true, but many mere inventions, of the traps that the Germans had left in dugouts to ensnare the unwary. Advanced dumps of stores and ammunition were formed as soon as the light railways could be pushed ahead. New gun positions necessitated by the changed situation were rapidly constructed.

On April 1st the Battalion marched to Achicourt and took over trenches in front of Beaurains which had been the British front line prior to the evacuation. The companies were employed at night in digging trenches in the assembly area for the forthcoming attack on Neuville Vitasse, and thus had time and opportunity to become familiar with the lie of the land. Battalion Headquarters was established in a dugout in the side of the railway cutting near the Achicourt railway bridge, a point which had been under enemy observation prior to the retirement, but over which lorries now ran in daylight on their way to Beaurains. On the 3rd the Battalion moved back into billets in Achicourt, and on the following day, known as V day, the bombardment of the enemy positions opened. Achicourt lies in a valley through which flows a small stream, and from well-camouflaged pits beside the stream the guns barked continuously day and night and helped to swell the full-throated chorus of gunfire all along the front. W day, the 5th, was fine and clear, and a steady bombardment was maintained all day. On the 6th, however, heavy rain fell and the attack was postponed for twenty-four hours. This meant that the 6th was also W day, and that the Kensingtons spent another day in Achicourt, waiting in readiness for the coming battle. The passage of the cavalry through the village aroused the usual hopes of a big advance, open warfare, and the end of the war. On the 7th the final preparations made, the Battalion moved up to the front line, A and C Companies occupying the front assembly trenches, with B Company in support and D in reserve. Y day, the 8th, was fine with good visibility, and as the trench occupied at the time by Battalion Headquarters was on the Beaurains side of the valley, on the opposite side of which in the distance a few tree stumps and a wall here and there indicated the village of Neuville Vitasse, there was opportunity to observe the devastating effect of our bombardment. A practice barrage at 3.15 p.m. was seen to be accurately placed on the enemy defences. Clouds of dust, smoke and flashes marked the intensity of the barrage, and it seemed that nothing could live under it.

Heavy shells had been heard throughout the day whining overhead in the direction of Achicourt as the German heavies retaliated on our back areas. The transport and reserve personnel of the Kensingtons in Achicourt had a bad time of it on this, the eve of the battle. A heavy bombardment, directed by an aeroplane, had fallen on the village, and an unlucky shell had struck an ammunition lorry, one of a convoy of twenty which had halted in or near the village square. As the lorries were loaded with 9·2 shells, the effect can be imagined. The lorries were shattered, immense masses of ironwork being hurled for hundreds of yards. Fearful havoc was wrought in a few minutes, and fire spread rapidly. The damage might have been much worse, but Major H. Campbell, who was in Achicourt at the time, took command of the situation and, with the assistance of N.C.O.s and men of the transport section, drove many of the lorries out of the danger zone. The decorations later awarded for this display of courage and presence of mind were well merited. In consequence of this holocaust all the buildings surrounding the square were in ruins and the Mairie was burnt to the ground. Many of the terrified civilians were not rescued from the wreckage of their homes until nightfall.

The battle opened at 5.30 on the following morning, April 9th. It was but Z day to the Kensingtons waiting in that shell-torn valley for zero hour, but at home in England it was Easter Monday. Away on the Vimy Ridge the Canadians stormed the enemy stronghold. On

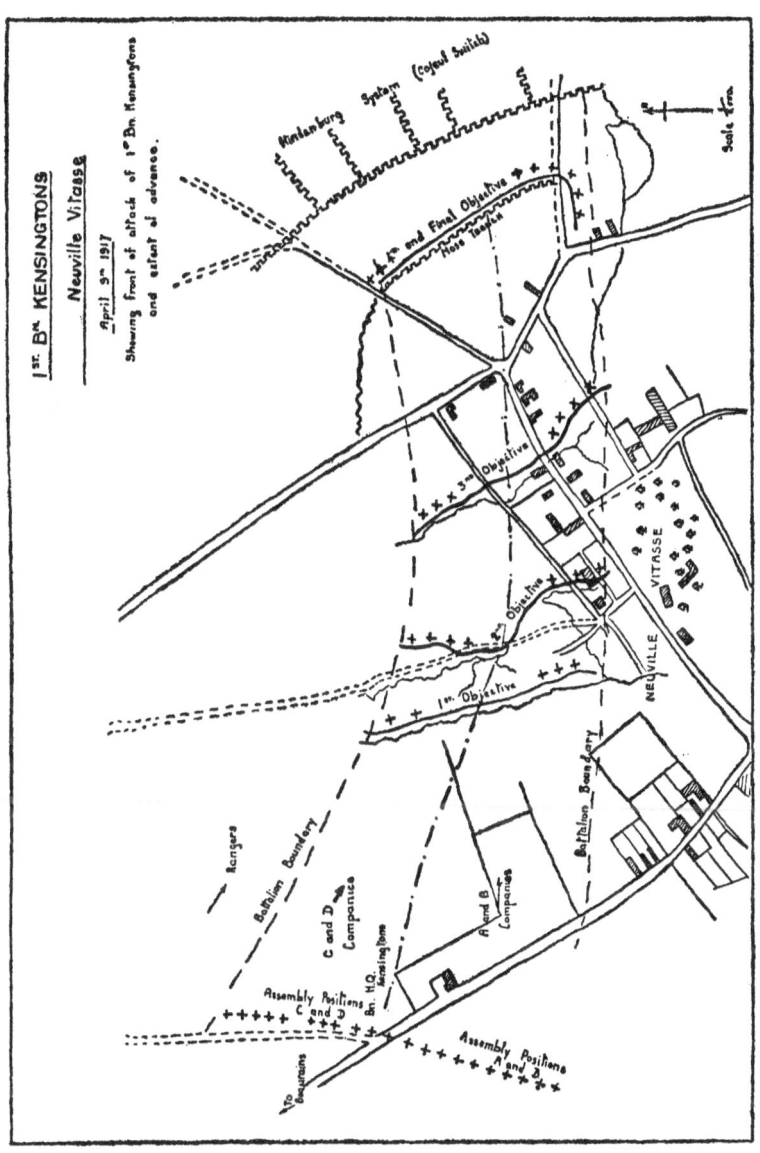

the Arras front the crucial attack was that of the 14th Division on Telegraph Hill, to the immediate left of the 56th Division. Anxious eyes strained to pierce the rain-laden atmosphere in an endeavour to detect the progress of the operations on the left. At 7.30 a.m. the attack on Telegraph Hill opened with instant success, and a quarter of an hour later the 56th Division, with the 168th Brigade on the left and the 167th Brigade on the right, entered the battle. On the 168th Brigade front were the Kensingtons and the Rangers in line, with the 4th Londons in support and the Scottish in reserve. The final objective of the Kensingtons was Moss Trench, to the north-east of Neuville Vitasse. When this was secured, the Scottish were to pass through the Battalion and attack the Cojeul Switch (Hindenburg Line). Neuville Mill, a strong point to the south of the Beaurains–Neuville Vitasse Road, was considered an obstacle worthy of special attention, and tanks were therefore directed against this objective.

For the first time in the campaign as far as the Kensingtons were concerned, the battle, at least in the early stages, went according to programme. On the preceding night 2nd Lieut. Mortlock and a small party of D Company had cut three lanes through the enemy wire in spite of machine-gun fire, and now the Battalion, disposed on a two-company front with A and C Companies leading, comprising four waves of two lines each, followed by B and D Companies similarly disposed, swept over the enemy's trenches, killing or capturing the enemy. Moppers-up followed the leading waves and dealt with dugouts. By 8.20 a.m. A and C Companies were through the village, and at 10 a.m. these companies were able to report their presence in Moss Trench in touch with the Rangers. Captain Clarke, commanding A Company, having been killed early in the fighting, Lieut. Farrar assumed command. B Company had already reported its objective gained, and at 9.50 a.m. this company was sent to the assistance of the 8th Middlesex on the right of the village. By 11.5 a.m., when news came from D Company of their success, the

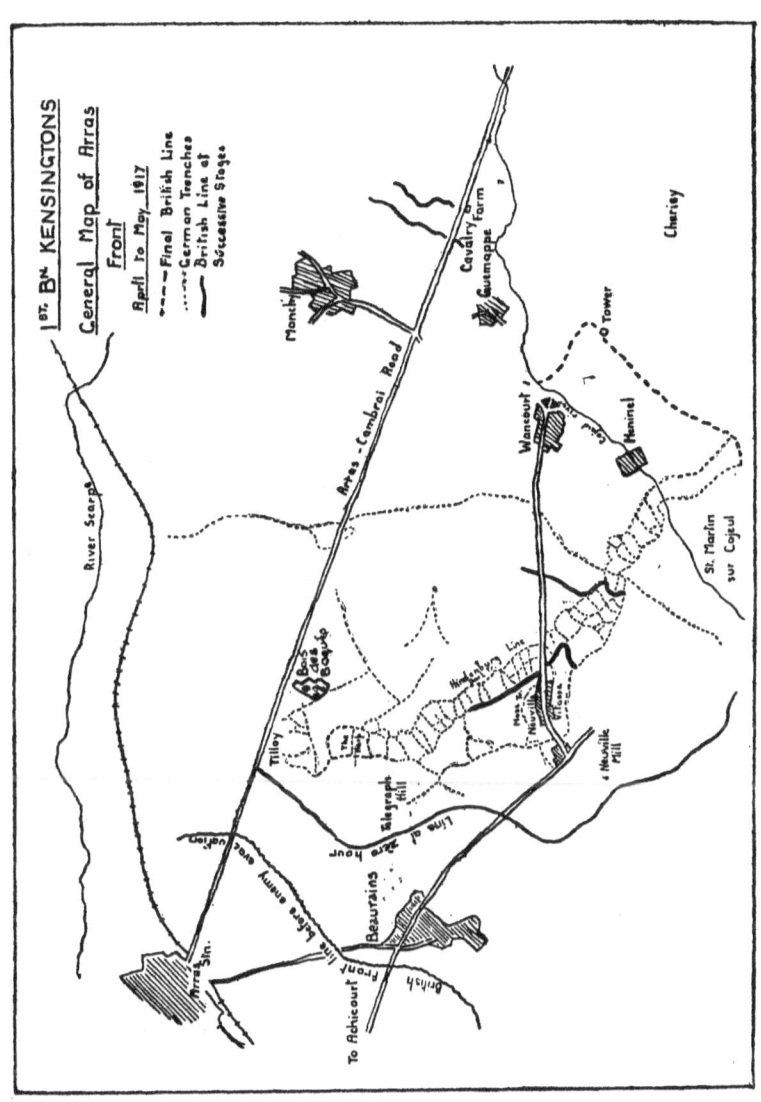

Battalion reported to Brigade that all its objectives had been won.

Four tanks had been allotted to the 168th Brigade, but of these only one started, and this was soon put out of action. In the operation against Neuville Mill, however, they rendered great service, and in subduing this strong point prevented the enfilade fire that would have rendered the attack of the Kensingtons very costly. As it was, the losses, amounting to 5 officers and 123 other ranks, most of whom were wounded, were accounted slight in view of what was undoubtedly the most successful day's fighting the Battalion had had since coming to France. Commenting on the attack, the Commanding Officer reported that the men behaved with the greatest coolness and dash throughout, in spite of the mud. The artillery support had been excellent and communications had been maintained throughout the day. As the result of the assault, the Kensingtons had taken 100 prisoners and captured 6 machine guns, 2 heavy mortars, and 3 grenatenwerfers. The prisoners were soon put to work in helping to carry the wounded to the dressing-station, a duty which they did well and carefully.

The second stage in the attack on the 168th Brigade front was allotted to the Scottish, who, passing through the Kensingtons at noon, assaulted the Cojeul Switch and fought their way against an increasing opposition to Back Trench, the final Brigade objective. Parties of this battalion penetrated the enemy system altogether on the right and disappeared towards Wancourt, but, the attack on their right having been held up, were compelled to return. In the early evening the Kensingtons were ordered to hold themselves in readiness to relieve the Scottish in Back Trench when this was cleared, but it was not until the early morning that this objective was fully obtained and contact established with the 14th Division on the left.

Rain had fallen during the day, and towards evening sleet fell and conditions became very bad for the men in the open in the captured trenches. The attack was continued

Battle of Arras, April 1917. 9·2 Howitzers, Neuville Vitasse.
Imperial War Museum photograph. Copyright reserved.

on the 10th by the 167th Brigade and the 14th Division in the direction of Wancourt, the 168th Brigade being in support. On this occasion it was on the left that the situation became obscure and a gap developed between the 167th Brigade and the 14th Division. The Kensingtons had re-formed around Neuville Vitasse during the day, and at 10 p.m. B Company with a company of the Scottish was ordered forward to fill this gap. The cavalry had been much in evidence all day, showing up in black masses in the wide snow-covered valley below Telegraph Hill towards Tilloy, apparently quite indifferent to the shrapnel that burst overhead. Away in the distance a pall of smoke hung over Monchy, plainly discernible on its hill, and witnessed to the intensity of the bombardment over the village.

The offensive was slowing down already, and the same difficulties accompanying an advance over country recently gained from the enemy as the result of hard-fought battles were arising as in the case of the Somme fighting. Guns had been rushed forward over roads softened by the late frosts and reduced to quagmires by the rain and snow, and the dead horses lying beside the Beaurains–Achicourt Road were silent witnesses to the fearful strain of transporting heavy loads to the fighting zone.

The Kensingtons spent a cold and miserable period until the 14th in reserve in Neuville Vitasse, the only protection against the incessant rain and sleet being such improvised shelters as they could construct from the débris lying about. On the 13th the line had been carried forward as far as Wancourt Tower, which, apart from a shell-hole through the middle, had escaped destruction and still stood as a prominent landmark. The enemy blew up the tower during this night, and some severe fighting developed about the ruins. When, on the 14th, the Battalion moved into trenches in the Cojeul Switch, the enemy was expected to counter-attack from the direction of Guemappe, and the 168th Brigade was disposed on a line facing north-east along Back Trench. This attack failed to reach thus far, however, and that night the Brigade took over the front line, a disconnected system of shell-holes and isolated pits, the Kensingtons being in support. During the night the enemy counter-attacked from the direction of Wancourt Tower, and B and C Companies were moved to the support of the Scottish and the 4th Londons in the front line. The attack was repulsed with heavy losses to the enemy on the Brigade front, but on the left he succeeded in penetrating between the Scottish and the 14th Division and regained the tower. The remaining two companies of the Kensingtons were moved up with the view to regaining this position. Heavy rain was falling and the night was extremely dark, and it was decided to postpone the operation till daylight. During the night, however, the task of recovering Wancourt Tower was allotted to the 14th Division, and this was accomplished by the Northumberland Fusiliers at noon on the following day. The Kensingtons were now in the front line, and attempts were made to improve and consolidate the trench system—very necessary, for the men were up to their knees in mud and water. The trenches, such as they were, were also badly sited and were under continuous observation, so that the Battalion received considerable unwelcome attention from the enemy artillery. All roads leading to the trenches were, in fact, subjected to a considerable bombardment from heavy artillery during this period, and ration parties were compelled to run the gauntlet in their nightly journeys to the line.

Relief came on the night of the 19th, when the front line was taken over by the Royal Scots Fusiliers and the Kensingtons marched back to Arras, a long and fatiguing journey which made the comfortable billets in an auxiliary hospital near Schramm Barracks doubly welcome. The Quartermaster, with his customary consideration for the men, had hot soup and tea prepared and blankets ready. It was needed, for all had been continuously exposed to most unseasonable weather since the 7th. General satisfaction was felt, however, for the objectives had been secured and a considerable number of prisoners and war material captured.

The famous Hindenburg Line had been penetrated, the perfection of the dugouts testifying to the expectation of the enemy to hold this line for a prolonged period. Some of these dugouts were approached by fifty steps leading steeply downwards, and below ground there were wire beds in wood-lined compartments, the whole work being of a very high standard. The larger dugouts would accommodate a company, and numerous entrances were provided. It was realised how the enemy had been able to survive the intense bombardment prior to the infantry assault when provided with protection such as this.

Arras at this time was not so badly smashed as might have been anticipated, considering the length of time it had been within range of the enemy guns. A house here and there was roofless, but it was the larger buildings that had suffered most. The Cathedral was a ruin, as were the station and buildings in the vicinity. The streets were alive with troops, a khaki stream flowing continuously in a vain search for shops. The relief from shell fire was, however, too recent for the civil population to return, though by the next time the Kensingtons came that way the city had regained much of its normal war-time activity.

The stay in the city lasted but two days, and on the 21st there began a series of moves in a sort of seven-day circular tour, ending up again in Arras on the 28th. These moves were occasioned by the transfer of the 56th Division to the VIth Corps, though at the time they were mysterious enough to the pawns that were thus moved about in an apparently aimless fashion. Bayencourt, well remembered from Hebuterne days, was the first stop in the tour, and the Kensingtons, conveyed thither in buses, found a quiet, almost post-war atmosphere about the deserted village which the year before had housed three reserve battalions. Grass was growing in the roadway and wild daffodils bloomed in the hedgerows. Billeting occasioned no anxiety, for comfortable huts abounded. The whole area seemed strangely quiet after the recollections of 1916, and explorers found Gommecourt, now well behind the line since the evacuation, a heap of ruins inhabited only by a Town Major in a cellar. On the 24th a sudden move to Gouy was ordered, and a long and trying march ensued to this crowded village, followed by a move to Simencourt on the 26th and the completion of the tour on the 28th by the march to Arras.

Further operations on the Arras front were contemplated. The offensive which began on the 9th had been staged in order to assist the great French offensive at Chemin des Dames under General Nivelle, but whereas the supporting operations on the Arras front had achieved great success, the main offensive had failed. In order to assist a further stage in the French operations on May 5th there was to be an attack on the Arras front on the 3rd. On April 28th the 56th Division took over a line east of Guèmappe, the 168th Brigade being in reserve, and on May 2nd the Kensingtons moved to Tilloy in reserve to the battle planned for the following day. This attack was opened by the 167th and 169th Brigades at 3.45 a.m. on May 3rd, when, following an artillery barrage, the assaulting troops advanced upon Tool Trench and Cavalry Farm, enemy positions astride the Arras–Cambrai Road. They were met by a withering rifle and machine-gun fire, and in the darkness the situation became very confused. Isolated parties penetrated beyond the objectives, but the enemy was holding the line in force with well-sited machine guns and a general advance was impossible. Such parties as did get through were surrounded and either killed or captured. In spite of the utmost gallantry on the part of the attack, the day resulted in the withdrawal of our men to their original line. The Kensingtons had been moved up during the fighting to the north end of the Harp, and on the following day they moved into support trenches, the 168th Brigade now holding the front line. On the 6th they took over the front from two battalions of the 8th Infantry Brigade to the north of the Divisional sector.

In the meantime our heavy artillery had been concentrating a steady bombardment on Tool Trench and Cavalry Farm. The enemy, no less active in this respect, bombarded our trenches with shells of a large calibre. Twenty of the Kensingtons were buried by one such shell, but were dug out unhurt. Parties had been seen leaving these positions, but patrols had found Tool Trench fully manned. On the 11th an attack was made by the Scottish and the Fusiliers without preliminary barrage. The enemy garrison was surprised, and both Tool trench and Cavalry Farm were captured. B Company of the Kensingtons was in support to this operation under the Scottish, but apart from this the Battalion was not called upon to enter the fighting. The sustained shell fire during the period, however, had occasioned the loss of 1 officer and 83 other ranks.

CHAPTER XII

THE THIRD BATTLE OF YPRES

ON the 14th the Battalion was relieved in trenches and moved to bivouacs at Tilloy, marching to billets in Schramm Barracks on the following day. Arras was an obvious billeting place for large numbers of troops, and the enemy showed his recognition of the fact by shelling the city with long-range guns. Several shells struck the barracks, fortunately without causing any casualties, and during the night the crash of a bursting shell and falling masonry awoke the echoes with persistent regularity. The Divisional band now played occasionally on the Place du Théâtre amidst the wreckage of the past gaieties of Arras. A fallen kiosk obstructed the footway, and the pre-war theatrical posters were shredding from the walls of the shell-battered theatre. The military crowd attracted to the spot was very varied, Welsh and Scottish regiments rubbing shoulders with Canadians and South Africans. A closer examination of the city revealed that many of the houses, apparently whole, were completely ruined inside. The roads in the vicinity of the ruined cathedral were buried beneath twenty feet of fallen stonework. Here and there a shell had penetrated to the underground tunnels which honeycombed the chalk under the Cambrai side of the ruined city. These tunnels and caves had been improved during the military occupation and were now very extensive, running to points right outside the city. Reliefs had been carried out by means of these tunnels when the trench line had been near the city. In certain sections electric lighting had been installed, and salvaged furniture and wire beds made these caves into desirable residences for troops in reserve. The Citadel, a French military school near Schramm Barracks, possessed a bathing-pool in the grounds, and Kensington swimming enthusiasts were quick to take advantage of the recreation thus offered. On May 19th the Battalion moved to Berneville and on the 24th to Simencourt, where all ranks entered with zest upon a fortnight of real rest and enjoyment in glorious weather. It is pleasant to record the events of this well-merited holiday, which came as an interlude between the recurring cycles of trench warfare, intensive training and battle. Apart from the physical and company training necessary to maintain military efficiency, the sunny days were given up to sport and recreation. There were Battalion and Brigade sports, inter-battalion cricket matches and shooting competitions.

An amusing incident occurred on the day of the 168th Brigade sports. The transport section, ever ready to furnish the comic element, attired themselves as Staff officers complete with red bands on their hats, red tabs, and an imposing array of medals consisting of empty blacking tins. Mounted upon heavy draught horses and carrying long poles as lances, the impressive cavalcade came suddenly upon D Company guard. The startled sentry at the first sight of the red tabs called out the guard, but the sergeant, more observant, perceived the hoax and hurried his men back under cover again, but not before onlookers had seen enough to enable them to spread the glad news abroad. It is reported that the sentry, smarting under the wrath of his superior, failed to turn out the guard when the real General came by, and was once more the subject of verbal castigation.

In the evenings the Bow Bells, the Divisional concert party, provided entertainment to packed houses of appreciative troops, to whom theatre-going was a thing of the past. This concert party had been formed at Souastre in 1916, and in barn, hut, or even, as on the Somme, in the open air on a G.S. wagon, had provided entertainment to the troops whenever possible. In an amazingly short space of time a miniature stage was erected and first-class shows given. " Miss " Holland of the Scottish, Dick Horne of the Westminsters, and Harry Brandon of the A.S.C. were especial favourites.

Battalion concerts were also arranged, and the Kensington drums gave an excellent concert, followed by a short play, on June 9th.

There followed yet one more tour in the line on this front. On June 10th the Kensingtons marched to Gouves and the following day to Arras. A week was spent in reserve in huts which had been erected near Beaurains among the barbed wire of the old No-man's-land before taking over trenches in front of Guèmappe.

During the first night in these Nissen huts a peculiar whining under the floor of a hut occupied by Headquarter details was noticed. Investigation on the following morning revealed a bitch of nondescript breed with a litter of four puppies. The family was enthusiastically adopted and carefully fed and transported during the frequent moves of that summer. The mother was duly named Nellie, and the youngsters, as they grew and flourished under the devoted attention of the men, became earmarked for issue to companies. The urgent question became that of deciding on the approximate breed and the necessary treatment of tails. A dog fancier was discovered in the Battalion (it was invariably possible to discover an expert on any conceivable subject among the troops), and he recommended and carried out amputation in the approved manner, having decided that the breed was mainly terrier. The family remained with the Battalion for some months, but never appeared able to distinguish one khaki-clad friend from another, and one by one they disappeared to go, doubtless, on the strength of other units. Nellie was the last to go, her nomadic instincts asserting themselves once more.

The tour in the front line was not a pleasant one. The glorious summer weather had broken and heavy rains flooded the sector. The position of the enemy was not very clear and the trench system was disconnected and badly overlooked, but things had quietened down considerably and the tour proved uneventful. On June 27th the Battalion moved back into support in Wancourt, two companies and Headquarters occupying an immense cave under the ruins of the village of Morlière, a mole-like existence in subterranean darkness which the meagre supply of candles utterly failed to dispel. Although the sector was quiet on the whole, the enemy artillery maintained a steady bombardment over the whole area, and the Battalion lost 2 officers and 30 other ranks from shell fire.

Relief came on July 2nd, when the Kensingtons marched to Achicourt, now quiet and peaceful, and, arriving in the dawn, enjoyed the morning air, scented by Madonna lilies now in full bloom in the gardens of the deserted houses. The war-time gardens of Arras and the surrounding villages were aglow with flowers in the summer months. Pounded by shells, with crumbling walls and houses about them, they yet ran riot in a wanton confusion. Nature appeared to hasten her efforts to replace the ruin of war with sweetness and beauty.

On July 4th, following a short march to Dainville, the Battalion was met by a convoy of motor-buses and conveyed to Liencourt, a village near Lignereuil, well remembered from the spring of the preceding year, when several weeks had been spent there prior to taking over the Hebuterne sector. Lieut.-Colonel J. C. King left the Battalion on the 14th to join the XIXth Corps, and Captain J. E. L. Higgins assumed command.

Towards the end of the month the 56th Division was transferred to the Fifth Army, and it was recognised that the end of this second period of rest was in sight. Events followed quickly. The Kensingtons marched to Monts en Ternois on the 22nd and, entraining on the following day at Petit Houvin, reached St. Omer and marched to the twin villages of Houlle and Moulle, a distance of about ten miles from the town. Intensive training now began, including field firing exercises at Tournehem, lasting two days. The long summer evenings, however, gave some opportunity for recreation, and the men, realising the wisdom of taking advantage of every facility that offered, enjoyed swimming in the river or fishing with improvised materials. Needless to say, no important catches were reported.

While the 56th Division thus enjoyed a few days of summer in a quiet and charming country-side, the final preparations had been completed for the third battle of Ypres.

The decision to stage a great British offensive had been made as the result of the definite failure of the French attacks in April and May. The British Army was now at its maximum strength, and the duty of maintaining pressure upon the enemy devolved upon Sir Douglas Haig, for our Allies were exhausted and discouraged by their losses on the Champagne front. Ypres, the very name of which was already a byword to the British Expeditionary Force, was chosen as the theatre of operations, not only because of the urgent necessity for making an attempt to clear the enemy from the Belgian coast to which the salient, once carried, offered immediate access, but because no other front appeared at the time to offer such promise of success. Arras was out of the question, for the enemy was known to be massed there and attacks were not considered likely to be successful without supporting operations farther south, support that the French were in no condition to give. The evacuated area south of Arras was ruled out because of the difficulty of establishing communications over such desolated country, while the densely populated character of the area behind the lines to the north would render any advance extremely difficult.

The great essential for a successful offensive in the Ypres salient was favourable weather, for the whole area is low-lying and, the normal drainage system being ruined by shell fire, it became a morass in rainy spells. Valuable time had already been lost, for, as has been seen, the Arras offensive was continued into May contrary to the original intention, and as it was hoped to obtain decisive results at Ypres before the fall of winter upon the area, preparations were pushed forward with the utmost speed. The enemy

THE THIRD BATTLE OF YPRES

held the slightly rising ground to the north, and thus had excellent observation over the whole area of the proposed attack. His artillery knew every inch of it, and the already crowded zone was subjected to continuous long-range shell fire. Bombing aeroplanes added their regular contribution.

The battle opened on July 31st with an attack on a wide front, when the enemy's new method of defence was at once detected. This consisted in holding the front lightly with machine-gun posts sited in " pillboxes," concrete emplacements of great strength, able to stand all but direct hits from very heavy shells. The main line of defence was concentrated farther back, to which the garrisons of these posts could, if they survived the assault, retire. The distances were so arranged that when the first waves of the attack, exhausted and disorganised, reached the main line of defence they received the full force of the counter-attack. However, in spite of this new development, substantial gains were made on the left and a footing gained on the Passchendaele Ridge, but on the right the advance towards the Westhoek Ridge was held up in front of Glencorse Wood and Inverness Copse.

The weather now took a hand in the battle. Rain fell heavily during the first day's fighting and continued without appreciable improvement for four days and nights. As had been feared, the whole area became a swamp with patches of dry ground here and there, and movement was possible only over tracks constructed of logs above the water level. Conditions were such that it was impossible to follow up the initial gains by a rapid succession of blows before the enemy had time to reorganise. Indeed, it was not until August 10th that the new line was consolidated, and the battle was not reopened until the 16th.

The 56th Division entered the arena on the 11th, when they took over the line facing Inverness Copse and Glencorse Wood and preliminary operations were carried out by the 169th Brigade, without, however, any appreciable measure of success.

"THE KENSINGTONS"

Meanwhile the Kensingtons left Moulle and Houlle on the 5th and, entraining for Abeele, marched thence to Steenvoorde, which was reached on the 6th. The village offered poor accommodation, and the inhabitants were unfriendly and strongly suspected of espionage. While here the command of the Battalion was taken over by Major V. A. Flower, D.S.O.

On the 12th the Kensingtons moved in buses to Canal Reserve Camp, about seven miles from the line, and the following day marched to Micmac Camp, near Ouderdom, where they stayed until the 15th, continuing training and preparing for the coming battle. The country here was typical of the salient, flat and monotonous, and intersected with frequent irrigation ditches, now swollen by the recent heavy rains. No building remained intact, and the concentrated troops were accommodated in camps of Nissen huts thickly scattered on the flat country.

At 6.30 p.m. on the 15th, the usual battle arrangements having been completed, the Battalion marched along the cobbled road leading to Ypres, passing Brig.-General F. G. Lewis, C.B., C.M.G., whose brigade was leaving that area, and as the sun set in a watery sky struck off along the Corduroy Track, four kilometres long, towards Half-way House, reserve positions for the attack on the morrow. The usual precautions to minimise losses from the shell fire, which swept the track as the sole route to the front, were taken, the men marching in small groups with long intervals between. The journey in the fading light became a memorable one, revealing, particularly in its later stages, the horrors of the sector. On either hand stretched a morass with large pools here and there, many of them showing the half-submerged remains of limbers, horses, and guns. On either hand shells burst around the batteries which occupied every dry patch, fully exposed to observation. Ahead the flash of bursting shells indicated heavy fire on the assembly positions. Half-way House, which served as Battalion and Brigade Headquarters, proved to be a large shallow dugout running with water,

THE THIRD BATTLE OF YPRES

which the efforts of a fatigue party, continuously at the pumps, failed to keep dry.

Company commanders had been ordered to report the safe arrival of their companies at the end of the track where it led into the support trenches, and the Commanding Officer, Major V. A. Flower, with Major J. E. L. Higgins and Major M. Harris, stationed themselves at this highly dangerous spot to receive these reports. At the moment when the last company was almost clear of the track a shell burst close to these senior officers. Major Flower was killed, and Major Higgins and Major Harris were so badly affected by the concussion that, after attempting to carry on, they were at length compelled to go to the dressing-station, whence they were evacuated to hospital. The Battalion was thus left without a Commanding Officer in unknown terrain on the eve of a battle. The preparations for the attack had been hurried, and apart from a reconnaissance of the ground about Half-way House during the morning by company commanders, there had been no opportunity to gain any knowledge of the part that the Battalion might be called upon to play. Captain Venables, as senior Company Commander, assumed command temporarily, and Brigade was hurriedly informed. Captain R. E. F. Shaw, who was attached to Brigade, was thereupon sent to take over the command, an office he filled with conspicuous success until his death about a year later.

In the meantime the companies struggled to their positions through the swamp. The enemy was shelling with gas shells, and box respirators had to be worn, still further increasing the difficulties. Men were constantly falling into shell-holes and searching for lost helmets. The rations even were lost, a clear indication of the bad going. Ultimately the required positions were occupied, and at 2 a.m. the barrage on the enemy front started, many of the batteries firing from exposed positions, close to the companies. At 10 a.m. the Battalion was ordered to move forward to positions in and around Château Wood. Heavy shell fire now fell on our trenches, the very names of which were suggestive of the uncertainty of the situation. A Company occupied Ignorance Trail, B Company Ignorance Row, and C Company Ignorance Reserve. The Battalion was now near the Ypres–Menin Road, with the ruins of the Hooge Château on its left flank. Battalion Headquarters was established in a pillbox about 400 yards behind the companies. Away in front the Westhoek Ridge sloped gently to the skyline, and through glasses little groups of men could be seen, now advancing, now retiring. During the afternoon D Company was ordered to move forward to Westhoek Ridge to reinforce the 7th Middlesex. As the men moved in file across the swampy, shell-torn ground, a gap in the Ridge permitted enemy observation of the movement, and he opened enfilade machine-gun fire on the men as they followed the only available track. However, few casualties were sustained and the men were disposed behind the ridge under cover from view, if not from fire. The trenches, smashed and unrecognisable as such, were literally filled with the dead of many units, testifying to the repeated efforts of many Divisions to carry this position. The night, fortunately, proved quiet, as did the next day, and the company remained on the ridge until relieved in the early hours of the 18th.

At 4.45 a.m. on the 16th the 167th and 169th Brigades in conjunction with the 8th Division on their left, had attacked, with Polygon Wood as the objective. Both London brigades almost at once encountered an unsuspected marsh which created a gap between them, and this, coupled with fierce enemy resistance in Glencorse Wood, brought the attack to a standstill. In some cases the leading waves penetrated to Polygon Wood, into which they disappeared, but it was not found possible to follow up their success. The Kensingtons awaited the order to move forward into the attack, but as the day wore on and no call came, it was realised that the battle had not gone according to expectation. In the late afternoon very heavy shell fire fell on the Battalion, and Headquarters suffered particularly heavy casualties.

THE THIRD BATTLE OF YPRES

At nightfall on the 16th the 56th Division was withdrawn from the line. The losses had been exceptionally heavy, 5 Commanding Officers being casualties. The Kensingtons marched wearily to bivouacs at Ouderdom for a few hours' rest, and then on to Cornwall Camp. The first and last experience of fighting in the Salient concentrated into an unforgettable day was ended. Two officers and 18 other ranks had been killed and 3 officers and 87 other ranks wounded or missing, although the Battalion had taken no part in the assault. At Battalion Headquarters the Regimental Sergeant-Major had been wounded and Sergeant Bryant, an old-time Kensington, killed.

A few days at Cornwall Camp offered a breathing-space before the next move, though enemy aeroplane activity served as a reminder of the proximity of the camp to the Salient. One night as the men lay tense in the flimsy tents and hutments listening to the droning overhead, a plane, clearly visible in the beam of the searchlights, let fall a bomb, which fell on a near-by ammunition dump. The concussion was terrific, and the morning revealed an immense crater where the dump had been.

The Battalion saw the last of this front without regret when on the 24th it marched to Reninghelst siding and entrained for Watten, near St. Omer, and marched thence to Houlle. On the 31st it was again on the move, this time by tactical train from Arques railhead to Bapaume. The records of the journey give some idea of the wearisome nature of such a move. The march from Houlle started at 12.30 a.m., and dawn came and found the heavily laden men jogging along the road to Arques. The train started at 5.19 a.m. and pursued a leisurely course to Bapaume, which was not reached until 4 p.m., via the reconditioned line through Arras.

The Kensingtons now found themselves on the scene of the 1916 fighting on the Somme. Bapaume was entirely destroyed, and no civilians were to be seen in the whole area. The camp which was the temporary resting-place of the Battalion was near Le Transloy, and from it could be seen the shattered stumps of Leuze and Delville Woods and a ruin or two of Les Bœufs. Nature had already clothed the ground with weeds and tall grasses, masking shell-holes, trenches, dugouts, and tangled wire. So featureless was the rolling country that distances were deceptive, and it proved an adventure to revisit a spot which by now seemed almost historical. Les Bœufs was a forgotten village. Rusty, shattered signs outside estaminets creaked in the breeze. The street was grass-grown. In one garden stood the dismal relics of a roundabout, and near-by gaudily painted swing boats, smashed and scattered here and there, told a tale of a village feast overtaken by war. Aeroplane Trench was located, and the remains of the aeroplane that gave it that name, but diligent search failed to reveal the remembered graves of men of the Kensingtons who had fallen during the Somme fighting. The grass had hidden everything in its rank profusion. Now that the front was afar off and it was possible to stand erect and look about the rolling country, it was easy to understand why such difficulty had been experienced in locating trenches when shattered woods, the only landmarks, looked so much like one another.

On September 3rd the Battalion left the Bapaume area and marched to Fremicourt, occupying a camp near the Fremicourt–Vaux Road, the following day relieving the 1st Northumberland Fusiliers in trenches in the Lagnicourt sector.

CHAPTER XIII

THE CAMBRAI FRONT

THE autumn of 1917 became associated in the minds of the Kensingtons with quiet tours in front, support, or reserve lines in the Lagnicourt sector. The area behind the line had been evacuated by the Germans in the spring, and there were no civilians within miles. The villages were all in ruins, just as the retreating enemy had left them, grass-grown and desolate. The front, however, was extraordinarily quiet, and, taking advantage of this, the Engineers had been busy in the construction of huts, dugouts, and light railways. The trenches themselves were well made and drained, and across the wide No-man's-land the enemy, comfortably ensconsed in his much-vaunted Hindenburg Line, gave very little trouble to the opposing forces. The weather, making some recompense for the wretched August, became warm and sunny in the early weeks of September, and this, coupled with lack of activity on both sides, made even trench warfare tolerable. The canteen, now a much-appreciated feature of army life, was installed in a sunken road near the line, and even baths were provided in the village of Lagnicourt for the men holding the line. The normal routine became six days in front line, six in Brigade support in a sunken road, and six in the Fremicourt Camp in reserve.

As tour succeeded tour, the front line became more and more comfortable. The ruins of Lagnicourt provided a happy hunting-ground for stoves, damaged chairs and tables. Supplies of fuel and water were left for the incoming relief, who reciprocated by similar provision for the subsequent return. Amusing incidents occurred to relieve the tedium. Rations were carried nightly to the companies in the line by pack animals, travelling " over the top." One of these mules, named Nelson, by virtue of his one eye, stampeded one night and was ultimately found hung up on the barbed wire in No-man's-land. To the amusement of all, the return to the camp after the first tour in the line was accomplished by means of a light railway which ran from Maricourt Wood, a short distance from the line, to Fremicourt, some kilometres farther back, and on to back areas. This was felt to be soldiering in luxury. The little open trucks, crowded with men in full marching order, were hauled and pushed by two diminutive engines, one fore and one aft. After a great puffing and emission of smoke these sturdy locomotives got the train under way, only to come to a standstill on the first slope. No amount of puffing enabled them to proceed. The two drivers dismounted and held a conference amid the ribald remarks of the troops. It was even suggested that perhaps they had been pulling in different directions. By unloading and pushing, the train was ultimately got under way again and triumphantly reached the camp. The end of this noble attempt to lighten the burden of the infantryman was inglorious, for, on a later journey to the line, the speed down the slope was permitted to exceed the customary six miles per hour, and at the bottom the train overturned and shot the surprised Kensingtons into the embankment. After this the troops marched to the line in the usual manner. An enemy attempt at propaganda occurred one day, when a number of red paper balloons came over our lines and were shot down. Each one was carrying a parcel of German papers printed in French. As there were no French, either soldiers or civilians, within fifteen miles, as an attempt to disseminate "kultur" it appeared to miss the mark badly.

Active patrolling was undertaken in the wide No-man's-land, and a series of advanced posts were connected. The greatest activity on the part of the enemy was manifested by a machine-gun post situated in Magpie's Nest. He also raided the Scottish on September 28th and secured 2 prisoners, though at a heavy cost. About a fortnight later the Scottish raided Magpie's Nest, which they found heavily wired along the parapet and the garrison very much on the alert.

On October 13th, while the Kensingtons were in the front line, a furious air fight developed overhead and three enemy planes were seen to be attacking a single British plane. After a few minutes of tense excitement the latter came down and crashed just in front of a Kensington post. Captain F. W. Heath, who was attached to Battalion Headquarters as works officer at the time, immediately went forward, in spite of shell and machine-gun fire, and crawled towards the plane. When within twenty yards of it, he discovered that the airman was lying wounded in a shell-hole, to which he had managed to crawl. Captain Heath was himself wounded, but was able to get back. Colonel Shaw now reached the post and called for volunteers to go out and rescue the airman. Corporal Legh, who had already made one attempt, and Sergeant Manzi undertook the task and, carrying a stretcher under cover of a white flag, succeeded in bringing in the wounded officer. Colonel Shaw was wounded, however, by a sniper's bullet while superintending the rescue. The wrecked aeroplane became a centre for activity on the part of patrols for some nights until destroyed by the Royal Engineers after instruments had been removed. The following letter was received by Major A. G. Symes, who was temporarily in command:

56TH DIVISION.

H.Q. 3rd Brigade R.F.C.

I wish on behalf of the 3rd Brigade R.F.C. to express our gratitude to the Division for the very gallant action performed by Captain Heath, M.C., Sergeant Manzi, and Corporal Legh of the 13th Battalion the London Regiment when they succeeded in bringing in to our trenches Lieut. Morrison, who was lying out badly wounded in No-man's-land after his machine had been brought down. This was done under heavy shell and rifle fire.

I regret very much that Captain Heath was wounded. I also wish to express our thanks to Lieut.-Colonel Shaw who, standing on the parapet at great personal risk, was superintending Lieut.

Morrison being brought back from the front line and who was also unfortunately wounded.

I should be very glad if these officers and N.C.O.s could be given some recognition for their gallantry, which undoubtedly saved Lieut. Morrison's life.

(Signed) Brig.-General Commanding 3rd Brigade
R.F.C.

16/10/17.

As the result of these recommendations Captain Heath was awarded a bar to the Military Cross and Sergeant Manzi and Corporal Legh each received the Military Medal.

The fine weather of early autumn had changed to rain and frost by November, and conditions became less congenial. The tents at Fremicourt had been replaced by huts, but in the bivouacs in the sunken road where the six days in support were spent, no amount of ingenuity could keep out the rain. When the Kensingtons took over the front line on November 12th, it began to look as though the whole winter would be spent in the unchanging routine of trench warfare. When, however, there arrived from the transport lines a collection of wooden effigies resembling the head and shoulders of soldiers, nailed in rows to boards, it was felt that something was in the air, and the arrival of the 3rd Londons in relief, equipped in full battle array, confirmed suspicions. The Battle of Cambrai was about to begin.

This battle was the first attempt to carry out a surprise attack on a large scale. It became a ten-day adventure which nearly succeeded in fulfilling the wildest hopes and as nearly ended in disaster. The general purpose of the attack was to relieve the situation in Italy, where our allies had suffered serious reverses, and more particularly to break through the Hindenburg Line from Gonnelieu to Hermies. In order to keep the immense preparations necessary for such an operation concealed from the enemy until the actual moment of the assault, very thorough precautions were taken. Gun positions were camouflaged, infantry bivouacs arranged under screens in woods. Ammunition was gradually assembled in hidden dumps and the necessary concentration of troops carried out with great secrecy. Instead of a preliminary bombardment, with its advertisement of impending attack, reliance was to be placed on tanks to flatten out the enemy wire defences. They were got forward by night just prior to the battle and their tracks obscured from aeroplane observation before morning.

On the eve of the battle the 167th and 169th Brigades were holding the front on the extreme left of the proposed attack, and their first task was to make a demonstration with dummy tanks and men, supported by smoke discharges and artillery fire. The 168th was in reserve in and about Fremicourt.

The battle opened at 6.10 a.m. on November 20th, and success was immediate, particularly on the right. The enemy was completely surprised and, following the tanks, the attacking troops penetrated the Hindenburg Line on a wide front. As regards the hoax on the 56th Divisional front, the dummy tanks, half obscured by smoke, and the dummy men, pushed over the top, called forth an intense bombardment which kept the enemy on that front busy until past midday. The " troops " thus bombarded stood their ground and perished at their posts in the approved style.

The 36th Division on the right of the 56th had advanced from the direction of Demicourt along the Bapaume–Cambrai Road, and the 169th Brigade linked up with them on the German outpost line during the morning. The end of the first day saw a substantial salient, some eight miles wide and four miles deep in places, made in the enemy line, with the cavalry through. The advance had stopped short at Bourlon Wood, the inevitable rising ground which dominated the situation on the left. Flesquières village held out in the centre, and on the right the Scheldt Canal still remained in the hands of the Germans.

On the next day, the 21st, further attempts were made to continue the advance. The crossing of the Scheldt Canal was extended and Flesquières taken, but on the left Bourlon

Wood still held out, and now appeared to be the key to the situation. Although enemy reserves might be assumed by this to have reached the area, and the resistance was undoubtedly stiffening, Sir Douglas Haig decided to carry on, and on the 22nd and succeeding days operations resolved themselves into determined attacks on Bourlon Wood. On the 22nd the 56th Division took a greater share in the battle. It must be realised that the two brigades in line, the 167th and the 169th, held the extreme left of the front. The 169th Brigade, which was on the right, was now ordered to attack the Hindenburg Line in an attempt to roll up these defences from the left. On the 23rd the 168th Brigade was moved forward into the battle zone, the Hindenburg system about Tadpole Copse now being the Divisional objective. The Kensingtons, with Lieut.-Colonel Shaw again in command, moved from the camp at Fremicourt, where they had been awaiting orders since the 20th, to Le Bucquière (Cinema Camp), and at 6.30 p.m. marched along the straight cobbled Bapaume–Cambrai Road with its fringe of poplars, to the ruins of Doignies. On the next night, November 24th, they took over the area vacated by the Rangers and the Fusiliers in the old British front line, Battalion Headquarters being established in dugouts in Louverval Wood. Hopes were still high that a great advance might be made. Fresh troops were being thrown into the battle, and the Guards had marched by while the Kensingtons were halted on the way to the line.

In the meantime the operations against Tadpole Copse were progressing. The London Scottish had established themselves in the Hindenburg Line and were pushing on through the trench system towards the Copse. In order to protect their flank C Company of the Kensingtons (2nd Lieut. H. B. Perry) had gone on ahead of the Battalion from Doignies to dig a trench from the old British front line to the crater. By 8 p.m. the rest of the companies were in position, A Company (2nd Lieut. J. B. Farrer) taking over the defensive flank, while C Company returned to Doignies to collect battle stores. At dawn on the 25th A Company returned to our lines, leaving two Lewis-gun sections to hold the flank. During the day the enemy counter-attacked

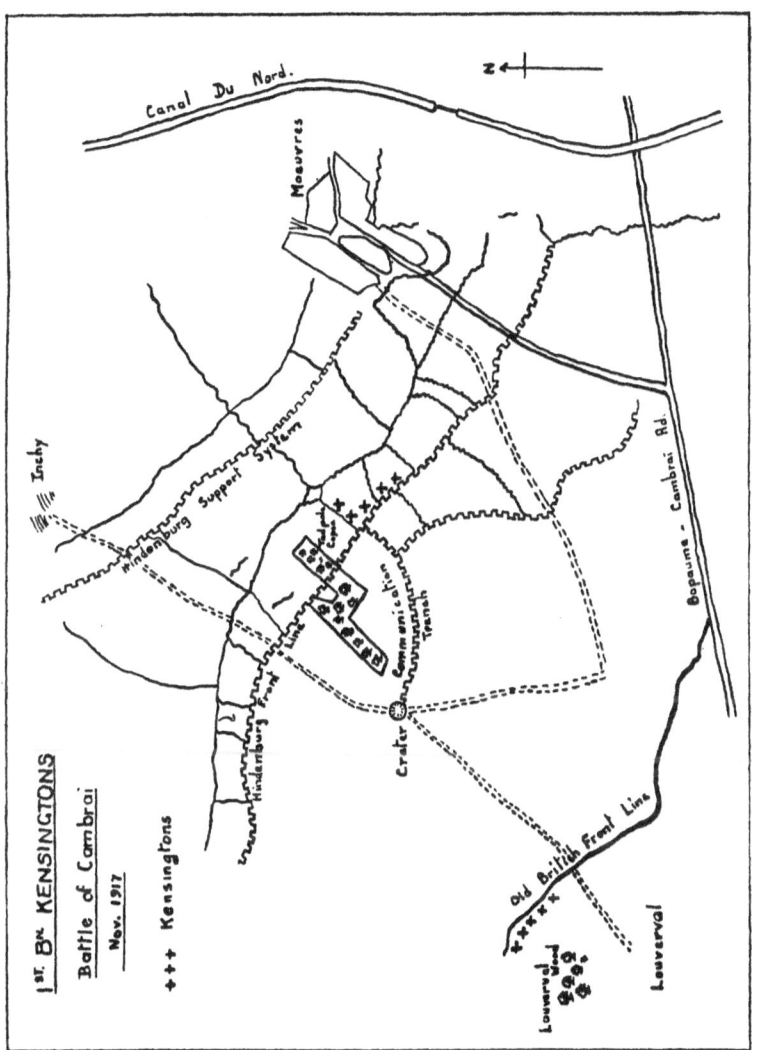

the Fusiliers and Scottish in the Hindenburg Line, and at noon D Company (Captain N. J. Inns) was moved to the old enemy outpost line in support to the Scottish. At 5 p.m. C Company took over a section of the second line in the Hindenburg system from the Fusiliers, and that night the rest of the Battalion moved across No-man's-land to relieve the Fusiliers. The Scottish had been relieved by the Rangers and B and A Companies of the Kensingtons were in touch with the latter battalion on the left and the Queen Victoria's Rifles on the right. As far as the crater, along the Louverval–Inchy Road, the relief had encountered only stray machine-gun fire from the left, where enemy guns were active as usual from Magpie's Nest, but on leaving the crater and entering a shallow communication trench leading to the Hindenburg Line, they had to run the gauntlet of heavy shells very accurately placed on the trench.

The Hindenburg system when at length reached proved to be a labyrinth of trenches well provided with deep dugouts. The trenches had to be hastily provided with firesteps on the side facing the enemy, but the dugouts, well fitted out with wire beds and furnished with the spoils of the adjacent villages, proved too dangerous to occupy in the forward zone. Short communication trenches led direct from the captured trenches to those still held by the Germans, who were in places but fifty yards away behind bombing-blocks. Their voices could be plainly heard. This unusual proximity added to the sense of tension, though it carried with it the advantage that the enemy batteries could not shell our men without danger to their own.

The night was cold and some snow fell. As the men were in battle order without great-coats, some difficulty was experienced in keeping warm. The situation, however, was very quiet and remained so during the following morning, but at 3 p.m. on the 27th the enemy concentrated a heavy barrage of 77-mm. and 4·2-in. shells on the front line of the Hindenburg system, which was occupied by Battalion Headquarters. There was also heavy shelling of the Hindenburg outpost line. At 3.20 p.m. the enemy attacked a block held by B Company (2nd Lieut. A. E.

Crouch) and attempted to rush the garrison. They were met by a vigorous defence and after several attempts were finally beaten off, although three of the bombing sections of B Company had been knocked out by shells from our own batteries. No attack developed on the blocks held by C Company, and by 4.30 p.m. all was quiet again. Some difficulty was experienced during the worst of the barrage in getting a signal through to the artillery asking them to lengthen range. The cables had been broken during the first few salvoes and the messages despatched by carrier pigeons brought no response. A wireless squad, however, which was attached to Battalion Headquarters, erected a short aerial on the parapet during the height of the bombardment and got the required message through. Further attacks on various bombing-blocks were made by the enemy during the following two days, but our men were on the alert, and they were all held.

The difficulty of getting up supplies across the old No-man's-land led to shortage of food and water. The latter was particularly precious, and washing was out of the question. The more fastidious were compelled to contrive a shave in the dregs of tea in the mess tin.

The general situation remained one of uncertainty. On the front as a whole the British offensive appeared to be virtually over. There were signs, however, to the discerning, that the enemy was contemplating a counter-attack. Low-flying aeroplanes came over with increasing regularity, and enemy patrols were very active. Yet although there seems to have been a general awareness along the front that the Germans might take advantage of the stagnation that had fallen on the situation, little appears to have been done by the Staff, and forward positions, well marked by enemy batteries, continued to be manned, though men were ordered to keep out of the dugouts and occupy the trench. In view of the tension of the situation it was with some surprise that the Kensingtons received sudden orders on the 29th that they would be relieved that night by the 8th Middlesex. An attack in conjunction with the London Scottish, now on the left, which had been planned was cancelled, and the Battalion, on relief, proceeded to the Louverval Wood positions. There was an unusual quiet during the relief and a suspicious lack of enemy artillery activity. It was the prelude to the suspected counter-attack, for at 3.6 a.m. gas shells began falling round the Louverval Wood area, part of a preliminary gas bombardment of artillery positions all along the front. The Kensingtons "stood to" in gas masks, and at 7.30 a.m. the enemy launched his great assault on the newly won salient. His intention, it afterwards appeared, was to penetrate the two flanks of the salient and, turning inwards, capture the troops within it. The attack was first directed on the British right, and, using similar tactics to those so recently applied to him, the enemy, after a very brief preliminary bombardment and using troops unobtrusively concentrated overnight on the front, swept forward in the early-morning mist and overwhelmed the British Divisions. By 9 a.m. he had broken through on a six-mile front and penetrated to Gouzeaucourt, three miles behind the line, capturing men and materials. Realising, no doubt, that the necessity for stemming this calamitous advance would occupy the full attention of the Staff, the enemy played his next card and at 9.45 a.m. concentrated a heavy barrage on the left of the salient at the junction of the Hindenburg Line and the old British front line, the front held by the 56th Division.

The 168th and 169th Brigades were in line, the Scottish on the extreme left holding the Hindenburg Line at Tadpole Copse. Next came the 8th Middlesex, attached temporarily to the 168th Brigade, in the positions occupied overnight. On their right were the 2nd Londons and the Queen's Westminsters. The 4th Londons held the defensive flank, and the Kensingtons were in support. At 10.15 a.m. the enemy advanced to the attack, wave after wave, with great determination. In that maze of trenches Germans appeared to attack from all directions, but the defenders were undaunted, and with rifle, Lewis gun, and rifle grenade broke up attacks from over the top, while the bombers dealt with such parties as came through the trenches. The situation at one stage looked grave when a party of the enemy overran the trench where the Middlesex Headquarters was situated. The dugout was bombed, but the Scottish counter-attacked and the Middlesex soon cleared the whole trench. D Company of the Kensingtons was at 11.20 moved across in the open to the Hindenburg outpost line in support to the Scottish, and in the afternoon a platoon of this company took over a block from the Middlesex. In moving across the old No-man's-land the third platoon of D Company was fired on by a low-flying German aeroplane and in addition was heavily shelled, 14 men becoming casualties. A Company was also sent forward to occupy the crater. No further calls were made on the Battalion, however, for the enemy attacks were held. The element of surprise was now absent, and any enemy movement was at once greeted with a vigorous rifle and machine-gun fire. The danger had passed by the late afternoon, and that night the Division was relieved.

It had been a triumph for the infantry of the Division, for the artillery had been able to give little support, so close were the combatants, and by their determined resistance they had saved the day from becoming one of disaster. The following extract from an official account of the battle shows that the heroism of the 56th Division was appreciated:

> The 56th Division had been in line prior to the British attack of November 20th and since that date had captured and held about a mile of the Hindenburg Line west of Mœuvres, including Tadpole Copse. Almost constant fighting had taken place in this area since our attack, and the Division, which at one time had been holding a front of 11,000 yards, had already been subjected to a severe strain. November 30th, 1917, will be a proud day in the lives of all those splendid British soldiers who, by their single-hearted devotion to duty, prevented what would have become a serious situation had they given way.

On December 1st the Kensingtons handed over their positions in the old British front line to the 5th Gordon Highlanders and moved into support in the open near

Lagnicourt. During the day the S.O.S. went up from the front line and B Company was sent forward. The situation had cleared by the time they arrived, and they rejoined the Battalion. At 8 p.m. the 7th Black Watch took over the support positions and the Kensingtons marched to the transport lines near Fremicourt. They had lost 18 men killed and 2 officers and 60 other ranks wounded. It had been a gruelling twelve days, and the men were exhausted. There had been little opportunity for sleep and the nights had been frosty. The provision of hot tea and soup, by the Quartermaster (Capt. A. Ridley), was very welcome.

There was little time for rest, however. The transport was already packed up for a move, and at 9 a.m. on the following day the Battalion entrained at Fremicourt siding for Beaumetz, near Arras, and marched to Simencourt, where the men were billeted in huts. After but two nights they were again on the move, this time by route march through Dainville and Arras to Ecurie, near the Vimy Ridge. Again two nights were spent in huts, and at 7 a.m. the Kensingtons marched for the first time up the slopes of the famous ridge to the Daylight railhead and into the long communication trench, Ouse Alley, leading down to the plain below and the trenches in front of Oppy.

CHAPTER XIV

THE OPPY FRONT; AND THE GERMAN OFFENSIVE, 1918

THE Vimy Ridge was well-known by name to the Kensingtons, for the Canadians in the spring of the year had achieved a wonderful victory over the enemy in this well-fortified position and had driven him to the plain below. From Arras towards Lens the land is undulating and rises gradually to a ridge running in a north-westerly direction. It then falls more or less abruptly to the level mining country stretching away to Lens. On the Arras–Lens Road the descent is steep through the little village of Petit Vimy, but at the Arras end of the ridge the slope is more gradual to a cluster of villages, Oppy, Arleux, Gavrelle, Bailleul, and Willerval. It was at this end of the ridge that the 56th Division took over the trench system, the front line of which ran approximately north and south close to the villages of Oppy, Arleux, and Gavrelle, the former being in the German lines and the two latter in the British lines. The Daylight railhead was the last point screened from observation on the Roclincourt–Bailleul Road whence access to the trench system was obtained by long communication trenches, some three miles in length, zigzagging down the slope to the flat ground below. Of these trenches Ouse Alley and Tommy Alley became best known to the Kensingtons as approaches to the Oppy sector. At night overland routes were used, and there was also a light-railway system for the transport of stores and ammunition. The front line consisted of a series of posts that had been hastily constructed when the fighting in the spring settled down to the normal trench warfare. Behind this system of trenches and posts a strong main line of defence had been constructed, the Bailleul–Willerval line, more popularly known as the Red Line. Other lines of defence lay behind this.

"THE KENSINGTONS"

On taking over the Oppy sector, the Kensingtons occupied Bradford Post (A Company), Beatty and Bird Posts (C Company), B Company took over Earl Trench, while D Company remained at the Daylight Railhead in reserve. The sector proved a quiet one, but the forward posts were a good distance apart, and this engendered a feeling of insecurity. Wood Post particularly, running as it did into Oppy Wood, with its shell-stunted trees, was an eerie spot, and the garrison, constantly on the alert throughout the long winter nights, could never be sure that enemy patrols were not moving about amongst the trees. The outgoing battalion on handing over had told tales of men who had mysteriously disappeared. Oppy and Bradford Posts were a little better in this respect, but Bird Post had its own peculiarities. It consisted of a long stretch of shallow trench held by small groups of men with long intervals between. It was really not a post at all, but a series of small strong points each with its own Lewis-gun section, and appeared to be very vulnerable to hostile attack. All these posts were ordered to be held to the last in the event of an enemy assault.

Much work was necessary to maintain the trenches in a state of repair. Frost came early in December and heralded what proved to be the severest winter of the war. The struggle to keep warm became as vigorous as the efforts to prevent the crumbling trenches from falling in.

On December 13th the Battalion moved into support in the Red Line and occupied old German dugouts in the side of a railway embankment. The railway line ran almost parallel to the main defence system and was littered with overturned trucks and débris as though the gunners of both sides had enjoyed a little target practice. The Germans had been to some pains to construct really comfortable dugouts, approached by a series of steps up the steep slope. The walls of many of them were wood-lined and canvas-covered, and had evidently served as observation posts, for stairs led up through the chalk to the top.

Conjecture was now busy as to the prospect of spending Christmas out of the line, and on the 16th news of a Divisional relief was hailed with joy. Within half an hour there came a cancellation, and on the 18th another spell in the frost-bound trenches commenced. However, relief came on the 22nd, and in the camp at Roclincourt, where the Battalion eventually spent the Christmas season in Divisional reserve, preparations were soon afoot for keeping the feast in the approved manner. The camp consisted of Nissen huts, originally wood-lined and furnished with stoves, into which no doubt the matchboarding had recently gone, for the cold was intense and fuel lamentably short. Snow fell on Christmas Eve and a frantic search amongst the débris of the country-side was made for firewood, but without much result. However, the low temperature could not quell the high spirits which graced the feasts that took place in the various Company messes. By some miracle the Quartermaster had provided roast beef, turkey, and the inevitable pudding. There was no lack of drinks. During the early evening the Commanding Officer, Lieut.-Colonel R. E. F. Shaw, went the rounds with Christmas greeting and was accorded an unusually hearty reception, a tribute to his popularity in the Battalion. A further fall of snow occurred during the evening so that when the drums, after serenading the camp, marched, still playing, into the huts, white with snow, their resemblance to the old-time waits was complete, and furnished a picture that will never be forgotten by those who saw them.

Arras was not far from the camp and provided opportunity for the purchase of the extras so dear to the heart of the troops. A Divisional cinema and the Bow Bells concert party offered good entertainment at very small cost. The latter produced a pantomime enriched with songs from the musical shows running at the time in London, and these gave inspiration for the nightly sing-songs in the crowded huts.

The Battalion was due to go into the line as " wiring " battalion on the 28th, but the bright moonlight, coupled with the frozen state of the ground, caused a cancellation of the order, and instead a move to Wakefield Camp, even

"THE KENSINGTONS"

bleaker and colder than the Roclincourt Camp, took place. The Nissen huts were decrepit, and the snow, driven by the bitter wind, drifted on to the sleeping men.

On January 6th, following a brief three-day tour in the line, the Battalion moved to Marœil, and on the following day entrained for Tinques on the Arras–St. Pol Road and marched to Magnicourt en Comte, a village to the north of the road and new to the Kensingtons. The whole Division had entered on a welcome period of rest, and many men enjoyed a brief spell of leave to England. The cold weather continued and the poor barns and stables of the village failed to keep out the snow. Nevertheless, the time was profitably spent in re-equipping and in company training.

During the Christmas season the following letter came to remind all ranks of the pride and affection with which they were regarded by H.R.H. Princess Louise.

Kensington Palace,
12/12/17.

Dear Colonel Shaw,

I am anxious to send my congratulations to all the 1/13th Kensingtons, and beg of you to convey the same from me to all officers, N.C.O.s and men on the splendid part you have taken in this difficult and arduous campaign. Please assure them that my thoughts and wishes are always with them, and the knowledge of the valiant way in which they are carrying on their work is a source of deep interest and pride to me and gives me the feeling that the power and courage they show is due to their faith in the Unseen Being ever with them.

Yours sincerely,
(Signed) Louise.

The following reply was sent to Her Royal Highness.

B.E.F.

To H.R.H. Princess Louise

From Lieut.-Colonel R. E. F. Shaw, commanding the 1/13th Kensington Battalion, the London Regiment.

On behalf of the officers, N.C.O.s and men of your Kensington Battalion, I thank you sincerely for your kind letter of encouragement and praise.

THE OPPY FRONT; AND THE GERMAN OFFENSIVE, 1918

The few who came out with the Battalion and are still serving remember your first message of God Speed read to us in 1914. That message has always been passed on to the new members of the Battalion, who realise as fully as those who marched out from Abbots Langley in November 1914 how zealously you have looked to our interests and how prompt has been your praise for what little we have been able to do.

I can assure you that every man in your Battalion is still filled with the determination to fight on until that peace is secured for which we came out to fight, and to maintain the proud traditions which the Battalion has built up for itself during its three years on Active Service.

I remain,
Your very obedient and respectful servant
(Signed) R. E. F. SHAW, Lieut.-Colonel.

19/12/17.

The spell of Divisional relief terminated on February 1st when the Kensingtons entrained at Tinques railhead for Ecurie and marched to Stewart Camp. On the 10th they moved once more to Roclincourt Camp. While here Brig.-General Loch, commanding the 168th Brigade, presented the ribbon of the 1914 star to officers and men who served in France before the end of November 1914. The veterans of the war were already distinguished by the chevrons worn on the lower end of the left sleeve, a red chevron indicating service overseas in 1914 and a blue chevron each year of service subsequent to that date. Gold vertical stripes were also worn to indicate war wounds. No little pride was felt by those entitled to wear these decorations, and the story which was current at the time, of the old lady who asked a man on leave to explain the meaning of the chevrons, is worth repeating. He was wearing one red and three blue chevrons, and, being a wag, he explained that the red stood for a wife and the blue ones for the children. " Oh! " ejaculated the dear old soul in horror. " I saw a man the other day wearing three blue stripes only."

On February 14th trench warfare recommenced for the

"THE KENSINGTONS"

Kensingtons with the usual periods in support in the Red Line, in the front-line posts, or in reserve at Roclincourt.

It is necessary now to glance at the general situation on the Western Front. The British Army was beginning to feel a shortage of man power, and many units were below strength. In consequence the drastic decision was made to reorganise brigades on a three-battalion basis and disband the fourth battalion. Divisional infantry would thus consist of a pioneer battalion and nine fighting battalions instead of the twelve to which all had grown accustomed. As the result of this order the Rangers, the Queen Victoria Rifles, and the 1/3rd Londons were lost as separate units, their transports and Headquarter personnel going to their second battalions and their fighting strength serving as reinforcements for other units. The Kensingtons thus received 3 officers and 150 other ranks from the Queen Victoria Rifles, a splendid draft of experienced men. It was one of the most regrettable incidents of the war that these splendid fighting battalions, each with a fine record, should thus lose their identity.

Germany also had her anxieties. Austria was exhausted, and Turkey could no longer be counted as a factor in the situation, for Jerusalem had fallen to the Allies. But, on the other hand, she was now definitely relieved of the burden of war with Russia, for, following the collapse of the Tsarist régime and the virtual cessation of any active participation in the war on the part of Russia, the Bolshevists, once in power, sued for peace as their first measure. But although Germany was thus able to transfer some thirty Divisions to the Western Front, it was realised only too well that American intervention would in time far outweigh any advantage the Russian débâcle had given her. But the American armies were not yet in the field in any number, and in the interval a lucky offensive might turn the scales in favour of Germany. The time factor was now of supreme importance.

Fully alive to this aspect of the situation, the British Staff had an anxious time during the early months of 1918 reviewing the arrangements for the defence of the front against the expected enemy onslaught. The first indication to the Kensingtons of unusual enemy activity was the amount of gas shelling that took place. The Red Line was frequently bombarded, and the heavy gas got into dugouts and caused numerous casualties. When shelling occurred, as it often did, during a frosty night, the danger would be deemed to have passed, only to recur on the following morning when the sun caused the evaporation of the gaseous fluids. Other units in the Brigade suffered more seriously from gas than did the Kensingtons. The casualties were none of them serious, but they caused a loss of men at a time when they could ill be spared.

Raids took place on both sides. A Kensington N.C.O. was suddenly attacked in Oppy Post by two of the enemy, but managed to fire his rifle, and the attackers fled. On March 9th the Battalion, then in the front line, had the opportunity of showing once more its skill in raiding. The raid was undertaken by 2nd Lieut. A. E. Lester and 2nd Lieut. W. E. Smith, with 42 other ranks, with the object of securing identification, an important matter at this critical time. The party had been sent out of the line to Roclincourt some days previously, where facsimile trenches were marked out to as near a copy as possible of the enemy trenches to be raided. The approaches from our line were exactly copied and the whole scheme fully explained with the help of maps and aeroplane photographs. In three days every man knew his job and was confident and keen to carry it out. In the meantime the artillery gradually cut the wire, and Lewis guns were posted in No-man's-land to prevent any attempts to repair it. This part of the work was so well done that the enemy front was devoid of wire at the points of entry.

The essence of the scheme was to attack at a time when the enemy would be taken unawares, and as at night he showed great nervousness and kept the spot well lit up, daylight was chosen as the time for the raid. At

6.45 a.m., under cover of an artillery diversion about a quarter of a mile away, the raiders quickly but silently crossed over to the enemy's front line and were clearing the trench before a shot was fired. An alert machine gun in the German support lines opened fire, but was quickly silenced by a burst of fire from the raiders' Lewis gun, but not before it had caused the only casualties of the raid. By this time the second party had worked round to the rear of the enemy front line, leaving the front line to be cleared by the converging groups of the first party. The clearing process was rapidly accomplished, and four Germans were soon seen hurrying back to our lines. This was the cue for the cessation of the raid and the recall signal was sounded by the buglers. In a few seconds the party regained our lines, the whole affair occupying only seven and a half minutes from start to finish, including the bringing back of the wounded men. One man had been killed on the far side of the enemy trench and Sergeant Calf tried in vain to bring him in, but was prevented by the weight of the man and the bad ground from doing so. It was estimated that about 25 of the enemy had been accounted for.

The anxiety of the Staff now began to affect the men in the front line. A great paper offensive started. Orders were given to cover this and that contingency, only to be modified or cancelled later. The posts which had originally been intended as outposts only and not as strong points, from which a stout defence could be put up, were now ordered to be held to the last, a costly proceeding, as experience showed. "Stand to" became a matter of real annoyance. The men were accustomed to the hour's stand-to at dawn and dusk when in the front line, but to find they were expected to do this from 4.30 a.m. to 9 a.m. when in reserve at Roclincourt was felt to be giving the enemy more credit than he was entitled to. Hourly-situation reports were expected from company commanders when in the front line, and they were deluged with correspondence filtering down to them from the higher command. In fact, of the two evils, an enemy attack from the front, and a paper bombardment from the rear, the fighting men felt they preferred the former.

As evidence that the Kensingtons preserved their sense of humour during the general nervousness that prevailed during these anxious days, the following situation report is quoted. It was sent in morse in the usual manner to Battalion Headquarters by Capt. F. W. Heath, M.C., commanding C Company, where it caused much amusement. Needless to say, it was not forwarded officially to Brigade.

C COMPANY SITUATION REPORT, 19/3/18

There is nothing I can tell you
  That you really do not know,
Except that we are on the Ridge
  And Fritz is down below.

I'm tired of " situations "
  And of wind entirely " vane,"
The gas guard yawns and tells me
  " It's blowing up for rain."

He's a human little fellow
  With a thoughtful point of view,
And his report, uncensored,
  I pass, please, on to you.

" When's old Fritz coming over ?
  Does the General really know ?
The Colonel seems to think so,
  The Captain tells us ' No.' "

" When's someone going to tell us
  We can ' stand to ' as before ?
An hour at dawn and one at dusk,
  Gawd Blimey, who wants more ? "

On the 21st the Kensingtons took over the front line again after five days in the Red Line, during which an officer and 44 men had been gassed by a bombardment of Bailleul East Post. The Battalion was now responsible for the defence of Bird and Bradford Posts, with the 4th Londons in Oppy, Wood, and Beatty Posts on the left. Yet farther to the left were the Canadians in Tommy and Arleux Posts. This day saw the opening of the great German offensive. The long-awaited blow had fallen, and even the sparse reports which filtered through to the Battalion holding the exposed posts were disquieting in the extreme. Attacking on a front of forty miles between Croisilles and La Fère with sixty-eight Divisions, the enemy by sheer weight of numbers had overrun the front-line system. Within a week the whole of the Somme battlefield was behind the enemy line and Amiens was threatened. The Fifth Army had borne the brunt of the attack and had been overwhelmed. The most heroic efforts were made to maintain a line. Pioneer battalions, transport men, and even labour battalions were called on to man the improvised defences. Battalions perished to a man and in so doing stemmed for an hour or so the oncoming flood. The 2nd Middlesex was one such unit, for the 8th Division since Christmas had been held as G.H.Q. reserve troops, ready at an hour's notice to rush to the first point of attack. They detrained in the midst of a battle and did yeoman service in delaying and finally stemming the advance.

The British positions about Arras now threatened the flank of the German salient, and the imminence of an attack on the defences around the city became evident. Sudden orders for moves and changes of disposition came, only to be cancelled. All attempts to secure identification were met with failure, for the enemy was too much on the alert. As a contrast to all the excitement and confusion which prevailed behind the line, the men in front remained calm. Their orders were so simple. They were to hold on to the end; there was to be no retreat. The word "retire" was not to be used, for rumour had it that Germans disguised as British officers had ordered troops to retire, a rumour probably without foundation. The defences were strengthened, wire put out, and trench mortars placed in the best positions for defence.

Meanwhile the receipt of the news in England caused a reversion of the policy which had hitherto insisted on the maintenance of a big defence force at home, and large numbers of troops were rushed overseas to the support of the hard-pressed Expeditionary Force. Their presence a week earlier might have avoided the sacrifice of the gallant troops holding the front and prevented this first German attack from coming, as it did, within measurable distance of inflicting a crippling blow upon the Allies.

The attack on Arras was anticipated on the 26th, and final instructions were issued. Before dawn the Kensingtons stood to in readiness for the expected onslaught, but the day dawned in comparative silence and nothing untoward materialised. The same thing was repeated on the following day. It looked as though the Staff had inside information of the abandonment of the attack when, late on the evening of the 27th, sudden orders came to the Battalion to side-step to the left round the 4th Londons and take over the front occupied by the 2nd Battalion Canadian Mounted Rifles. The London Rifle Brigade were to relieve the Kensingtons in Bird and Bradford posts. The move was caused by the receipt of orders for the 56th Division to extend its front to the Souchez River on the left. For the Battalion it involved a return along Ouse Alley to the Red Line, and then, a short distance along this main line of defence, striking off to the front again along Tommy and Tired alleys and taking over Tommy and Arleux posts.

The relief was far from complete and the Kensingtons were strung out along these communication trenches when, at 3 a.m., a furious gas and high-explosive shelling opened on the whole system. Box respirators were hastily donned and, thus impeded, the men blundered along in the darkness to take over the forward positions from the Canadians.

As the hour of dawn approached, the barrage increased in intensity, and in the growing light it was seen that the whole front was deluged with shells of all calibres. It seemed impossible that men could live through such a

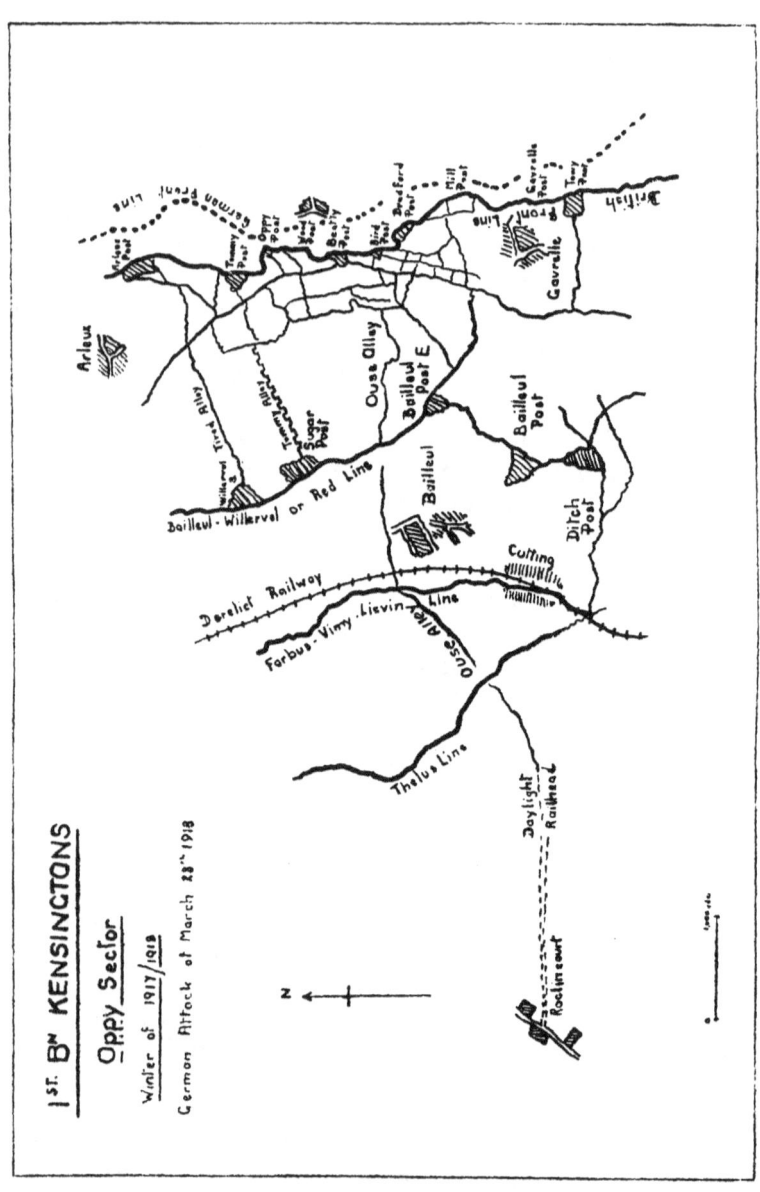

torrent of bursting steel. Our own artillery added to the deafening volume of sound as, at 7 a.m., the S.O.S. went up from Towy Post, held by the Queen's Westminsters, on the right of the Divisional front, and our guns concentrated an intense fire on the enemy front and support lines and artillery positions. The German infantry attack rapidly developed from Towy along the line of posts to Oppy Post. The Kensingtons awaited the spread of the onslaught to Tommy and Arleux posts, manned by A and B Companies, every weapon in readiness for the first sign of the grey masses of the enemy. But apart from an attack by a party against Tommy Post, an attack which melted away before the furious fire directed on it by the alert garrison, no general assault developed. It soon became apparent that the posts held by the Battalion were just outside the front of attack, and as the need for repelling frontal assault became less urgent, they were able to assist the hard-pressed troops on the right by Lewis-gun, rifle and rifle-grenade fire on the German supports as they emerged from the cover of Oppy Wood. By 9 a.m. reports came to hand that the enemy had reached Clarence and Beale trenches, and A Company posted bombers on the Battalion's right flank to deal with any enemy penetration in their direction.

On the rest of the front the situation was "obscure." Obviously heavy fighting was taking place, but it was impossible to determine the extent of the German advance. It must be realised that most of the fighting took place in trenches, and a battalion fighting for its life finds it difficult to report frequently on the situation. The only means of communication was by runner, and runners got lost, wounded, or captured. However, contact was established, and it was soon learnt that the story was one of heroic resistance against heavy odds, desperate hand-to-hand fighting, and a fierce defence of every inch of trench. In the early stages the intensity of the barrage had all but obliterated the forward posts, and their garrisons, reduced to a handful of wounded men, were overrun, and the enemy was soon in the front lines and communication trenches. Bradford and Bird posts, with their garrisons barely in position, were practically destroyed by the bombardment, and the London Rifle Brigade, sadly depleted in numbers, was slowly forced back. Beatty, Wood, and Oppy posts suffered in varying degrees. In the case of Wood Post the garrison had fortunately been moved and thus escaped the barrage which smashed up the old post. They were thus able to put up a stout defence, which was badly needed, for the other two posts had been battered out of recognition by shell fire, and the half-dozen or so survivors had to fight their way out. Elsewhere much the same thing happened—the enemy got into the trench system, but was held by the vigorous efforts of the infantry, who exacted a heavy toll from the attackers.

At 12.15 orders were received for a withdrawal to the Red Line. Covered by the right company, the Kensingtons moved back along Tommy and Tired alleys and took up positions in this main line of defence, where they soon got in touch with the London Scottish in Ouse Siding. The withdrawal was accomplished without enemy interference, but a renewal of the attack was felt to be certain. The withdrawal had served to clear the situation; the Division was in touch with the 4th Division on the right, and the prospects of putting up a stubborn defence on the Red Line were felt to be good. However, no further enemy activity was manifested during the afternoon and evening apart from a few feeble attacks which were easily subdued. The night was an anxious one, for the morrow was fraught with possibilities. It seemed incredible that the enemy should give up, without further effort, his aims on the Arras positions. Early morning, however, brought no signs of renewed action, and the Kensingtons pushed out patrols to investigate the situation more fully. They returned with the surprising news that they had penetrated as far as the old Company Headquarters in Baron Trench and had encountered no one. It soon became apparent that the enemy had indeed given up the idea of further offensive

THE OPPY FRONT; AND THE GERMAN OFFENSIVE, 1918

action on this front, at least in the immediate future, and that Arras was once more saved from enemy occupation.

The 56th Division could again claim to have broken a German offensive. It was afterwards found that five German Divisions had attacked the front held by the 56th and 4th Divisions, and it had been the intention to carry the Red Line on the first day and Vimy Ridge on the following day. The attempt had failed in its early stages and was perforce abandoned. By a curious coincidence the battle had resembled the Cambrai counter-attack in several details. The 56th Division had in both cases been on the extreme left of the front attack, which had followed close upon changes in disposition. The folly of holding advanced posts which were well known to the enemy was again demonstrated, and General Loch, commenting on the day's fighting, drew attention forcibly to this danger and to the risk attaching to changes of disposition at the eleventh hour. So sudden had been the orders to move that the rations, dumped in the open in the rear of the front line, were temporarily forgotten, though harvested later by D Company.

During the night of the 29th the Kensingtons were relieved by the Canadians and marched up the Ridge for the last time to a camp at Ecoivres, near Mont St. Eloi, where they revelled in the luxury of comfortable huts but recently vacated by a Corps Headquarters. The rapidity of the move by the latter was evidenced by the amount of gear that had been left behind, including, as it did, a large hut completely fitted up for badminton, rackets, etc. On April 6th the battalion marched to Duisans for the night, and on the 7th moved forward in battle order to a position in support to the 167th Brigade, which was holding the Telegraph Hill sector. They were now once more in the zone between Achicourt and Beaurains, where a year ago preparations had been made for the battle of Neuville Vitasse. The changing fortunes of war had once more delivered the village into enemy hands, and it almost seemed as though the efforts and sacrifices of Easter 1917 had gone for nothing. The ground was in a terrible state. The trench system had been used, abandoned, and was now to be used once more, although the trenches were crumbling and ankle deep in mud. Shell-holes and rusty wire half concealed by a year's growth of weeds made movement in any direction a precarious undertaking.

The 56th Division had taken over the Tilloy-Beaurains sector, and much labour was called for to put the ruined trenches once more into a state fitted for defence, for it was realised that a further enemy attack was imminent, though none could tell where this blow might be delivered. When it did fall, it was on the front between La Bassée and Armentières, and, on April 9th, the Portuguese Division holding the front near Armentières was driven back, and the attack spreading north and south, another great salient was made in the line before the enemy was finally held. Passchendaele Ridge to the east of Ypres, won at such cost in the summer of 1917, had to be abandoned.

Until the middle of July the Kensingtons remained in the Tilloy–Beaurains area and there followed tours in the trenches, interspersed with periods of rest in Arras. The line held by the 56th Division was now roughly astride the Arras–Cambrai Road, running through the Bois des Bœufs to the east of Tilloy and on to Neuville Vitasse, and during the early summer months the Kensingtons occupied various positions within the Divisional sector. The periods in the line were very active, for an aggressive policy was pursued and raids became the order of the day. The enemy was to be given no rest. The first of these took place on April 19th, when the London Scottish and 4th Londons carried out an attack on the enemy line and succeeded in securing a number of prisoners.

When in support or reserve, the Battalion occupied the St. Sauveur Caves or other part of the vast labyrinth of underground workings under the city, for the whole area was shelled regularly. These workings, in parts, were of considerable antiquity, but during the war they had been developed and extended and provided not only billeting areas for troops in reserve, but a safe means of communicating between different parts of the city and the suburbs. The Engineers had fitted up wire beds and rough furniture, and a light-railway system was installed. Here and there the tunnels widened out into lofty caverns large enough to accommodate a company, and in an emergency more than a Division could have found cover, either in the St. Sauveur or the Ronville caves. The system had been divided into areas named after the great English cities—London, Manchester, Leeds, etc.—and were interconnected by the light-railway system. The main thoroughfares were lit by electricity generated underground, and canteens and messes were established at various points to serve those troops permanently employed in maintenance. Signposts at the crossings indicated the direction to " Manchester," " Leeds," or " London." Exploring off the beaten track by candle light, one could wander for considerable distances and, climbing a flight of steps, emerge into daylight in a cellar in an unsuspected quarter of the city. In the St. Sauveur suburb, which became very familiar to the Kensingtons during the summer, the caves passed under the ruined church, and Headquarters was established in the cellars. Heads of saints gazed upwards from the tumbled heaps of stones, a gaudily painted Sainte Vierge stood propped up in a corner. Outside on the level ground the frame of a grand piano served as a bridge across a trench. The havoc wrought by war was never more clearly demonstrated than in this ruination of the handiwork of past generations. In the city itself the ruins increased daily as the ever-falling shells found their marks. But though the buildings suffered, the gardens flourished in rank profusion. Unpruned fruit trees showed promise of a good crop, and in the market gardens near St. Sauveur it was worth the risk of occasional shrapnel to hunt for strawberries growing amongst the weeds, to serve as a welcome addition to army rations. Other periods of reserve were spent at Dainville, which was much as it had been in 1916 when the Kensingtons first visited it. Civilian friends were still there to welcome the men, and some merry evenings were spent in the local estaminets.

Early in May the Kensingtons took over the line for the usual period of trench duty. The positions held were astride the Arras–Cambrai Road just in front of the village of Tilloy. In pursuance of the policy of maintaining aggressive action, outposts were manned in No-man's-land during the night, the garrisons taking cover during the hours of daylight in order to maintain secrecy. One such post was established in disused gun pits in front of the Bois des Bœufs, and during the tour in question was manned by a platoon of D Company, under the command of Lieut. A. E. Lester, an officer who had shown great dash in recent operations. Just before dawn on May 9th Lieut. Lester and the platoon sergeant (Sergeant L. Drew) were withdrawing the posts, and had reached the Lewis-gun post in a pit near the wood and commanding the road, when they encountered a patrol of D Company under 2nd Lieut. Symons. At that moment a grey-clad figure was seen running along the road towards our lines. On being challenged, he replied with an obvious Scotch accent, and proved to be a corporal of a Scottish battalion who had been but recently taken prisoner by the enemy at Monchy. He had been working during the night with other prisoners carrying ammunition to batteries at Vis en Artois. Seizing an opportune diversion created by a British air-bombing attack on the dump, he, with a companion, had eluded the vigilance of their guards and, taking a German great-coat and cap apiece, had made for our lines, following the main road. They had almost reached safety when they ran into a German post, and in the firing his companion had been wounded. Lieut. Lester ordered the sergeant to remain with the men and with 2nd Lieut. Symons set off towards the enemy lines in a heroic endeavour to locate and rescue the wounded man. It was now getting light, and they were fired on by an unsuspected enemy post or patrol, Lieut. Lester being mortally wounded and the other officer barely escaping with his life. On learning of this, Sergeant Drew at once set off in the increasing light and, taking cover in the deep ditch flanking the road, managed to reach the point where the firing had taken place. Lieut. Lester's steel helmet was lying in the road, but of the officer nothing was to be seen. The sergeant succeeded in recovering the equipment, but in so doing was seen by the enemy, now thoroughly aroused, and was fired on by rifles and a machine gun. By a miracle he escaped, though a trench mortar was directed on the ditch as he wormed his way back among the bodies of Germans lying there just as they fell in the advance of March. Patrols on succeeding nights made every effort to locate the officer's body, but without success, and there can be no doubt that his wounds were fatal and that he was buried by the enemy. The Scotch corporal was able to give very valuable information as to the position of enemy batteries, and was afterwards awarded the D.C.M.

On June 1st, the Kensingtons carried out the last and most successful of their raids. During the first six days in the sector there was great patrol activity and an enemy machine-gun post was located and destroyed and 2 prisoners captured by a patrol under the leadership of 2nd Lieut. A. D. James (D Company), Lieut. James and Sergeant F. Brownjohn (who was wounded) being awarded the M.C. and M.M. respectively. Plans were now made for a more ambitious operation on what was known as the Stone Dump area, for A and D Companies had established the fact that there were forward enemy posts in the area north of the Cambrai Road near a number of heaps of stones. On the evening of May 26th it was decided that C Company (Captain F. W. Heath) should attempt a raid on this area, provided a jumping-off place could be found. On the following day Captain Heath was unfortunately seriously wounded by a shell fragment, and 2nd Lieut. W. E. Smith succeeded him. On the night of the 27th, accompanied by one N.C.O. from each platoon, this officer explored the gun pits and dugouts in the forward area and decided that the necessary accommodation was there. No. 9 platoon was to take up a position due north of the dump, Nos. 10, 11, and No. 1 Platoon (lent by A Company for covering purposes) in gun pits and trenches due west of the dump. All platoons would thus be brought within 500 yards of the objective. No. 9 Platoon was ordered to clear the Stone Dump and some shelters west and east of it, and then cover the withdrawal of Nos. 10 and 11. The former of these two platoons had the task of crossing the Cambrai Road at the south end of the dump and destroying enemy trench mortars and trenches on that side, while No. 11 was to proceed along the road and attend to the many shelters in the area west of the dump. On the succeeding nights each platoon sent out strong patrols and reconnoitred its area thoroughly.

Meanwhile Lieut.-Colonel Shaw made all necessary arrangements with the artillery and machine-gun company, while Major Prismall worked indefatigably with the platoon officers and N.C.O.s, ensuring that all duties were thoroughly understood. The very thorough nature of the artillery and machine-gun support reflects great credit on the excellent liaison between these two arms of the service. 18-pounders, 4·5 howitzers, and 6-inch howitzers, as well as the machine guns, fired on carefully arranged lines to give the maximum support to the operation.

On the night of May 31st the whole party took up its position in No-man's-land without mishap, Major Prismall establishing a forward headquarters in telephonic communication with Battalion Headquarters. Throughout that night and the following day, the raiders remained in position unperceived and unmolested, and at 9 p.m. on June 1st the barrage opened promptly and effectively and the raiding party issued from its widely scattered lairs, the men greatly relieved to be able to stretch their legs and get on with the job in hand. As the barrage lifted from the objective the platoons rushed in and proceeded to carry out the carefully prepared programme. This was done with great thoroughness, and prisoners were soon taxing the speed of their guards in a race to the raid headquarters.

THE OPPY FRONT; AND THE GERMAN OFFENSIVE, 1918

One or two enemy machine guns beyond the reach of the attacking party remained in action and caused a few casualties, who were attended to and brought back safely. The company withdrew after its work was done with the same steadiness and precision that had characterised the whole operation. One man was killed and later 3 died of wounds, while 11 others were slightly wounded. As an offset to these losses 1 officer, 1 sergeant, and 29 other ranks were taken prisoners, and many who refused to leave their dugouts were bombed. A minenwerfer was destroyed by No. 10 Platoon.

Altogether it was a most successful raid, during which the artillery and machine-gun company engaged put in some remarkably accurate work, which alone must have wrought havoc in the enemy's lines.

Meanwhile another enemy offensive had materialised and been held in check by the determined and self-sacrificing resistance of British divisions. This time it was an attempt to drive a wedge between the British and French Armies, and was delivered on a very quiet sector on the French front near the Aisne River, a sector which was at the time held by exhausted British divisions, among them the 8th Division. As has been stated, this Division bore the brunt of the German attack of March 21st on the Somme and sustained very heavy losses. Again on April 24th they were in the final thrust of the enemy towards Amiens, and at Villers Bretonneux were again largely responsible for holding the German advance.

The imminence of this new offensive was apparently not suspected by Marshal Foch, who was now in supreme command on the Western Front. Before supports could be rushed up the enemy had driven back our line and reached the Marne. The fighting was of the fiercest description, and before it was ended the gallant 8th Division had ceased to exist as a fighting unit. Its Commander, reporting on this last self-sacrificing defence by his Division, says: " It may be said without exaggeration that all the gallant battalions of this Division have ceased to exist as fighting units." The 2nd Devons and 2nd Rifle Brigade of the 23rd Infantry Brigade perished to a man, and by the time it was relieved the Division comprised a number of staff officers and about 200 men, sprinklings from a great variety of units, all holding grimly on to a line beyond which the enemy never penetrated. This experience of old friends of the Kensingtons is quoted to show what happened when the front line of defence was pierced and the enemy poured his massed troops through the breach.

On the Arras front, in spite of a scare period at the beginning of May, the enemy evinced little activity, and, apart from raids, the tours in the trenches were quiet. The Kensingtons became accustomed to the surrounding scenery. In front of the trench system stretched the valley before Monchy, the ruined encampments and gun pits standing out clearly in the bright sunshine amidst the trench-seamed waste. Monchy itself, ruined and deserted, showed up plainly, a sentinel watching the Scarpe valley. Beyond the Cambrai Road the change in the subsoil from chalk to the brown alluvial soil of the river valley was clearly to be seen in the changing colour of the trenches in the distance. Behind the line lay Arras, and farther off the towers of Mont St. Eloi. In the immediate vicinity Tilloy Wood and Bois des Bœufs (known as Bully Beef Wood) were but collections of splintered stumps.

Towards the end of June a few days were spent in Berneville, and the opportunity was taken to hold Brigade sports. At the beginning of July the whole Division was relieved and, after three days in Arras and five in Dainville, the Kensingtons marched to Lattre St. Quentin on the 13th, Grand Rullecourt on the 14th, and Bailleul aux Cornailles on the 15th. These marches were useful from a training point of view, but were not popular with the men, entailing as they did long journeys in the hot sun. On July 18th the Battalion marched to Château de la Haie, where a stiff period of training began. There was time for plenty of sport, boxing, baseball, and football, and concert parties to be visited during the evenings. The whole Brigade infantry were in close proximity in hutments among the trees of what was really a delightful spot, but though the days were enjoyable, the nights were less so, for the huts were infested with rats. Inter-hut competitions were organised in rat-trapping without any appreciable diminution in their numbers. After candles were extinguished, the men sleeping on the boarded floors were overrun, and although they lay with bayonets and flashlamp ready, it was rare that a successful blow was delivered. Enemy aeroplanes also indulged in bombing during the night, and although the Kensingtons escaped, troops near-by suffered serious losses when a bomb fell on a hut crowded with men.

It was during the Château de la Haie period that the " brass hats " began to take an interest in the mental welfare of the troops and an educational scheme was initiated. It is difficult to understand what results were expected in the arduous conditions under which the infantry lived, but, nevertheless, in obedience to orders a few lessons were given by qualified instructors in French, arithmetic, and science.

The training period, though short, had worked wonders, and the Kensingtons were fit men again, refreshed mentally and physically, when on the 31st of the month they were taken by light railway to St. Aubin and marched thence to the line, relieving the 10th Canadian Battalion in the familiar Tilloy sector.

The month of July had seen the last of the great German offensives. On the Somme, against Arras, in Flanders, or on the Aisne, the enemy had tried his strength against the Allied Forces and, although gaining ground, he had ultimately been held. In spite of huge losses nothing had been achieved. This last attempt to break through took place in the vicinity of Rheims on July 15th. But Foch was ready, and after crossing the Marne the advance was checked by the joint efforts of French, American, and Italian Divisions. In three days Foch launched his counter-offensive, and from that date the tide turned.

"THE KENSINGTONS"

The offensive had passed again to the Allies, and once started there was no looking back.

Until August 17th, the Kensingtons remained in the Tilloy sector, and the usual periods were spent either in the line or support positions in caves and dugouts on the outskirts of Arras. The Brigade front at the time was held by one battalion in line, one in support, and one in reserve.

A sporting event came off on August 15th, when a cross-country race of three miles was run for the Gropi Cup. Twenty Kensingtons were released from the line to train at Berneville, and the best runners were selected to represent the Battalion in the race. Other units in the Division sent teams in proportion to their ration strength, and the field totalled in all about 400 men. They lined up for the start and were soon strung out in the rough country about Berneville, jumping trenches or ploughing across the neglected fields. The first 25 to get in scored 3 marks each for their unit; the next 50, 2 marks; and the next 25, 1 mark. The Kensington team scored 14 marks and were the first in the 168th Brigade, but failed to secure the cup, which was won by a team from a field ambulance. The fine turn-out of the men and the excellence of the performance were a testimony to the physical fitness of the Division.

CHAPTER XV

THE FINAL BRITISH OFFENSIVE—BOYELLES AND BULLECOURT

MARSHAL FOCH opened the last great offensive of the war on July 18th, and it met with remarkable success. Not only did the enemy sustain severe losses, but was compelled to evacuate some of the more advanced of his newly won positions and, on his own admission, reverted to the defensive on the whole front. There is no doubt that the German morale was already showing signs of weakening. On the other hand, the spirit of the British troops was still high. Admittedly the year had, up to the present, shown no gains on French soil, but rather the yielding of hard-won ground, in itself a demoralising undertaking. It had meant the loss of the fruits of hard fighting and tremendous effort in the preceding years. The gain of a few yards of ground had assumed possibly an undue importance, but in this war of armies locked up in trench systems it was only natural to look on a small advance as of great moment, overlooking the wider aspects of morale and man power. In spite of this the men, though many of them were war weary and disillusioned, were still as determined as ever to go through with the task in hand and achieve victory, no matter what the cost.

Further demands on the endurance of the Kensingtons were about to be made, for the success on the right was to be followed by vigorous action by British, French, and American Armies, each on its own particular front.

Operations on the British front opened with an attack on the enemy line to the east of Amiens on August 8th, and was followed within an hour by a great French attack on their right. Success was immediate, and by the end of four days a large number of prisoners and much war material had been captured and an advance of twelve miles made to the positions of 1916. We were back on the Somme front of that year, but in a much better position on the left, so that it was decided to extend the attack in this direction. Rapid decisions were made. Existing plans to attack Orange and Chapel Hills, near Beaurains, were scrapped, and the 56th Division, caught in the maelstrom of activity, was hustled about until in a surprisingly short space of time it found itself committed to an attack on Boyelles and Boiry Becquerelle, villages about three miles to the south of Neuville Vitasse.

The Kensingtons did some speedy moves. Relieved on August 17th in the Tilloy sector, they marched to bivouacs at Berneville, and the next day entrained on the light railway for Liencourt, via Lattre St. Quentin, and marched to Gouy en Ternois. On the 20th a sudden move to Liencourt was ordered, and after but one night there the whole Brigade marched ten miles to St. Amand, a village close to Souastre, where the Battalion had awaited the battle of July 1st two years earlier.

It must be explained what sudden moves such as this involved. If the men were billeted on civilians, billets had to be arranged beforehand, and with some care if general satisfaction was to be achieved. On leaving, there were billeting forms to be completed and a copy handed to the Maire, often a peasant dragged from his fields, to affix the official stamp. Rations had to be obtained daily by the Quartermaster and issued to the men, and the transport frequently had to hunt about to find the ration dump. A certain amount of unloading of wagons necessarily took place when the Battalion spent a night or more at one place. The inevitable correspondence flowed between Brigade and Battalion Headquarters, and orders for the morrow had to be issued to companies. An early move meant an orgy of packing, and dismantling of improvised kitchens.

August 22nd was a day of ultra-rapid action on the part of the Staff, for the Divisional Commander, General Hull, received but verbal orders less than twenty-four hours

THE FINAL BRITISH OFFENSIVE—BOYELLES AND BULLECOURT

before the attack was due to be launched. The prolonged deliberations preceding earlier battles were thus short-circuited. Hurried conferences were called, and as the result the Kensingtons left St. Amand at 5 p.m. and joined the rest of the Brigade in a concentration area near Blairville, a village ten miles to the north-east, at 10 p.m. About midnight they moved again a further distance of four miles to assembly trenches south of the village of Boyelles. They were heavily shelled with gas shells during the last mile of the march and, wearing box respirators, were unable to move with any speed, so that it was not until 4 a.m. that they reached the assembly trenches, A and B Companies being in front with C and D in support. There had been no time to reconnoitre or indeed even see the ground over which the attack was to be launched.

The objectives of the 168th Brigade which was to attack with all three battalions in line—the Kensingtons on the right, 4th Londons centre, and London Scottish left—were the villages of Boyelles and Boiry Becquerelle and, when these were captured, a line of posts beyond. As the daylight strengthened, it was seen that, from the assembly trenches, good observation of the enemy's positions was possible.

At 4.55 a.m. the barrage commenced, resting twelve minutes on the enemy front line, and then, in stages of 100 yards, moving to the final objective, where it dwelt for an hour. Tanks went over with the attack and cleared the way well for the infantry. A and B Companies attacked in the new " blob " formation; that is, in sections in small groups instead of widely extended lines. This was found to give better control and minimise casualties. C Company followed similarly in support, D Company occupying the old front line in reserve. By 6 a.m., with but slight opposition, all the first objectives of the Kensingtons had been gained and consolidated, and patrols were pushed out some 500 yards in advance. The left company, however, now encountered heavy machine-gun fire from the left flank and were compelled to withdraw their advanced posts, though these were re-established later. The 4th Londons on the left, with the village of Boyelles confronting them, had met with a more determined resistance from a sunken road and other low ground which had escaped the barrage. Two platoons of D Company were sent via

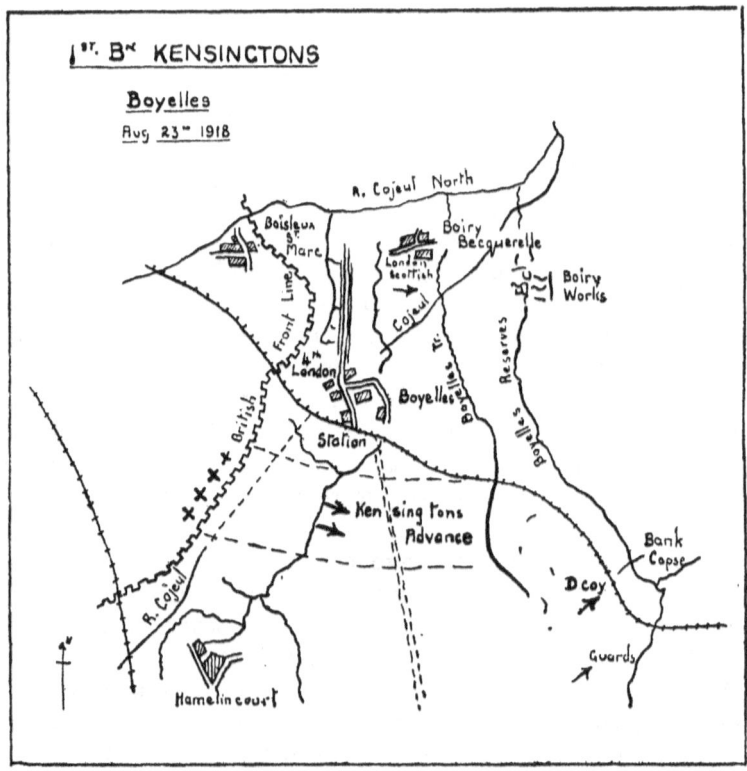

Station Trench to attack the village from the south, and this, coupled with the timely arrival of tanks on the scene, caused the garrison to surrender. Numbers of trench mortars and machine guns were captured, and by about 7 a.m. the objectives of the 168th Brigade were all gained.

Orders were now issued for the continuation of the advance to new objectives. The troops were, however, separated by considerable distances and the message, carried by runner, did not reach the Kensingtons until almost noon, so that it was not until 1.30 p.m. that the Battalion again advanced with orders to link up with the Guards Division on the right. D Company moved forward from reserve to the right front, with instructions to established this contact and capture Boyelles reserve trench. C Company was to advance to Boyelles reserve on the left of D Company and get in touch with the 4th Londons on the left. A Company was to support these forward companies, B remaining in reserve in the old German front line. Strong opposition was now encountered. Both C and D Companies came under heavy artillery and machine-gun fire and were soon fighting in scattered groups. The ordered advance to Boyelles reserve was found to be out of the question, but two platoons of D Company succeeded in working round to a position in touch with the Guards at Bank Copse and with them rushed the railway embankment, driving the enemy out to Boyelles reserve. No contact had, however, been made with the 4th Londons, and C, D, and A Companies endured very heavy shell fire all the afternoon and evening. The situation remained obscure. At 5 p.m. the Commanding Officer, Lieut.-Colonel R. E. F. Shaw, M.C., proceeded from advanced Headquarters with a runner and signaller to reconnoitre the forward situation. While so doing he was hit by a rifle bullet fired from a distance and killed. The Kensingtons had been the worst sufferers in this second stage of the day's fighting, the other battalions gaining their objectives with but slight opposition and small losses. By about 9.30 p.m. it was found possible to establish a line on the Battalion front in conformity with the Brigade front.

During the early hours of the 24th the Kensingtons were relieved by the 8th Middlesex and marched to Hendecourt, near Blairville. Here for a space the Battalion weighed its successes and mourned its dead. Apart from the disastrous loss of the Commanding Officer, the day had been a costly one. Captain F. Roseveare, commanding B Company, 2nd Lieut. Wilson, and 12 other ranks had been killed. Captain F. J. Goddard, commanding C Company, 4 other officers and 91 other ranks had been wounded. On the other hand, 2 officers and 174 other ranks of the enemy had been captured, together with 6 heavy machine guns, 5 light machine guns, and several trench mortars.

At 2 p.m. the Battalion paraded for the funeral of Lieut.-Colonel Shaw at Blairville Cemetery. Colonel Shaw had served with the Battalion since the early days of the war, first as a subaltern and finally for a year as Commanding Officer, and he typified the fine young men of England who served her even unto death in her hour of need. He had a high sense of duty, never sparing himself, and expecting from others the same standard of devotion to the cause of winning the war. His death and that of others who fell on that day of victory cast a gloom over the Battalion, though one realised that Colonel Shaw himself would have issued the order to " Carry on."

The command of the Battalion now passed to Major M. A. Prismall, who, as has been seen, had served with the Battalion since Neuve Chapelle and was in all respects " one of ours."

On the 24th the attack was continued by the 167th Brigade, Croisilles now being the objective, following the capture of intermediate positions. Enemy reinforcements had, however, arrived, and the garrison in the ruined village maintained a stout resistance. No progress could be made, in spite of attempts to surround it, and troops advancing met with heavy machine-gun fire. Gas was used freely by the enemy, and this prevented much support being given by tanks.

The following day brought no better success on the 56th Divisional front, though on the left the Hindenburg system to the immediate north was reached and the possibility of working along this system became apparent as the only method of subduing Croisilles, which still held out

THE FINAL BRITISH OFFENSIVE—BOYELLES AND BULLECOURT

against frontal attack. On the 27th the Kensingtons, who on the preceding evening had been moved from the old assembly positions of the 23rd, were moved forward into Summit trench, overlooking Croisilles, with the Queen's Westminsters on the right and the London Rifle Brigade on the left. The 169th Brigade had relieved the 167th and were to continue the operations against the village. Very little progress was again made, but, as on the preceding day, success followed the attack of the 52nd Division on the left, who reached Fontaine Croisilles. Attacks by the Guards on the right were less successful, and the enemy counter-attacked them fiercely. In the late evening a change of disposition was decided on. The 167th Brigade was again to confront Croisilles, but the 169th was to enter the Hindenburg Line and, supported by the 168th, attack along this trench system towards Bullecourt. Croisilles was in process of being surrounded.

At 11 p.m. the Kensingtons were ordered to occupy a position in the Hindenburg Line in rear of the 4th Londons and in advance of the London Scottish. These positions were not reached until 4 a.m. on the 28th, for the Hindenburg system was extremely congested, the trench system very complex, and, to add to these difficulties, it was a very wet, dark night.

Due to the impossibility of getting the troops into position earlier, the attack did not commence until 12.30 p.m., by which time the 8th Middlesex, after a stiff fight, had succeeded in occupying the village of Croisilles, and the 167th Brigade was thus free to support the advance towards Bullecourt.

The task allotted to the Kensingtons was that of mopping up, a very necessary procedure, for in the maze of trenches, abounding with deep dugouts, small parties of the enemy escaped the front waves and, emerging, attacked the supporting troops. With A Company on the right, B Company on the left, and D in support, the Battalion progressed steadily along the system. C Company cleared Sensee Trench and Sensee Avenue on the right of the advance, thus

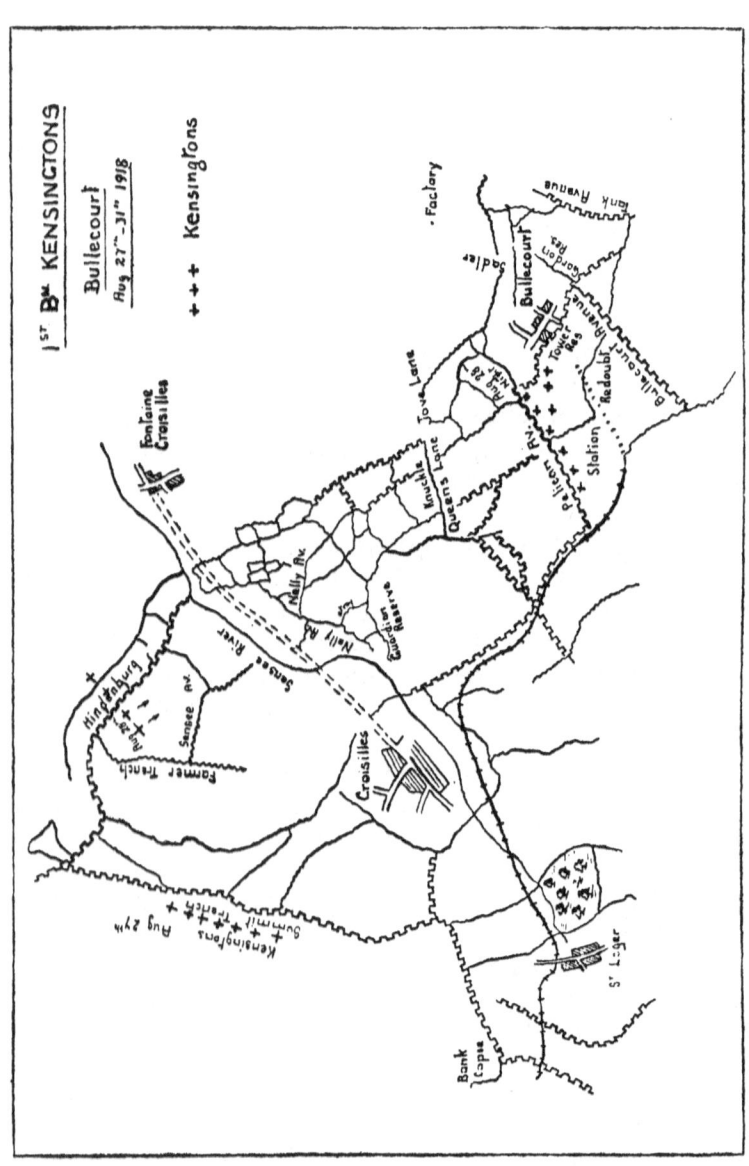

protecting the flank. The advance thus continued across the Sensee valley and the Fontaine Croisilles Road, but with every step the resistance increased, due, no doubt, to the support received from the garrison of Croisilles. C Company was at this stage ordered forward to assist the right flank of the attack and mop up Nelly Avenue, Guardian Reserve, and Stray Trench, while B Company was despatched to the help of the 4th Londons for similar duties in the support and front lines of the Hindenburg system. A strong enemy post now held up the right flank of the advance with machine-gun fire, but the supporting trench mortars compelled its surrender. A platoon of B Company, under 2nd Lieut. C. A. G. Wilde, cleared one of the many posts. They rushed it, and after a lively scuffle secured 19 prisoners and several machine guns.

In the meantime several battalions of the 57th Division on the left, which was attacking in conjunction with the 56th, were in the Hindenburg Line behind the advancing battalions, and the congestion became acute. Troops could not be moved with the celerity that the situation demanded, and the day ended with the Kensingtons, in common with the rest of the attack, holding on to various positions about Pelican Avenue. It must be realised that the ground was seamed with trenches, pitted with shell-holes, and overgrown with long grass, so that the fighting resolved itself into a large number of minor operations against scattered machine-gun posts and small groups of the enemy.

With the morning concerted action was again initiated, and at 7.15 the Battalion assembled in Pelican Avenue in readiness for the resumption of the attack on Bullecourt. A and B Companies were to be in front, with C in support and D in reserve. However, the confusion caused by the mixing of units in the Hindenburg Line delayed the attack, which did not open until 1 p.m., when, following the lifting of the barrage, the 168th Brigade, with the Kensingtons on the right and the Scottish on the left, the 1st and 4th Londons supporting, began the attack. A and B Companies of the Kensingtons, advancing from Pelican Avenue, at once encountered heavy rifle and machine-gun fire from Station Redoubt and Station Reserve. A platoon of D Company was sent to reinforce B Company in an attempt to silence these posts, but without achieving the desired result. The 1st Londons were asked to send a company to take Station Redoubt. The advance, however, was definitely checked, and at 7.5 p.m. the Battalion was ordered to consolidate on the line Tower Reserve–Pelican Avenue. At the same time two platoons, accompanied with light trench mortars, were sent to clear Station Redoubt and work eastwards along Station Reserve. They succeeded in capturing Station Redoubt, but progress beyond it was found to be impossible. By nightfall the 1st Londons operating on the right flank had got into touch with the Division on the right.

In the meantime the Scottish on the left had reached Bullecourt and during the early afternoon cleared the village and linked up with the Kensingtons on their right at Station Redoubt and the 169th Brigade on their left in Sadler Lane.

The day had been a successful one in view of the late start, and during the night the 168th Brigade handed over to the 167th. The relief was the signal for an enemy counter-attack, and at 5 a.m. on the 30th, with a vigorous assault, the Germans drove the line back to Pelican Avenue, capturing Bullecourt and Station Redoubt. Attempts by the 167th Brigade to regain the lost positions failed, for Station Redoubt covered the front of the village and the garrison maintained a strong enfilade machine-gun barrage which effectively prevented any advance.

The Kensingtons had spent the day reorganising and re-equipping in Stafford Lane. That evening orders came to hand that the 168th Brigade was to attack on the morrow and regain the lost positions. The ultimate objective was the rising ground to the east of the village, and in the attack the Battalion was in support to the London Scottish, who were to attack Station Redoubt first and then Bullecourt.

The 4th Londons were centre battalion, with the 7th Middlesex on the left.

At 1 a.m. the Kensingtons moved into the assembly area, A and B Companies in Knuckle Avenue, C in Queen's Avenue, and D in Jove Lane. At 5.15 a.m. the barrage fell on the enemy positions and was replied to by the enemy with heavy shell fire, including a large proportion of gas shells. The attack, however, made good progress at once, and Station Redoubt, which had had a night of intense bombardment, was soon cleared by the Scottish. Meanwhile the 7th Middlesex, advancing towards the factory, were held up, for the enemy posted there maintained machine-gun fire on the approaches. C Company of the Kensingtons was sent to the assistance of the 7th Middlesex, but before their arrival the enemy had evacuated the factory. C Company remained in Beef Alley, in reserve to further operations by the Middlesex.

The Scottish advance had continued, and they were soon in Bullecourt Avenue, though attempts to get beyond here met with considerable opposition. They consolidated on this line. The 4th Londons, after some stiff fighting, had succeeded in reaching the eastern extremity of the village. During the afternoon the enemy had been observed concentrating troops in Tank Avenue, and, suspecting a counter-attack, a heavy bombardment was concentrated on the position by the 56th Divisional artillery. The counter-attack did not materialise.

During the early evening B Company received orders to take up a position 200 yards short of Gordon Reserve and, under cover of a trench-mortar bombardment, rush that position. Before it was possible to comply, the order was cancelled and the company moved instead to the support of the 4th Londons in Bullecourt.

The result of the day's work was very satisfactory. Although the line reached and consolidated was short of the final objective, the enemy strongholds in Bullecourt and Station Redoubt had been captured and the situation was clear for an early resumption of the advance. That night

"THE KENSINGTONS"

the Kensingtons were relieved by the 4th Royal Scots Fusiliers and marched back to Boyelles Reserve and Boyelles Trench, east of the Arras–Bapaume Road, the 56th Division having been relieved by the 52nd.

In this second stage of the fighting on this front the Battalion had suffered most severely. Lieut. W. E. Smith, M.C., commanding D Company, and 42 other ranks had been killed, while 2nd Lieuts. G. B. Cameron (commanding B Company), A. E. Phillips (commanding C Company), 3 other officers, and 103 other ranks had been wounded. During the operations 60 prisoners, 10 machine guns, 1 light trench mortar, and 1 field gun had been captured.

CHAPTER XVI

THE CANAL DU NORD

DURING the few days that the 56th Division spent about Boyelles, resting, bathing, re-equipping, the advance continued. The enemy found himself compelled to yield up his carefully chosen strongholds. During the later stages of the operations against Bullecourt the armies on the right had reached such familiar villages as Combles, Fremicourt, and Les Bœufs, and the French farther south had advanced to the left bank of the Somme. By September 1st Peronne had fallen to the Australians. On the left, on the Arras front, similar progress had been made, and the line was now established through Plouvain and Eterpigny. It is thus seen that, between these limits, the line now ran practically due north and south and the Drocourt–Queant line was the immediate obstacle on what may still be called the Arras front, though the city itself now lay some ten miles behind the line.

It is important that the nature of these defences should be appreciated. In the early days of the war the Germans had begun to establish behind their line a formidable system consisting of well-constructed trenches amply provided with dugouts and strongly wired. They were sited to include every natural advantage that the ground offered, and, when completed, presented a barrier to an attacking army that, if defended with spirit, might well be considered impregnable. In parts they were as much as ten miles in depth. Events, however, had shown that a courageous attack might break through this complex system, and now that the morale of the defenders was low, they proved less of an obstacle than the Germans had anticipated. The main system ran from St. Quentin to Queant near Cambrai, and thence westwards towards Arras. Here it turned north again and, running towards Vimy Ridge, continued via Lens to Aubers Ridge and Lille. Following the penetration of the northern part of these defences at Lens in 1915, a new line was constructed running from Queant to Drocourt, near Lens, and thence direct to Lille. In its course this system followed the Canal du Nord. It became known to the British Army as the Drocourt–Queant line, while the main system south of Arras was called the Hindenburg Line, though the Germans referred to them as the Wotan and Siegfried positions respectively. By the end of August 1918 the original defence system about Arras had, despite a determined resistance, been reached and passed, and now, on September 2nd, Canadians and British attacked the Drocourt–Queant line between Queant and the Sensee river with immediate success, though the positions were held in force. This occasioned a withdrawal of the enemy to the line of the Canal du Nord. Farther south there were more withdrawals. This success and the subsequent retreat brought the Canadians to the swampy zone at the confluence of the Canal du Nord, the Cojeul and Sensee rivers, and the Sensee Canal. This area was taken over by the 56th Division, and on September 6th the Kensingtons left the Boyelles area and marched to trenches about one mile north of Vis en Artois, via Croisilles, Fontaine Croisilles, and Vis en Artois, a noteworthy journey, for the ground traversed had been recovered only in the last few days. On the 7th the Battalion took over trenches in the Lecleuse sector from the 2nd King's Royal Rifle Corps, A and D Companies occupying the front line, with B and C in support. The trench system consisted of an outpost line, and the platoons were disposed in short lengths of trench and shell-holes. Active patrolling was carried out across the flooded Sensee valley to the north of Lecleuse in order to locate the position of enemy posts. Enemy artillery was very active, and any movement in the open in daylight drew immediate shell fire.

After but a brief tour in the front line the Kensingtons were relieved by the 8th Middlesex and on the 13th September were transported in buses from St. Rohart

Factory at Vis en Artois to St. Laurent Blangy, a suburb of Arras, along the familiar Arras–Cambrai Road, with its well-known landmarks. The tide of war had ebbed once more on this front, leaving in its wake an area of indescribable desolation and ruin. Monchy was a deserted ruin, but Arras was already showing signs of recovery.

At St. Laurent Blangy the time was spent in cleaning up and training. Battalion Headquarters was established in wine cellars under the ruins of a château. The grounds were delightful and contained a number of small lakes. The weather having turned fine and warm the men took advantage of the opportunity to enjoy bathing and swimming in the clear water. Some even attempted fishing until an enterprising bomber discovered the unsporting but efficacious results of a Mills bomb cast into the water. An improvised boat race, using old washing tubs with spades as oars, provided much amusement and frequent overturnings. Even in such stirring times as these, the Bow Bells were still going strong, and in an improvised theatre gave an excellent show much appreciated by the troops.

On the 19th the Kensingtons, refreshed and ready once more for battle, embussed for the Vis en Artois sector and relieved the 1st Canadian Mounted Rifles in support positions south of Rumancourt. The 56th Division had extended its front to the right, taking over from the Canadians. The Divisional front now extended to the Arras–Cambrai Road on the western side of the Canal du Nord.

The Rumancourt area was less devastated than those farther back, and it was somewhat of a novelty to find the villages largely intact. Rumancourt and Ecourt St. Quentin, near-by, showed very few signs of shell fire. The houses had not been damaged by the retreating enemy—there had been no time for systematic destruction—but they were stripped of furniture, much of which had gone to furnish a field hospital. This latter was remarkable for the thorough way in which it was fitted up, bearing in mind its proximity to the line. A German light-railway system ran through Rumancourt, and the small station showed signs of the bombing activities of our aircraft. The sector was quiet save for some registration on our battery positions by the enemy, and aerial activity on both sides. Some fierce fights overhead were witnessed, though it was not possible to determine whose airmen were victorious.

Plans for an attack on the 27th on a large scale were now mature. The main assault was to be delivered on the right, the 56th Division being on the extreme left, next to the 11th Division. As the enemy was known to be holding the angle between the Sensee and Nord Canals in force, it was decided that the main crossing of the canal should be made by the Canadians at Mœuvres, to be followed by a crossing near the Arras–Cambrai Road, from which point the 56th Division would advance due north astride the canal, with the 11th Division on its right, as far as the confluence of the two canals. The 168th Brigade was to clear the west bank, and the 169th, crossing on pontoon bridges made by pioneers and engineers, to advance along the eastern bank.

On September 26th, the Kensingtons moved into assembly positions to the west of Sauchy Cauchy, with B and D Companies in the front line, A Company in support, and C Company in reserve, and at 5.20 on the following morning the barrage began and, following it, the Canadians crossed the canal near Mœuvres. There had been no secrecy about the preparations, and the enemy was on the alert, but the Canadians overcame all opposition and advanced on their objectives. Six hours later action began on the 11th and 56th Divisional fronts. The former Division crossed the canal and deployed facing north and north-east, whereupon the Engineers began the construction of the pontoon bridges, one on each side of the Arras–Cambrai Road, for the crossing of the 169th Brigade. Marquion proved to be still occupied by the enemy, and this delayed the work, so that the Brigade did not get across until just after noon and the advance along the canal did not commence until 3.28 p.m., nearly an hour late.

The Kensingtons had the duty of clearing the western

THE CANAL DU NORD

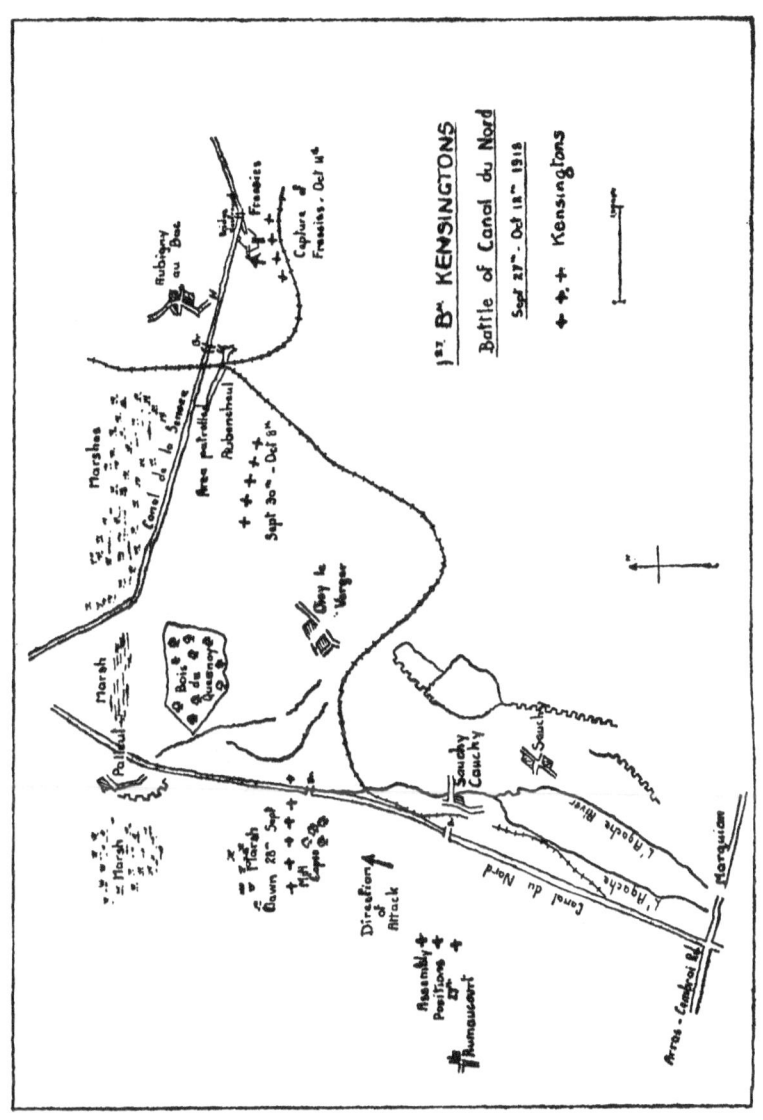

bank while the Queen's Westminsters of the 169th Brigade were working along the eastern bank. Attacking on a two-platoon frontage with B Company leading, followed by D and A, the Battalion advanced steadily northwards. Very little opposition was met as far as the Sauchy Cauchy–Rumancourt Road, which was the first objective. Here B Company halted and consolidated. At 4.40 p.m. the advance was resumed, A and D Companies passing through B and advancing along the canal bank towards Mill Copse, the final objective. During the whole of the advance, touch had been maintained with the Queen's Westminsters across the water. The leading companies had not proceeded far before they came under machine-gun fire directed from a strong enemy post on the canal bridge, near the copse. The ground also became very marshy as the companies neared the objective. By 6.20 p.m. the leading company, D Company, had succeeded in reaching a line in the marshes about 500 yards short of Mill Copse. It was now definitely ascertained that the firing came from a machine gun on the canal bank and a group of guns on the bridge, but it was impossible to rush them, for there were but two approaches, one along the towpath and the other along a paved lane partially flooded, and both were in view of the enemy posts. There was no cover anywhere. After dark, however, D Company worked up the paved lane towards the copse, and at the same time orders were given to C Company to advance from its reserve position, astride the canal, at moonrise, when the light would be sufficient to enable the men to deal with the posts on the canal banks. Their assistance was not required, however, for D Company reached the copse at 2.30 a.m. and cleared it, and then, turning their attention to the post on the bridge with a few well-directed bombs, caused the garrison to flee. The company was thus able to establish itself on its final objective north of Mill Copse, and A Company moved forward a corresponding distance in support with its flank on the canal bank. They were thus disposed when C Company arrived, having left Sauchy Cauchy Bridge at

THE CANAL DU NORD

2 a.m., and having worked systematically over the ground cleared that day.

During this successful operation on the west bank the 169th Brigade on the eastern side had cleared that area of scattered posts of the enemy and by early morning had reported their objective gained. They had reached the vicinity of Palleul and the Bois de Quesnoy was clear. The Division was now astride the canal and in the swampy area between the two canals.

September 28th was a day spent by the 168th Brigade mainly in consolidation. The 4th Londons cleared the ground northwards, while A, D, and B Companies of the Kensingtons mopped up the area advanced over on the preceding day. During the day the 169th Brigade reached the marsh south of the Sensee Canal and the 8th Middlesex captured Palleul. No organised resistance had been encountered during the two days' operations, but rather a delaying action by scattered machine-gun posts. During the course of the action the Kensingtons had captured 71 prisoners and 8 trench mortars.

On the following day the Kensingtons withdrew to the old assembly positions near Rumancourt, a flat area dominated by one isolated and prominent hill popularly known to the men as the "Pimple." This gave a brief opportunity for cleaning up and re-equipping in readiness for the next move, which all knew would not be long delayed. At 8 p.m. on September 30th, the Battalion paraded under Lieut.-Colonel J. Forbes Robertson, V.C., D.S.O., M.C., who had been in command since September 28th, and marched to the pontoon bridge at Sauchy Cauchy, where guides conducted the companies to the sector north-east of Oisy le Verger, in relief of two companies of the 5th Dorsets. The 56th Division had extended its front to the outskirts of Aubencheul, thus relieving part of the 11th Division on the right. The London Scottish were in the line on the right of the Kensingtons, the London Rifle Brigade on the left, and the 4th Londons in support. Active patrolling was carried out towards the banks of the

Sensee Canal, which now lay immediately opposite the Divisional front, with the view to finding out if the villages of Arleux, Aubigny au Bac, and Brunemont were still occupied by the enemy. All patrols reported that the enemy was on the alert and that machine guns opened fire on any approach to the canal bank. However, flames were seen at Aubencheul on October 6th, which indicated a possible retirement, and D Company at once pushed out patrols to raid the bridge near the centre of the village. Here they got in touch with patrols of the 4th Londons, and a post was established commanding the bridge.

The 4th Londons took over the Battalion front on the 8th, and the next day the Kensingtons moved east again to the immediate south of the village of Fressies, where they relieved the 9th Sherwood Foresters. There had been a further extension of the Divisional front. The whole of the 11th Division left the sector in order to follow up the enemy retreat which followed the entry of the Canadians into Cambrai.

Fressies was found to be held by the Germans, and it was decided to clear the village on October 11th. The operation was carried out by two platoons of C Company and two of D Company, under command of Captain C. M. Hemsley. Light trench mortars were used in conjunction with artillery to deal with the enemy posts located by the patrols.

At 7 a.m. the barrage descended on the approaches to the village and continued for five minutes, after which it lifted and the platoons advanced from their assembly positions, which were along the line of the railway. The C Company platoons on the right advanced up the road through the village to the canal bank, while the D Company platoons made similar progress. An observation post was established on the railway line, which was manned by the remaining platoons of the two companies, and communication was maintained by wire with Battalion Headquarters throughout the operations.

On reaching the canal bank the leading platoons established posts on the bridge near the village and then, leaving a section to patrol the bank of the canal, turned back through the village, clearing cellars and dugouts and finally establishing posts at the chapel and in the main streets.

At 9 a.m. the agreed signals, consisting of red and green Verey lights, indicating the arrival at the various objectives, were seen from the observation post, and the conclusion of a successful enterprise was assumed. It was now reported by Captain Hemsley that the right front platoon, which had been engaged in clearing a dugout, was imprisoned by an enemy machine gun firing into the entrance. Artillery fire was directed on the offending post, and by noon the platoon was able to extricate itself from an unenviable position. The remainder of the two companies now advanced into the village and finished the work of consolidation.

The operation had been completely successful. The Kensingtons had cleared the village to the banks of the canal and captured 47 prisoners, including 2 officers, in addition to 13 machine guns, at the cost of 3 killed and 12 wounded.

During the night the London Rifle Brigade took over the front and the Battalion marched back to the Rumancourt area, surprised to find how great a distance now lay between the front and the familiar "Pimple."

The enemy resistance was lessening daily. Such opposition as was encountered came from isolated machine-gun posts established in advantageous positions. The dugouts were littered with provisions, papers, and personal property, left behind by the retreating Germans, and German field glasses, revolvers, and other impedimenta became objects of much bartering amongst the men.

Three days were spent in damp shelters and holes in the ground near the "Pimple." Baths were provided, however, and on the 12th the Kensingtons went *en masse* to a performance given by the Bow Bells at Villers Cagnicourt.

Good news came on the 14th that the 56th Division was to enjoy a brief rest in Arras and that the journey was to be accomplished by train from Marquion Station, in itself an astounding possibility indicating some fast work by the railroad engineers.

The train was due at 5 p.m., and the Kensingtons, believing in an early arrival, had marched from the "Pimple" in high spirits to Marquion, reaching the siding at 3 p.m. Night came but still no train, and without tea or rations other than those carried by the men, spirits tended to be damped. However, a large amount of waste wood was collected from the vicinity and huge bonfires lit, around which community singing, led by a musical corporal, aroused echoes in the quiet night. Welcomed with ringing cheers, the train eventually materialised at 10 p.m., but it merely afforded some shelter from the night, for it did not leave until 8 a.m. on the following day with its load of cramped, frozen, and hungry humanity. The men were accustomed to the vagaries of French trains in the military zone, but it was felt that this one really exceeded the limit for time-keeping. One thought enviously of the transport, having covered the twenty-odd miles by road, enjoying the amenities of Arras.

However, Arras, when at length reached, offered its customary welcome of good comfortable billets. The civilian population was returning, shops were opening, and the Y.M.C.A. was established in several parts of the city. A number of theatres, run by the concert parties of Divisions stationed in or near the city, and Divisional cinemas, offered a variety of entertainment to those with a little money to spare. An aged photographer did good business with the Kensingtons. Groups of all kinds were taken, with extraordinarily good results considering the difficulties under which the old man must have worked. As it happened, it was the last opportunity for a permanent record to be obtained of groups of N.C.O.s and men who had worked together for so long, for, after the Armistice, none of the poverty-stricken villages of the frontier in which the Battalion was billeted possessed a photographer. Indeed, it is doubtful if, had one existed, he could have obtained supplies.

The city had already taken on the air of an old ruin. Grass grew over the tumbled stones, and the deserted cobbled streets, away from the main thoroughfares, echoed dismally as the iron-shod heel of the exploring soldier clattered on the pavé. The Cathedral, Hôtel de Ville, and the Grand Place, the latter but recently called "Barbed-wire Square," were being preserved from souvenir hunters, and notice boards abounded. Large numbers of evacuées had returned and were accommodated in the Schramm Barracks. Although so familiar, it was an Arras with a difference. It was the absence of gun fire. No bombardment was audible in the distance, no air raids disturbed the night, and there were no reverberations from the heavies in the Citadel grounds. Schramm Barracks was at last free from the attention of long-range artillery.

The influenza epidemic, which invaded Europe in the autumn of 1918, now began to take toll of the British Army. Many men who had endured battle and hardship without hurt fell victims, and the hospitals, fortunately freed from large numbers of battle casualties, were invaded by crowds of men in the throes of influenza.

CHAPTER XVII

OPEN WARFARE AND THE END

SEPTEMBER had been a bad month for the Central Powers. Austria sued for peace; Damascus fell on the 20th, and on the 29th Bulgaria surrendered. On the Western Front the main lines of defence had been broken. The month of October brought further disasters for the enemy. The progress on the front attacked by the 56th Division has been seen. It was followed on the 13th, while the Kensingtons were in reserve, by a bold and successful attack by the 169th Brigade on the village of Aubigny au Bac on the northern bank of the Sensee Canal. Crossing on a floating bridge constructed in the darkness by the Engineers, close to enemy positions, the assaulting party raided the village and captured 207 prisoners, more than double the number of those actually engaged in the attack. On the Oppy front our troops had advanced, and Douai was entered on the 17th. The town had been mined, but had not been destroyed prior to evacuation. It seemed that the Germans were already considering terms of armistice. An Allied force under the King of the Belgians was advancing through Belgium; Ostend had fallen, and before the end of the month the Dutch frontier had been reached. On the Lys front the enemy had evacuated his formidable defences in order to conform with the advancing line of the main British attack, which had now reached the Forêt de Mormal and was nearing Maubeuge. British troops were in Lille.

The Germans had made their first tentative requests for armistice and peace at the beginning of the month, but while the negotiations dragged on, the vigour of the Allied attacks continued unabated, and every day brought further news of successes. It was open warfare at last, the enemy endeavouring to withdraw his main forces for a stand farther

OPEN WARFARE AND THE END

back, leaving a screen of outposts to fight delaying rearguard actions.

On October 31st the Kensingtons, fit and ready to take their share in this arduous fighting, paraded under Major F. S. B. Johnson, who was now in command, and marched to the Baudimont Gate, near the Citadel in Arras, and journeyed thence in buses with the rest of the Brigade to Noyelles sur Seine. They marched from this point to Douchy, a village not far from the Belgian frontier and south west of Valenciennes. Fighting was going on while the Battalion awaited further orders in billets, the attack being pressed in the zone lying between the Scheldt and Sambre Rivers. On November 2nd Valenciennes was cleared of the enemy, and the 56th and 11th Divisions were now to advance, with the general line of the Aunelle River as the objective, and attack in an easterly direction on a line south of Valenciennes. This implied clearing the villages of Estreux, Saultain, and Preseau, by a converging movement on the part of these Divisions on the right and the Canadians on the left. The latter were to attack Estreux. The enemy was countering the tank as a weapon of attack by holding river fronts, against which tanks were useless. During the night of the 2nd/3rd the Kensingtons relieved the 7th West Riding Regiment on the high ground east of the River Rhonelle, near Famars, in readiness for the operations of the morrow. In the early morning news came from Brigade that the Canadians were in Estreux, and the Battalion was ordered to advance on Saultain, sending forward strongly supported patrols to locate the enemy, and if possible establish a line on the Ferme du Moulin Ridge on the far side of the village. Early contact was to be established with the Canadian Corps patrols. This duty was successfully carried out by A Company, with one platoon as patrol and three in support, and at 11.15 a.m. the officer commanding the company reported that he was advancing in touch with the 4th Londons on the left and the Queen's Westminsters on the right. Within half an hour the company had reached Saultain and the remainder of the Battalion moved up in closer support. Midday, however, brought news of enemy resistance in Estreux and in Ferme du Moulin, and the Kensington advance was ordered to cease while the supporting artillery fired on both targets. B Company was very near the Ferme du Moulin Ridge at the time, and the platoons dug in as ordered. A Company was still in the village. By nightfall the situation had cleared, the enemy machine-gun posts surrendering or retreating, and the main body of the Battalion entered the village of Saultain, to find it full of civilians, who acclaimed the entry of British troops.

During the day the Kensingtons had moved through country unspoiled by war, for there had been little shelling on either side. It provided a sharp contrast to the devastated areas which in the preceding years had become so familiar. Neuve Chapelle, Aubers, Neuville Vitasse, Oppy, had been mere names. No conception could be formed of the original appearance of these villages, they being but crumbling heaps of masonry. Here, however, the pretty villages stood amongst trees, now gaunt and dripping in the November mists, but still natural and undefiled by war. The roads, though mined here and there, were passable to infantry, and the fields still showed signs of the summer crops. To find the villages inhabited came as a shock, and what these people had endured during the rapid passage of the battle line through their midst can be imagined, and the thankfulness with which they greeted their deliverers after the long years of invasion understood. They pressed forward to cheer the British Tommy, giving him hot "coffee," little realising that they were now cut off from their war-time source of supply—Belgium—by a retreating army which had left in its wake a trail of ruined roads, bridges, and railways. From the new source now available they were separated by a wide zone similarly ruined and taxed to its utmost capacity by convoys of lorries bringing rations and supplies from the distant railheads to the ever-advancing infantry. The duty of feeding this civilian population added further burdens to the transport.

OPEN WARFARE AND THE END

By November 6th the 56th Division alone was rationing 16,000 civilians.

The transport difficulty was becoming acute, for the Germans had destroyed communications with typical thoroughness. Huge craters had been blown at crossroads, road bridges and culverts mined, and trees felled across roads. Rations, ammunition, and supplies of all descriptions had to be brought within reach of the horse transport of the fighting units by motor-lorries, and as railheads were now many miles back, this entailed long and difficult journeys. The roads were never intended to bear such a weight of traffic, and now that their pavé surfaces were slippery, owing to the rain and mud, and with craters at every stream crossing, they became well-nigh impassable. The M.T., A.S.C., had all along been a subject of mirth to the infantry; but they accomplished heroic tasks during this advance and had as little sleep as the fighting men. They steered their cumbrous vehicles over muddy tracks, by-passing the frequent obstructions, halting to drag one another out when sunk axle-deep in mud, and always by prodigious efforts managing to keep the troops supplied. Labour battalions and the Engineers laboured incessantly to repair roads, bridges, and railways, so that the advance should not be impeded.

As soon as the Ferme du Moulin Ridge near Saultain had been captured, cyclist and cavalry patrols pushed forward to the River Aunelle and came in contact with the enemy, who was found to be established on the far bank. During the night the line Ferme du Moulin–Cemetery was consolidated, and at 5 a.m. on the 4th the advance was continued to the river, the Kensingtons being in reserve. The Brigade objective was a line running north and south through the villages of Angre and Angreau, and the 4th Londons, the foremost battalion, were to clear the ground behind the mounted troops. The London Scottish were then to pass through the 4th Londons and gain the final objective. The advance proceeded well and the Fusiliers captured the village of Sebourquiaux, near Sebourg, but came under heavy machine-gun fire from the direction of Rombies. The Queen's Westminsters met with a similar experience. They crossed the river and captured the village of Sebourg, meeting with but slight opposition, but attempts to continue the advance in an easterly direction met with heavy rifle and machine-gun fire from rising ground beyond. The Canadians were also held up. Pending artillery co-operation to deal with these enemy posts, the advance halted just east of the villages. In the meantime the Kensingtons had been awaiting orders since early morning, and at 10.30 a.m. they moved forward to cover the left flank of the Brigade during the crossing of the river, protection rendered particularly necessary by the failure of the Canadians to capture Rombies. Heavy shell fire was encountered, but the casualties fortunately were few. Night came, bringing with it the urgent necessity for getting in touch with units on the flanks, the Canadians on the left and the 169th Brigade on the right. 2nd Lieut. J. H. Wright with a runner set off to find the latter brigade, but both officer and man were wounded. 2nd Lieut. Osborn, who went to get in touch with the Canadians, never returned, and his dead body was found on the following day. These incidents serve to show the difficulties of keeping in contact with constantly moving troops on the flanks. The front was very wide and considerable intervals existed between companies, and between companies and adjacent units. The nights were dark, and rain fell with monotonous regularity, the ground was entirely unfamiliar, and there were no trenches to follow or barbed wire to give a hint of an enemy post.

During the night the Scottish took over from the 4th Londons on the east bank of the river and in Sebourquiaux, and the Kensingtons moved into support to the Scottish, with orders, as the advance proceeded, to move up and fill the gap which was now known to exist between the left of the Scottish and the Canadians. 2nd Lieut. F. Garside, the Battalion Intelligence Officer, and one officer per company went forward to reconnoitre the river crossing at

OPEN WARFARE AND THE END

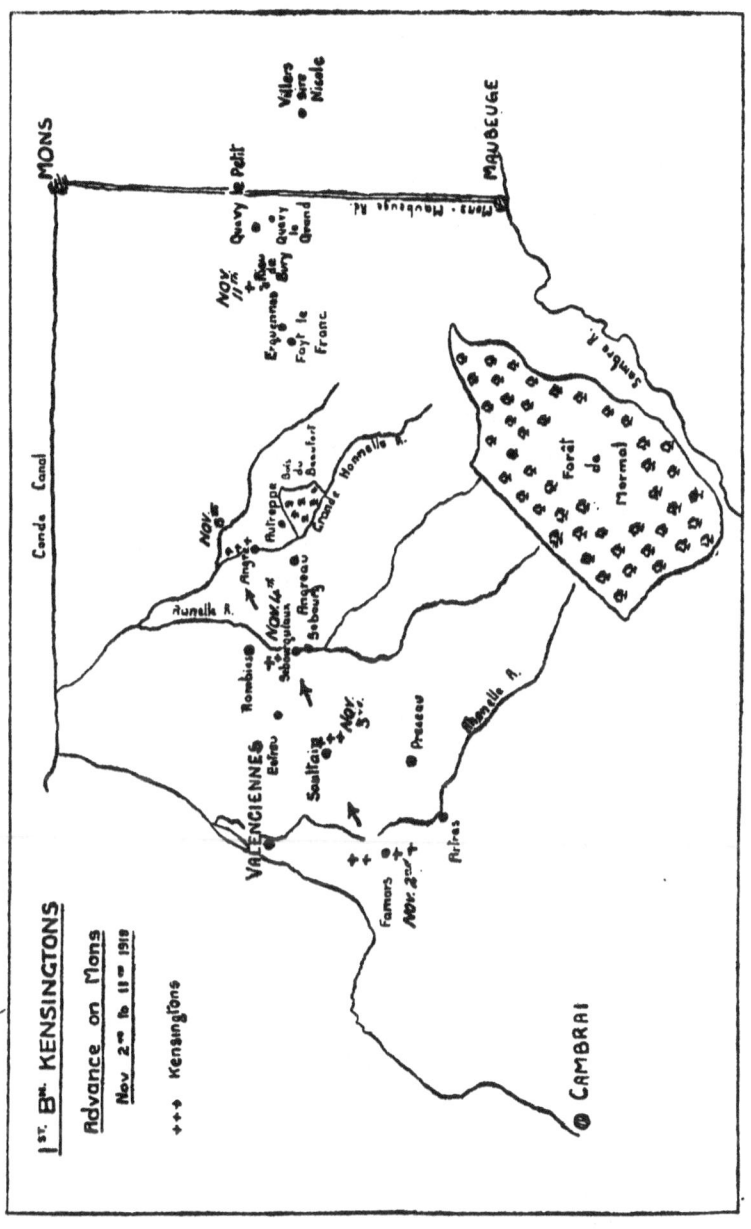

Sebourquiaux, but in the darkness they missed their way and entered Rombies, where they were fired upon by the enemy. In the early morning of November 5th the Battalion moved off and crossed the Aunelle at Le Pissot. An artillery barrage had been arranged to deal with the enemy on the high ground east of the river, and, following this, the 169th Brigade at 7.30 a.m. captured the village of Angreau, but were unable to get beyond it. Roisin was taken by the 11th Division on the right, but on the 168th Brigade front the enemy held out in determined fashion. At 8.40 a.m. A Company of the Kensingtons established contact with the Canadians on their left and the Scottish on the right, the latter having gained the high ground, found machine-gun fire from the direction of Angre a barrier to further advance. B Company was sent forward to join A Company, C and D Companies remaining in support. The forward positions were found, however, to be untenable in face of the intense fire from both machine guns and artillery. There was no cover of any description, and the enemy fire made digging-in impossible. However, the capture of Rombies by the Canadians eased the situation, and by nightfall the Kensingtons and the London Scottish had advanced the line to the west of the village of Angre and the Grande Honnelle River. C Company established a post with two machine guns, in contact with a similar post of the Canadians, which was engaging an enemy post, and D Company moved forward to locate the Scottish at 10 p.m., but was fired on from the direction of the river and thereupon dug in on a line facing the enemy.

The following day, November 6th, saw the last battle of the Great War for the Kensingtons, and proved an exhausting day for men who had been in the open, continually on the move, with no opportunity for proper sleep, for three days and nights. The enemy was prepared to resist the passage of the River Grande Honnelle, and in the early morning a heavy barrage of gas shell compelled the attacking troops to don gas helmets. At 5.30 a.m. the attack commenced with the 169th Brigade on the right and the 168th on the left. The former brigade, on crossing the river, encountered heavy fire from the Bois de Beaufort, which was held by the enemy in force. They made little progress during the day. The 168th Brigade, with the Kensingtons and London Scottish in line, advanced towards the river bank at 5.30 a.m., the Canadians operating on the Battalion's left, the Scottish on the right. A and C Companies of the Kensingtons, leading the Battalion advance, had special orders to maintain touch with units on the flanks, A Company with the Canadians, and C Company with the Scottish. Heavy shell fire fell upon the whole line of advance, and machine guns across the river were particularly active against these two companies, A Company finding its advance seriously impeded. C Company extended and directed covering fire on the enemy posts in order to assist the advance of A Company. The firing was so intense that great difficulty was experienced in gaining touch with the Canadians, and Captain H. B. Perry, who set out in an endeavour to locate them, was fired upon from a German machine-gun post and killed. C Company, however, was able to subdue the enemy on its immediate front, and at 6.30 a.m. crossed the river and entered the village of Angre, being joined by A Company, which had crossed by the same route. Moving ahead, C Company succeeded in reaching the high ground to the east of the village, and there got in touch with the London Scottish on its right, and A Company was soon in position on its left. D Company was now moved up in support, and, reaching the village, two platoons were sent round the northern outskirts, where they found the enemy still in possession.

The Germans now rallied and delivered a counter-attack which compelled C Company of the London Scottish to withdraw to the river and back across the bridge. The flank of the two companies of the Kensingtons was thus exposed, and they fell back to conform with the new line. C Company, however, left a strong post on the bridge while the remainder of the Company withdrew to the west bank of the river. A Company, following, took up a position on the right of C Company. The village was heavily shelled at this juncture by enemy artillery. In the meantime D Company was still on the east side of the river close to the village, and, pushing on, they surprised what was at this time a large body of the enemy, numbering about 150. The Kensingtons at once opened fire, but the Germans were in no mood for fighting and at once scattered, but not before a considerable number had been hit by rifle fire. About 70 were made prisoners. This enterprise on the part of D Company cleared the situation about the village, and A and C Companies again crossed the bridge and were soon in possession of the high ground to the east of Angre. The time was now 8.30 a.m., the village was securely held, and a strong line established to the east of it in touch with the Scottish. Of the Canadians on the left, nothing was known and all efforts to locate them failed. Battalion Headquarters was moved into the village and took shelter in the cellars of the church, for the enemy artillery again shelled the village heavily. The telephone line to Brigade was broken in several places, and communication was maintained by the aid of wireless.

During the afternoon the artillery attached to the 168th Brigade fired on what was believed to be the enemy positions on the east of the village. Unfortunately the shells all fell on the Battalion outpost line, compelling a withdrawal until the lifting of the barrage permitted its re-establishment. At nightfall B Company, which had been on the west of the river during the day, was ordered to cross the river and extend the line to the left and link up with the Canadians. This they did, but though two platoons were despatched in different directions, they located the enemy, but not the Canadians. The state of affairs on this flank was still shrouded in mystery when the Kensingtons left the front. Guides had been ordered to Sebourquiaux during the evening to meet the Drake Battalion of the Royal Naval Division, and at 3 in the morning of the 7th a weary but triumphant Battalion handed over their

OPEN WARFARE AND THE END

positions and marched away from the fighting line through the mud and the darkness for the last time.

In this last battle the Kensingtons had lost 2 officers and 9 other ranks killed, and 2nd Lieut. J. H. N. Wright and 30 other ranks wounded. Their captures included 80 prisoners and 16 machine guns. The weather had been atrocious and the men were worn out, but the advance was forging ahead and a prolonged halt was impossible. After one night in billets in Sebourquiaux, on the 8th the Battalion marched to Autreppe, on the 9th to Erquennes where a particularly good welcome was received from the inhabitants, and on the 10th to Rieu de Bury. The 167th Brigade, attacking, had gone forward on the 7th, clearing the Bois de Beaufort, which had been strongly defended by the enemy and reached the village of Montignies. The enemy resistance now stiffened somewhat and compelled a brief halt, but during the night, fires and explosions behind his lines indicated evacuation, and on the 8th he was found to be in full retreat, and little opposition was encountered. It became a steady march east, Maubeuge had fallen, and Mons was within reach. By November 10th the 56th Division, preceded by cavalry, had reached Harmignies, and there they were ordered to halt while the 63rd Division carried on the advance.

Thus, halted in the different frontier villages, thankful to be in billets with the opportunity to rest awhile, the units of the London Division received the Cease Fire order for 11 a.m. on November 11th.

It was received by the Kensingtons in Rieu de Bury with a deep sense of thankfulness, but no great display of emotion. It meant too much to men who had endured as they had, and thoughts of comrades who had helped to achieve this day, but who lay in hastily dug graves scattered over the whole area of operations between the Lys and the Somme, intruded, as they always will on the anniversary of this day of relief from war.

It is doubtful if the advance could have continued much longer at the same pace. During the whole of the November fighting, the 56th Divisional railhead had been at Aubigny au Bac, and the convoys of lorries were confronted with a journey which, each day, was miles longer than it had been on the preceding day. Roads, in spite of the constant efforts of the labour battalions, were fast deteriorating. The difficulties confronting the railway engineers were enormous, and it was a remarkable achievement that by the 10th the line from Arras to Valenciennes was repaired. Not only had the bridges been demolished by the retreating enemy, but joints between consecutive sections of rails had been bent up by well-placed bombs and re-laying was necessary over long sections of metal. Arras was thronged with men discharged from hospital, and reinforcements, all vainly endeavouring to find the whereabouts of their Divisions. When a crowded train did ultimately leave for a railhead, a further problem ensued in finding the location of the particular unit.

The days immediately following the Armistice passed quietly. There was no longer any need for training for battle, and the general shortage of supplies prohibited much re-equipping of the men, badly as they needed it. There was plenty of other work to do, however, in repairing roads and cleaning up. The men were able to make themselves tolerably comfortable in billets, but the food shortage, both among the troops and the civilian population, prevented any celebrations centring round a hearty meal. A Brigade service of thanksgiving for the cessation of hostilities was held on the 17th at Sars le Bruyère, and on the 22nd a party of 10 officers and 13 other ranks, under Major M. A. Prismall, proceeded to the Mons battlefield, where a description of the battle in that area on August 23rd, 1914, was given by Brig.-General Elkington, who had fought there on that date. For him the wheel had truly come full circle. The Kensingtons also sent a party to join in the triumphal entry into Mons on November 15th. Under Captain G. A. Beggs, 3 officers and 80 other ranks took part in the First Army march through the town. Some comment was made by members of the party on the lack of enthusiasm of the crowds. There was no cheering. The populace were either too overcome with joy to give vent to their feelings in the customary manner, or else their phlegmatic characteristics asserted themselves on this, for them, remarkable occasion. In any case, it made an unfavourable impression on the men.

The sound of the guns had hardly died away before rumour was busy as to the probability of the 56th Division marching to the Rhine and forming part of the army of occupation under the terms of the Armistice. The rumour was confirmed by preliminary orders that the Division would move on the 17th and, marching for thirty days, arrive on the Rhine at the conclusion of the thirty-six-day Armistice. Hot on the heels of this came further orders, more gratifying still, that the journey would not be by route march, but by train from Valenciennes. However, it was not to be, for the 56th Division as a whole remained in approximately the same area until demobilised, and the London Scottish, selected to represent the London Division on the Rhine, left for Germany in January 1919.

On November 27th the Kensingtons left Rieu de Bury and marched to Villers sire Nicole, where they remained for a month, a month which was enjoyed to the full, covering as it did the last Christmas season overseas. The inhabitants made the men welcome in their billets and, with skilful cooking, made the meagre army rations palatable, for the transport situation was still acute and the food supplied was just enough for a bare subsistence. The civilians were even more short of food than the troops, and the men were glad to share what they had with Madame in return for her services as cook and needlewoman. As Christmas drew near there was some anxiety on the score of the provision of seasonable fare for this, the best Christmas yet, with its real message of "Peace on earth." Individuals with well-known "scrounging" propensities were despatched into the blue by the various messes with a supply of cash to convert into food and drink. Their efforts were successful enough to ensure a Christmas dinner which, reigned over and shared in by Madame, was satisfactory in every way. The Quartermaster miraculously produced a small supply of 1914 rum, a potent vintage in which the health of the Regiment was drunk. Rain had fallen heavily in the days preceding Christmas, but on Christmas night it turned to snow, and the footprints of homeward-bound Kensingtons were not found to be in straight lines when viewed in the cold morning light of Boxing Day.

Sport and education served to pass away the wintry days. G.H.Q., which had first thought of education in the preceding summer, now thought that the men should be prepared to resume civil life, and after much correspondence, equalling in volume that hitherto devoted to orders for battle, the scheme came into being. Under the control of an Education Officer, qualified instructors taught the three R's, modern languages, and science in an improvised school. The idea underlying the scheme was a good one, but the upheavals caused by the frequent change of billeting area and later the disorganisation introduced by demobilisation interfered with that continuity of teaching and study without which any system of education is doomed to failure. The afternoons were devoted to sport, and some well-contested Soccer matches were played. On December 27th a very successful concert was arranged in the hall of the village school. Among other items, a clever pantomime entitled *Babes in the Wood*, presented by the Signal Section, drew much applause. Interspersed with songs specially written for the occasion, the dialogue rich in humorous references to life in the army, the effort was a worthy expression of the spirit of comradeship that prevailed in the various sections of the Battalion, a spirit that had so largely contributed to the fine *esprit de corps* of the Kensingtons.

Opportunity occurred, in the close contact with the peasants which was necessarily made, to discover what the war had meant to these people in the invaded territory. Food had become terribly deficient towards the end, and the only meat many of them had was derived by breeding rabbits, and these had to be concealed from the Germans.

Coffee was non-existent, and roasted wheat was used as a substitute; for sugar they extracted a sugary syrup by boiling down slices of sugar-beet, a favourite crop in this territory. Many had made friends with the Germans billeted on them and had thus enjoyed preferential treatment. They now reaped their full meed of scorn from their neighbours, and the " Greffier " of the village, a sort of village clerk, well known to have gained favours by his partiality for the invaders, fled one night before a massed attack on his house by the villagers, who had long awaited this opportunity. The people all agreed in their stories of the loss of morale by the Germans. There had been much talk of revolution and, towards the end, the infantry, ordered to attack the oncoming British, had been mutinous.

On December 28th the Battalion was ordered to move to Quevy le Grand and on January 16th to Givry. In neither of these villages was there a welcome from the inhabitants. Many of them refused accommodation to the men, and it was not until the Maire was called in to talk to them that they grudgingly complied. They regarded the British soldier as another type of foreigner come to disturb them. In one billet an N.C.O. was compelled to sleep on the stone floor of the kitchen, and in the early hours of the morning the disgruntled woman would proceed to swill the floor with water and commence to scrub, disregarding his blankets and other possessions. In excuse for such a poor reception one can only conclude that they had received bad treatment from the Germans and had, as yet, no opportunity to find out the accommodating character of the British " Tommy." In conjunction with other incidents, however, it created a bad impression in the minds of the men, who concluded, naturally, that it arose from a partiality for the departed Germans and that, perhaps, the Belgians had been spoilt by the kindness and pity that the whole world had showered upon them.

With the coming of the new year, the thought uppermost in the minds of all was that of home. Bearing in mind the fact that most of the men had had no leave for a year, a year that had been so crowded with incident that in retrospect it seemed like two, it was but natural that home ties should assert themselves and hopes of a speedy demobilisation be aroused. Thoughts, now that the war cloud had lifted, turned to civilian life and work, and many wondered if the post that was supposed to be kept open for them was still vacant.

And so, classified in groups according to employment, the Kensingtons slipped away as demobilisation allotments came through, to be scattered throughout London and the Provinces. Certain groups had priority over others, but with a few men leaving each day, the number on the strength in Givry dwindled until a mere skeleton of the Battalion remained, designated the Cadre. The departing Kensingtons, after a hasty farewell, proceeded to Mons, where the troop train carried them in leisurely fashion to the concentration camps at Dunkerque or Calais, and here, after a clean up and the issue of new clothing, they embarked for England where they passed through demobilisation camps. There was to be no spectacular homecoming of the Battalion as a whole, no marching up the High Street behind the drums to the well-known Battalion March, as so many had hoped.

Thus the Kensington Battalion, a mere shadow of its former self, lived on at Givry enjoying sports, with Corps and Divisional race meetings at Mons, until March, when the Cadre moved to Cuesmes, a suburb of Mons. On May 16th, 1919, only 5 officers and 32 other ranks strong, under the command of Major M. A. Prismall, it moved to Antwerp and sailed on the S.S. *Sicilian* for Tilbury on the 20th, there awaiting the arrival of the transport vehicles which followed on the S.S. *Calix*. After spending a night at the Guards' Camp at Purfleet, this small band entrained for Newhaven, and on the 27th left for Kensington, where a civic reception was accorded. The colours, which had been in safe custody at the Town Hall since 1914 and recently despatched to the Cadre in Belgium, were now brought home again to Headquarters. Her Royal Highness,

OPEN WARFARE AND THE END

Princess Louise, was awaiting the Cadre in the drill-hall and, in welcoming the Battalion home again, said how proudly she had followed the fortunes of her Regiment throughout the war. Sir William Davison, K.B.E., Mayor of the Royal Borough, was present in his official capacity, and with an enthusiastic crowd of Old Comrades accorded the home-comers a hearty reception.

The 1st Battalion of the Kensingtons was home again. The Battalion had spent more than four and a half years in France, had been through fourteen battles, and had endured long periods of trench warfare in rain, frost, and sun. Throughout the long campaign all ranks had proved themselves worthy to bear the arms of the Royal Borough of Kensington, for they had truly lived up to the motto

QUID NOBIS ARDUI.

3RD BATTALION OFFICERS

Standing (Left to Right).—E. A. R. Wilson, N. O. C. Mackenzie, W. G. Mager, F. B. Goddard, H. G. L. Prynne, L. B. Bluett, N. J. Ims, G. K. Clifford, L. T. Elvy, C. S. David, C. T. Tate, J. P. Williams, L. B. Hawkes, A. F. Moss, E. R. Kisch, G. P. Bryer.
Sitting (Left to Right).—A. E. Watts, Capt. E. C. Bratt, Capt. M. R. Harris, Capt. C. M. Miller, Capt. R. Spofforth, Major V. Flower, Lieut.-Col. H. Lumley Webb, Major C. M. Mackenzie, Capt. F. H. Ware, Capt. H. Graves, Capt. C. N. Joseph, Lieut. W. A. Morgan.
On the Ground (Left to Right).—C. M. B. Byles, S. L. Vincent, P. E. Leggett, A. de F. Macmin, A. W. Tosland.

THE 2ND BATTALION
By H. M. HOLLIER

THE 2ND BATTALION

By H. M. HOLLIER

CHAPTER XVIII

ENGLAND—FORMATION AND TRAINING

THE 2/13th Battalion London Regiment, like all second-line units of the Territorial Force, owed its existence to the Great War and closed its short but vigorous history shortly after the termination of hostilities. Born of a national crisis, it grew swiftly into lusty manhood, both eager and ready to plunge into the welter of great events which reverberated through the world; was held, restless and impatient, for nearly two long years in the fields and plains of the Homeland, and finally plunged into an overseas military career lasting some thirty-odd months, during which its members trod a multitude of foreign fields such as fell to the lot of few other units of Great Britain's Forces to cover.

With no early history of its own, the 2/13th was bound by ties of duty and affection to its senior battalion, of whose years of honourable service to the Crown it was very proud, and the fact that the formation and training of the Second Battalion was undertaken entirely by serving and time-expired members of the former naturally strengthened the ties that bound together the two battalions of Kensingtons. Although the fortunes of war never threw the two sister battalions together in the field, they were never far from each other in thought, and especially during the interminable days of training in England, the welfare and progress of the First Battalion was ever the first concern of the men, held long against their will, or necessity, at home. As the process of supplying drafts for the Kensingtons in

France began and proceeded, this feeling deepened, and continued to the end. . . .

By a singular coincidence, the outbreak of war found the majority of the Territorial Army already in uniform and under canvas—the annual training camps having just begun. The Kensingtons were indeed recalled from Salisbury Plain to await the call for mobilisation at Headquarters, so that the night of August 4th, 1914, found the drill-hall at Adam and Eve Mews, Kensington, filled with men clad in the khaki that (they little dreamed!) they were not to doff for four and a half years. The Battalion was much under strength, and recruiting commenced at once.

The response was overwhelming, and the deficiency in strength was made up as quickly as attestation forms could be completed and the men passed through the medical inspection. It was at that moment that the 2/13th came into being. Whilst the First Battalion enjoyed the first hardships of a soldier's life, billeted in the local schools and route-marching through the sober squares of South Kensington and the wildly enthusiastic High Street, the men who were to form the Second Battalion of the Kensingtons were queuing up in the drill-hall, where Captain Lesser was feverishly working against time at the job of attestation, or were similarly engaged at the Town Hall, where Major MacLean had the same work in hand. Many of the men, therefore, made a very early acquaintance with that choleric but dearly-loved man who was to command the Battalion throughout nearly the whole of the long period that was destined to elapse before it finally left England.

Once accepted and sworn in, the immediate daily life of those first members of the 2/13th was exactly similar to that of their (judged more fortunate) colleagues who had succeeded in obtaining entry to the First Battalion—already described in the History of the 1/13th Battalion.

It can be said, without fear of contradiction and without boastfulness, that no finer body of men could be found than those who so promptly and enthusiastically answered the call to the Colours in those early days of '14. Their physique must have gladdened the hearts of the drill instructors, but did not, however, deter the latter from indulging in the traditional forms of " frightfulness " so dear to the heart of the Sergeant-major! The awkwardness of those very " awkward squads " must have been maddening on those long, hot August days, but what the recruits lacked in training was abundantly made up by their enthusiasm, and if their instructors found them exasperating at times, they were nevertheless very proud of the manner in which their charges acquitted themselves as the days wore on.

Many of the recruits were never intended for the Kensingtons at all, but had applied at other Territorial Headquarters, and, becoming tired of waiting as the weary process of attestation dragged on, had hurried down to Kensington, where the work was perhaps proceeding more expeditiously. Hence the presence of many in the Battalion who had no local connections at all; men who had left City offices determined to join up that day, and had visited one headquarters after another before being accepted at Kensington. There they were quickly at home, and in congenial company quickly became as good Kensingtons as any born within the sound of St. Mary Abbots' bells. It is to the lasting credit of Captain Lesser that the work of recruitment was carried forward so smoothly at the 13th Headquarters that both battalions were brought up to full strength in an amazingly short time.

Major MacLean was appointed to the command of the Battalion with Major H. Lumley-Webb as second-in-command. The grounds of Holland House furnished the drill-ground for the Battalion, the members of which continued to disperse nightly to their homes, until November 10th, when the White City was made available for troops, and thither the 2/13th moved, to live together for the first time as a complete unit, and from that date Army life proper may be said to have commenced. The First Battalion, having meanwhile completed a period of intensive and exceedingly hard training at Abbots Langley, in

Hertfordshire, left for France early in November, being among the first of the Territorial Battalions to strengthen the British Forces on that front. It left behind a small company of men, some of whom for various reasons had seen fit to decline to serve overseas, and some who were temporarily on the sick list, or who were too young to go abroad. This party was ordered to join their second-line comrades and arrived at the White City under the command of Captain G. Thompson, where their complete equipment aroused the envy of the Second Battalion men, some of whom were still clad in uniforms purchased by themselves.

Training at the White City, although perforce stricter than during the earlier care-free days at Holland House, was still very easy, although the innovation of the pre-breakfast run was not popular, and soon considerable numbers learned how easy it was to miss it. Here a great many men undertook their first guard duties, and everyone made his first acquaintance with that awful and sickly concoction known as " Gun-fire." " Beds " were provided which consisted of three planks laid on two small trestles, together with a straw palliasse; and although many men found these but poor comfort after the beds of home, days were to come when they would have been considered the acme of comfort, and, indeed, decidedly effeminate.

Evening and week-end leave was plentiful, and as Shepherd's Bush and Hammersmith furnished much in the way of amenities dear to the heart of a soldier (to say nothing of other and even brighter places but a twopenny fare away), life was very congenial. Whatever it lacked as an ideal training camp for troops, the White City lent itself most admirably to that species of torture known as " Kit Inspection " and its allied amusements, and however rudimentary their general training there may have been, the men of the Second Battalion mastered that part of a soldier's duties thoroughly. The dressing of the long lines of little beds in those great halls was checked and counter-checked in a manner that must have proved extremely satisfying to those of the warrant officers and N.C.O.s who found life's keenest

ENGLAND—FORMATION AND TRAINING

pleasure lay in straight lines. Be that as it may, the 2/13th formed habits of tidiness which they never quite lost afterwards, and which is an important trait in a soldier.

The preparation of East Coast defences was actively in hand during this period, and in common with many other Territorial units, the Battalion was called upon to furnish very large trench-digging parties for this work. These parties, with haversack rations, entrained early in the morning at Uxbridge Road Station, from where they were taken down into Essex for the day's work. On detraining, a short march would be made to the engineers' dump and tools drawn and working parties formed. The weather conditions were generally very bad, and as the work chiefly consisted of trench-digging in almost solid clay, it is to be feared that often the results achieved at the end of the day hardly seemed to warrant the long journey from the other, and extreme, end of London. However, the journeys were pleasant enough, and great were the cheers that daily greeted the passing of Clarnico's factory, where the hundreds of girl employees used to line the windows, gaily cheering, waving, and blowing kisses to the troops *en route* to the Essex front! Whether the trenches that were dug (and which immediately filled with water) were ever intended to be occupied, or whether the work was all part of the general scheme of training, was never ascertained; but if the trenches as a defensive system may be questioned, the value of the training was real, for no other reason than that it accustomed the men to conditions that approximated more to the real thing than anything hitherto encountered.

Three exciting incidents disturbed the even tenor of life at the White City. The first was the call for a draft to go out to the First Battalion in France. This draft included all original members of the First Battalion who had been invalided from Abbots Langley and were now fit, together with the first men of the Second Battalion selected for active service. Naturally there was intense competition to be among the chosen, and many were the " personal interviews " requested in order to lay before Lieut.-

"THE KENSINGTONS"

Colonel MacLean the applicants' sound reasons for being included. The draft, however, was a small one; it had a stirring send-off, and its going served to sharpen the anticipations of the Battalion of an active share in the war, and focused the minds of all at the White City across the Channel, to where the 1/13th were already fighting a grim battle with the mud of Flanders.

The second wave of excitement came in December, when German cruisers bombarded Scarborough. The air was electric; rumours of invasion flew round, all leave was stopped, and visions of occupying those awful trenches so recently dug in Essex began to fill the minds of the 2/13th. The excitement passed, but the stopping of Christmas leave put a real damper on the spirits of the troops. Had it not been for this confinement, however, the Battalion would have missed one of the most impressive, and delightful, moments of the war. Chief of the legacies which the First Battalion had to leave to their newly formed sister battalion was the band of the Kensingtons ; it was, rightly, the pride of the regiment, a band such as few Territorial units possessed, and an asset which Colonel MacLean valued highly and used, be it said, on every possible occasion to the utmost advantage!

By prearrangement, the band had risen and paraded very early on Christmas morning, and whilst it was still dark outside, the lights were switched on and shone down upon the hundreds of sleeping Kensingtons, who awoke to hear the strains of "Christians, Awake!" sweeping gently through the great halls, softly at first, but swelling louder and louder. The bewildered men sat up in their beds, rubbing their eyes and wondering where they were. No one who was present on that occasion can ever forget the almost painful sweetness of those first moments, when the soft strains of the well-known tune stole upon their awakening consciousness. Not a word was uttered. Men lay quietly back on their funny little beds and gave themselves up to thoughts of home, of families left behind, of parents, wives, or sweethearts, from whom they were parted—perhaps for ever. The music ceased; the spell was broken and the familiar murmur of voices broke out. The "interlude" was brief, a mere drop in the ocean of time that was to measure the long war, but while it lasted it was very beautiful. The 2/13th never forgot it and their gratitude to the band lasted always.

The third incident was concerned with the march of the Battalion to the Tower to draw rifles. True, they were Lee-Enfields and in no way to be compared with the short service rifles that were "the real thing," but they were rifles, and their possession meant that civilians in uniform became soldiers. The march, from Shepherd's Bush to the Tower and back, was a long one, and was carried out with the fullest display of military ardour that the Battalion could muster. Colonel MacLean was a proud man riding at the head of his fine regiment through the busy thoroughfares of the West End and the City, with the famous band of the Kensingtons giving of its best. Woe betide the ignorant citizen who tried to break through the line of marching men; one such unfortunate aroused the full ire of the Colonel, and was compelled to march for miles between a guard of four men. The populace was at that time still full of enthusiasm, and altogether the march proved a great tonic to the Battalion.

In the middle of January 1915, orders were received to proceed to Maidstone, and the Battalion entrained at Addison Road for the Kentish capital, and on arrival were allocated to their first billets. This proved a very pleasant experience, and to their great surprise the 2/13th found themselves sleeping between sheets once more. Training, carried out chiefly in Moat Park, became sterner, but the men were becoming hardened and bore it all lightly. One may perhaps except a certain famous march from Maidstone to Rochester and back, a distance of some twenty-two miles. It was Colonel MacLean's delight to accompany the Battalion on route marches, but on this occasion he was held in Maidstone by other duties, and the Battalion was under the command of Major Thompson. It proved a very gruelling day and easily the hardest experience of the 2/13th at that time. They managed it successfully, but only just. The gallant Colonel was out on the road to meet the incoming Battalion in the evening, and was plainly very concerned as to the condition in which they would march in. If he had any qualms, they were baseless, and the Battalion proudly made the first notch on a long list of famous marches that it was destined to undertake before the end of the war.

The Battalion was called upon to provide another draft for the First Battalion from Maidstone, and many early friendships were perforce severed. Few of the men who formed those early drafts for France ever saw their colleagues of the 2/13th again. A good deal of wet weather was naturally experienced at this time of the year, and many were the hours spent in musketry and other instruction in Foster Clarke's empty factory at Maidstone. Time began to hang a little drearily, and although the billets were generally very good, few in the Battalion were particularly sorry when the time came to leave Maidstone, especially as a return was made (surprisingly) to London. The second sojourn in town was a very short one, but they were halcyon days indeed, for the Battalion was billeted in a number of private hotels and boarding-houses in South Kensington, not merely the empty shells of houses, but all occupied by their usual inhabitants. The latter, far from resenting this intrusion, gave the troops a warm welcome and treated them generously, and even luxuriously. The Battalion lived in sumptuous style for several days, indulging in a little training in Hyde Park and a number of route marches through the populous thoroughfares of West London. A very fair proportion of the residents in the private hotels that formed the 2/13th's billets were dear old ladies who were plainly thrilled at this close contact with the war, and did their best to spoil their gallant and temporary fellow-boarders, so that it was perhaps as well that the Battalion soon moved out of London to a fresh training area, this time at Leatherhead.

ENGLAND—FORMATION AND TRAINING

Quarters were again found in private billets, and life was very happy and comfortable. The open commons of the area provided excellent training ground, and with improving weather conditions, greater opportunities were provided for the officers to develop their tactical knowledge, and as a result the daily work became far more interesting to everyone. The men were in fine fettle, although leave was now far more restricted than formerly.

At the end of April 1915, the Battalion moved once more. The new (60th) London Division, of which the 2/13th was a part, concentrated in the St. Albans area, the Kensingtons being billeted in Watford. On May 2nd the newly formed Transport Section, which had already received separate training at Westerham, drew horses from St. Albans. Things were taking shape and the Battalion now looked very workmanlike. Curiously enough, the present billets were located but a few miles from Abbots Langley, where the 1/13th had undergone its severe ten-weeks' training, and by taking a pleasant walk across the fields, the curious could find the old Company Headquarters and other landmarks still chalked on farm gates. As if to emphasise this nearness, the news of the Kensingtons' engagement at Aubers Ridge on May 9th followed swiftly on the Battalion's arrival at Watford. At an impressive parade in Clarendon Park, Colonel MacLean read out the glorious but heartrending news of the achievements of the senior Battalion, which, in covering itself with "imperishable glory," was practically wiped out, with losses of 500 killed and wounded. This tragic news only served to render the men of the 2/13th more eager than ever to get out and take their part "over there," but another twelve long months were destined to pass before the call came.

On June 7th, 1915, the Battalion was ordered to Saffron Walden, in Essex, and this journey was accomplished by march, occupying four days. Service conditions prevailed, and the Battalion slept on succeeding nights at Ware and Hertford in barns and any similar accommodation that could be found. The weather was hot and the march proved a severe trial, despite the long months of training, without which, indeed, it would never have been accomplished so successfully as it was. Arriving at Saffron Walden on June 10th, the Battalion moved into billets once again, and commenced a five-months' stay in the sleepy old Quaker centre. After a few weeks a camp was prepared close to the town, and here the 2/13th found themselves under canvas for the first time. It proved a very happy experience. Training was now much harder, although it never approached the rigours undergone by the First Battalion in those now far-off days at Abbots Langley. The other three units of the "Grey Brigade" were also under canvas in the same camp, and a good deal of field training was undertaken.

Colonel MacLean's song, "The Uniform Grey," had long been adopted as the regimental march, and its familiar strains were soon whistled by every errand boy in Saffron Walden. A good deal of amusement was got out of the dear old Colonel's well-known irritation at the near presence of the London Scottish (the 2/14th), which was shared to a hardly less extent by his peppery Adjutant, Captain David Devis. Both officers were deeply respected, and both were excellent soldiers, but they possessed in common an explosive temper that was frequently aired in public, sometimes to the chagrin and sometimes to the amusement of the troops—it all depended on the situation! On one occasion when both battalions were out on the march the London Scottish, by accident or design, just cut across the Kensingtons' line of march, causing the Battalion to halt for some moments and inhale the considerable dust raised by their rivals; it proved, however, to be nothing to the "vocal dust" raised by the choleric Colonel a little later, when he got the 2/13th halted in mass and told them just what he thought of them for allowing such an insult to his *amour propre!*

Later that summer the Division took part in manœuvres, marching out of camp one cold morning in September to repel "invaders" advancing from Billericay. The Kensingtons were absent three days, during which they marched

2ND BATTALION OFFICERS

Back Row (Left to Right).—2nd-Lieut. H. Gordon Clark, 2nd-Lieut. L. C. Gates, 2nd-Lieut. W. Read, Lieut. F. R. Rosevear, Lieut. L. F. Baker, Lieut. S. M. Green, 2nd-Lieut. K. A. S. Rivington, 2nd-Lieut. A. S. Lancaster, 2nd-Lieut. R. P. Shute.

Front Row (Left to Right).—Capt. the Rev. C. R. Harding, Lieut. Quartermaster A. C. Cattermole, Capt. R. P. Gladstone, Capt. P. M. Slade, Major P. A. Hopkins, Lieut.-Col. W. R. J. McLean, T.D., Capt. and Adj. W. E. David-Devis, Capt. C. E. Brockhurst, Capt. G. W. Collier, Capt. C. T. Foster, Capt. A. G. T. Hanks (M.O.).

Inset.—Lieut.-Col. C. M. Mackenzie.

[219]

and "fought" under service conditions, an experience which proved stiff but interesting, and from which they emerged, it was thought, not without credit. But the months were passing, the war was dragging on, and the Battalion was becoming rather fed-up at its rôle to date, and in danger of becoming stale. It was, therefore, with general relief that at last came the news that they were not, after all, to be buried at Saffron Walden "for duration," and on November 9th a light-hearted Battalion set out on the march south to Sawbridgeworth, albeit it was still in Essex, a county they were heartily tired of. The weather was surprisingly good for November, and the two-day trek proved uneventful. Once more the Battalion found itself in billets, for which it was very thankful, as the weather changed and was mainly wet during its two-months' stay in the village.

A series of N.C.O.'s promotion classes were held at Saffron Walden and Sawbridgeworth, in which Colonel MacLean took the keenest personal interest, and these were responsible for the quickening of interest on the part of many fine men in the ranks, whose early enthusiasm had been dulled by the mechanical routine of the endless months. The subsequent examinations were compiled and conducted by Colonel MacLean with unflagging zeal, and, despite his advancing years, a light could be seen burning in his office into the small hours for many nights on end. The fine old gentleman put in a tremendous amount of good work for his beloved regiment both before and after that time, but perhaps none of it was more valuable than the work he did in those dark days of the winter of 1915, when he set himself to build up a splendid body of non-commissioned officers who were to serve the Battalion in good stead in the trying days ahead. Not that he neglected his officers, whom he also trained to a fine pitch, and who bore his choleric outbursts with equanimity, knowing him for a leader whom they could respect and serve and love to the end.

That end, alas! was not far distant, for when, in January 1916, the 60th Division was called to Warminster, on Salisbury Plain, to undergo its final training and reconditioning prior to departure overseas, the time came for Colonel MacLean to part company with the 2/13th, the Battalion he had himself largely attested in August 1914, and for whom, and with whom, he had since lived his entire life. It was quite a personal bereavement for the Battalion, but it had to be, for the Colonel was obviously too old to undertake the hardships that lay ahead, although, as he confessed, with tears in his eyes, he had himself " moved heaven and earth " to go to France, but " those damned old women at the War Office " thought he was too old.

The departure of the Battalion from Sawbridgeworth, which furnished the last inhabited billets occupied during the war, seemed to sever the one remaining link with civilian life, and from that time onwards the men became " pukka " soldiers. Life in the great training camps outside the town of Warminster needs little description, and the lot of the 2nd Kensingtons was the same as that which fell to hundreds of other units on the Plain. The Battalion was actually quartered near the village of Sutton Veney, but the whole country-side was so overrun with camps and dumps of the Army that all but the merest vestige of civilian occupation had long been lost to sight, and the little group of cottages and tumbledown buildings which formed the village appeared utterly out of place amid the endless lines of huts which encircled them.

The almost total lack of local amusements kept the men in camp and threw them together much more than formerly. It was surprising to find how little the men of one company knew the men of another; one would become used to familiar faces seen always on parade with another company, but the billeting system had tended to keep the companies apart, and unless a man had friends in other companies, he knew surprisingly little about any other than his own. For officers and N.C.O.s, of course, the mess began to play an important part in their lives. Life was much harder in Camp and far less congenial in many respects, but the sense of comradeship quickened considerably, and altogether the period spent at Warminster was immensely valuable to all ranks. The command of the Battalion was taken over by Lieut.-Colonel C. M. Mackenzie, D.S.O., O.B.E., a First Battalion officer who had returned from France. With his quiet voice and meditative habits he appeared the very antithesis of the late Commanding Officer, but the Battalion quickly sensed in him the qualities of a soldier, and he became popular in a very short space of time. The 2/13th was certainly fortunate in the choice of Commanding Officers.

There was a feeling in the air that the time was nigh, and this was quickened by the arrival of drafts from the H.A.C. and the Artists' Rifles to make the Battalion up to overseas strength. The physique of these men was astoundingly good, and there is no doubt that their arrival strengthened the Kensingtons in every way. The feeling that France was drawing near was heightened by the formation of a Snipers' Section, chosen from the best shots in each company. Nevertheless, another three months passed away, and the 2/13th was beginning to wonder if once again it had been "forgotten" when there occurred a dramatic interlude to its training which threw everyone into a ferment and acted as a curtain-raiser before it took the stage in real earnest. This was the Easter Week rebellion in Ireland, when the Irish rebels so nearly threw a monkey wrench into the Empire's machinery of war. Nipped firmly before it did much damage, the rebellion was yet touch and go for a few days, and the 2/13th was called from Salisbury Plain to cross to Ireland and take a hand in quelling the trouble.

At 3 a.m. on April 28th the Battalion marched out of camp, to entrain at Warminster with no knowledge of its destination. Dawn revealed to the astonished eyes of the men the platform of Cardiff Station, and later they arrived at Neyland, the station for Pembroke Dock. Here the Battalion encamped by the seashore, where it spent Sunday and was an interested spectator of the towing in of a submarine, whether British or German it knew not. Late that afternoon, it embarked on H.M.S. *Snowden*, and as it steamed down Milford Haven in the gathering dusk, many thought that they were having a last glimpse of the Old Country. The bewitching beauty of Queenstown Harbour under a glittering sun greeted them the following morning, and a few hours later they marched through the crowded streets of Cork City to the boos and cat-calls of a hostile populace. Arrived at Fota Park, the weary and thirsty troops were issued with a mess tin of real old Dublin stout. Drunk under the rays of a hot sun, the somewhat amusing result was to put the entire Battalion to sleep in a very short time! That night they encamped at Coachford in tents that had been left standing by a battalion called away for service farther north, and the following day commenced one of the hardest marches in their history. Oh! those Irish " miles." A " kip down " in bare barracks at Ballincollig preceded another eighteen-mile march to the market town of Macroom, where they encamped within the Castle Grounds. The attitude of the inhabitants necessitated strict and armed guards being mounted here, where the Battalion lay for six days. The duties consisted in providing armed parties to escort the sorely tried members of the R.I.C., who were busily rounding up known rebels. The work took place entirely at night, long marches being carried out in complete silence to isolated farmhouses, usually reached just prior to dawn, which was heralded by the worthy sergeant of R.I.C. hammering on the door and demanding the inmates to " Open in the King's name !"

The next march was to Mill Street, a straggling little town in Co. Cork, reputed to be the headquarters of the most desperate of the fleeing rebels. For three days the Battalion was without regular rations, and to add to the general discomfort the blanket convoy broke down some sixteen miles from camp, whilst the weather was wretched, the men being drenched to the skin half the time. Similar escort duties to those at Macroom were carried out, and the acute misery of those night tramps into the Bochtagh Mountains was seldom excelled in later experiences. However, the back of the rebellion was by now broken, and on

ENGLAND—FORMATION AND TRAINING

May 14th the 2/13th were recalled and, returning via Rosslare and Fishguard, arrived back at Warminster on the 17th. It had proved a wonderfully interesting and useful experience and was certainly no picnic. Amongst other things, the foundation of the 2/13th's future reputation for hard marching had been well and truly laid.

The Battalion now entered upon its final month in England. Any lingering doubts that the period of training was drawing to an end were dispelled by the inspection by General French on May 23rd, which was followed on June 11th by an inspection by His Majesty the King. Everyone knew what that meant, and the loyal cheers with which they greeted His Majesty were intermingled with expressions of relief that at last they "were off." The intervening period was occupied with the final four days' leave, taken in turn. The anticlimax which was the lot of those returning to camp after bidding good-bye to their dear ones, and having perforce to take up the camp routine once more, was terrific. It seemed a pity that the whole Battalion could not go on leave at once, for those last two or three weeks were a long-drawn-out agony to men who had been on final leave. But much still remained to be done, even now, and No. 12 Camp was a hive of activity during the whole of that last month following the Irish "excursion."

On June 10th and 11th the Battalion received two large drafts of 104 O.R.s from the 2/28th and 101 O.R.s from the 2/5th London Regiment. These brought the 2/13th up to overseas strength and completed the final preparations. Lieut. Clark took over command of the Transport Section, vice Lieut. Caldbeck, who did not accompany the Battalion to France.

But the end came at last, and on June 22nd, 1916, the Second Battalion of Kensingtons left for France. The majority of the men never saw England again for nearly three years, their service eventually taking them across submarine-infested seas, whence leave was very scarce—like water, which simple beverage they were to come to prize highly.

"THE KENSINGTONS"

As the transport rounded the forts in Southampton Water, many of those on board realised with the shock of discovery that there was a war on. For twenty-two months they had been in it but not of it. Among the very first to bear arms, they had seen others wait, six months, twelve months, and even longer before joining up, and yet go out before them. Strange were the ways of the W.O.! But now the past was forgotten and every face strained eagerly forward into the gathering darkness, somewhere in the gloomy folds of which lay France. That magic name—FRANCE.

CHAPTER XIX

FRANCE

It was still dark when *La Marguerite* steamed into the harbour at Le Havre on the morning of June 22nd, 1916, carrying the 2/13th Battalion, and the troops were sufficiently chilled after their uncomfortable night on board to pay scant attention to the welcome which the little red and green harbour lights winked at them as the boat came alongside the quay. The raucous voice of the pilot, however, shouting out directions in French, which were answered by dim figures busy with ropes on shore, awoke in them that thrill so familiar to all who see a foreign land for the first time.

The tedious business of disembarkation lost its weariness owing to the strange setting in which it took place, and the blue uniforms of a few French Territorials who were to be seen on duty conveyed the sense of an exciting unreal atmosphere to the men fresh from England. Here at last was France—magic name! What strange sights and deeds lay ahead? How long—and how soon—were they to plunge into the welter of bloodshed that lay but a few score miles beyond the sleepy-looking town at their feet?

Actually, the experiences of the 2/13th in France proved as uneventful as any that fell to the lot of any British troops there. After but four months the currents of war were to draw it farther afield, away from its sister battalion and the carnage of the Western front, to the battlefields of the Near East, where it was finally to prove its mettle in more open and satisfactory warfare.

But in June 1916 nothing was known of this, and so far as the 2/13th knew it was in France "for duration." By this time it was well seasoned to the changes of Army life and looked forward philosophically to whatever the future might hold. The war was at an intermediate stage. Gone were the fresh enthusiasms of the early days, whilst the grim bitterness of mind wrought by the warfare of the Somme and the Ancre was yet to come. No one had any doubt as to the eventual issue of the war, and no one had the slightest idea how long it would last; speculation on that point had practically ceased. It had grown like some huge, grim monster, slowly but steadily devouring relatives and friends, enveloping the lives of everyone, until any other existence but this seemed unreal and not to be thought of. It was better not to think, anyway. The 2/13th, like the hundreds of other battalions now pouring into France, perceived dimly what it " was in for," and went forward steadily but without enthusiasm, prepared to take its medicine.

After some hours in a rest camp, it entrained that evening in the familiar trucks (" Hommes 40—Chevaux 8 ") and, after a fifteen-hours' journey to Mont St. Tournois, marched to its first French " billets " at Penin. From here the first sound of the guns could be heard—thrilling moment! Men began to wonder how far they were from the line, but no one seemed to know anything, and then it began to rain pitilessly and everybody was so tired that they soon ceased to wonder about the guns, and wondered only instead when they were going to get a really good sleep. How many times they were to wonder that during the next two and a half ears.

Another march brought them to Mont St. Eloi, whose ruined towers convinced many that they were really under shell fire by now. They afterwards learnt that the damage was done in the war in 1870. Actually, the Battalion was now six miles behind the line. The weather became very bad, and the shelter provided by some French huts that night proved more than welcome. The next day, the 26th, the Battalion moved to a " camp " two miles distant, whilst the 27th saw it billeted in the ruins of the village of Neuville St. Vaast, relieving Indian troops, who moved out of the cellars as the Kensingtons moved in.

FRANCE

Only a week later the Battalion would have considered itself comfortably situated in such quarters, but coming straight from home into the eerie atmosphere of that battered village, with its shell-scarred stumps of trees and half-ruined remnants of trenches left by the French, and living for the first time underneath the ground it was accustomed to walk upright upon, the discomfort and sense of danger were acute. The Battalion was at once put to work as carrying parties for the mining engineers, and was so divided and split up among the hundred and one cellars and dugouts in the village that it seemed as if a mighty shell had hit the Battalion as it entered Neuville St. Vaast and blown a familiar and united body of men into a hundred strange little fragments, each of whom seemed to have lost touch with the others. No doubt the Adjutant could have put his finger on any one of his platoons at any moment, but such was the unreality of those first few days among the ruins that it seemed like that to the men in the ranks. It was an experience common to most new-comers to France.

The strangeness wore off very quickly, and between their spells of duty men were soon carrying out local exploring expeditions of their own. Neuville St. Vaast was at that time full of mementoes of the early days of the war and provided a rich harvest for the inquisitive. Some of the " finds " were distinctly gruesome to the new arrivals, who were not then familiar with the habit of the French of burying some of the dead in the walls of trenches. Neuville St. Vaast was in the area of the famous operations around Souchez, and evidence was not lacking of the heavy losses the French had sustained. It also fronted Vimy Ridge, where the R.E.s were engaged in vast tunnelling operations underneath the front line, and it was carrying parties for this work that the Kensingtons were called upon to provide. It was eerie work down there, far under the ground, watching the white-faced miners picking away at the chalky soil, which was filled into sandbags as it fell and carried away, especially when it was known that the German engineers were engaged in similar work only a few yards through the soil! The working parties were fascinated by the listening apparatus used by the miners, through which the faint thud of the German picks could be plainly heard, and by which means their progress could be gauged to a foot. The work was extremely hard and unhealthy.

On July 1st, when the never-ceasing gun flashes lit up the sky like a great bonfire, telling of the opening of the holocaust in the south, the 2/13th sustained its first casualties. Fatal luck seemed to dog new drafts and a shell struck one of the carrying parties, killing five men and wounding several more, most of whom were just out from home. The bodies were taken back by the light railway which brought up rations to the forward dump, and buried at Bray, near the Transport lines. The long toll had at last commenced for the Second Kensingtons.

July 5th saw the Battalion move back to Bray for its first rest, which proved very brief, however, for the following day it moved into support at the Maison Blanche, and the 8th saw two companies in the line for the first time. It was on July 12th that the 2/13th took charge of a complete sector of the line, taking over the centre sub-section opposite Thelus village from the 1/5th Gordons, with Battalion Headquarters situated in the Boyau des Abris. The following night a party of the Gordons returned for a sort of farewell salute to the Boches, in the form of a raid, carried out from the 2/13th sector.

Although not directly concerned in this operation, the Battalion received the benefit of the accompanying artillery action, and to the inexperienced men it seemed a great "strafe"; it served to illustrate how meaningless was the phrase "the monotony of trench life." Indeed, the subsequent few months proved that life in any sector of the trenches, however quiet, was anything but monotonous, and few indeed were the hours when the weary troops could lay down in their dugouts for rest. The trench-mortar activity of the enemy was ceaseless, and although actual casualties from this source were comparatively few, it meant work, work, work all the time.

FRANCE

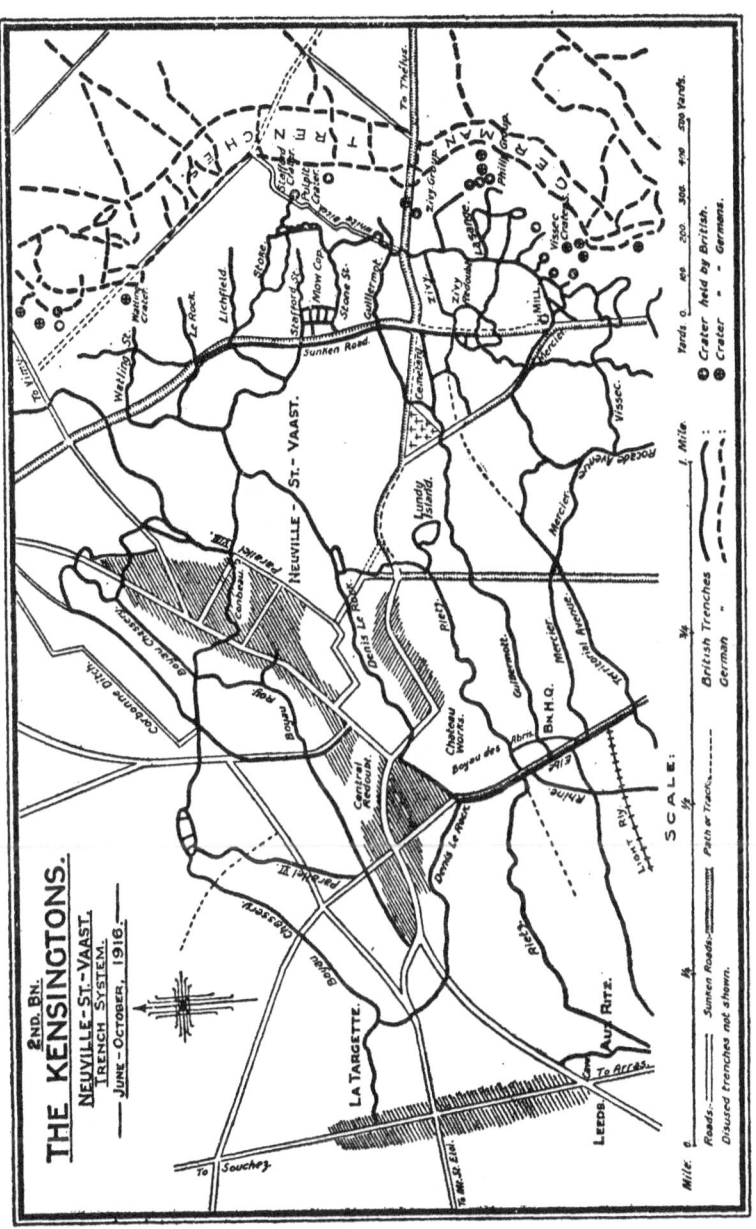

"THE KENSINGTONS"

The 60th (London) Division had taken over from the 51st (Highland) Division, whose ranks had been well thinned, and consequently the condition of the trenches left much to be desired. In many places they were definitely bad. No blame for this could be attached to the Highlanders, who were hard put to it to find enough men to hold the line securely, but it was the first job of the fresh division to put the trench system in order, and so every available moment was occupied in digging and wiring. This unusual activity did not pass unnoticed by the Germans, whose minenwerfers and trench mortars were set to work systematically to destroy the newly built trenches as fast as they were completed. They did not succeed in their object, and after the 60th had been in occupation of the line for two or three weeks there was a marked improvement both in the fire trenches and the communication trenches.

It was about this time that the Allied Forces made a determined bid for the supremacy of the air, and each day saw one or more aerial combats immediately over the sector of line held by the 60th Division. They were intensely exciting to the men in the trenches, who often forgot to keep well down as they watched the rival pilots circling round and round, plugging away with their machine guns. The Germans had two or three snipers well posted opposite the Kensingtons, and a few casualties resulted. The Battalion had its own Snipers' Section, picked from the best riflemen in the old Scouts' Section, and in addition to manning the observation posts these men took the work in hand of subduing the enemy snipers, using the rifles provided with special telescopic sights, and armour-piercing bullets for use against the armoured plates which protected the enemy sniping posts.

On July 16th the Kensingtons were relieved by the 2/16th (Queen's Westminster Rifles) and moved back along the four-mile Territorial Trench to rest huts at Bray. The accommodation here was quite good, and a fair night's sleep in the huts proved a godsend. Those who had any idea that rest time out of the line meant a slack time had a rude awakening, for the following morning the order was given for a general clean up, and numerous parades were the order of the day. The moral effect of once again seeing smart companies on parade was undoubtedly good, and with the evenings mostly free to visit the various local estaminets, life at Bray was to prove an event to be keenly anticipated. The only drawback was the presence of an enormous naval gun mounted on a railway which had been run into the little wood at the back of the Battalion camp site.

The Kensingtons moved up into the line again on July 20th in good spirits, taking over the same sector of trenches, with Battalion Headquarters in the Boyau des Abris. Seven days later they moved back into reserve, with Headquarters at Maison Blanche, and the following day witnessed a sad sight, albeit a common one farther south, when a British aeroplane was brought down in flames. The second anniversary of the outbreak of war saw them again in the now familiar front line, and two nights later a party of Kensingtons undertook their first offensive action in the form of a bombing raid.

The raiding party consisted of two officers and 33 O.R.s from A and B Companies, the officers being Lieut. W. Read and 2nd Lieut. F. R. Stockwell. The party had carried out careful and extensive training at Aubigny, where a facsimile set of trenches to those about to be raided was prepared. Day after day the whole party rehearsed the entire operation, until each man knew his own job to the last inch. Eventually a full-dress rehearsal was carried out, and this nearly had a fatal sequel, for a piece of Mills bomb about the size of a shilling flew back and caught Lieut. Read on the bridge of the nose, where it embedded itself and caused the unfortunate officer a few days' pain and anxiety. Happily he recovered sufficiently to be able to accompany his party as arranged. The men were lightly clad for the occasion and all evidence of identification was removed from their clothing. Coming up with the ration party on the night of August 6th, their faces blackened on arrival at Battalion

Headquarters, they then made their way to the front-line trenches to await zero hour, which had been fixed for 22.00 hours.

A short but sharp box barrage was laid on the section of enemy trench to be raided, and a 60-pounder from a trench mortar gave the signal to go over promptly on the hour. The night proved, as expected, to be very dark, and in order that the party should not be lost on the return journey, "tape-men" had been provided, carrying a metal drum of 1½-inch white tape, one end of which was secured to our own fire-trench and the other carried to within 15 yards of the German line. The party had not been over a few seconds when the first tape was broken by shell-fire, the enemy retaliating immediately and vigorously, and although this was replaced with gallantry under heavy fire by Private Tufnell, it was subsequently found to be hopelessly broken in many places. The raiders were divided into two flanking and one "body-snatching" party, the latter reaching the German trench, into which they jumped and bombed their way along until a dugout was reached, which was also bombed, with presumably good effect, judging from the cries.

No opportunity of taking the desired prisoner had occurred at this stage, and the time limit fixed for the raid was up. With the certainty of German reinforcements appearing at any moment, and the necessity for getting his party back to our own line before it became impossible, Lieut. Read gave the signal to retire. He was the last to leave the German trench. Scrambling back over the parapet, he found that the German artillery had done its work so well that there was no trace of the tape which was to guide the party back, and it became a case of every man for himself. Lieut. Read discovered Private Sharpe wounded and in danger of being left behind, and delayed his return to assist the wounded man, although his own wrist had now been broken. He was helped by Privates Barham and Field, but the delay nearly cost the little party their lives, and, cut off by the enemy barrage, they were forced to seek refuge in a shell-hole, where they remained throughout the whole of the next day, finally reaching the safety of the British line at 1.30 a.m. on the morning of the 8th. In the meantime, 2nd Lieut. Stockwell, accompanied by some half a dozen men, lost their direction and, mistaking the German trenches for our own, vanished into the darkness and were never seen again. The remainder of the party was stumbling back across No-man's-land in twos and threes, amongst them being Corporal R. O. Wills, who assisted three wounded men to safety. Also losing his direction, Wills struck the German trench and found himself confronted by an armed enemy; his own rifle had been blown out of his hand, but, armed only with a pair of wire-cutters, the gallant N.C.O. secured the German prisoner and guided him and the three wounded men back to the right sub-sector. For his act Wills received the Military Medal. Lieut. Read was awarded the Military Cross.

Captain Hanks, the M.O., and 2nd Lieut. Shave were " mentioned," the former for attending wounded men under heavy trench-mortar fire, and the latter for occupying an exposed position in the " Pulpit " crater for two hours, whence he rendered great assistance by supplying the Commanding Officer with news. Privates Barham and Field were also " mentioned " for the assistance they rendered to Lieut. Read during the nerve-racking experience they shared whilst they were " missing " for twenty-seven hours. The raiding party lost one O.R. killed, one O.R. died of wounds, whilst 2nd Lieut. Stockwell and seven O.R.s were posted as " missing." The raid accomplished its objective, but at a tragic cost for the 2/13th.

In addition to the casualties sustained during the actual raid, a further blow was the loss of four of the Battalion police, who were killed by a trench mortar whilst waiting to escort prisoners.

Less than a week later there was further " liveliness " on the Kensingtons' sector, occasioned by the blowing up of a mine from the Pulpit Sap. Parties of A Company (Major P. A. Hopkins) and B Company (Capt. C. E. Brockhurst) were detailed to rush the crater. The explosion was timed for 12.30 a.m. and promptly on the half-hour there was a terrific roar and masses of earth shot skywards. A brisk fire immediately opened from the German lines as the occupying parties went over, whilst our artillery put down a barrage on the far lip of the crater. In just under twenty minutes the crater was reported taken, and shortly after Lieut. Killingbek of the Royal Engineers was killed. The work of consolidating the crater went on feverishly for four hours and was successfully carried out, and at 4.30 a.m. the " all-in " was reported.

On August 12th the Battalion was once more relieved by the Queen's Westminsters and moved back to Bray for a well-earned rest of eight days. At a full Battalion Parade on the 16th, Corporal Wills was decorated with the Military Medal. The now familiar cycle of front line, reserve trenches, and rest billets carried on evenly for over two months, yet no man would call them " uneventful." Casualties became fairly numerous, whilst the state of the trenches called for incessant work of repair. Towards the end of August the weather broke and rain became unpleasantly frequent. The trials of the 60th Division in the water-logged trenches facing the lower slopes of Vimy Ridge could not be compared to the sufferings of the Army on the Somme, where the costly British offensive was now checked in seas of mud, but they were real enough to the Londoners, who were meeting their first experience of bad trench conditions, aggravated by daily increasing activity of the German trench mortars.

The trenches in which they had taken such pride were rapidly becoming mere battered mud-holes which they strove day by day to build up, with increasing lack of success. After " stand down " each morning, the weary men, lying huddled in wet dugouts or crouched uncomfortably on muddy fire-steps, would see the results of a whole night's hard labour wrecked and laid waste by half a dozen well-placed " Minnies " or " Flying Pigs." The Germans were apparently much better equipped in the matter of heavy trench mortars than we were, and used them with great skill and accuracy. Our own Stokes' mortars were too light for effective retaliation, though they were often called upon for this purpose, and the soft swish of their shells leaving the gun was as music to the ears of the men irritated by the incessant and unpleasant attention of the German mortars. The Stokes' were, of course, immensely valuable in many ways, but they could not batter the opposing trenches sufficiently to satisfy the urge for revenge felt by men who saw the results of their own immensely difficult and irksome labour dissipated so easily and so quickly.

During their tenure of the line the Kensingtons were interested to see one of the mines exploded which they had earlier had some small hand in excavating. The result scarcely seemed worth the time and money which it had cost; another crater was added to the trench maps, and another obstacle or friendly shelter was provided for the night patrols, which were an unceasing feature of trench life. At least it provided the Divisional artillery with a good " shoot."

The command of D Company was now taken over by Captain E. R. Kisch.

On September 20th, the Adjutant, Captain W. E. David Devis, was appointed Town Major of Marœuil, and was succeeded by Captain R. P. Gladstone of D Company. In Captain David Devis the Battalion lost its most outstanding personality, and his going was felt with great regret by those who had known him through the long days of training at home. He never rejoined the Battalion, but survived the war, and was subsequently appointed a judge in the Sudan, where he died at Khartoum a year or two ago.

Two further incidents marked the closing weeks of the period spent in the line facing Thelus, widely differing in character. On October 6th, during one of the usual rest periods at Bray, the 2/13th was inspected by the Divisional Commander, Lieut.-General Sir Chas. Ferguson, an occasion which immediately produced the inevitable crop of rumours, chief and most probable of which was that a move south to the Somme was in prospect. It would be untrue to say that such a prospect was welcomed (too many tales of almost unbelievable sacrifice and hardship had dribbled north for that), but the Battalion was now thoroughly seasoned and was ready to more or less cheerfully accept whatever the fates had in store. The second incident was an attempted raid by the enemy on the sector of trenches held by the Kensingtons. This occurred on October 11th, and whatever the object may have been, it was not achieved. A hot barrage was laid down by the German artillery and the Battalion stood to. The enemy left their trenches and came over, but the combined effort of our artillery and machine-gun fire was sufficient to break up the attack, and after a gruelling half an hour comparative peace descended over the line, although double sentries were maintained throughout the night, which was lit up by an unusual expenditure of Verey lights.

It may be that the Germans had an inkling of a change in front of them and wished to verify their suspicions, for it was not long afterwards that confirmation of the many rumours came, and on October 24th the Kensingtons handed over to the Canadian Scottish and left the trenches of France for good. They were not to know this for some weeks, however, and when the 60th Division was relieved by the Canadians, it was ostensibly bound for the Somme. The Canadians proved to be the happy-go-lucky fellows rumour had indicated, and the relief was quickly and easily accomplished.

On October 16th the Battalion lost another senior officer who had been with it since its inception, Major P. A. Hopkins, commanding A Company, being invalided home. Major Hopkins was an old Kensington, who was on the retired list before the war and offered his services on the outbreak, and threw himself into the arduous work of raining recruits with an energy that many far younger men might have envied. Major Hopkins was a fine example of the old Volunteer officer, immeasurably just in his dealings with his men, by whom he was loved.

FRANCE

While the 2/13th was still near Abbeville, only two weeks later, news was received that the Canadians were making no attempt to carry on the herculean efforts made by the Kensingtons to preserve the front line with some semblance of a trench system, but were manning a few well-chosen places as outposts and had retired generally to the reserve trenches to live in. This was probably a very sensible thing to do under the circumstances, the circumstances being continued rain accompanied by the collapsing of long stretches of the cherished trenches.

Marching back along the Arras–St. Pol road, the Kensingtons were in high spirits at the thought of the rest ahead and the prospect of spending arrears of pay among the amenities of civilisation. The Battalion marched via Savy–Buneville–Neoux Frevent to Prueville, sleeping in fairly comfortable barns *en route*. A stay of five days at the latter village included a roadside inspection by the C.-in-C., Sir Douglas Haig, a prelude to the final departure from France. On November 3rd, the march was resumed to Vauchelles, via Riquet, a village a few kilometres outside Abbeville. Leave into the town was freely granted, and the sight of real shops and good food proved more than welcome. Rumours concerning the Kensingtons' destination had been rife for some days, and when it finally became known that the 60th Division had been ordered to Salonika, the liveliest curiosity was aroused as to the nature of the experiences which lay ahead. A scene of great activity ensued at Battalion Headquarters; on the 6th all the horses were handed over to the remount depôt at Abbeville, but another nine days elapsed before the Battalion entrained for the south.

Major G. Thompson bade farewell to the Battalion, returning to the Third Battalion in England, and Captain R. P. Gladstone was promoted to second-in-command, with the rank of major. He was succeeded as Adjutant by Lieut. E. W. Phillips, who was to hold the post for the ensuing twelve months. The Battalion had a gruelling march to Longpré, where entrainment took place, and the seemingly interminable fifty-five-hour journey to Marseilles began. The Battle of the Somme had strained the resources of the French railways to the utmost, and, packed like sardines in the familiar trucks, it proved an uncomfortable and monotonous journey. But discomfort and monotony were the only things that one could really count on in any theatre of the war, and the inevitable cards and loud choruses of song enlivened the time as usual. It was hoped that the train might pass through, or even stop at, Paris, but it was only the suburbs that the train skirted, and these were generally voted to be unexciting. There were many, however, who fully appreciated the glorious scenery of the Rhône Valley, which was seen bathed in sunshine. Marseilles was reached at night, and in pouring rain, and it was a very disconsolate Battalion that marched into a rest camp in pitch darkness, where small rivers of water ran through most of the tents.

No leave into the town was possible, and on the following morning the Kensingtons embarked on H.M.T. *Transylvania*, which anchored in the harbour for the rest of the day and the ensuing night. They had as sailing companions, Brigadier-General Edwards, his Brigade Staff, and various odd units of brigade troops. The *Transylvania* was a fine boat and the trooping accommodation was on the whole very good, as was the food. The sea proved a little choppy in the Gulf of Lyons, although the weather was glorious, and there were many absentees at meals during the first day. It was not long before every seat was filled, and, with appetites whipped up by the sea air, full justice was done to the excellent fare which was served.

Everyone enjoyed the sea voyage, for although the days were fairly well filled by parades of one sort and another, there still remained plenty of time for games, and the excitement of spotting for submarines was a game in which all joined with zest. The Kensingtons' brass band played each night for the officers' mess. On the 22nd Malta was reached, and the *Transylvania* anchored in Grand Harbour on a sweltering day; that evening a most successful ship's concert was held, at which one of the artists was Arthur Prince, the celebrated ventriloquist, who was attached to the Brigade Ammunition Column from the R.F.A. This halt on the voyage was entirely unexpected, and it seemed that a submarine scare was responsible; on the 24th the ship steamed round to Valetta and once again anchored. A three-days' stay was made here, and opportunity was given to all officers and some N.C.O.s to go ashore for a few hours on the 26th. It was a wonderful opportunity and was fully appreciated. Valetta holds a good deal of interest, but there was no time for the usual round of the sights, and the Kensingtons were mostly content to stroll about and interest themselves in the bizarre crowds, although numbers went into cinemas and were surprised to find that the sub-titling was in Italian; the atmosphere of the harbour was so British and naval, that it came as quite a shock to many of the men to realise that the actual inhabitants were by no means English. Rumours of submarines being in the neighbourhood were effectively confirmed by the appearance of a French passenger ship which had been badly holed and had limped into Valetta. By the 27th a destroyer escort was available, and the *Transylvania* steamed away from Malta with all ranks on board grateful for the pleasant interlude which had effectively broken the monotony of war. As darkness fell news was wirelessed that the boat ahead of the *Transylvania* had indeed been torpedoed and sunk; course was altered to due south, and every possible ounce of steam was raised. A swell got up, and altogether it was quite an exciting night for all on board. The following morning it was seen that the ship was running parallel with the northern coast of Africa, which was within view all that day, until a northerly course was again set for the Ægean Sea. Threading her way through the Archipelago, the *Transylvania* made the Gulf without further incident, escorted during the last day by a British submarine, and Salonika was reached after breakfast on November 30th.

CHAPTER XX

SALONIKA

The voyage through these waters of the classics had been beautiful, but everyone was anxious to see the city that was their destination. Rising gently from the water at the head of the Gulf, it was a fair, even a noble sight, and the question was eagerly discussed as to the distance of the ultimate camp site, for, without exception, everyone keenly anticipated their first visit to so fair a city.

Alas, for hopes! When disembarkation was finally completed and the Battalion marched into and through Salonika, it proved on closer inspection to be the filthiest and most uninteresting place so far encountered on their travels. There was undoubtedly good reason for the order which practically placed the town out of bounds for the troops of the 179th Brigade during the subsequent ten days which they spent in Dudular Camp, a few miles to the north-west of Salonika. Leave was restricted to officers and to other ranks whose duties took them into the town, and as there was nothing to see and practically nothing to do there, the restriction was not felt as a hardship.

From first to last the Salonika Expedition was a depressing "show," and at the time of the arrival of the 60th Division a general air of neglect and disillusionment hung over everything. Had the Expedition been undertaken in sufficient time, it might well have served an important and even a decisive rôle in the war, but, after months of hesitation, it was finally landed too late to save the Serbian Army or prevent Bulgaria from throwing in her lot with the Central Powers, and from the outset was starved of both ammunition and equipment vitally necessary for its success, and provided with scarcely enough for its continued existence. This neglect, indeed, proved to be the reason

SALONIKA

which drew the 60th Division out of France at short notice, for the Central Powers had gauged its weakness, and in the late autumn of 1917 there was a real danger of an enemy offensive which would drive the Salonika Allied Forces into the sea, and give to Germany the outlet on the Mediterranean for her submarines that she so badly wanted. Greece was still neutral, and with the notoriously pro-German King Constantine on the throne might at any moment declare against the Allies. The danger had to some extent been obviated, and at least postponed, by the action of M. Venizelos in declaring a revolution and setting up a Provisional Government with his headquarters at Salonika. The forces at his command at this stage were, however, more moral than military, and the 60th Division were sent out post-haste to stiffen the military defences. A more motley force than the Allied Army at Salonika could scarcely be imagined, and soldiers of the French, British, Italian, and Serbian Armies, intermingled with Greek volunteers, were to be seen in all stages of equipment. There were also large numbers of Russian troops.

The London troops were not concerned with high politics, or they might have felt more depressed than they did in their new surroundings, and these gave them full cause for both wonder and misery. Their camp was pitched on bare, inhospitable-looking ground, which rapidly became an absolute quagmire as soon as the rains commenced, which happened almost as soon as they arrived. The allowance of tents was far below normal, and men were herded twelve in a tent, the floors of which were soft mud. The Transport Section was the first to feel the full benefit of conditions in the new country; on landing, the Division was, of course, without horses for transport, and in two days after arrival drew 129 mules from remount. These were entirely unbroken and had never worn harness, and the trials of the unfortunate Transport Section may be imagined. In addition to breaking in these animals, it was necessary to train a number of new men to transport work, and as many of these had never had anything to do with animals, the following week provided many lively incidents. On December 7th a regular deluge broke, many tents were blown down, and the mud problem became terrible. Conditions in the transport lines, where many of the mules broke loose, were indescribable; harness and blankets floated in a sea of mud and water, which was churned deeper and deeper as the mules lashed out in all directions in their misery. The troops were in scarcely better plight; nevertheless, a certain amount of training work was carried out, so far as conditions permitted, whilst the Transport Section grappled daily with their refractory mules, until something like order in the lines was restored.

Then, unexpectedly, on December 10th, came a welcome diversion, which was probably without parallel in any theatre of the war. The 179th Brigade was detailed to make a forced landing farther down the eastern coast of Greece, to proceed, not against a declared enemy, but to ensure the continued neutrality of that uncertain country, or, at worst, to block the only road from the south which would enable Greece, entering the war, to deal a blow at the unprotected rear of the Salonika Force. In an area of the war concerning the operations of which many hard things have been both said and written, the fullest credit must be given to the Allied Command for conceiving a bold stroke which was successful in averting a grave danger before it actually arose. In an expedition of which vacillation was unfortunately the keynote, this operation, although of minor dimensions, was carried through with a rapidity and decisiveness which caused it to stand out like a shaft of light against a dull, uncertain, and sombre background. Brilliantly conceived and skilfully carried out, the entire plan was executed without a single hitch, and reflected great credit on Brig.-General F. M. Edwards, C.B., C.M.G., D.S.O., and the four battalions of the 179th Brigade under his command.

The difficult position of the Salonika Forces should the Greeks declare war and march northward has been alluded to, and the tension at this stage having become acute, it was decided to end it once and for all, by seizing the initiative and throwing an Allied Force across the only possible line of approach open to the Greeks. The country dividing Greece and Macedonia is exceedingly difficult, being composed of a mountainous range, of which the historic Olympus is the centre and the peak. To the east of Olympus runs the railway along the shore of the Gulf of Salonika, to the west the only road through the Petra Pass; these two possible approaches converge north of the mountains and pass through the town of Katerina, which became, therefore, a point of vital importance. The seizure and occupation of Katerina was the first objective of the raiding force, for which the complete 179th Brigade was chosen.

A company of the 2/14th London Regiment (London Scottish) formed the advance guard, which left Salonika on December 10th. The Kensingtons followed on the 11th on board H.M.S. *Endymion*, together with the rest of the Brigade, minus Transport, which was ordered to march by an inland route. The whole operation was shrouded in secrecy, and the Battalion moved at an hour or so's notice. None of the men had the slightest idea of their destination, and the crowded embarkation on the cruiser in Salonika harbour was an added and unexpected thrill; the sailors were very curious to see what equipment the troops carried, and, after trying it on, magnanimously declared that they had the best of the war! Crowded and difficult as the conditions on board were, the naval ratings did everything possible to make the men of the 179th Brigade comfortable, and very cordial relations were quickly established, so that the troops were sorry when the short voyage was over. The destination proved to be a village named Vromeri, a mere collection of tumbledown cottages huddled together on a deserted part of the western shore of the Gulf of Salonika. The advance guard of the Scottish reported all quiet, and the *Endymion* dropped anchor a few hundred yards from the shore. The troops were transferred into lighters, but even their shallow draught did not allow them to get sufficiently close in, and in the end every man had to wade ashore, carrying his rifle

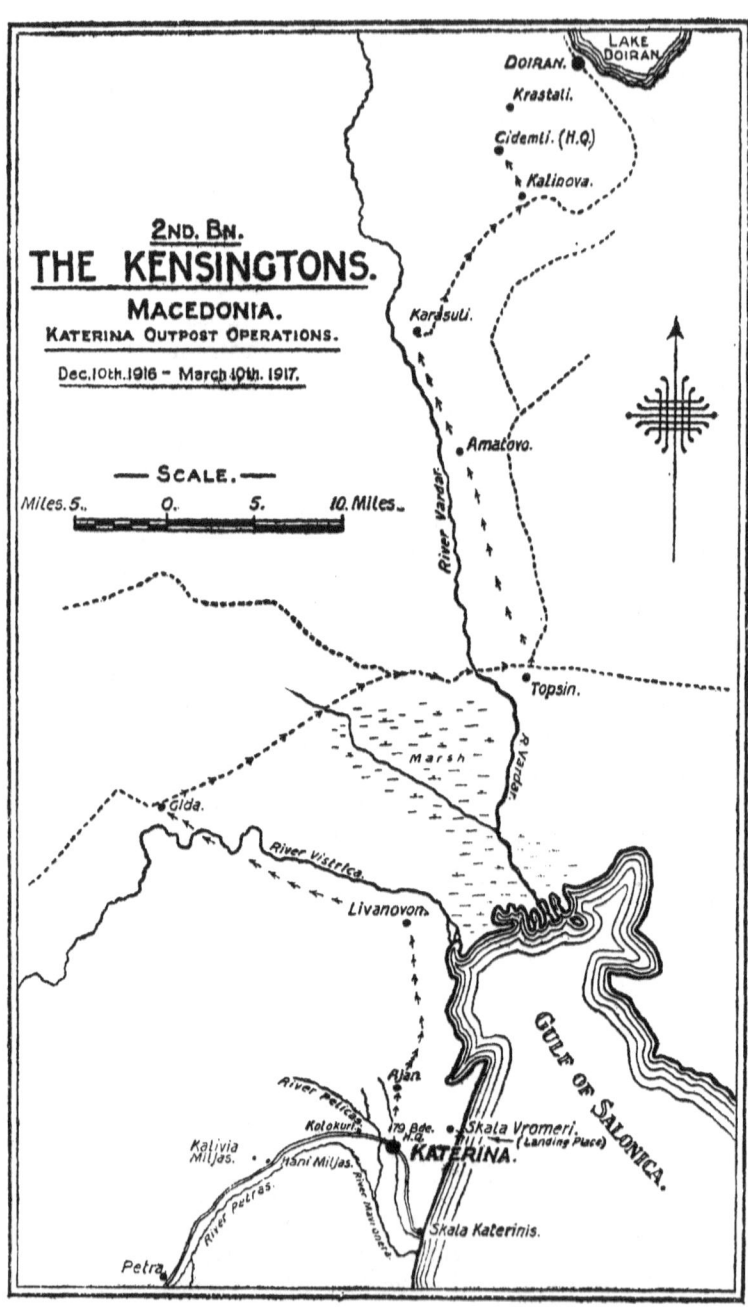

high above his head. There were a number of laughable calamities, and it was a wet body of men that eventually landed.

The Kensingtons were ordered to make the first advance inland, and seize Katerina that same night, and so, leaving the remainder of the Brigade hard at work landing stores, the Battalion moved off in their sodden clothes through the fast-gathering dusk. Progress was slow, the country being quite unknown and the night dark, whilst the fording of a river took time and added to the general dampness of the little expedition. There was no sign of any opposition, and Katerina was reached and occupied by midnight without incident, such few inhabitants as were encountered being very friendly. The following morning the Kensingtons had opportunity to examine their new surroundings, which proved to be a typical little Greek town, most of the houses of which displayed a Venizelos flag. An outpost line was established to the west of the town, whilst the rest of the Battalion settled down to dry themselves and await the arrival of the London Scottish, who marched in later on the 12th. The Kensingtons were then ordered farther west, to the village of Kolokuri, on the far side of the River Pelikas; where Battalion Headquarters was established, while a new outpost line was thrown out across the Petra Road and linking up with the River Mavroneri, a clear, fast-flowing stream running through a rocky defile. The following day work was commenced on defences covering Kolokuri. A week was spent in this position, the Battalion sleeping under bivouac sheets. A few French troops were also in occupation here and received their Allies warmly; the weather, which had been both wet and cold, improved and, with the arrival on the 16th of the Transport from their long march south, conditions became more pleasant. Work there was in plenty, for apart from the outpost duties up in the surrounding hills, the whole Brigade set to work on road-making, the existing roads being in a very primitive state and totally unfit for military operations.

After a week occupied in this manner, the Kensingtons

were relieved by the London Scottish, and went into reserve at Katerina a week before Christmas. Here they enjoyed their first real rest for a considerable time, for although a certain amount of training work was carried out, they were relieved from all duties in connection with the object of the expedition. The weather was exceptionally good and opportunities for addition to the army rations not lacking, a brisk trade being done in the local poultry, and even sheep. On Christmas Day every possible attempt was made to reproduce something of the spirit of the festive season, and Brigade Sports were held, to which all the battalions of the 179th Brigade were able to send some proportion of their strength. This was the first Christmas Day that the Kensingtons had spent away from England, and they were fortunate to enjoy such congenial circumstances.

For the next two months the Brigade passed an uneventful existence, filled with much hard work it is true, and marred by most unpleasant weather conditions, but life in and around Katerina was very peaceful, and it was difficult to believe that the World War was raging; no through traffic passed near this remote country-side, no aeroplanes roared overhead, and so sparsely populated was the area that very few peasants were ever met, save an occasional lone shepherd, outside Katerina, which was the gently stirring centre of Army life. Katerina itself did not, could not, respond in the usual way of towns and villages which suddenly become the base of thousands of troops. Had the occupation lasted, there is no doubt that the inevitable appendages would have appeared—the cafés and saloons and cheap "souvenir" shops—but it remained unspoiled during the three months' stay of the 179th Brigade, and there was nothing more innocuous to do than sit and idly sip Russian tea, a delicacy to which the local bigwigs were much addicted, the while they interminably counted the string of black beads which they all, without exception, wore.

On January 3rd the Battalion again took over outpost

duty at Kolokuri. The weather broke two days later and there followed a fortnight of miserable conditions; the bivouacs were all but washed away and a fresh camping site had to be sought for Battalion Headquarters. The duty of rationing the outpost companies out on the hills became arduous with the rising of the River Mavroneri, which had to be forded. An interesting experiment was tried at this time by the Regimental Quartermaster, Lieut. Cattermole, with a view to exterminating the lice with which the men were still plagued; although there were now ample facilities for washing in the icy waters of the Mavroneri, little headway could be made against these pests whilst they still enjoyed the cosy warmth of the sheepskin coats which were part of the clothing issue. Q.M. Cattermole hit upon the ingenious idea of withdrawing and burying these coats in deep trenches, arguing that, deprived of human society and dependent for succour on wet clay, the vermin would perish ignominiously in time. The sequel proved the reverse of his hopes, for, when the coats were unearthed two months later, they were found to be literally alive, millions of eggs having been hatched out in the warm seclusion of the soil! The unfortunate men who were forced to don the coats on their return to Salonika still had sufficient sense of humour to join in the laugh which greeted the result of the well-meant but misdirected effort of the worthy Q.M.

In addition to the ceaseless road-making which went on, the respite from active warfare was utilised for a considerable amount of specialist training, the signallers in particular getting all they wanted in that direction, while the period in the Katerina area proved a godsend to the Scouts Section, who set to work to map the area occupied by the Kensingtons, and gained valuable training which later stood them in good stead in Palestine, where their services were of great value as guides. Company training was carried out whenever practicable, and on their last day at Kolokuri even the luxury of a field day for the Battalion was indulged in. Football provided a great deal of relaxation for the troops not actually on outpost duty, and Major Gladstone, who was a Soccer enthusiast and a referee of merit, carried through a programme of inter-platoon competitions. On January 17th the M.O., Captain D. F. C. Nielson, R.A.M.C., left the Battalion on the termination of his engagement, and was succeeded by Captain Spencer.

On February 13th orders were received to strike camp and march westward to the village of Kolivia Miljas, where the London Scottish were relieved. This was situated farther up the Petra Pass and just north of the Petra Road, almost at the foot of Mount Olympus. The scenery was indescribably beautiful, and many were the pleasant walks and expeditions undertaken when duties permitted. The summit of Olympus is above the snowline, and the view at dawn, when the first rays of the rising sun tinted the snow with a delicate pink, was some compensation for the men who were forced by military exigencies to live for so many weeks among the wild mountain fastnesses of northern Greece. The weather turned very cold and snow fell in the middle of February, so that the men shivered in their frail bivouacs and began to regret the lack of the verminous sheepskins hidden in the soil at Kolokuri. Further field operations were carried out on February 23rd, and on the 28th orders were received to move farther up the Pass, but these were cancelled later in the day, and the Battalion wondered what was going to happen. It meant that the end of their sojourn in the hills had arrived, and two days later the return to Katerina was made.

The period of anxiety occasioned by the pro-German sympathies of King Constantine was judged to be over, and the threat to the Allied rear was no longer existent. The timely measures taken at the beginning of December had had their effect, and although for three months the 179th Brigade had not heard a shot fired in anger, their time had not been wasted, but had, in fact, undoubtedly been better spent than in swelling the numbers in the line of somewhat useless trenches which lay well under the too-observant eye of the Bulgars entrenched on top of the highest hills twixt Vardar and Doiran, from where they had

2ND BATTALION BRIDGE-BUILDING AT KATERINA, JANUARY 1917.
Imperial War Museum photograph. Copyright reserved.

the whole Allied area from front line to Salonika under easy observation.

The 179th Brigade left behind them as a legacy a series of small bridges and the finest roads which the inhabitants of the Katerina area had ever seen. Mention must be made of the "Chelsea Bridge" at Hani Miljas over the Mavroneri, which, although not built by the Kensingtons, was left as a lasting memorial to the skill of the Royal Engineers attached to the Brigade, who rebuilt it, assisted by two companies of the London Scottish. It was a fine stone-built structure which replaced a primitive bridge which the swift floods of the Mavroneri had carried away, and which was essential for military movement along the only road through the Petra Pass. It carries an inscription commemorating the event, and should outlast several generations.

Save for essential duties, the Brigade had a complete week's holiday at Katerina, the Kensingtons being encamped on the banks of the River Pelikas, the cold waters of which they had forded on that dark landing night three months earlier; now it carried a substantial bridge sufficient for the needs of the military. It proved a pleasant, restful week, broken only by a fierce gale on the night of March 5th, which blew all the tents and many of the bivouacs down; however, by this time the Battalion was quite used to little upsets of that sort. The past three months of life in the open had rendered them almost impervious to weather conditions—but their hardihood was to be severely tried during the following week.

On March 10th, 1917, the Brigade set out upon its march north to rejoin the Salonika Army. The history of the British Army teems with wonderful marching feats, and it is not suggested that the present march of the 179th has not been excelled on many occasions, both in length and conditions, but it is doubtful if Territorial troops had ever previously been called upon to undertake such a feat of endurance. In seven consecutive days the Brigade marched ninety miles, finishing up with two very severe night marches carried out in very bad weather. The equipment carried by the troops was enormous, weighing no less than 103 lbs., and including, in addition to the regulation full marching order, a sheepskin coat or jerkin, a waterproof cloak, and a bivouac sheet with pole. The march was carried out over bad roads, which for the first three days were little better than cart tracks, deeply rutted, whilst the metalled roads which succeeded these were indeed metalled but not rolled, so that the sharp flints cut wickedly into tired feet. Sand-flies and mosquitoes added to the general discomfort, and supplies of fresh water were strictly limited. The low marshy country was dreary in the extreme. On the 14th the British G.-O.-C. Salonika, Lieut.-General G. F. Milne, drove out and watched them on the march near Topsin, but few of the men knew of his presence. On the morning of the 15th the Brigade set out from Amatovo in intense heat on the penultimate stage of their march to Karasuli; the final approach to the latter place being under enemy observation, a long halt was ordered at midday until dusk. By this time the weather had completely and quickly changed, so that the rest of the day's march was carried through in rain; on this occasion the usual good work of the Staff broke down, so that when the weary column arrived in pitch darkness at Karasuli the guides who were to take them to their allotted bivouac areas were at first not to be found, and when found proved themselves to be hopelessly lost! The wind increased to gale force, the teeming rain turned to sleet, and so dark was the night that scarcely two yards ahead could be seen; the troops were at first led round in circles, slithering through the mud and trying in vain to protect themselves from the icy elements. At last the whole Battalion sank down by the side of the road and, wet through, waited for the dawn, when bivouacs were pitched.

The following day, March 16th, was probably the most uncomfortable ever spent by the Battalion. The trying conditions of the previous few days had levied toll upon the reserves of energy of everyone, and the men fully expected that a halt of twenty-four hours would be called; but that same afternoon the Brigade was ordered to proceed forward on the last stage of the march to Kalinova, and the cramped and weary troops crawled out of the sodden bivouacs to resume once more the equipment that by now seemed to have doubled in weight. A cold and piercing rain, falling from a leaden, forbidding-looking sky, greeted them, and as the tired feet dragged off—squelch, squelch—in the mud, the rain gradually turned to snow in the fast-gathering gloom. The conditions were appalling, and were so described by the *London Scottish Regimental Gazette* as follows :

> Scarcely had we started when it began to snow, and ere we had made two miles we were moving in the teeth of a Balkan blizzard. The Battalion will not readily forget that night, and to crown all, it was on this of all nights that our usually perfect Staff arrangements must needs miscarry. We reached the end of our march only to find that our guides had been taken away by Brigade Staff, and we had to wait for upwards of an hour before they were found. The final seal to our discomfort was set when, led on to a bare snow-swept hillside, we were informed, " This is your area; you bivouac here."

The experience of the Kensingtons was identical with that of the Scottish. The blizzard was indeed one of the worst ever experienced, and when at 2 a.m. the Battalion finally came to a halt, men and animals were absolutely " all in," and huddled together in a strange medley in a vain effort to escape the icy teeth of the storm. The finest tribute that can be paid to the 2/13th for their endurance on that memorable night is to record that every man completed the march safely, albeit some weary stragglers came stumbling in through the snow until dawn broke. Unfortunately, one private of the Scottish, although completing the march, fainted and died from cold and exposure before medical aid could reach him.

The extreme vagaries of the Balkan climate were aptly demonstrated by the fact that when morning came, a hot sun blazed out of the sky, and quickly dried the drenched troops and soddened equipment, and brought cheer to the hearts of all. The "powers that be" decided that a rum issue would further improve the occasion, but unfortunately this, taken on empty stomachs, produced dire results, and at 7 a.m. the Battalion was scarcely able to stagger to a fresh bivouac area which had been allotted half a mile away. Possibly unwittingly, the enemy chose this moment to make a daylight air raid on the camp, and the harassed troops had to hastily seek what scanty cover was available against the dropping bombs. Happily there were no casualties, at least in the Kensington lines, but the few transport men still fit for duty had a lively time with the frightened mules. A twenty-four hours' complete rest was ordered for all ranks.

The following day the Battalion moved into the line and took over positions from the 12th Argyll and Sutherland Highlanders, with Battalion Headquarters at Cidemli. Conditions were very different from those experienced in France, the trenches and support lines (particularly the latter) being in a half-finished state. Most of the Battalion had corrugated-iron shelters dug in the reverse side of the hill, the Bulgar lines being a considerable distance away. The enemy obtained a direct hit on one of these shelters on Bastion Hill, killing six men and wounding several others. The line was fairly quiet, but movement was difficult owing to the fact that the Bulgars occupied much higher ground, and had almost perfect observation over the whole area. They were strongly entrenched in an almost impregnable position on the western slopes of the mountain covering the Doiran front, known as the "Pip" Ridge. The line taken over by the 60th Division (which the 179th Brigade had now rejoined) ran from the low, broken ground facing this formidable ridge, westwards to the Vardar Valley. The intervening country was very hilly, and trench digging was extremely difficult owing to the rocky nature of the subsoil. The wire left much to be desired. The Division was set to work to improve these scanty defences, and it took a month of hard labour to render them even passably safe; the use of gelignite was resorted to as much as supplies permitted, but it was typical of the whole state of the supplies for the Salonika Army that gelignite proved very scarce, and worth its weight in gold.

During this period in the line, the Bulgars raided the 2/16th (Queen's Westminsters) and proved themselves adept at this branch of trench warfare. A further raid by the enemy was carried out on April 6th, this time against a post of the London Scottish, and after two days of intermittent artillery preparation. The raid was gallantly repulsed with the loss of one killed and six wounded. On April 9th the Kensingtons were subjected to a fairly stiff artillery " strafe " which seemed to suggest further raiding activities, but nothing resulted. These minor events pointed to the fact that the enemy morale was strong, and it is not too much to say that they held the whip-hand, owing to their strong positions and also to the fact that at this period they undoubtedly held a marked and irritating superiority in the air. Daily air raids, even on the frontline trenches, were carried out, and although these did not pass unchallenged (many thrilling aerial combats were witnessed), on the whole they did pretty well what they liked in the air. Rightly or wrongly, the Allied High Command were obsessed with the idea of a grand breakthrough on the Western Front; the ghastly carnage of the Somme had failed to eradicate this " idée fixe," and in consequence the unfortunate Allied Army on the Salonika Front were kept shorn of all but the barest necessities of defence. The fact that this information was no doubt well known to the enemy facing them, coupled with the formidable strength of their position, kept the Bulgarian tail " well up."

Notwithstanding this somewhat depressing position, it shortly became known that the British were about to make a frontal attack upon the Bulgarian position on the famous " Pip " Ridge. It also was known that the 60th Division would not be directly concerned, but would " stand to " in readiness to take advantage of any break through that might be made. The 2/13th, having been relieved by the 2/16th, were in reserve at Dache when the first preliminary British bombardment was opened on April 21st. The next day the enemy sent over a strong aerial squadron to bomb both the line and the railway dumps at the rear, and succeeded in doing considerable damage. The British bombardment and the accompanying enemy aerial activity continued daily for a week, and the Kensingtons, spending a most uncomfortable time in consequence of their close proximity to the forward dumps, began to wish that they were in the line. The ill-fated attack was launched on the night of April 24th–25th, and continued intermittently for four days until the final assault was made on the night of April 28th–29th. It proved a costly failure, the Bulgars stubbornly maintaining their positions on the " Pip " Ridge. The 179th Brigade, standing to, were interested spectators only. Whatever slender chance of success this attack might have had seemed, to the watching Londoners, to have been irretrievably lost by the full week's warning which the enemy was given by the bombardment.

Everybody in the Battalion was saddened by the news of the sinking of the *Transylvania*, the fine ship which had carried them from France a few months earlier. The German U-boat campaign in the Mediterranean had reached its height about this time, and ships were being sunk daily, so that the already depleted supplies for the Salonika Forces were becoming further, and seriously, jeopardised. So many mails were being sunk that many men instituted a system of numbering their correspondence with the folks at home, and the missing numbers told their own tale.

During this action, the Kensingtons again moved into the line, taking over from the 2/15th (Civil Service Rifles) on April 26th, with Battalion Headquarters in Clichy Ravine. The weather was vile, and all got a good soaking going up. A quiet week followed the British attack against the " Pip " Ridge, but early in May it was learned that the 60th Division was shortly to undertake a minor offensive and advance their line by seizing a good slice of the extensive No-man's-land which lay between them and the enemy.

SALONIKA

A good deal of surprise was occasioned when the operation orders disclosed the proposed new front line, which was to run across a lower-lying line of hills than those held previously, and which seemed to men who had had much practical experience of patrolling the area to offer a much inferior line of defence. It was thought by many that this " British advance " and seizure of uncontested territory might be required to cover up the failure of the major action against " Pip " Ridge.

Despite this feeling, all threw themselves into the preparations with the greatest goodwill, and the operation was carefully planned, and the share of the 179th Brigade was successfully carried out. The new position had first to be seized and then put in a state of defence and adequately wired. The solid nature of the soil would prevent this being carried out in one night, and so in order to lose no single moment once the ground was taken, forward dumps of material were made beforehand, and for two or three nights prior to the " advance " the area in front was a scene of great activity. So carefully was this veiled, that no hint of the forthcoming move seems to have reached the alert Bulgar patrols who nightly shared the wide stretch of No-man's-land with our own patrols. The advance was scheduled for the night of May 8th–9th, the 179th Brigade operation orders providing for three battalions (the 2/13th, 2/14th, and 2/16th) to advance, with the remaining unit (the 2/15th) in reserve. An early attempt by the 180th Brigade to take a salient on their front had already been repulsed, so that, despite the secrecy which had attended the preliminaries, a " walk-over " was by no means certain.

The advance of the three battalions was not contested, however, although their unusual presence in front of their wire in such strength was noted by the enemy, whose artillery was soon in action and caused a number of casualties. This did not in any way hamper the predestined work from going on, and outposts having been posted well in front of the new line, every remaining man was quickly hard at work digging or wiring. Despite the utmost despatch, it was impossible to complete the work by dawn, and the Brigade withdrew to the old trenches according to prearranged plan, leaving strong posts to hold the newly won positions through the day. On the night of the 9th the work on the new line was resumed and practically completed.

The action of the enemy artillery against the new positions was so half-hearted that it was assumed the Bulgars were not unduly worried about the nearer approach of the British to their line, but at " stand to " the following evening a counter-attack was launched against part of the line held by the 2/16th (Queen's Westminsters). The Kensingtons were not directly concerned, but it transpired that an advanced post of the Westminsters had been wiped out, the few occupants gallantly refusing to give way against much greater numbers. The post was almost at once counter-attacked and retaken.

Very hot weather had now set in, and the Battalion was glad to be relieved on May 12th by the Royal Welch Fusiliers, moving back to the ruins of Cidemli village, where they remained in support in most uncomfortable surroundings. Two days' rain followed, and on the 16th another move was made to Dache; here they stopped for a fortnight, undertaking the usual support duties. A return to the front line was made on the last day of the month, and the Kensingtons found themselves on Crow Hill in fairly good quarters. The improvement effected in the trenches during the sojourn of the 60th Division was striking, and the general defences were much improved, although many thought a false move had been made in May when the front line was advanced on to lower ground. That there was some ground for this opinion seemed to be proved by the fact that the relieving Division subsequently abandoned the ground prepared with so much labour, and reverted to the original line.

This proved to be the final tour of duty in the front line at Salonika, and the usual trench routine was broken by an action on June 4th.

Immediately facing the Battalion's right lay " Goldies

Hill," a prominent position in No-man's-land, which it was the object of both British and Bulgar patrols to occupy during the hours of darkness. On the night of June 3rd A Company, occupying the right of the line, sent out a party of three N.C.O.s and nine men to occupy the hill as usual. This party was split into three, under Sergeant Major, Corporal Key, and L/Cpl. Newham respectively, and without opposition took up positions on the top and the right and left sides of the hill. About 11 p.m. a Bulgar rocket went up, putting the Kensington party on its guard, and shortly afterwards Corporal Key and three men on the left observed a patrol of some thirty to forty Bulgars advancing up the slope of the hill. Key and his men at once threw their few bombs and opened rapid fire, which was followed by yells from the enemy. Finding their ammunition running low, Corporal Key decided to make his way across to the sergeant for instructions, and in doing so nearly ran into a party of Bulgars who were working their way round the hill. Wriggling his way under cover of darkness, Key was inadvertently fired upon by his own party, but luckily was not hit, and the entire party was able to get back to its own trenches in safety. It appeared that a runner who had been sent to warn them to withdraw had lost his way and failed to deliver the message. Our trench mortars then opened fire on Goldies Hill, and after a brief rest our party returned there, to find that the Bulgars had withdrawn.

The following night the same party again went out from A Company wearing full equipment, as they were to be relieved during the night by B Company. This time they found that the enemy were there first. During the relief the Bulgars on Goldies Hill opened fire, and the party under L/Cpl. Newham found themselves in difficulties and had to fight their way back. Newham himself was badly wounded, and Private Bytheway was unfortunately captured, whilst most of the party were hit by splinters in the face and chest. Captain Brockhurst, commanding B Company, thought it advisable to strengthen the Goldies patrol to twenty-five N.C.O.s and men, and this party was led out by Corporal Key. From some twenty-five yards below the summit of the hill the position was rushed with the bayonet, but was found to be unoccupied, the Bulgars having retired with their prisoner.

The next day the Battalion was relieved by the 8th South Wales Borderers, and moved back into reserve trenches, known as "Sandbag City." Rumour was rife that the 60th Division was to be withdrawn from the Salonika Front, but the secret of their destination was well kept. On the evening of June 8th the march back to Salonika commenced, the first destination being Janis, where bivouacs were pitched. The march lasted five days and proved tiring but uneventful; the column rested during the day and marched in the comparative cool of the evening, bivouacs being pitched at Sarigol on the 9th, Sarimaule on the 10th, Naresh on the 11th, and Uchantur being reached on the 12th. This spot was some three miles from the original camping ground of unhappy memories, occupied by the Battalion upon its arrival at Salonika seven months earlier. The weather was now very different and the ground was as hard as iron. Flies proved a terrible pest, and the men began to suffer severely from dysentery. Whilst the Transport Section had previously had their hands full with refractory mules, they were now busily engaged in re-equipping. The Battalion was occupied daily with tactical exercises, chiefly in attack formations, which hinted at more stirring days to come.

There was no leave granted to Salonika, neither was any really desired; but the neighbourhood was very desolate and, once the day's work was over, time hung heavily. There was plenty of excitement occasioned by air-raid scares, the enemy aircraft being very active at this stage of the campaign, enjoying as they did a marked superiority. A full-dress raid occurred on the 18th, when the whole Brigade scattered in artillery "blobs," raising a terrific cloud of dust which must have proved quite useful to the raiders, whilst the following day another air raid took place, bombs being dropped on the harbour. The authorities apparently expected a further raid of serious dimensions, and on the night of June 22nd the Brigade was turned out and spent a back-aching night endeavouring to dig shelter "slits" in the unyielding soil; the efficiency or otherwise of these was never put to the test, for the anticipated super-raid did not materialise, although spasmodic enemy aerial activity continued. On the 17th an inspection was carried out by Major-General Bulfin, G.O.C. the 60th Division, and it became certain that the Division was to leave the country, but the actual destination was still kept secret. On the 24th orders were suddenly received for half the Battalion to move down to the docks, where it was rumoured they were to embark for Egypt—one of the few rumours that subsequently proved to be correct, although confirmation was lacking at the time. The remainder of the Battalion, together with the Transport, stayed on at Uchantur and endured one of the worst storms in its experience on the 28th. The wind attained a great velocity, accompanied by torrential rain. Dozens of tents were blown down, and articles of equipment, together with various personal belongings, were blown all over the camp, which presented a sorry spectacle afterwards. This was followed by a spell of intense heat, during which the plague of flies nearly drove the men mad. Oh, this blighted Salonika! Would they never get away from it? With the exception of some halcyon days at Katerina, the Battalion had experienced nothing but discomfort of every possible kind since landing on these inhospitable shores eight months earlier and yearned for the merest breath of civilisation, even though it be the prelude to sterner days in France. Dysentery had ravaged the ranks, leaving but a skeleton Battalion to carry out the numerous guards and duties, so that no one had any rest and all were weary and heartily sick of their present life. July 1st brought the welcome orders to prepare to move, and the next morning every man was able to plunge into the sea at Salonika, where a brief halt was made before embarkation on the

Manitou. Whereas the advance half of the Battalion (under Major Gladstone on board the *Minominee*) had a very pleasant crossing to Alexandria, the rear half was not so fortunate, and found that they had to share a not very commodious boat with the transport animals. Less than three days, however, sufficed for the voyage, and on July 5th at midday the *Manitou* berthed in Alexandria Harbour, and another phase of the war had opened for the 2/13th.

Although the period spent as part of the Salonika Forces was almost uniformly miserable, it was undoubtedly very valuable in helping to mould the Battalion into an efficient fighting unit. Of actual fighting there, it had seen very little, although a considerable number of casualties were sustained during the period spent in the trenches; but as it turned out subsequently, the varying experiences they had encountered in Macedonia were of just the right type to fit them for the strenuous days ahead. Particularly was this true of the long and arduous marches, which were destined to be repeated in another three or four months under even more trying conditions. One would hesitate to say that the Battalion could not have carried through the Palestine campaign without their Salonika training, but that it proved of inestimable benefit, and fitted them for the job as nothing else could have done, can hardly be denied. The sufferers from dysentery quickly recovered, and within a very short time the whole Battalion was as fit a body of men as could be found anywhere.

They landed in Egypt quite ignorant of the state of the campaign there, or of the immense forces which were slowly being gathered under the command of General Allenby, and which were destined finally to rout the Turkish Armies on that front, and so break the Turks' hold on Syria and Palestine for ever. The general impression was that it was even more of a " side-show " than Salonika, would be much more pleasant, and altogether something of a picnic. They were soon to be undeceived.

CHAPTER XXI

PALESTINE

THE troops sensed a new spirit of orderliness and of purpose as soon as they set foot in Egypt. Hardly three hours after disembarking they were entrained and, even more significant, the train was moving. They found themselves comfortably settled in quasi-luxurious rolling-stock of the Egyptian State Railways, which proved a pleasant change from the dirty and cold trucks which served to transport the military of France. The weather was very hot, it is true, but the wonders of the unfamiliar landscape drove away monotony, and a number of stops were made at wayside stations where quantities of native produce, such as eggs, tomatoes, and melons, were readily obtainable. When a troop train stopped in France, it was usually at some desolate spot where the only thing obtainable was hot water from the engine driver, secured, for tea-making, after a hurried sprint up the line, followed by a breathless leap back into moving trucks. Here in Egypt the first impressions were decidedly more pleasing.

A seven-hour journey brought them to Ismailia, where they detrained and marched to Moascar Camp, just outside the town. Tents were found standing, and conditions generally were all that could be desired. No leave passes were necessary to go into Ismailia, and everybody availed themselves freely of the privilege. It proved a pleasant little place, with plenty of shade and several quite good places where a decent meal could be obtained. At the same time leave was at once opened for Cairo, and although the Battalion did not remain long enough for more than a proportion of its number to take advantage of this, those who were lucky enough to make the journey returned with glowing accounts of the attractions offered by the capital city. Indeed, it would perhaps be true to say that at this stage of the war, leave was to be spent more pleasantly in Cairo than at home, where the pinch was beginning to be felt and the heartbreaking gaps in almost every home threw a shadow over leave days.

Re-fitting on an extensive scale began immediately. A welcome issue of khaki drill was made, and the members of the Transport Section departed into the desert to be instructed in the mysterious ways of camels. Every day a little light training was undertaken, but light as it was it proved burdensome, owing to the intense heat and the heavy sand, to both of which the troops were as yet unaccustomed. It was their first experience of the desert, which ran right up to Ismailia, and they found it heavy going and productive of great thirst. This was readily quenched at Ismailia, but was to prove the greatest trial of the ensuing fifteen months.

It will be fitting here to leave the Battalion at Ismailia for a moment and consider the circumstances which led up to the arrival of the 60th Division in Egypt and the military position as it was known to exist at that time. The British Forces there were known as the Egyptian Expeditionary Force (the E.E.F.), and in the early days of the war were charged with the duty of holding the Suez Canal and protecting Egypt against the attack which the Turkish Army essayed soon after the declaration of hostilities. The attack had been easily defeated and was followed by a British advance to the eastern side of the Canal, and thence onwards across the Sinai Desert to the borders of southern Palestine. The Turks had offered no very determined resistance, but had proved themselves adept in the art of getting away, so that no matter how rapidly the British attacks were pressed, it was seldom that anything beyond abandoned trenches were taken. This facility of the Turks to make a good clean retreat was to manifest itself throughout the campaign, until that final day when, chiefly through the operations of the Royal Air Force, it proved no longer possible, and nothing but a scattered and thin remnant of the Turkish Armies escaped. It proved a constant source of surprise to the British troops throughout the campaign, and quite a legend grew up about the powers of "Johnny's get-away."

The Sinai Desert is a most inhospitable region in which to wage modern warfare. It is all but waterless, and therefore without trees or shade of any kind, and the heavy sand renders wheeled transport impracticable. The age-old caravan route from Egypt to Palestine which closely follows the coast-line is but the semblance of a " road," but it was along this route that the British advance continued, based on Kantara, at first merely a native village of mud huts on the banks of the Suez Canal, but by July 1917 an Army base-town of imposing dimensions. The speed of the advance had been governed by two factors—the provision of water and of facilities for transport. Both presented almost overwhelming difficulties which had been overcome in a remarkable manner by the British engineers and railwaymen concerned, and which were reminiscent of the wonderful work on the Upper Nile which was a necessary prelude to the final and successful Sudan Campaign of the late '80's. The first was met by the laying of a pipe-line reaching from the Canal right across the desert; the second by the building of a railway alongside the vital pipe-line, and by the provision of a " wire road " which would take wheeled transport, or greatly facilitate the marching of troops should the railway be out of action or required for other traffic. By the early spring of 1917 the railhead was at Deir el Belah, a distance of roughly 150 miles from Kantara. At that time but a single track existed, but work was being feverishly pushed forward, and in mid-November a double track was opened as far as El Arish (100 miles). It may also be mentioned at this point that the latter place was made into a hospital centre to ease the transport of sick and wounded from railhead to the base hospitals.

So far everything had gone smoothly, but once across the frontier of Palestine a definite, and it seemed a permanent, check was encountered. The whole of the barren and waterless Sinai Desert had been relinquished easily by the Turks, but with this awkward line of communication transferred to the British, the enemy soon showed that he had no intention of prolonging his retreat into Palestine. A stand was made at Gaza, on the coast, which was heavily entrenched and strongly fortified, and thence a line was established eastward along the Wadi el Ghuzze and bending back north-eastward to the town of Beersheba. In March 1917 what was known as the " First Battle of Gaza " was fought; it proved unsuccessful. In April Gaza was again attacked by the British, who were once more repulsed, this time with heavy loss. The town appeared to be impregnable, at least against frontal attack without heavy artillery. The British retired and dug themselves in on a trench line facing the town in the low-lying coastal area, whilst the Turks redoubled their efforts to strengthen their defences at Gaza, and proceeded to extend their efforts along the line. The short spring passed, to be succeeded by the unbearably hot days of summer. The two armies lay facing each other sullenly, and the position seemed to be one of stalemate.

This was the general position when, in June 1917, General Sir Edmund H. H. Allenby, G.C.B., G.C.M.G., commanding the Third Army in France, was sent to take over command of the E.E.F. and to report to the Government upon the position in Palestine, together with the action he recommended should be taken. A happier choice could not have been made; General Allenby had established a great reputation on the Western Front, where more reputations were lost than made, and all knew that his command of the moribund E.E.F. meant action, strong, resolute, and definite. We should either get on or get out. Arriving in Egypt at the end of June, he lost not a single moment. Visiting the front, he consulted with the Commander of the " Eastern Force " (Lieut.-General Sir Phillip Chetwode, Bt., K.C.M.G., C.B., D.S.O., later to win fame as Commander of Allenby's XXth Corps), and by the second week of July had telegraphed his proposals to the Cabinet.

These embodied offensive operations to be undertaken against the Turkish Army in the autumn, contingent upon reinforcements of two British Divisions, together with certain units of Yeomanry and other arms. His proposals were accepted with commendable (and unusual) promptness and his request for reinforcements granted. The 10th (Irish) and 60th (London) Divisions were ordered from Salonika to Egypt forthwith. Major-General Bulfin was given the command of the XXIst Corps and handed over the 60th Division to Major-General J. S. M. Shea, who had come over from France with General Allenby.

From that moment the entire area covered by the E.E.F. became a hive of activity. The most extensive and formidable preparations were undertaken consistent with the forces available. These, although considerable, were none too many for the great task ahead. General Allenby had at his disposal six British, one Indian, and three mounted Divisions. Opposing him were the Turkish Seventh and Eighth Armies, later reinforced by the Fourth Army. The British Forces were divided into three Corps, the XXth, the XXIst, and the Desert Mounted Corps. The 60th were drafted to the XXth, under the command of Lieut.-General Sir P. Chetwode, on the right of the British line. Here, as the extreme right-flank infantry, it was their duty to link up with the Desert Mounted Column, and upon them subsequently fell the brunt of the important opening operations against Beersheba, and the honour of capturing the town and rolling up the Turkish left flank.

Kantara itself became a base of gigantic proportions, the Canal being widened and deepened to permit the passage of ocean-going ships right up to the base, and from that great centre poured masses of material along the railway, for the doubling of the track itself, for the opening up of advanced bases and hospitals, and the transport of heavy siege guns and every kind of war material. All the important base depôts had been previously situated in Egypt, and these were transferred to Kantara, the work being carried on feverishly and against time, in order that the Army in the field might derive full benefit from their activities when the new campaign opened. Advanced depôts were opened at Rafa, Khan Yunis, and at Deir el Belah, whilst a double track as far as El Arish was actually completed by mid-November, a fortnight after Beersheba had fallen. A fresh railhead at Shellal was established two months earlier.

During this time, the strategic position had undergone important alterations, and this time not to the advantage of the Turks. It has been seen that the Turks, having heavily fortified the town of Gaza on the coast, went on to extend their defences along the line of the Wadi el Ghuzze eastwards towards Beersheba. They could not be blind to the nature of the preparations which were being carried on in front of them, and evidently deciding that the Wadi el Ghuzze, which was but a dry watercourse until the rainy season set in, did not offer a sufficient natural defence against the forces which were now likely to operate against them, withdrew their line of defence to the hills north of the Wadi. Here they commenced to dig and wire what were subsequently proved to be formidable defences, which ran almost unbroken to Beersheba. By forcing this bloodless withdrawal General Allenby gained control of valuable additional water supplies which existed in the Wadi itself, and which greatly eased the water problem for the XXth and Desert Mounted Corps. It also enabled him to bring the railway up to Shellal, where there were important wells, and finally to take the line across the Wadi to Karm. This piece of daring was abundantly justified and was protected by the strong cavalry patrols which General Allenby kept going throughout that summer in the Wadi el Ghuzze area.

The reader will realise that conditions varied greatly along the length of the Palestine front during the summer of 1917. In the west, or coastal sector, the armies faced each other from entrenched positions, which grew farther apart as the line stretched eastwards, until on the British side the entrenchments ceased altogether. Several miles divided the opposing armies and the British flank was pro-

PALESTINE

tected by cavalry patrols and isolated defensive positions manned by the infantry. It was the latter conditions with which the 60th Division were concerned and which became their first and main duty to assimilate.

Picking up the thread of our narrative again at Ismailia, we find the Battalion completely re-equipped there by July 16th, 1917, and packing up ready to move off on its long, long trail northwards, to be pursued now until the war is over. The march to Kantara from Ismailia took three days, the route lying alongside the Suez Canal and through the desert. Leaving Moascar Camp about 5 p.m., they plunged into the sandy wastes for the first time with full equipment, and although the march was carried out during the cool of the evening, the experience was trying. The landscape was extremely desolate and the Canal, lying between the two sandy ridges, was hidden from view, so that the eye met nothing but sand, not an inconsiderable quantity of which seemed to get into the throat. El Ferdan was reached about 9.30 p.m. the first night, and the Battalion bivouacked under the stars. In the morning the waters of the Canal looked inviting and provided an excellent bathe. Resuming the march the following night, bivouacs were pitched at Balah, and again a welcome swim was possible. Reveille sounded the next morning at 3.30 a.m., and the final stage of the march was completed to Kantara. Here the Suez Canal was crossed for the first time, and the remainder of the march was through the dreary wilderness of the vast base-camp to the railway station, where the troops entrained at once in open trucks which were, however, provided with temporary and very necessary head-cover from the sun. The train journey through the Sinai Desert to railhead at Deir el Belah took fourteen hours, and, uncomfortable as it was, one could not help comparing this luxurious mode of transit with the lot of the men who had taken months to cover that same distance, laying the railway, the wire road, and the vital pipeline as they went. Save for occasional glimpses of the sea, there was absolutely nothing to be seen *en route* but sand

and more sand, until the train passed through El Arish, which was quite a pleasant-looking oasis, and was very soon to form an advanced hospital base.

Railhead was reached about 1 a.m., but it was three hours later before the weary troops lay down to rest. One of those unfortunate contretemps arose when the best-laid plans of the Staff seem to go wrong, and for some little time the Battalion was led aimlessly about in the darkness, to be told again and again to "lie down on packs," until it seemed that they were indeed literally lost "in the Desert of Sin." But eventually the right area was found and in a few minutes all were fast asleep—their first night in Palestine. The glories of the morning amply compensated for the experiences of the night; the 2/13th found itself camped on the shores of the Mediterranean, with very little to do save bathe in the glorious breakers and lie on the soft sandy beach, where the sand was very different from the soft dust of the desert. Standing out beyond the line of breakers was a Naval supply ship landing stores, an operation which provided a considerable amount of interest and a certain amount of danger. It also gave a thrill to be once again in close contact with the Navy, some of the ships of which were to render valuable assistance during the bombardment of Gaza three months later. The bathing on the coast was rare fun, albeit somewhat dangerous, and a system of beach patrols was necessary to prevent fatalities. The Brigade spent a week amid these delightful surroundings and benefited immensely. The front line opposite Gaza was only some ten miles distant, and the rumble of occasional guns served as a reminder that the "picnic" was temporary. The most important item of interest which occurred during the stay near railhead was the issue of camels to the sorely tried Transport Section, who, as one member of which remarked, "only wanted a few 'ruddy' elephants to complete the blinking menagerie!" It may be remarked that at this time General Allenby had some 30,000 of these wonderful beasts, and nearly all were allocated to the XXth Corps, as vital adjuncts to the transport facilities of his eastern force. They were managed by fellahin of the Egyptian Labour Corps, marvellously tough and wonderfully dirty, who went through the rigours of a Palestine winter, clad for the most part in a solitary garment.

During the stay at Deir el Belah numbers of officers were able to visit the coastal sector, held by the 54th Division.

On July 29th this pleasant stay came to an end and the whole of the 179th Brigade moved off to take up duties at the right of the line. For sheer discomfort this march was one of the worst endured up to this time. There was no road, of wire or otherwise, and the desert was just powdery sand similar to very thick white dust on an old country road, into which the feet sank at every step. The marching column raised a cloud of dust some fifteen feet high, which hung motionless in the still air, forming a thick curtain which caused a choking sensation and made breathing difficult. When the usual ten-minutes' halt was called and there was opportunity to look about, men could scarcely recognise their fellows, so thickly coated were they with dust. The contrast with conditions at the camp just vacated on the coast could hardly be greater, but a soldier's life was ever thus. Bivouacs were pitched that night in the desert, and the march resumed the next evening to Tel el Fara, where the 2/13th were in Brigade Reserve, taking over from the 1/7th Battalion Cheshire Regiment. At this time the strength was 34 officers and 888 O.R.s. The 179th Brigade took over from the 159th (53rd Division) holding an entrenched position in the Shellal-Gamli defences on the eastern edge of the Wadi el Ghuzze, which had been strongly wired, and which protected the water supply at Shellal. The Turks were a long distance away, and the sentries in the trenches saw no more of them than did the 2/13th in reserve, for the Yeomanry patrolled the stretch of desert which lay between the Turkish positions and the Wadi. The latter, although actually a water-course, was, in fact, a stretch of country varying in width from a mile to a mile and a half, lying between two sheer faces of cliff in the desert. It was a bewildering piece of country, composed of sandhills and gullies, all looking exactly alike and amazingly easy to become lost in.

A fortnight later the Battalion moved back to a fresh camp position near El Gamli, relieving the 2/15th on the right sector, where a period of twelve days was spent before another and final move was made to El Shauth, after being relieved by the 2/17th, which was to be the home of the Kensingtons until the time came for the offensive to be taken. Here the camp site was situated in flat desert scenery, the monotony of which was extreme. In every direction the eye met the same seemingly endless vistas, with not a tree to break the even monotony of the landscape. The slight relief which the arid, broken ground of El Gamli had afforded was gone, and nothing remained but sand—and flies. The number of flies which were to be found in this inhospitable region was amazing, and these were not only a serious menace to health, but a continual source of irritation. A further source of acute discomfort was the regular dust-storm which the afternoon wind brought in their train. The troops were, of course, living under bivouacs, and some protection was sought by scooping out holes in the sand and covering these with the bivouac sheets, but everything was covered with sand, whilst swarms of flies settled on every particle of food. Water was severely rationed, not only on account of the necessity for conserving supplies, but because it was important that everybody should become accustomed to existing on the smallest possible quantity.

The 179th Brigade had been relieved from their duties in the line by the 180th Brigade, and from the end of August took up serious training for the great attack in the autumn. For the most part this consisted of night work, and as it was of vital importance that the officers should be able to overcome the great difficulty of finding their way across the featureless desert by night, marching by compass and stars became the main feature of the work. On the whole it was very monotonous work for the ranks, who had only to march and march, night after night, with no intelli-

PALESTINE

gent interest in the route, which usually lay between two points on a somewhat barren map. It proved absorbing enough to those whose difficult job it was to locate the given points and arrive there at the appointed time, and many were the weary and circuitous marches undergone before reasonable accuracy was attained.

During the daytime the heat was intense and little could be done except lie under the scanty shelter provided by the bivouac sheets and swat the innumerable flies which made life almost unbearable. For this purpose every man was issued with a gauze fly swatter, but although the havoc wrought by these was immense, it never seemed to have much effect upon the numbers of the pests. Time hung heavily and letter writing languished for lack of something to write about. Leave to Cairo was commenced and brought a bright episode into the lives of most, for there was plenty to see and do there, and as opportunities for spending money in the desert were practically nil, pay accumulated and provided the wherewithal to enjoy the five or six days which most men were able to spend in the capital.

Despite the barren nature of the country, every effort was made to provide some relaxation, and a number of successful Battalion concerts were held, whilst it was here that the Brigade concert party, " The Roosters," made its name by providing a show which was far above the average army entertainment. The 60th Division already possessed a first-class concert party in " The Barnstormers," and produced comparatively lavish entertainments, but in the nature of things the Divisional troops saw more of these than the infantry units, and " The Roosters " filled a long-felt gap in splendid manner. When they entertained their regimental colleagues under the desert skies during that summer of 1917, they probably had little idea that the name of " The Roosters " was in later years to become known throughout the length and breadth of the Home Country. They did their job exceedingly well, and the survivors of their Palestine audiences will never cease to thank them for their efforts to dispel the weary monotony of those long weeks.

No matter what the circumstances may be, if the British soldier is given half a chance, he will produce a game of football, and Shellal proved no exception. In spite of the unfavourable conditions (and less propitious circumstances could hardly be imagined!), football loomed large in the activities of the Kensingtons when the sun had passed its zenith.

On August 31st, after a practice attack at dawn, the Battalion marched past the G.O.C. 60th Division, Major-General Shea, and repeated the performance on September 4th. A change in the Adjutancy took place at this period—Lieut. Phillips was posted to 179th Brigade Staff and was succeeded by Captain C. E. Brockhurst. This led to some reshuffling of Company Commanders, who were now as follows: A, Captain C. T. Foster; B, Capt. E. R. Kisch; C, Captain A. W. Tosland; and D, Captain S. M. Green.

An interesting experiment was carried out on the night of September 4th, the Brigade concentrating in the Wadi Shanag, where each battalion in turn advanced to within 100 yards of a row of wire in attack formation. Our artillery then opened fire on the wire over the heads of the infantry, who observed the effects. Not a very pleasant experience!

Brigade field-firing schemes occupied the next day or two, while on September 11th the Battalion was inspected by the G.O.C. Division. The eyeglass of Major-General Shea, and the twinkling eye behind it, were by now familiar to the troops. A few days later bayonets were withdrawn for sharpening by the 519th Company of R.E.s, which looked like business.

September 19th saw an inspection by the Colonel in order to select the smartest company to attend a Divisional Church Parade. This honour was won by C Company, under Captain Tosland, and they were away for two days attending the ceremony in question. A further decisive step in the great preparations was taken on the 20th of the month, when three officers and 109 O.R.s were withdrawn to Brigade Reinforcement Camp, to form the nucleus of a fresh battalion in the event of heavy casualties. The party included 33 per cent. of all specialists.

While the 60th Division was engaged in its necessary but somewhat monotonous training and finding time hang despite all its efforts, preparations in other directions were being pushed ahead with all possible speed. Masses of material were pouring into the desert area, work on the railway was proceeding feverishly, and the Royal Air Force was carrying out frequent reconnaissances of the Beersheba area, from which large numbers of aerial photographs of the Turkish positions were obtained. From a collection of these at 179th Brigade Headquarters a splendid relief model of the entire Turkish trench system in front of Beersheba was built up. This work was done by the Intelligence Section at Brigade Headquarters, the members of which were drawn from the Scout Section of the Kensingtons. The model was made of clay and had to be kept moistened daily to prevent cracking, but by means of constant attention it was maintained in good condition until parties of officers and N.C.O.s from all the brigade units had had an opportunity of visiting it. This was but one example of the meticulous care which was taken during the course of the preparations to ensure that, so far as was possible, everyone thoroughly mastered the details of the work to come. Towards the end of the period spent in training a series of mounted reconnaissances was undertaken in the direction of Beersheba; the chief of these, on October 2nd, was carried out on an ambitious scale, for in addition to the full Divisional and Brigade Staffs, each unit was represented by its C.O., Second in Command, Adjutant, officers commanding companies, and specialist officers and N.C.O.s of all kinds. To secure this important party against attack from the strong Turkish mounted patrols which were known to be active in the hills and wadis fronting Beersheba, it was necessary to provide a screen of Yeomanry outposts.

A rendezvous was fixed at a ruined house, known as Rashid

Bek, for 9 a.m., and in order to reach this in time it was necessary for most of the parties to leave their units before dawn. The first part of the arrangements was carried out according to plan, and in the early afternoon the objectives were reached and little knots of men were to be seen on the foothills facing the Turkish trenches, carefully taking bearings and comparing them with the maps in their hands. Seldom can such a large-scale reconnaissance prior to an important attack have been carried out with such insolent disregard of the enemy. Had the Turks realised exactly what was happening in front of them and taken prompt action, it is probable that they would have made some important captures that day, but from the large numbers engaged in the reconnaissance they may be excused for perhaps thinking that an actual attack was imminent. Be that as it may, no attempt was made to interfere with the reconnaissance, which then began to penetrate much farther than had been originally proposed, so that various small parties went through the Yeomanry screen and underwent the rare privilege of actually going over the approaches to the ground allotted to their units in the scheme of operations. Darkness fell while this work was still in progress, and with it the issue of sundry Turkish patrols. No sort of contact had been maintained between the various odd parties now dispersed throughout the rocky wadis leading up to the Turkish position, there was no moon, and it was impossible to distinguish between friend and foe except at close quarters; the position of the entire reconnoitring force became one of extreme peril. There were several close brushes with enemy patrols and a few stray shots were heard. The position of the Yeomanry covering the reconnaissance was one of difficulty; fronting them and completely screened by the darkness was a stretch of unfamiliar country in which were numerous small parties of both Turks and British, and it was hardly a matter for surprise that before the withdrawal of the reconnoitring force some at least of the latter came under fire from the Yeomanry, but happily without a casualty. The various small units had so far exceeded the original intention that any concerted withdrawal was impossible under the circumstances, and eventually all made their own way back to their lines. It was 7 o'clock on the following morning when the weary little band of Kensingtons returned to camp, having been absent some twenty-eight hours, a large number of which were spent in the saddle. Some of the N.C.O.s were mounted on mules borrowed from the transport lines, and as for several it was their first real experience astride an animal, their feelings the following day may be imagined!

The observations taken during this reconnaissance were invaluable, and the clocklike precision of the subsequent Beersheba operations was in no small measure due to the information which the officers and N.C.O.s engaged in it obtained on this occasion. From now onwards the attack formation training of the Battalion proceeded apace and several night " stunts " were undertaken. The senior officers were called to Brigade Headquarters and received from Brig.-General Edwards their battle disposition. On October 20th the Kensingtons left their old camp, after parading for a few final words from the G.O.C., and joined the other three battalions of the 179th Brigade at El Gamli, camping in the wadi by day. The following night they trekked forward to Bir el Esani, where a certain amount of cover was provided by scrub and broken ground, and here bivouacs were pitched for a week, most of which was spent in resting and completing final preparations. The halt at Bir el Esani was made to protect the R.E.s, who were developing water supplies there. As much secrecy as possible was observed, the camp being camouflaged and all unnecessary movement during the day prohibited.

It may be thought that this was a somewhat unnecessary precaution in view of the fact that the enemy could scarcely be unaware of the nature of the preparations of the preceding months, culminating in the elaborate reconnaissance in front of the Beersheba positions already described. That the Turks knew that an attack was imminent was certain, but it was subsequently proved beyond all doubt that he was kept guessing right up to the last, and never knew that the main attack was to be launched against his left flank until he was swept in a few hours from his carefully prepared defences at Beersheba. Intelligence was well aware that the enemy was becoming jumpy, and on October 27th the Turks themselves attempted to carry out a large-scale reconnaissance, no doubt with the view of setting their doubts at rest and finding out exactly what was happening in front. On the morning of October 27th a strong force, consisting of two regiments of cavalry and two or three thousand infantry, with guns, issued from the direction of Kauwukah towards Karm, and attacked an outpost near El Girheir, held by Yeomanry. General Allenby was throwing out a railway line to Karm, and the unwonted activity had aroused the Turks' curiosity. One post was rushed and cut up; another, although surrounded, held out all day and inflicted heavy losses on the enemy. The 53rd (Welsh) Division was hastily summoned and, coming up, caused the Turks to withdraw. That same day the bombardment of the Gaza defences commenced and continued daily; on October 30th the warships of the Royal Navy joined in. The bombardment was the heaviest ever carried out in Palestine, and its intensity convinced the Turks that the main attack was to be against their right flank, and so their left flank at Beersheba was left without the reinforcements which could easily have been hurried there and by their presence have made the task of the Desert Mounted Corps well-nigh impossible.

Lying huddled in their flimsy bivouacs at Bir el Esani, the Kensingtons listened to the rumble of the guns on the coastal sector and knew that the hour was near. After the three long months of irritating monotony and hard training on the desert every man was eager to be getting a move on; few realised the immensity of the great task which lay ahead, but it is true to say that all were very confident of the final issue, and that this confidence persisted throughout the year which was to follow before the Armistice. Of hardship there was to be plenty, but the Army was all the time moving forward, and save in the case of the Jordan raids, there was never any of the sense of frustration which followed all the big offensives on the Western Front.

The final march commenced on October 28th, the 179th Brigade concentrating around Abu Ghalyun, on the Wadi Khalasa, a point about eight miles south-west of the advanced Turkish post at Ras Hablein. Here the Brigade lay low for forty-eight hours. During the day on October 30th, the battle orders were made known. The attack from the 60th Divisional front was to be made by the 179th and 181st Brigades, with the 180th Brigade in reserve; the 179th was allotted the extreme right flank of the infantry, linking up with the Yeomanry Mounted Division, with the Anzac Mounted Division engaging in a flanking movement to the east of the town. The 179th was to move forward in brigade order with the Kensingtons as advanced Battalion, followed by the 2/14th (London Scottish), 2/15th (Civil Service Rifles), and 2/16th (Queen's Westminsters).

As advanced Battalion, the Kensingtons had the duty of clearing the ground by engaging and driving in the Turkish patrols. There was real disappointment that they were not in the actual first attack, this duty being delegated to the 2/14th and 2/15th, but as support Battalion the duties of the 2/13th included the pursuit of the enemy once the front-line trench system was carried, and this part of the operations was looked forward to with the greatest interest.

Shortly before dusk fell on October 30th bivouacs were struck, water-bottles filled, bully beef and biscuits issued, and the Battalion stood ready assembled for its first real action, under the command of Lieut.-Colonel Mackenzie. Haversacks were carried on the back, in battle order, and a small piece of biscuit tin was fastened to each, in order to let the gunners know the progress of the infantry. The night was exceptionally still and the faintest sound seemed to carry a hundred yards; that the jingling of the animals' harness would be heard a mile away seemed certain!

Punctually at 8 p.m. the column moved off, strict silence being enjoined. There was not the suspicion of a breeze,

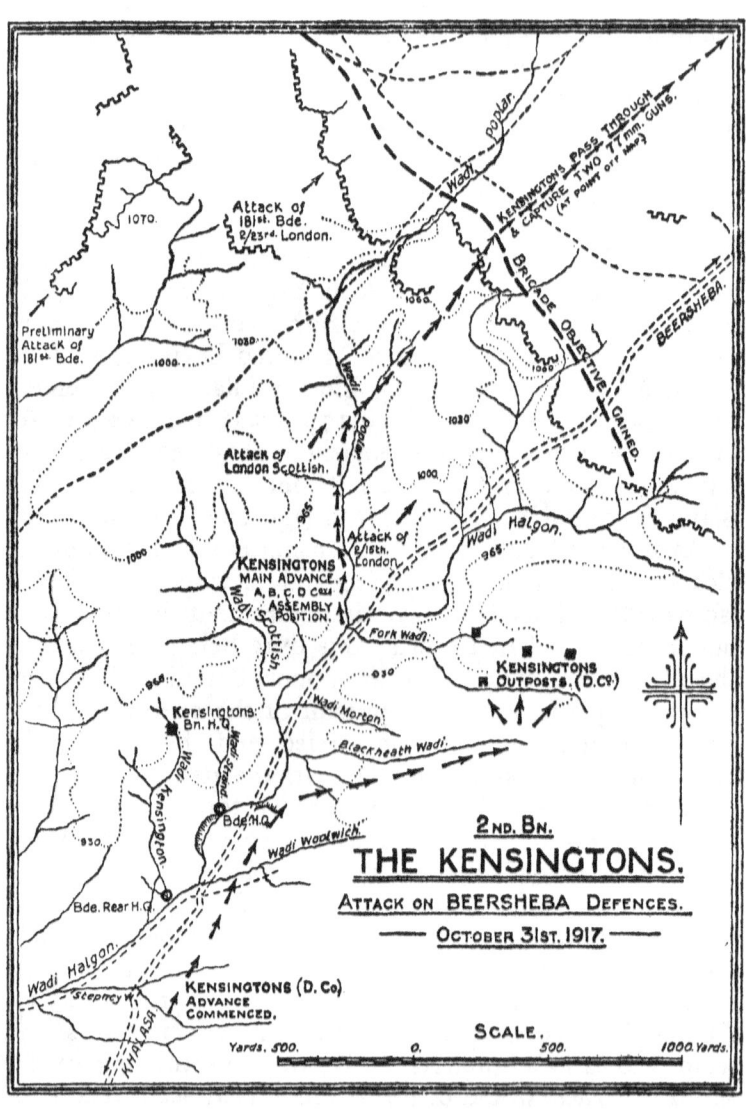

PALESTINE

and soon the laboured breathing of the marching men appeared to fill the air with sound. For two hours the Battalion moved slowly over the heavy ground and officers began to consult their watches anxiously, for less than five miles had been covered, and at this rate it did not seem possible that the point of deployment could be reached according to schedule. The column was threading its way across country in a due easterly direction, until the Beersheba–Khalasa road was struck, when this was followed, the direction then being north-east in a direct line to Beersheba. Having some experience of the "roads" in the country, the Battalion expected little from it, and it was therefore a pleasant surprise to find it in comparatively good condition, so that the rate of progress improved a great deal and Point 960, south of the Wadi Halgon, was reached in good time and well before midnight. Here the remainder of the Brigade was to rest a short time, while the Kensingtons pushed cautiously forward to cover the deployment, A and D Companies forming the advanced guard, astride the Wadi Halgon. No contact with the enemy was made until about 2 a.m., when the first Turkish patrol was encountered, who, before making a hasty withdrawal, fired a few shots at random. The Brigade having now all reached the point of deployment, the Kensingtons proceeded to carry out their second duty, which was to protect the right flank. For this purpose outposts were flung out along the Khalasa road, disturbing other Turkish patrols, so that stray rifle shots now began to re-echo through the night, followed by a few bursts of machine-gun fire from the enemy posts on the hills.

Following the deployment of the Brigade, B and C Companies entered Kensington Wadi, whilst A Company moved into Strand Wadi and D Company formed the outposts mentioned, on the high ground east of Wadi Halgon. The latter was under direct orders of Brigade and was detached temporarily from the 2/13th. Captain G. V. Thompson acted as liaison officer with the 2/14th.

D Company was under the command of Captain Green,

and carried out its outpost duty without a hitch. Proceeding in the pitch darkness by compass bearing, it found and occupied its allotted position on the hill. The company had been fired upon during the approach, and as the crest of the hill was reached, dark forms could be seen disappearing down the reverse slope. Long afterwards it was found that the Turks thought that the noise made by the approaching party was but one of the usual British cavalry patrols, proving that at that hour they had no inkling of the great attack which was being launched. Had the Turks decided to hold that hill, events might have turned out very differently; so much depended upon the surprise nature of the attack. Fortunately for D Company it was not engaged, although many casualties were suffered during the subsequent shelling.

By midnight the outpost line was in position. The hour that followed saw the whole of the attacking force taking up its position in the wadis leading up to the entrenched positions on the hills facing them. Although the utmost care was taken to avoid noise, there was an unmistakable murmur and faint jingling in the air as the ammunition mules were off-loaded, and the companies, one by one, dumped their packs and moved off to their positions. The spasmodic bursts of fire from the Turkish trenches made it clear that the enemy was by now thoroughly uneasy and aware that something momentous was taking place under cover of darkness and immediately beneath them. The preparations for the attack went forward smoothly and easily, however, and by 3 a.m. the assault battalions were reported to be in position. At a few minutes after this hour the Kensingtons sustained their first officer casualty, 2nd Lieut. M. S. Lissack being wounded, followed shortly afterwards by 2nd Lieut. Carroll. As dawn approached the Kensington outposts were withdrawn and the whole Battalion assembled at the foot of the Wadi Poplar and lay down to snatch what rest it could. This was little, for very soon the sun was rising over the hills beyond Beersheba, and at 5 a.m. the battle opened with a fierce artillery bombardment of the heavily entrenched Turkish position on Hill 1070.

This was a rocky eminence immediately to the left and formed the first objective for assault by the 181st Brigade. It enfiladed the whole of the ground to be covered by the 179th Brigade, and its capture was essential before the operations of the latter could commence. The artillery preparation lasted for three hours and presented a wonderful sight to the waiting infantry; columns of smoke and dust enveloped the Turkish positions, and it could be seen that the fire of the British artillery was remarkably accurate. Shortly after 8 a.m. long lines of tiny figures could be seen toiling up the steep approaches—the 2/22nd (Queen's) having commenced the assault. What was happening subsequently could only be surmised, for the figures disappeared into the smoke and were lost to view, but by 10 a m. the artillery fire was pounding away at the main Turkish position along the ridge in the rear and news came that Hill 1070 was ours, and the moment for the main assault was approaching. Actually two more hours were to elapse before the second bombardment had been deemed sufficiently effective. Meanwhile the position of the 179th Brigade was distinctly uncomfortable. Lying along the bare slopes of the Wadis Scottish, Poplar, and Halgon, it was exposed to the fierce rays of the sun, the men afflicted with thirst which orders definitely forbade them to quench with the precious contents of their water-bottles. The Kensingtons, assembled at the bottom of the Wadi Poplar, were in better case than the Scottish and Civil Service Rifles, who, being farther up the wadis awaiting their turn to attack, were somewhat exposed to rifle and machine-gun fire, from which they both suffered some casualties. Many of the British guns had to be moved up to fresh positions for the bombardment of the main trenches, and had to undertake fresh registration, so that the delay was unavoidable and, of course, foreseen. The Turks were by now aware that their entire position was menaced and opened a fierce fire over the whole front; they evidently had little idea of the disposition of the attackers, for much of their fire was misdirected, although shells began to burst up and down the wadis. These troubled the waiting troops less than the sun, the heat from which was now almost unbearable, scorching the rocky surface of the ground, and making it almost impossible to lie down, and as standing up or walking about was even more out of the question, everyone was acutely uncomfortable.

It came as a tremendous relief when the assaulting battalions were ordered over at 12.15 p.m. From their positions at the beginning of the attack the Kensingtons could see very little of what was going on, but they were soon following hard on the heels of the Scottish and toiling up the steep slopes of the wadi bank.

As they topped the first hill a magnificent panorama lay before them. In front, on the left and on the right, were long and apparently endless lines of khaki figures, moving forward steadily and with the utmost precision. The sun picked out the shining pieces of equipment and flashed along the rifle barrels and bayonets, until it appeared as though hundreds of heliographs were busily winking back messages. At this stage the Battalion was perhaps some 1,200-odd yards from the Turkish front trenches, which lay just under the crest of the farther ridge, wreathed in smoke, and from which a murderous fire was being maintained, despite the accuracy of the British artillery bombardment.

Perhaps half of the total casualties at Beersheba were sustained during the approach to the assault, which perforce had to be made across open ground, the hilly nature of which kept the pace of the advance a steady one. The Turkish artillery was not at this phase of the operation particularly troublesome, but the rifle and machine-gun fire was heavy, and all along the attacking waves figures could be seen dropping. There was, however, not the slightest check to the advance, which continued steadily and relentlessly. It was an impressive sight. As the Kensingtons first emerged from the wadi and came under fire, the Scottish in front were negotiating a deep wadi bed, from which their kilted figures could be seen scrambling up the farther slope. A quarter of an hour had now passed since the commencement of the assault, and the artillery barrage lifted from the first- to the second-line trenches. The great moment had come and the Kensingtons almost stood and cheered as they watched the hodden-grey men in front dash forward up the last slopes which separated them from the Turks, the long lines of bayonets flashing in the sun. The issue was never in doubt, and scarcely a few moments seemed to pass before the Scottish were sweeping on to the second line. By this time the Kensingtons were themselves making the difficult crossing of the last wadi, and as they toiled perspiringly up the slope, it was seen that the Scottish were manning the Turkish trenches and firing like mad at the fleeing figures of Turks racing towards the town of Beersheba, the roofs and minarets of which could now be plainly seen in the far background.

The smell of the battle was now thoroughly in the nostrils and with a whoop and a yell the foremost waves of the Kensingtons leapt over the trenches, where the panting Scottish lay waving them on. The Turks, however, made no stand, and when nearly a mile had been covered, the order was given to stand fast and dig in. They had now arrived on a broad rising plateau, across which the fleeing Turks were racing a zigzag course; the Battalion flopped down and opened a rapid fire in which the Lewis gunners joined and enjoyed excellent practice at the moving targets in front. Soon there remained nothing to shoot at and by 1 p.m. the whole of the enemy entrenched position was captured, and with relatively little loss. The ease with which the Turks had been dislodged from their trenches was surprising, but they had been subjected to a fierce and remarkably accurate artillery bombardment all the morning and had evidently little stomach left to face a bayonet attack. Moreover, the swiftness of the attack had taken them completely by surprise; quite evidently they had absolutely no idea of the proximity of so large a force.

But although the entrenched defences had fallen, Beersheba was not yet captured, and it was not long before the whole of the 179th Brigade came under a fairly heavy fire, from concealed machine guns and field artillery, especially from the right flank. Another machine gun on the left was particularly troublesome, and eventually B Company was ordered to try to dislodge it, but was unable to do so until dusk fell. Had the British force been in a position to sweep on to Beersheba from the first assault, it is probable that the town would have fallen to the infantry, and several hours earlier than it did. But it must be remembered that the country was very hilly and was intersected by deep wadis which were impassable for wheeled traffic, so that once the artillery had performed its work on the enemy lines, a considerable period elapsed before fresh positions could be taken up. The infantry too had moved a long distance forward from their advanced base and were without replenishments of ammunition or tools. Before the attack there was no accurate knowledge of the strength of the Turks, nor was it supposed that they would so quickly yield their entrenched positions on the ridge, leaving the road open to Beersheba.

The attack on Beersheba was twofold. Firstly, the direct assault on the trench line, allotted to the infantry; and secondly, a wide encircling movement to the south and east of the town by the cavalry, who were to ride down into Beersheba in the early afternoon. The infantry gained all their objectives in the minimum of time, but the cavalry after an all-night ride of twenty-five miles for some, and thirty-five for others, were held up after arriving at their rendezvous five miles east of Beersheba. Here an underfeature in the Wadi Saba, called Tel el Saba, was found to be strongly held and fortified, and was not taken until after some hours of fierce fighting.

This was the position throughout the long, hot afternoon, when the 60th Division, having gained all its objectives, found itself exposed on the high ground, the men digging themselves in as best they could in the rocky soil. No one knew quite what was happening except that it was evident that Beersheba was still in Turkish hands. The harassing fire of the Turks' field artillery caused a good many casualties during these anxious hours of waiting. From their high position, the Kensingtons had a most unusual view of an enemy battery in action, far away down in the foothills on the right flank, and in a position almost parallel with their own. The enemy gunners could be seen, darting to and fro, loading the shells which a few moments later came whistling over the heads of the watching infantry. The distance was too far for rifle fire, and although the F.O.O. sent back frantic messages, our own guns were evidently unable to get into action against them, and about five o'clock the battery could be seen limbering up, and soon disappeared round a hill in a cloud of dust. Meanwhile, No. 8 Platoon, led by Sergeant W. H. Godfrey, moved forward eight hundred yards to occupy the ridge from behind which the guns were firing. On reaching the crest, they were able to bring a Lewis gun and rifles into action, preventing the enemy from getting their guns away, and killing most of the crews. Later a patrol was sent forward and chalked the words " The Kensingtons " on the two captured 77 mm. field guns. The casualties of the platoon were slight, being one killed and two wounded. Sergeant Godfrey was awarded the Military Medal and had the unusual honour of being decorated by Major-General Shea on the actual battlefield. The General has subsequently confessed that he was well " slated " for his presumption by the War Office, but " thought it well worth it."

Save for this interesting diversion nothing much happened, and as the hours wore on the digging operations began to languish, for it became evident that the danger of a counter-attack was remote. The enemy fire, which had been continuous, slackened off and the machine guns ceased entirely, the Turks contenting themselves with dropping shells along the line of their old trenches, and with keeping up a steady shell fire along the Wadi Halgon and Wadi Poplar in the rear, along which supplies were now coming up. A sustained musketry fire could be heard on the other side of the town, and everyone wondered what was taking place. As dusk fell this entirely ceased and shortly after 7 p.m. news came along that Beersheba had fallen and there was no further cause for anxiety. The sky was lit by the glare of a large ammunition dump which the Turks had fired, and which later exploded; the pumping station was also blown up, but the damage proved less extensive than was feared, and the R.E.s soon had it working. It was afterwards learned that the Turkish cavalry had been defending the ground to the east of Beersheba, and had managed to hold Tel el Saba until the late afternoon. While this action was in progress, several attempts had been made by small parties of horse to cross the low-lying ground towards the town. In the early evening a mounted attack by the Australian Light Horse, riding straight at the town from the east, was completely successful, and Beersheba fell to them at 7 p.m. on the night of October 31st.

As a result of the action, 2,000 prisoners and 13 guns were taken, whilst some 500 Turkish bodies were buried on the field. The enemy left flank was laid open by the loss of Beersheba, and the way was now clear for the final big blow at Gaza. That the Turks were to the last unaware of the real British intentions is made clear by the following official Turkish appreciation, based on reports received from their air service before the operation:

" An outflanking attack on Beersheba, with about one infantry and one cavalry Division, is indicated, but the main attack, as before, must be expected on the Gaza front."

The main success of the Beersheba operation lay, however, in the complete secrecy which shrouded the actual date of the attack, coupled with the swiftness with which it was delivered. When the 60th Division left its camps in the desert, all the tents were left standing in order to deceive enemy aircraft, and it is certain that the Turks had no idea that the whole of the XXth Corps and the Desert Mounted

Corps were assembled under their noses on the night of October 30th.

Not least important among the captures at Beersheba was the invaluable water supply. This was found to be damaged, but was quickly repaired by the Engineers. Even so, the shortage of water during the following week was to prove acute; had the Turks been able to hold out at Beersheba sufficiently long to destroy the wells, Allenby's rolling up of the Turkish flank would have taken months, instead of under three weeks, and the whole history of the Palestine Campaign would have been changed.

Although it was the fate of the Kensingtons to be allotted but a secondary part in the Beersheba attack, they came through their first ordeal under open fire very creditably. Their casualties were surprisingly light—2 officers wounded, 6 O.Rs. killed, and 23 wounded. The Battalion captured 27 prisoners, including a medical officer. Lieut. L. C. Gates was awarded the Military Cross.

CHAPTER XXII

KAUWUKAH—SHERIA—HUJ

THE fall of Beersheba was followed by a lull in the activities of the 60th Division, which bivouacked on the battlefield for two days. The time was spent in cleaning up and hunting around for souvenirs, which were fairly plentiful, but nothing of great value, sentimental or otherwise, was found. Dumps were formed of captured material, and 26 enemy dead were buried. The weather was good, but the food was not, bully beef and biscuits still being the order of the day, whilst the shortage of water, far from being overcome, grew daily more acute. The large number of cavalry engaged in the Beersheba operations threw a terrific strain on the water supplies of that place, which proved insufficient to meet the demand, and while none of the infantry actually suffered from lack of water at this stage, nevertheless, supplies were so restricted as to make things very uncomfortable. They were to get worse.

The next important stage of the operations against the Turkish left flank was the assault on the strongly fortified Rushdi and Kauwukah trench systems, which covered Tel es Sheria. This was allotted to the 60th Division, but before this task could be undertaken there were numerous strategic and strongly defended posts to be cleared up, this duty being assigned to the 53rd Division, with the Imperial Camel Corps, which moved out from Beersheba to take up a position protecting the right flank of the forthcoming attack. Although Beersheba was lost, the Turkish defence was by no means broken, and they defended every possible point tenaciously, so that two clear days elapsed before the ground was sufficiently cleared for the further advance of the 10th, 60th, and 74th Divisions.

The 179th Brigade moved out from the captured

positions overlooking Beersheba late in the afternoon of November 3rd, and marched down towards the town about which they had heard so much during the past months. They saw little but a few dilapidated buildings, indescribably dirty, but the place was a hive of activity, with long lines of bored-looking camels laden with fantasses (water-tanks) awaiting their turn at the wells. Dusk was falling as the marching columns trudged through the town, raising clouds of dust which settled in the nostrils and gave rise to pangs of thirst which could not be assuaged. About two miles on the other side of the town the Battalion halted and bivouacked in a wadi. The march, although short, had taken a long time, and everybody was thoroughly tired out, and, above all, terribly thirsty. Water supplies were now entirely dependent upon the camel section of the transport, and as soon as the Battalion arrived at its appointed bivouac, the camel section set out again on its long trek to the Brigade water rendezvous. The night was pitch dark, the rendezvous but a map reference in an entirely unknown country, and the water column dependent upon the compass marching of the Battalion guides furnished by the Scout Section. These men had, of course, undertaken the same march as the Battalion, but duty called sternly that night, and without a moment's rest they set out in silence at the head of the ghostly string of animals, across the undulating, stony country-side, their faith pinned to the instruments they held in their hands and their knowledge of the stars. Upon this and countless other similar errands they carried the heavy responsibility of their sleeping comrades, and to their credit be it said that they never failed. On this occasion dawn was breaking when the weary little convoy got back to camp.

That afternoon a further short march was made to Wadi Welfare, and here bivouacs were pitched for thirty-six hours. It was a dreary place, quite featureless, and as there was nothing to do time passed slowly; rations still consisted of bully beef and biscuits, with a little over half a normal water ration. Most of the men wrote letters home with accounts of the operations at Beersheba and, more particularly, urgent requests for Harrison's pomade and other "remedies" to combat the lice nuisance, which, owing to the entire lack of washing facilities, began to get more than merely irritating. Lieut.-Colonel Mackenzie attended a Brigadiers' conference and came back with operation orders for Kauwukah. The following day, accompanied by his senior officers, he rode forward for a preliminary reconnaissance. No approach could be made to the positions themselves, and little was to be seen, but valuable information was obtained regarding the ground to be covered in the initial advance.

Operation orders revealed that the Kensingtons, together with the Queen's Westminsters, were to be the assault battalions, with the Civil Service Rifles in support and the London Scottish in Brigade reserve.

The Kensingtons were to go over in two waves, C and D Companies forming the first, and A and B the second. Every man carried two water-bottles, together with an extra fifty rounds of S.A.A. and one bomb each. The Kensingtons were the right assaulting battalion of the 179th Brigade. On the evening of the 5th, D Company was thrown out to occupy works and cover the deployment of the Brigade.

The attack on the Kauwukah position was dated for November 6th, and the Kensingtons moved out from their inhospitable wadi at 3 a.m. on that morning. When the Brigade reached its place of assembly, it was found to be already occupied by the 180th Brigade, and the 179th had to move a little farther on.

It was very cold with wisps of damp mist curling through the stony defiles through which the Battalion at first moved in column of route. As the dawn broke and the sun came swiftly up over the Judean hills to the east, the mist dispersed and all knew that they were in for another "scorcher." Men felt furtively at their water-bottles, regarding which the most rigorous orders had been issued, and wondered when they would next be filled.

All knew that a trying day had commenced. In front lay a formidable defensive position, fortified during months of preparation, the approach to which lay over miles of open country—to be taken at the point of the bayonet under what promised to be a scorching sun, with further supplies of both water and food problematical. Every officer and man carried his own succour, and none knew how long it must be made to last. As the Battalion moved into artillery formation at 8.45 a.m. sounds of lively firing commenced away on their right front.

The attack on Kauwukah was carried out by the XXth and Desert Mounted Corps, and the 60th Division was temporarily attached to the latter, together with the Australian Mounted Division. The order of battle was the 10th, 60th, 74th Divisions, in that order, with the Yeomanry on the extreme right. The 74th Division were to attack first on the right, and it was the opening of the artillery preparation for this attack that the Kensingtons heard as they moved forward. It was known subsequently that the 74th encountered fierce resistance, which held up the attack for some time, but before this was finally carried to a successful conclusion the 60th attack had begun. The British force was opposed by the entire Turkish Seventh Army.

During the early stage of the advance towards Kauwukah, the Battalion was able to move up under cover of wadi beds in file, but the character of the ground changed, becoming gently undulating and giving little cover. By 10 a.m. the sun was shining fiercely and the Kensingtons went through our own Divisional artillery, whose gunners were hotly engaged in wire-cutting operations. At this point they came under severe shell fire, most probably intended for the artillery, and they were glad to move on away from the guns. Numbers of walking wounded began to trickle back from the 74th front, who, in answer to excited questions, reported that things were pretty hot in front. Shortly afterwards the Kensingtons came within rifle range and deployed. From their position on gently rising ground

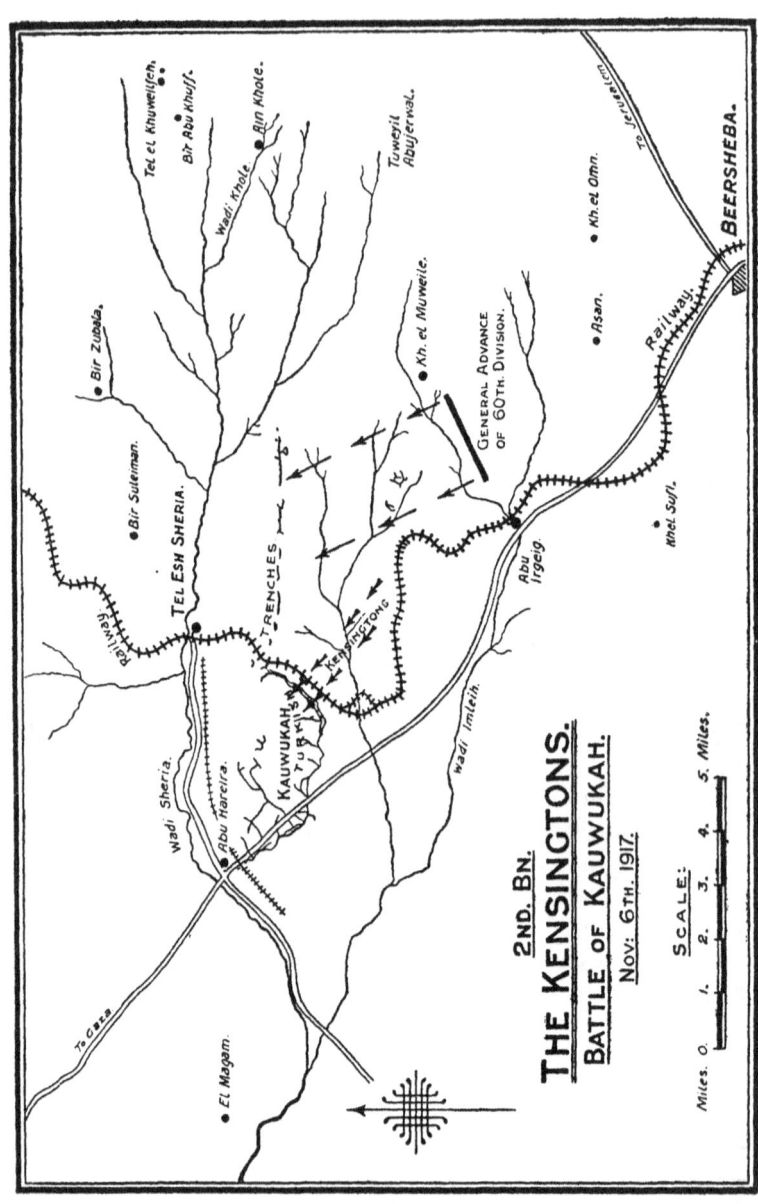

they could now plainly see the Turkish trenches, which our guns were pounding with terrible vigour. Instead of the hard, stony ground over which they had moved since the commencement of the attack on Beersheba, the Battalion now found itself on soft, reddish soil, which every explosion sent up in clouds, so that a red dust hung all about the Turkish position, clearly marking out the line of trenches, but hiding everything else. It is at least probable that this made it very difficult for the Turks to see clearly what was going on in front and rendered accurate sighting impossible.

It soon became clear that the enemy was very strong in machine guns, and in view of the open nature of the ground to be covered, substantial casualties were anticipated. It was hoped that the artillery was making a good job of the wire-cutting, for at this distance it could be seen that there was plenty of it. When the distance to the enemy trenches was perhaps 1,200 yards there came a slight check in the rate of advance, owing to the difficulty of maintaining touch with the 180th Brigade on the right, and whilst it lasted the Battalion had to lie flat in the open, with bullets tearing up the ground in all directions. At this stage of the battle Captain S. M. Green, commanding D Company, was wounded. It proved a most uncomfortable time, but the advance was resumed very steadily when ordered, and another 200 or 300 yards brought them to a slight declivity some 600 yards from the Turkish line, where a pause ensued until the moment for the final assault arrived. Lieut.-Colonel Mackenzie, with the Adjutant, Captain Brockhurst, and the Headquarters Staff, were gathered behind a small ruined hut in the centre of the Battalion's line of advance, and here the Colonel earned the real admiration of his men by his extreme coolness and quiet jocularity.

Puffing at a cigarette and carelessly swinging his walking-stick, Colonel Mackenzie moved about nonchalantly, making a few joking remarks here and there, and glancing ever and anon at his watch.

The attack at Kauwukah was absolutely of the textbook

order and similar to those practised over and over again by the Battalion in the fields of Essex, on the commons of Surrey, and the plains of Warminster. Every man felt that he knew his own particular part by heart (as indeed he did), but it meant that at this stage of the attack the Battalion had already perforce moved under prolonged shell fire and then heavy rifle and machine-gun fire; it was the supreme test of those years of training, and the Battalion came through without an outward tremor. As the men lay there in that slight drop in the ground, with that last open, bullet-swept space still to cross, every man's heart was pounding, and those who were near enough to see their Colonel's utter indifference to danger could scarce forbear to cheer wildly. The unusual sight was witnessed of the Brigade artillery galloping over open ground and going into action.

Brig.-General Edwards now rode up and consulted briefly with the Colonel. A hitch of some kind had occurred on the right, and the 180th Brigade was behind its schedule. After a few moments' conversation the Brigadier ordered an immediate assault.

The Colonel's whistle was in his mouth; the shrill blast was followed by his " Kensingtons—Advance! " and with his walking-stick waving high in the air, he was up the bank in front, leading the Battalion forward. As one man the lines of Kensingtons were up and over too; and so were the Westminsters on their left, and the Civil Service in the rear, until the whole plain was suddenly alive with trim-looking lines of khaki figures, moving forward with the precision of the parade-ground. It was a never-to-be-forgotten sight, and, apart from the columns of smoke caused by the bursting shells (the Turkish artillery was now in final, frantic activity) and the spurts of dust kicked up by the bullets, might easily have been taking place on Salisbury Plain. As they went over, a rousing cheer broke out all along the ranks, but soon every man was saving his breath for the grim business of reaching that line of trenches in front. It seemed a long way off.

Immediately in front, and running parallel with the trenches, was a cutting carrying a narrow-gauge supply railway, which was an unsuspected obstacle. A machine gun posted here maintained a murderous fire across the Kensingtons' line of advance, and for some moments checked progress, but when it became evident that nothing could stop them being overwhelmed by that line of bayonets, the machine gunners waved a white handkerchief and surrendered. Over the cutting and on again, the first wave was then held up by wire, which was incompletely cut by the artillery. From a view earlier on it had seemed to the advancing troops that nothing could have survived our artillery preparation, at least in the matter of wire, but here was unfortunate proof that much of it was little damaged. Hand-cutters were quickly in action, and but a few moments sufficed to clear several gaps, but slight as was the check, it resulted in many casualties. Very few yards now separated the first and second waves from the Turkish fire trench, in which two machine guns were in action at almost point-blank range. The crew of one of these were guilty of a despicable action for which they paid the just penalty. They waved a white rag, and on being approached by a group of Kensingtons treacherously opened fire again, causing several casualties before they were shot down.

The Turks obviously pinned their faith to their wire and machine guns, and, when both these failed, put up very little fight against cold steel. One of the first Kensingtons to leap over the parapet was 2nd Lieut. C. M. Wright, acting Intelligence Officer; pursuing some fleeing Turks with his revolver, he was shot dead at the very moment of victory. A quiet, charming man of middle age and considerable experience, his loss was very greatly regretted. Captain Tosland, commanding C Company, was badly wounded in the leg, but was carried back by stretcher bearers, cheerily waving his hand to his men. They were very sorry to see him go, for he was a popular officer, possessing a magnificent flow of language which earned him the respect of even the oldest soldiers ! Another bad casualty was Lieutenant L. C. Gates. It was afterwards learned that Captain Tosland had had his leg amputated, and neither of these officers rejoined the Battalion. Lieut. Gates subsequently recovered and was posted to the Lincolnshire Regiment (Regular Army). Captain Tosland survived and lives to-day to take a foremost part in the ever-increasing work of succouring old comrades who have fallen on bad times. No man since the war has done more for the men who loved him in those stirring times.

The final assault had been launched at 12.35 p.m., and exactly twenty minutes later the objectives were carried. The holding up of the 180th Brigade left the Kensingtons' right flank exposed, and for some little time they had to endure enfilade fire from machine guns. Immediately the front-line trenches were carried, work was commenced on consolidating the position; a post was pushed forward along a communication trench which ran back from the trench now occupied by the Kensingtons, whilst the fire trench was hastily reversed to meet an expected counter-attack. This did not materialise, however, and at 5 p.m. B and C Companies were sent some distance forward to act as a cover to the captured position. An hour later orders were given for the whole Battalion to concentrate at the communication trench; the enemy was definitely on the run, but the 60th Division was not in a position to carry out a pursuit that night, and the Kensingtons remained in the captured position all night. The retreat of the Turks did not render it necessary actually to occupy the trenches, which was a relief, as the enemy dead were still lying where they fell and attracted myriads of flies. The Brigade bivouacked on the spot and got what sort of a meal it could from the rations carried.

The Kensingtons' casualties consisted of 98 killed or wounded; 15 prisoners were captured, together with two machine guns.

In a special Order of the Day published shortly afterwards by the Commanding Officer of the 3/13th at home, extracts were given from a letter written by Lieut.-Colonel

Mackenzie, commanding the 2/13th, in which he wrote: " My Battalion has made a name for itself, second to none in this Army. I have been congratulated on all sides on the behaviour of my boys and have been told by the Staff that my Battalion has covered itself with glory. . . . The men are splendid, and I love them all. I am indeed a proud and lucky man to command so fine a Battalion. Our Brigade has been in all the fighting and has not been in reserve once. We are tired out, having done miles and miles in pursuit; only a quarter of an hour for letters. We are all tip-top and in the best of form. They call us the Flying Division now, and we are the pride of the East. Hoping to have a decent wash to-day; the men have had none since we started. . . ."

At 8 o'clock on the morning of the 7th, after a hasty and scanty impromptu meal, the Battalion paraded and moved back to the Brigade area of concentration about half a mile or so in the rear of the captured trenches. They hoped to be able to draw a water ration here, but were disappointed. Rigorous orders had been issued that the reserve water-bottle was not to be touched, but every man had by now emptied his first bottle, and another hot day was in prospect. It was clear that the wells at Beersheba could not provide for the needs of the three Divisions, with all the auxiliary troops now in action, and hopes were fastened upon the early capture of Tel el Sheria, where good water supplies were known to exist; it was even said that there was water in the wadi itself. The Turks had fallen back on Sheria, some two or three miles in front, and were gathering their scattered forces with a view to a stern resistance. Whilst the 179th Brigade lay all the morning in the sun, awaiting further orders, the 180th Brigade was pressing forward on its right to meet once again with great resistance, and at 2 p.m. orders were given to the 179th to continue the advance and capture Tel el Sheria.

The Brigade moved forward in two columns of artillery formation, the 2/15th and the 2/13th on the right, and the 2/14th and the 2/16th on the left. Crossing the trenches captured on the previous day, they commenced the advance over an undulating plain, completely destitute of cover save for a few scattered hovels about half-way across. Their appearance was a signal for a heavy fire from the Turkish artillery on the other side of the Wadi Sheria, who had a clear bird's-eye view of the approaching columns. Once again the eye beheld a splendid panorama. Reaching out farther and farther into the plain, the artillery " blobs " moved steadily forward in perfect squares, whilst puffs of shrapnel smoke gathered over their heads like balls of fluff. The luck of the Brigade on this occasion was marvellous, for although the Turkish gunners had an open view and accurate range, the casualties were very few indeed. Three-quarters of the shells seemed to burst in or over the open spaces between the " blobs." It was a new experience to march a couple of miles or so in the open under direct artillery fire, and not at all a pleasant one, but after a while they got used to it and took to betting where the next shell would burst.

The Turks were entrenched on top of the steep slope on the far side of the Wadi Sheria, a position which might well be considered almost impregnable when defended by determined men against attacking infantry, unsupported by artillery, but although the Kensingtons were not in a position to see what was going on, it was evident from the short time that rifle and machine-gun fire was in progress that the Turks were not putting up much resistance. This is in no way to detract from the assault carried out by the London Scottish and the Civil Service Rifles, who accomplished what appeared to be a nasty piece of work with their customary gallantry. Crossing the wadi bed in the fast-gathering gloom, they had to scale the steep bank and meet an entrenched enemy at the top. The privations of the past week, finishing with the three-hour advance across the open plain, and coupled with the shortage of water, were not the best preparation for so arduous a task, but fortunately the enemy was not in a position or perhaps the mood to withstand the assault, and after a brief but sharp engagement, the

Scottish and Civil Service carried the position. The Kensingtons and the Queen's Westminsters crossed the wadi about 6 p.m. and bivouacked on the high ground. B and D Companies were thrown out for local protection, and the night passed without further incident.

There was, however, a busy scene at the Sheria wells, where the whole of the Brigade camel transport was able to water during the night. While the tired infantry lay sleeping, every possible receptacle was being filled in order that the advance might be continued the following morning. Sheria was the only known water supply of any dimensions between Beersheba and Junction Station, the latter still being in Turkish hands. Most of the troops were too tired to care about anything but sleep, but before they dropped down they were glad to learn that Allenby's great coastal offensive had developed successfully and that Gaza had fallen.

Had the troops known it, the situation on the night of November 7th was most interesting. The 52nd and the 54th Divisions had pushed well forward on the coast, but the 75th (which was the right Division of the XXIst Corps) had not, so that the Turks in front of them were still holding most of their positions. The rapid advance of the Desert Mounted Corps (to which were attached the 60th Division) from Beersheba to Sheria had broken the Turkish centre and landed the 60th actually in the rear of the Turkish 26th and 54th Divisions, the Desert Mounted Corps advancing in a north-westerly direction, in the rear of and parallel to the old Turkish front line. This situation, although known at G.H.Q., could not be pressed home to full advantage owing to the wide nature of the country involved, and the impossibility of moving the infantry sufficiently quickly, although they did their best! From a Western Front standpoint the two Turkish Divisions were doomed, but expeditiously as the advance was pressed the following day, a surprisingly good proportion of the enemy managed to squeeze through the gap between the XXIst and the Desert Mounted Corps before it could be closed. It was at this period of the operations that the British troops first began admiringly to appreciate the ability of the Turks to extricate themselves from seemingly hopeless positions and make a "get-away."

The next day, November 8th, was an important one, when an attempt was made to press home the advantage gained. The 60th Division was ordered during the night to continue the pursuit and give the enemy no rest. Accordingly, the first streaks of dawn saw the Kensingtons, together with the remaining units of the 179th Brigade, assembling after a hurried scratch meal and facing east. After their exertions at Kauwukah, the 2/13th was again in Brigade reserve, although this meant little, for every unit had to press forward at the same speed, the 2/14th and the 2/15th being actually in touch with the Turkish rearguard. The same featureless country was covered under the same hot and dusty conditions; the arid plain stretched for as far as the eye could see, the nearest Turks being in position on top of a small ridge behind the village of Muntaret el Beghl, whence they opened fire at the steadily advancing British columns. Slight resistance was encountered by the London Scottish and Civil Service Rifles, but on the foremost wave approaching the line of trenches, the enemy was observed to abandon them and mount, galloping eastwards. A considerable number of enemy guns remained in action and caused a number of casualties; it soon became evident that the gunners were making a stand, and about midday, as the toiling column of infantry were halted in the blazing sun, enduring a heavy shell fire, they were witnesses of one of the most heroic episodes of the whole campaign. Major-General Shea and his staff had ridden up, and their presence, accompanied by the standard bearer, attracted a most unwelcome fire. The party was fully exposed to the view of the enemy gunners. Amid the din of the exploding shells a dull rumble could be heard, which turned into the thunder of galloping hoofs, and the watching infantry was transfixed by the sight of the gallant Warwick and Worcester Yeomanry charging straight at the guns, which were now firing through open sights. It was a magnificent spectacle, to live for all time in the memories of those who were privileged to see it. The thunder of the hoofs, the flashing sabres and hoarse yells of the charging Yeomanry, might well have struck terror to the hearts of the gunners, but they stuck to their job and continued firing to the last second, when they were sabred almost to a man. On, through the guns and up the hill, to a nest of machine guns, the Yeomanry swept and captured the lot. Their toll was terrible, as the riderless horses bore witness, but their bravery had saved the infantry incalculable casualties and smashed the last enemy resistance in southern Palestine. The heroism of victor and vanquished had been magnificent. This epic over, the infantry moved forward through the carnage of the guns, of which they counted twelve, and noted that many of the dead gunners were Austrians. Many machine guns were included in the capture and a number of prisoners, nearly all of whom were wounded.

It was now the hottest part of the day, and a brief halt was enjoyed before the march was resumed. Some of the Battalion had the joy of a glimpse of the sea away on the left —Allenby's pincers had met, but swift as the advance from Beersheba had been, it was not quite quick enough to enclose the main Turkish force, which, although beaten and broken, was now some ten miles to the north and retreating rapidly.

The spot where the historic charge of the Yeomanry had been made was but a stone's throw from the village of Huj, which had housed Turkish Eighth Army Headquarters before the advance. The entire column now turned right and continued the march due north until nearly 5 p.m., when the welcome order to halt was received. Throwing out C Company as local protection, the weary Battalion bivouacked and, snatching a scrappy meal, was soon fast asleep. Something like seventeen miles had been covered since dawn, in full marching order, and under continuous and at times heavy shell fire; no man had fallen out, but all were absolutely dead-beat.

For the moment the 60th Division was out of action, and November 9th and 10th were spent resting on the same site. The flies and the heat together made the long days very irksome, whilst water was still severely rationed, but for the rest the Battalion was well content. It was on the march again on the 11th, moving to the Wadi Jemmameh, where there was water. This place had been captured after a stiff fight by the Anzac Mounted Division, who had literally to fight their way to water on the 8th or go without. The general privations were greatly increased during these two days by the coming of the "sciroque," or hot winds.

The Brigade was bivouacked on an old enemy camp site, where the dirt and confusion were indescribable, and the ground badly fouled. During the two days which were spent there, 50 per cent. of the first reinforcements rejoined the unit. News from the front was scanty, but it was learned that the advance had eased up and the Turks were holding a line which ran roughly from south of Jaffa to Beit Jibrin. Allenby's greatest concern was the water supply, for the advancing troops had to "live on the country" in this respect, and there had been no rain for months. Conditions were so bad that a further move on the 13th was hailed with joy; this was to Tel el Nejileh, a few miles almost due west from the dirty Turkish camp.

At this point there were no troops between the 179th Brigade and the enemy at Beit Jibrin, some ten miles away, so that it was necessary to form some sort of defensive position. The duty of finding outposts fell to the 2/16th, the 2/14th forming the main line with the 2/13th and 2/15th in reserve. There was a large number of dead carcases to bury here, and this essential duty and generally cleaning up the area took up all spare time. A further short move was made on the 14th to a fresh bivouac on the Wadi Muleihah, where for two days the Battalion furnished working parties to assist the R.E.s, who were organising the water supply available there. The remainder of the Battalion took part in company parades and—drill!

KAUWUKAH—SHERIA—HUJ

Something more of the general position now became known. The enemy line was again split in two, their Eighth Army being grouped around Jaffa, whilst the Seventh Army was still in retreat and was reported to be retiring through the hills towards Jerusalem. The problem of supply for the British had now become so acute that only the XXIst Corps and Desert Mounted Corps could be kept on the offensive. The XXth Corps was ordered to fall back in order to leave all available water supplies up country for the troops in the line, and the 60th Division had to retire to near Sheria. This move was made on November 16th, a march of some ten miles being made across the same dry and featureless country with which they were now becoming familiar. At Sheria the first mail for over a fortnight awaited them, and the edible portion proved much too heavy to be consumed during the two days the Battalion rested. It had been anticipated that the 60th would be out of active events for perhaps two or three weeks, and a prolonged stay at Sheria was expected. When it became known on the second evening that the advance had been ordered again on the morrow, there was a great scramble to consume the quantity of foodstuffs available, and each bivouac that night became the centre of a feast in turn. After the half-empty stomachs of the last week it was a wonder that the whole Battalion was not *hors de combat* the following morning, but it was not so. When it was realised that the march was one of only four miles, the language was lurid; who couldn't carry a couple of parcels for four miles ? But, alas! the good things were gone beyond recall, and perhaps it was as well in view of the stern marching which lay immediately ahead.

The Division marched for seven successive days, at the end of which their front line was gazing at the roofs of Jerusalem; during that short time weather conditions changed from those of midsummer to something approximating to an English December. But neither Jerusalem nor rain was in the minds of the column as it set out in the usual dust and heat on the 18th, to arrive in mid-afternoon at Diah, where it pitched camp for the night. The next day's march was about ten miles, covering almost the same ground as during the pursuit to Huj. Indeed, that night it was bivouacked between that place and Gaza. Whilst here, striking evidence of the efficiency of supply work was furnished by the sight of the railway, which already ran right through Gaza—twelve days previous in the rear of a heavily fortified Turkish front line! Here then was the explanation of their renewed advance.

The following day, shortly after the march had been resumed, the column passed Deir Sineid, which had been the Turkish railhead and had, in consequence, suffered the heaviest bombardment. Everything had been pounded to pieces, and lying derelict by the side of the line was a burnt-out ammunition train, which had apparently been the object of attention from the British monitors at sea. Several of the naval shells had failed to explode, and they looked huge things, indeed. This was a memorable day in the campaign, for that afternoon rain began to fall, and a heavy downpour continued, so that marching conditions soon became most unpleasant. At first everyone welcomed the first sign of rain after so many weary, hot, and dusty days, but it soon became clear that this was no passing shower, but genuine rain of the old " Blighty " variety, and fears were expressed that the rainy season had started, which in fact proved to be the case. From now onwards the campaign was to be conducted under conditions of cold and wet; unfortunately the Battalion was still in summer drill and shorts, and so it was to remain until Jerusalem had fallen. That night bivouacs were pitched on the wet ground, and all turned in cold and shivering.

The march on the next day took the column to Junction Station, on the main Jaffa–Jerusalem line. Here branch lines went to Beersheba and Gaza. It was, therefore, of the greatest strategical importance, and had been the scene of fierce fighting some days previously. The Turks had not left much behind, and devastation was everywhere apparent. Pushing on again the following day, the column passed through Latron. The advance was now definitely headed east towards Jerusalem, and the ground began to rise; in consequence the bivouac site that night was situated on dry, rocky ground, and a comparatively good night was spent.

From here the character of the country changed abruptly, and the next morning the troops were winding their way upwards through a rocky defile, the road taking several dangerous twists. At odd intervals little groups of crosses were passed, marking the resting-place of British troops who had fallen in the first advance through these Hills of Judea, some days earlier. Better country for defensive purposes could hardly be found; a few resolute machine-gun sections could have held the road against an army, and everyone marvelled that the Turks had allowed it to pass into our hands so easily, until it was known that the assault had been carried out by the Gurkhas of the 75th Division, who had accomplished marvels in swarming up the steep hillsides. The resistance on the plain had been desperate enough, and the rout of the Turkish Army must have been almost complete for them to have given up these hills, which formed such a natural defensive position. But it was now known that the enemy had fallen back upon Jerusalem, where their communications were assured, the centuries having taught that it was a most difficult place to take. On the afternoon of November 24th the weary Brigade arrived at Kuryet el Enab (a former resting-place of the Ark of the Covenant) and the Kensingtons were deputed to take over the village of Soba from the 58th (Vaughan's) Rifles, (Indian Army) on the extreme right flank. The 2/15th and 2/16th moved into the line on their left, with the 2/14th in Brigade reserve. A and B Companies took over outpost duties that evening. The Brigade had relieved the 232nd Brigade of the 75th Division, which had fought its way up through the hills.

The 2/13th was now posted some seven or eight miles from Jerusalem, the outskirts of which could be plainly seen from Soba. Between the British line and the Holy

City lay very difficult country, intersected by deep wadis, flanked by stony hillsides, on which rose terrace after terrace of cultivated ground, each terrace bounded by stone walls. Only one road existed on this side of the city, that running from Jaffa, and both Armies were now astride this. From time immemorial the steep hills had been terraced to enable the peasantry to gain a precarious livelihood from the cultivation of olives and figs, and this fact rendered the provision of wheeled transport extremely difficult. It was a problem that had to be solved before Jerusalem could be taken.

In the meantime it was established that the enemy had not only decided to halt the retreat, but to resist any further attempts on the part of the British to advance. Only that morning the 52nd Division had made an attack upon El Jib (on the Jerusalem front), following two fruitless assaults of the 75th Division, and had been beaten back. On the coastal sector the British advance had been held up at the Wadi Auja (north of Jaffa) and the Turks, counter-attacking, had forced the Anzac Mounted Division to relinquish ground won the previous day, and the infantry who were called up to cover their retirement had suffered very severe casualties. On yet a third sector, the main road north from Beersheba through Hebron to Jerusalem, the 53rd Division was having a very unhappy time, having advanced little more than ten miles from Beersheba. The cold and wet weather, and the heavy casualty list, were combining to hold up the whole advance, whilst the difficulties of supply across over forty miles of captured and devastated territory were, of course, enormous. A pause in the operations was clearly necessary, whilst many thought that it might be decided to winter on the new line, prior to a fresh advance in the spring. No such thought, however, was in General Allenby's mind, and it soon became known that Jerusalem was to be taken as quickly as the necessary preparations could be completed.

At this time the city was threatened only from the west, although it was hoped that the 53rd Division would soon

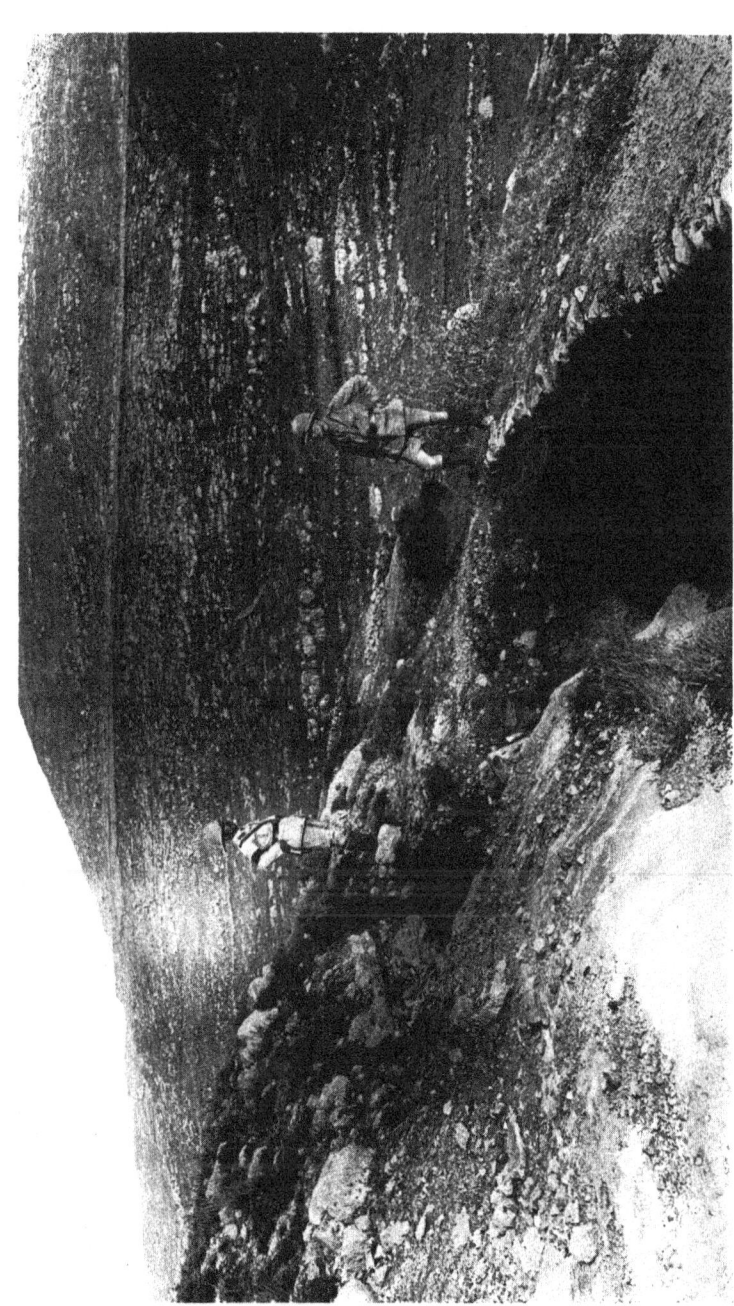

Turkish Positions to the West of Jerusalem.
Imperial War Museum photograph. Copyright reserved.

be able to advance from the south. The Turkish line formed a semicircle facing west and south, with the main line of communication open to Nablus in the north. To the east of Jerusalem lay mountainous country falling away to the plain of Jericho, and then up again to Amman and the open desert, where the Arabs, under Colonel Lawrence, were reported to be operating. In the line facing Jerusalem were the 52nd and 60th Divisions, with the 75th in reserve; then there was a great gap of open country where the situation was obscure, and the ground patrolled by the cavalry of both sides; on the coastal sector the Desert Mounted Corps were operating, with the 54th Division (less one brigade assisting) in reserve. The 53rd Division has already been alluded to as fighting its way slowly up the Hebron Road. The two remaining Divisions (the 10th and the 74th) were being hurried up country from the neighbourhood of Gaza. On the left of the Kensingtons' position lay the famous hill of Neby Samwil, from the summit of which can be seen the Mediterranean Sea to the west and the far mountains of Moab to the east. It had been occupied only after bitter fighting, and the Turks attached so much importance to its possession (commanding as it did a fine view of Jerusalem itself) that a series of fierce counter-attacks had been launched against it for three days in succession, without attaining their object.

This, then, was the position when the 2/13th again took up duties in the line at Soba. Soba itself was a typical Arab village, consisting of a few stone and mud hovels, and in an extremely dirty condition. It was still in occupation by the inhabitants, and the Battalion's bivouacs were, of course, pitched well outside the village. From the extreme point of the village a commanding view was obtained, and an excellent observation post was at once established here. During the first day of the Kensingtons' occupation there was a scare about a concealed enemy telephone, and every house was thoroughly searched (to the great disgust of the troops taking part!), but without result.

The Turks continued to shell Neby Samwil heavily, and

there were constant rumours of counter-attacks, but Soba was left in comparative peace and the line duties there were nominal. The Kensingtons, however, were responsible for patrolling the open country on the right flank, and on the 25th 2nd-Lieuts. Moody and McQueen took out the first patrols to the hills in the direction of Ain Karim. They reported that the village was not occupied, and that the country was impassable for artillery. During the night working parties were occupied in building stone sangars as defences, and in generally cleaning up the ground as much as possible. The weather, although cold, was now fine, and bright moonlight nights made patrol work easier than it might well have been in such difficult country. In addition to the Battalion's fighting patrols, the scouts of the Intelligence Section were out every night in the direction of Ain Karim, endeavouring to secure as much knowledge of the ground as possible, and produced a map which proved very useful.

It has been mentioned that the inhabitants of Soba were still living there, and it became difficult to distinguish wandering Arabs from Turks, especially after darkness had fallen. It is more than probable that some of these Arabs were carrying information to the Turks, for there was no real contact between the two lines on the flank, and for three days running it became necessary to arrest natives on suspicion of being spies. On the 27th the enemy again counter-attacked the 180th Brigade on Neby Samwil, after artillery preparations, but without success. After this the Turks seemed to give it up as a bad job, but every day the formidable hill was subjected to a heavy " strafe " at intervals. C Company relieved B Company on outpost duty on the night of the 27th, and the normal routine, chief of which was sangar building, went on.

On December 3rd the Brigadier called a Brigade Conference, at which the plans for the attack on Jerusalem were made known to the Commanding Officers. Once again the 179th Brigade was to be the right flank of the assault, and once more the Kensingtons were assigned the rôle of advanced guard, driving in enemy patrols, securing the right flank, and establishing communication with the 53rd Division, which, it was hoped, would by then have advanced sufficiently to be able to join in the final assault on Jerusalem from the west. That night Lieut.-Colonel Mackenzie, with Captain C. E. Brockhurst, the Adjutant, and fourteen O.R.s, undertook a reconnaissance along the route from Soba in the direction of Ain Karim, which had seen so much patrol activity during the past week. The great attack was timed for just before dawn on the 8th, and for the next four days little was done other than preparing for it. Work on the sangars was abandoned, as it was now clear that there was little danger of attack from the Turks, who had not ventured beyond their own line, save for an odd patrol or two. Whilst everything was done to ensure success, it was unfortunately found impossible to bring up serge clothing and overcoats, and, the weather continuing cold, the privations of the troops in their light drill uniforms can be imagined.

CHAPTER XXIII

THE BATTLE OF JERUSALEM

A "RIGHT COLUMN" of the 179th Brigade was formed, under the command of Lieut.-Colonel Ogilby of the London Scottish, and consisted of the Kensingtons, London Scottish, and Civil Service Rifles. The objectives of this column were the hills of El Jurah and Tumulus Hill (on the summit of which lay the left-flank Turkish trenches), then linking up with the Queen's Westminsters, who were assigned a separate first objective on the left of the Brigade, to wheel half left, skirting Jerusalem, cross the Jaffa–Jerusalem Road, and advance to a position astride the Jerusalem–Nablus Road north of the city, and finally to take Ras el Tawil, some three and a half miles along the latter road. The Kensingtons were to be the advanced guard, and their job was to seize the first two hills (believed to be but lightly held), thus clearing the way for the Scottish to make the main assault on the trench position at the top of Tumulus Hill, with the Civil Service in support.

Soba lay due west from Jerusalem, and El Jurah and Tumulus Hill south-west, so that the advance was to be first in a south-easterly direction. Between Soba and El Jurah ran the Wadi es Surar, a declivity over 700 feet below both places, the sides of which were steeply terraced, as mentioned. From Soba to the Wadi bed was just about a mile as the crow flies, and probably twice that distance to march; from the wadi to Jurah Hill it was nearly half as much again. To ensure a surprise attack, therefore, something like two and a half direct miles had to be traversed in silence, the best part of a brigade of men in full equipment moving in single file, accompanied by mules carrying Lewis guns and tools, jumping down a long succession of four-foot terrace walls on the one side and scaling similar obstacles

THE BATTLE OF JERUSALEM

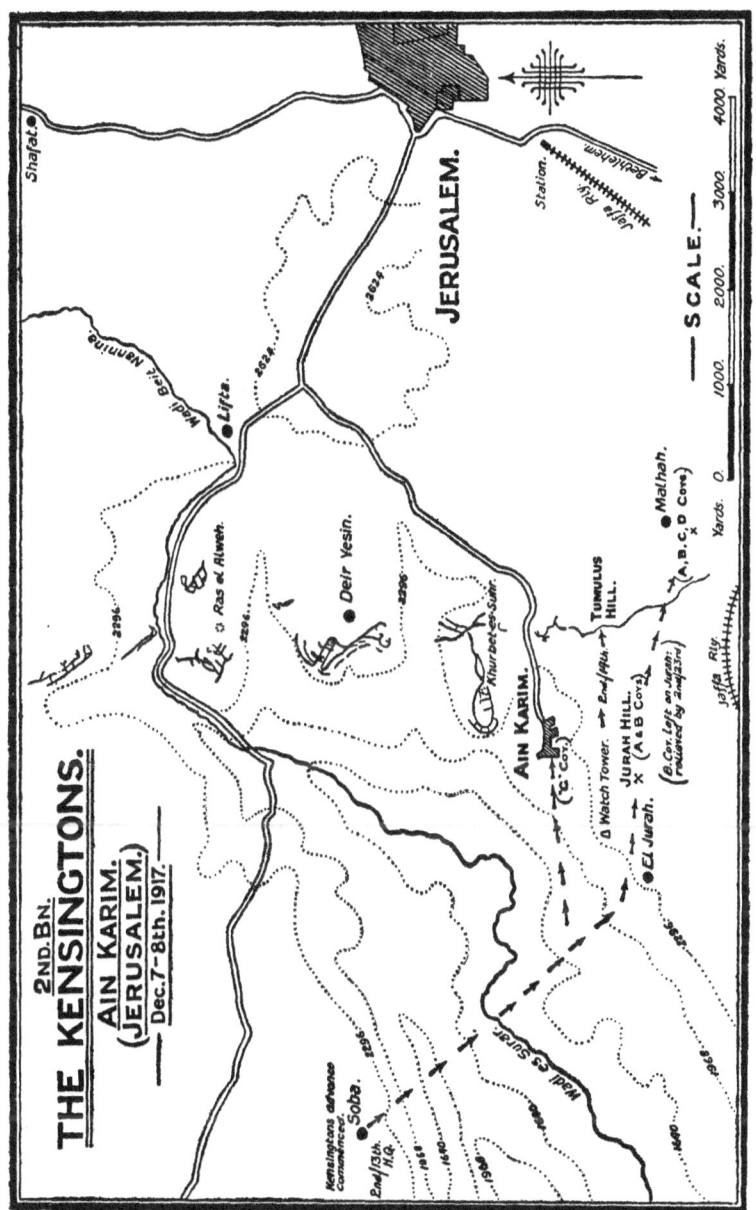

on the other. It was a formidable task, and everyone prayed that the good weather would hold, although the bright moon was likely to prove a treacherous ally. To assist the passage of the column, however, one company of the 1/12th Loyal North Lancs Pioneers was told off to level places in the terrace walls which should prove too difficult.

The morning of December 7th dawned cold and grey, and to the dismay of the whole Brigade, a cold drizzle set in soon after midday which persisted throughout the afternoon. By 3 p.m. bivouacs had been struck and the men stood about waiting for dusk to fall, wet through to the skin and perished with cold. A more inauspicious commencement to the great operation could hardly be imagined. About tea-time a cheery, laughing figure came riding up, which proved to be none other than the G.O.C. Division Major-General Shea, with his staff. Riding about the camp site, he chatted informally with the groups of shivering men, and his hearty demeanour did a great deal to cheer everybody up. Hanging around the camp were a number of Arab women carrying great baskets of luscious Jaffa oranges, which few could buy for lack of money. Calling several of these women over, General Shea purchased their stock and threw the oranges into outstretched hands until the supply was exhausted, at the same time cracking jokes and bringing smiles into the benumbed faces around him. The General's smiling face hid a worried mind, for he afterwards told the Kensingtons that when he rode into Soba and beheld the soaked and shivering troops, and knew the privations which awaited them that night on the exposed hillsides, he wondered if any men could attack the formidable positions held by the enemy with any chance of success. The Kensingtons were under no illusions as to the nature of the task which confronted them, but the action of the G.O.C. that afternoon at Soba endeared him to them.

That desolate day came to an end at last, and at 5 p.m. the advanced guard, consisting of B Company under

THE BATTLE OF JERUSALEM

Captain Kisch, the company of Loyal North Lancs, and one section of the 521st Company of Royal Engineers, pushed forward along the first stage of the descent into the Wadies Surar. Contrary to expectations, the evening turned out to be very dark, with rain still falling, and the going consequently very heavy. The mules, essential as they were, proved a great nuisance and behaved as only mules can; each animal had to be pulled and pushed down the terraces, and the resulting jingling and scuffling seemed loud enough to alarm all the Turks round Jerusalem. The Pioneers, however, were a great help, and it was a wise thought that included them in the advanced guard. If the descent into the wadi had been difficult, the ascent on the far side was incredibly so, and miracles of patience and endurance were performed as the long column slowly wound its way in single file towards El Jurah. Between there and the village of Ain Karim stood an ancient watch tower, which had been named the White Tower, and which had been appointed as the assembly position of the Right Column. When the ground had been patrolled it was clear of enemy, but as the advanced guard slowly approached, a challenge rang out, followed by shots. This meant a tremendous difference to the main operations, for all chance of a complete surprise was now clearly at an end. The night was very dark, and a white mist shrouded the hill, reducing visibility to less than a hundred yards. A pause ensued whilst scouts were sent forward to reconnoitre.

At midnight the rest of the 2/13th came up with B Company. By this time Captain Kisch had cleared the Turkish post out of the White Tower (which they had been using as a guard-post), capturing the first two prisoners. He reported that the enemy was holding Ain Karim, which had certainly been unoccupied previously, so that the Turks had taken alarm or had received information as to the British intentions (which is more than probable), and thus the assembly of the main column was jeopardised. Time was now of supreme importance; the Scottish were toiling up behind the Kensingtons in readiness for the main attack, and the prearranged schedule was already behind time. Lieut.-Colonel Mackenzie decided to send one company forward under Lieut. Baker to clear Ain Karim, the remaining three companies now having reached the vicinity of the White Tower. Patrols sent up the hill from the White Tower reported that the enemy were in strength, estimated at a battalion, farther up the hill. Everything was very confusing, owing to the incessant rain and complete darkness, accentuated by the abominable mist, and for a time communication with Brigade was lost. Lieut.-Colonel Mackenzie hurriedly set to work to reorganise the Battalion under the White Tower. One platoon under Captain Kisch was sent to act as protection to the right flank of the Brigade, one platoon of D Company was attached to the 2/14th, now coming up, the remainder of D Company was held in reserve, whilst A and B Companies were ordered to advance and clear Jurah Hill. They were met with heavy rifle and machine-gun fire at close quarters, to which they replied, and a desperate action resulted, the Kensingtons fighting their way up the hill yard by yard.

At this juncture Lieut.-Colonel Ogilby of the 2/14th came up to find out what was happening, the position to him being extremely confusing. The clear-cut plans had gone all awry owing to the unexpected presence of the enemy in such large numbers, and instead of the way being cleared for the Scottish attack on the main trenches on Tumulus Hill, a battle had suddenly developed almost on the site of the Brigade assembly point. For the moment nothing could be done whilst the enemy was in occupation of both Jurah Hill and Tumulus Hill. The fight for Jurah continued, the Kensingtons struggling up the hill finding themselves badly enfiladed. As a result, two platoons of D Company were ordered to attack up the opposite spur of the hill and clear the enemy. The fight proceeded in the mist. The enemy was maintaining a heavy fire from the summit of Jurah Hill from a force estimated at least three hundred men. It became clear that it was going to take some time to capture the hill, if indeed it could be managed with only two companies, and Lieut.-Colonel Ogilby decided to push ahead with the 2/14th to his first objective on Tumulus Hill, leaving the flanks still in action.

At 3.15 a.m. Captain Foster reported that he had captured his objective, but was hard pressed. The Turks counter-attacked twice in rapid succession. The Adjutant, Captain Brockhurst, going up the hill to establish the position, was wounded, and his place was taken by Lieut. E. J. Smith, M.C., an officer of the 10th Royal Fusiliers, who had been posted to the 2/13th in France. Captain Kisch also reported that he was hard pressed and being counter-attacked. A and D Companies were now on top of the hill under severe machine-gun fire from both flanks. They were shelled at point-blank range from a mountain gun in position on Tumulus Hill. Captain Foster reporting that the position was becoming critical, the remaining platoon of D Company was sent up to reinforce, leaving the Battalion without any reserve at all. Lieut.-Colonel Mackenzie, determined to retain the hard-won ground at all costs, now called for reinforcements from the 2/15th, and one company of this battalion, under Captain Wills, arrived and went up the hill. The position at this stage was extremely critical.

The 2/14th had by now reached the approaches to Tumulus Hill and proceeded to the assault in gallant manner, capturing the Turkish trenches on top of the hill, and thus rendering great assistance to the 2/13th. An exciting incident now took place on the Kensingtons' front, where Captain Foster, observing the enemy creeping up under Captain Kisch's position, collected some thirty men and charged down the reverse slope of the hill and drove them off. His own company was next counter-attacked again, but this was also successfully repulsed.

The whole action was still enshrouded in mist and darkness, no lamps were available, and the battalion was still out of communication with Brigade. It was a case for individual initiative all the way round, and there were many examples of stirring personal gallantry which perforce went unrecorded. The wonder is that organisation within the Battalion was maintained. At 6 a.m. C Company rejoined the Battalion, having completed its work of clearing Ain Karim, and bringing in five prisoners. Fierce fighting continued at the top of the hill, where the Turks were maintaining a stubborn attempt to recapture the lost position, and by 6.30 a.m. A and B Companies had repulsed no less than seven counter-attacks.

The situation easing somewhat, B Company, under Captain Kisch, together with the company of the 2/15th, were ordered to hold the heights whilst Lieut.-Colonel Mackenzie with the rest of the Kensingtons went forward to Tumulus Hill. The 2/14th had by now triumphed over its difficulties—during which Corporal Train had accomplished his gallant task of engaging a Turkish machine gun and crew single-handed, a deed which won for him the Victoria Cross—and had advanced to its second objective and carried it. B Company was relieved a little later by the 2/23rd London Regiment and rejoined the Battalion, which then moved on to the high ground south-west of Malhah in which direction the retiring Turks had fled. Here it remained, protecting the right flank of the attack, with D Company under Captain Thompson and C Company under Lieut. Baker thrown out as outposts on the forward slopes overlooking the village of Malhah. To advance to this last position they had to proceed along a single track and were heavily shelled by enemy batteries from the direction of Jerusalem. It was now nearly noon and the general situation rather obscure. The 179th Brigade lay on the open ground awaiting orders to continue to advance, which, it transpired, was held up owing to the initial repulse of the 180th Brigade on the left. The attack of the 180th was launched afresh during the afternoon, its objective of Deir Yesin being finally carried about 5 p.m. The final assault on Jerusalem proved to be unnecessary, the Turks evacuating the city that night. This, however, was not known at the time, and the Brigade spent a most miserable and uneasy night on the exposed hills, without rations,

THE BATTLE OF JERUSALEM

fires, or bivouacs, while the keen wind searched through light summer clothing.

Men paced up and down to keep warm or crept beneath the shelter of heaps of stones for what cold comfort they could find. Many fell asleep from exhaustion and had to be roused because of the danger of frost-bite. It was a terrible experience for the wounded, some of whom it is feared must have succumbed to exposure, although the medical orderlies worked hard to bring them all in and tend them. Dawn broke on a cheerless landscape on the 9th, and it soon became known that Jerusalem was evacuated, and the Brigade concentrated on the Ain Karim–Jerusalem Road about 10 o'clock. Here at last rations were brought up, together with water, and soon steaming dixies of tea brought solace to the benumbed troops. The actual surrender of Jerusalem was not without its quixotic side, for with the departure of the Turks, the Mayor came out of the city towards the advancing British forces, carrying the keys of the city with him. It is on record that he presented these to the first British troops he met, who proved to be two sergeants of the London Regiment, and that the startled Tommies were so embarrassed by the unprecedented offer that they did not know what to do with the keys and refused to accept them. They were, in fact, accepted later in the morning by the Brigadier of the 180th Brigade, only to be returned to the worthy Mayor for re-presentation to Major-General Shea, commanding the 60th Division. In any case, the honour of accepting the surrender of the Holy City, which had been in the hands of the Turks for centuries, fell to the lot of London troops, and never was honour more worthily earned.

At 2 p.m. on the afternoon of December 9th the Kensingtons moved forward into Jerusalem with the rest of the Brigade, the route taking them through the modern Jewish quarter on the north-western outskirts of the city. The Jewish population naturally turned out in great numbers to welcome the British " deliverers," and if their welcome lacked the enthusiasm of a London crowd, it seemed warm enough and occasionally sufficiently embarrassing. After the privations of the previous days the Kensingtons were delighted to find that they had been allotted billets in the Ellaline Rothschild School, and their exuberance at once more finding a roof above their heads knew no bounds. Although the enemy had only retired to positions just outside the northern outskirts of the city, the war was almost forgotten for the time being, and already there were many who wanted to start exploring the city. When the rolls were called it was found that casualties had been heavy. Unfortunately, there is now no record of what the Kensingtons' losses on this occasion really were, but among the killed were 2nd Lieut. Sutherland, C.S.M. Moss, and Sergeants Withy, Alsop, and Moody.

The rest from action was but brief, and on the following day the Brigade moved out to take over from the 180th in the new line north of Jerusalem, astride the Nablus-Jerusalem Road. The weather was now continuously wet and cold. The 2/13th relieved the 2/19th in support to the left sub-sector, with Battalion Headquarters in Shafat. The 2/14th was in the line immediately in front of the 2/13th. Five days were spent in this position, the line being quiet; both sides were without doubt exhausted by the efforts of the previous few days and lay quietly "licking their wounds" and gathering up strength for the next Battle of Jerusalem, which was to see the positions reversed, with the British fighting to hold the city against a Turkish attack.

The Battle of Jerusalem was the third major action of the present campaign in which the 60th (London) Division had taken a foremost part, and it can be said without rhetoric that the Division had covered itself with glory. Whether engaged in the fierce frontal assault on the left or the inconceivably difficult flank attack on the right, all had borne themselves splendidly. If the 180th had to face the strongest defences at Deir Yesn, the 179th can claim to have settled the fate of Jerusalem by the success of its flank attack at Ain Karim, carried out across mountainous country under appalling conditions, against tremendously strong natural defences which were held by forces at least equal to its own in strength, and without the aid of artillery support, which the character of the country rendered impossible. Looking back upon the action, one is compelled to admit that the chances of success were small, and that the inner forebodings of Major-General Shea on that wet afternoon at Soba appear to be justified. In the earlier part of the account of the action, mention was made of the hope that was entertained that the 53rd Division would have advanced sufficiently by the night of the 8th to link up with the Kensingtons and co-operate on the right flank. This hope was not fulfilled, and the action of the 179th Brigade was carried out with the right flank entirely exposed. It was not until the evening of the 9th that the head of the 53rd Division made its appearance from the direction of Bethlehem, south of Jerusalem, just in time to render gallant assistance in clearing the Turks off the Mount of Olives to the east of the city, where they had maintained a stubborn resistance. It was now at last linked up with the 60th Division and the British ring of defence around the Holy City was completed.

CHAPTER XXIV

THE DEFENCE OF JERUSALEM

DURING the five days which the Kensingtons spent at Shafat, the time was mainly occupied in path-making; the country was similar to that traversed at Ain Karim, consisting of stony hills, intersected by deep wadis, the sides of which were terraced and fairly well wooded with olive and fig trees. On the 11th sounds of firing to their front told them that the Scottish were busy, and it was learned that they had advanced their line in places to a depth approaching 1,000 yards. The position that the Brigade had taken over was little more than a series of outposts, and the action of the Scottish was undertaken with a view to establishing some semblance of a continuous line. Nothing else happened of interest during this period, and on December 15th the 180th Brigade relieved, the 2/19th again taking over from the 2/13th, which marched back to the city, and to its joy was billeted in the Bishop Gobat Schools and the Abyssinian buildings. It found that during its absence the city had quite settled down under its new rulers, and a peaceful atmosphere prevailed.

The men made themselves comfortable in long dormitories, and once again enjoyed the privilege of dressing their kits by the right. Scrupulous tidiness was insisted upon. Very strict orders were issued as to behaviour in and about the many and varied historic places of religious interest, and sight-seeing within the old city itself was confined to parties escorted by officers. The Padre became in great demand, for practically everyone wanted to see the spots made familiar by the Bible, and such historic places as the Church of the Holy Sepulchre and the Mosque of Omar within the old Temple Area. The latter, as a Moslem holy place, was forbidden to English troops. It can be said that never were conquering troops more quietly behaved, and the utmost deference was paid to General Allenby's order that the religious susceptibilities of the various sects, Christian, Moslem, and Jewish, were to be respected. On December 11th, during the last period of the 179th in the line, the Commander-in-Chief had made his official entry into Jerusalem in humility, on foot, and the occasion had been most impressive. On the whole, the troops were not impressed by the religious places of interest, which too often seemed to be the centre of racial greed and jealousy, and in the care of none-too-clean priests of the Orthodox Church, who were clearly out for what they could make under these favourable circumstances. The age-old city within the walls, however, unchanged through the long centuries, proved of inexhaustible interest. It was not that the British troops were lacking in religious feeling, but rather the reverse, and in after-days when occasion permitted, large numbers of men loved to roam about the hills round the city in twos and threes, and try to pick out for themselves the places mentioned in Biblical narrative.

On December 17th the Battalion was addressed on parade by Major-General Shea, who spoke in glowing terms of the behaviour of the Kensingtons at Ain Karim. Attention was now directed to the training of further specialists, especially reserves for the Lewis-gun and bombing sections, whose ranks had been sadly depleted. The next week also saw the Battalion called upon to provide large working parties for the area immediately in rear of the line, and also search-parties for hidden arms. Captain Collier took a party of two hundred to south of Beit Hannina on the 20th, to commence a new road. The next day Captain Foster took a party of one hundred to the village of Jura to seize arms from the villagers, whilst another hundred went with Captain Collier to Ain Karim on the same errand. Fifteen arrests were made altogether. General Allenby had issued a proclamation calling for the relinquishment of all arms from civilians, and search was carried on throughout the city and the surrounding villages. The " bag," however, was small. The Brigade was informed that it was to take over again in the line on Christmas Eve.

Whilst the 179th Brigade had been quietly engaged in road-making and gaily sight-seeing in Jerusalem, the British position there was absurdly precarious, and throughout this period minor actions were constantly in progress to the north-east of the city on the farther slopes of the Mount of Olives with a view to relieving the Turkish pressure and giving a little more elbow room. Even as late as December 21st, a fierce action was taking place just outside Anata, only two and a quarter miles from Jerusalem itself! On the left of the 60th line, the 74th Division was also continually engaged in pushing forward here and there, whilst a considerable action was taking place on the coastal sector. Here, although the Turks had lost Jaffa weeks earlier, they had maintained themselves, in the very strong position immediately north of the town on the Wadi Auja, whence they were able to menace the harbour and roads leading out of the town. The Auja was forty feet wide and ten feet deep, and formed a formidable obstacle which took the XXIst Corps over two weeks to negotiate and finally drive the enemy to a position which left Jaffa free from menace.

The fact of being billeted in a large city gave a false sense of security, and the Kensingtons were certainly completely carefree during this time. But those employed at Divisional and Corps Headquarters knew that the position was causing some concern, and it was obvious that matters could not rest as they were. Actually, General Allenby had decided upon a fresh general attack on the night of the 24th, but the troops at least went into the line in blissful ignorance of any such intention. At midday they took over the left sub-sector, D Company (Captain Thompson) and C Company (Captain Collier) being in the line, with B Company (Lieut. Baker) in left support and A Company (Captain Foster) in right support. At dusk, warning was received that an enemy attack was imminent and the sangars were manned. The weather was atrocious, torrential rain being experienced, and the men were thoroughly soaked in a little time. Probably on account of weather conditions, the enemy attack did not materialise; it is quite certain that the British advance was cancelled for the same reason! The curious position thus arose of two hostile armies scheduled to attack at the same time, one to capture and the other to relieve Jerusalem, and both being forced to cancel their programme. Conditions grew steadily worse, if that was possible; where the ground was anything but rock it became a sea of mud, whilst the bottom of the wadis were almost impassable. Attempts were made to rig up some sort of shelter with bivouac sheets, and men lay down as they were in pools of water.

On Christmas Day the Brigadier visited the line and made some alteration in the dispositions. Heavy rain continued all day and night, and a cheerless Christmas dinner was made off short rations of bully beef and biscuits; fires were out of the question, so that tea was off the menu. As a result of the visit of the Brigadier, B Company was introduced into the line between D and C Companies, whilst one company of the 2/15th under Captain Rimmington was attached to the Kensingtons and took over B Company's old position in support. Rumours of the impending Turkish attack flew round and the situation became tense ; it was clear that any assaulting troops would be under a great handicap from the weather, but rumour had it that the enemy was in great strength and had sworn to recapture Jerusalem; our line was known to be but thinly held. At 10.45 p.m. that night a party known as the " Bridge Post " was fired upon and the sangars were manned, but nothing further happened for two and a half hours. Brisk firing from the listening posts which were out indicated that they were in touch with the enemy, and shortly afterwards one post was practically wiped out. Rifle and machine-gun fire now developed along the whole of the 179th front, accompanied by heavy artillery fire. The Turkish attack on Jerusalem had commenced.

The attack continued for eighteen hours, during which

time wave after wave came over and the situation became so critical that back in Jerusalem arrangements were made for hastily evacuating the wounded. The first general attack was made at 1.15 a.m., the enemy force assaulting the Kensingtons' front being estimated at between five hundred and six hundred. The right of the sector was difficult to defend, the ground being broken by a series of slag-heaps and quarries, and in one of these a party of Turks succeeded in effecting an entry with two machine guns and bombs. They were quickly ejected by a bayonet charge. At 2.20 a.m. the Kensingtons' line was reported again intact, and messages were despatched to Brigade requesting further supplies of ammunition. The Battalion ammunition reserve was carried up to the ridge by runners, scouts, and batmen, who had to run the gauntlet of an artillery barrage which the enemy laid down across the intervening wadi. At 4.20 a.m. the enemy again was reported to be advancing on the right, in the neighbourhood of the Nablus–Jerusalem Road, and the 2/16th was ejected from a portion of its line. This Battalion was holding two important little hills, Ras el Tawil and Tel el Ful, which it appeared the enemy was determined to recapture. As Turkish possession of them left the 2/13th right flank exposed, it can be imagined that the Battalion's position became exceedingly uncomfortable. Shortly afterwards A Company reported that it had repulsed the enemy.

A quarter of an hour later the enemy attacked on the left, accompanied by heavy artillery support, but was again beaten back. At 5.30 a.m. it again attacked along the whole front and, the situation becoming serious, two companies of the 2/15th were sent to reinforce the line. Held up on the Kensingtons' sector, the attack progressed towards Tel el Ful, where the Queen's Westminsters were having a very hot time. Fierce hand-to-hand fighting ensued for half an hour, at the end of which the enemy was seen to be retiring, and a British armoured car made its appearance along the Nablus Road, firing rapidly. This success was but short-lived, for at 6.30 a.m. it could be seen that the

THE DEFENCE OF JERUSALEM

enemy had again gained a footing on Tel el Ful in large numbers, and the 2/13th was subjected to enfilade machine-gun fire, which caused a number of casualties. The attack on the Kensingtons' front had eased up, and by 8.30 a.m. four platoons of the 2/15th were withdrawn to their original position. Shortly afterwards the Kensington forward posts commenced to crawl back to our lines in daylight to escape shrapnel fire. A lull now ensued, although it was clear from activity in the Turkish line that they were not finished yet. At 12.55 p.m. they were seen to be again advancing from the direction of Kh Adaseh; a heavy barrage was laid on the reverse slopes of our position and on the support ridge, where Battalion Headquarters was situated. Every man " stood-to." The enemy attack broke in full force on the 2/13th line and a fierce action followed, the Kensingtons hurling bombs on to the enemy swarming up the slopes of the hill, whilst many hand-to-hand encounters developed; The front-line companies sent out an urgent S.O.S. and at Headquarters Lieut.-Colonel Mackenzie telephoned to the Brigadier that he would hold out to the last man.

Gathering round him a little knot of Headquarters Staff, signallers, scouts, batmen, and runners, the C.O. prepared to defend the support ridge should the front-line companies be swept back. No sooner had this message got through to Brigade than all communication was cut off. The artillery bombardment had cut all lines, and when the Brigade line was again re-established some two and a half hours later, no less than thirty-six breaks were found. At this point the support company of the 2/15th was again called into action; two platoons were sent forward into the line, whilst the remaining two were held for the last desperate defence if required. This proved to be almost at once, for the first two Civil Service platoons had barely time to arrive in position before runners brought news that the Turks had at last gained a footing on the forward slope. The Turkish barrage at this time was as heavy and as accurate as any experienced during the campaign, and the reinforcements had to make their way through a curtain of shells. With the exception of the loss of a few light guns, the enemy had been able to withdraw his guns from Jerusalem, and these were now concentrated on a much narrower front.

It was now 1.15 p.m. The most critical moment in the defence of Jerusalem had arrived, and things did not look too good; anything might happen during the next half an hour. The Kensingtons were not beaten yet, however, and with the assistance of the valuable company of the Civil Service, the C.O. judged the moment opportune to stake all by taking the offensive against odds. A few moments later, the order was given for the whole front line to charge over the top of the ridge it had defended so stubbornly. The bold move succeeded, and the panting Turks, unable to face the oncoming bayonets, broke and bolted down the boulder-strewn hillside, followed by a fusillade of rifle fire and bombs from the defenders. At this moment the remaining three companies of the 2/15th arrived post-haste and were thrown into the right of the sub-sector; this settled the issue beyond all doubt, and by 1.30 p.m. the Battalion's front was reported to be securely held. Fifteen minutes later a company of the 2/14th arrived under the command of Captain Robertson.

The Turkish attack, maintained with remarkable stubbornness in the face of repeated repulses in shocking weather conditions, had finally failed, and from that moment the safety of the city was assured. The enemy artillery was by no means done with, and for the next three hours a hail of shells of all calibres rained upon the Brigade's front; an unusual number of these proved to be "duds." It should be mentioned that the 2/15th had had a particularly trying time in support, being called upon in turn to assist first the 2/16th on Tel el Ful, where it had two platoons wiped out, and then the 2/13th on the left of the Nablus Road; its support duties had been no picnic. A lull ensued as darkness fell, and Lieut.-Colonel Mackenzie was glad to utilise the services of the company of the 2/14th in patrol work on the left of the position, a duty which the

THE DEFENCE OF JERUSALEM

exhausted men on the ridge were in no fit state to undertake. To this London Scottish company fell the delight and honour of capturing a Turkish machine gun and crew that had been worrying the exposed left flank. Very heavy firing was heard away on the left, and it was learned that the 10th and 74th Divisions were counter-attacking on a big scale. General Allenby was not the man to let an opportunity slip, and his postponed plan for a further advance to finally relieve Jerusalem was now put into operation. On the 60th Divisional front the night passed quietly and the Turks were allowed to fetch in their wounded without molestation. Many were brought into our own lines from the immediate front, and it was interesting to find that they all carried three days' rations, consisting largely of coarse milled flour, and to learn that they had confidently expected to consume these in Jerusalem. The Kensingtons' casualties during this action were found to total some 70 killed or wounded.

The following day, December 28th, passed quietly, the Battalion sending out a strong patrol to Kh Adaseh, which was not fired upon. The hill was occupied by D Company under Captain Thompson. This young officer had behaved with great coolness and gallantry during the Turkish attack on the previous day, and was seen to be hurling bombs over as methodically as if he were bowling at a wicket on the village green. Whilst the 179th Brigade was resting on its original position, the two other brigades of the 60th were ordered to advance, the 181st on the left, whilst the 180th passed through the 179th lines. The morale of the enemy was badly damaged, and he retreated some thousands of yards that day, his artillery affording him the usual excellent protection, so that the two advancing brigades did not pass unscathed. By nightfall they had captured Er Ram.

On the morning of the 29th the 179th was ordered forward in support of the 180th and the 181st, who were attacking Ram Allah and Bireh, which lay on the top of the last ridge which commanded a view of Jerusalem.

Scrambling down the wadi sides, the Battalion witnessed many distressing sights on its slow progress. The Turks had had enough to do to clear the wounded, and the dead lay everywhere unburied, British and Turks together. Many of the former were practically stripped of clothing and the bodies maltreated, whilst some of the enemy dead lay clothed in uniforms pillaged from the British. It was noticed that many of the 2/18th (London Irish) had suffered in this way. By midday the Kensingtons were at the village of Kulundia, and here a halt was made, and subsequently bivouacs were pitched. This was not done until the issue of the fight in front was decided, without requiring the assistance of the 179th Brigade. The final assault on Ram Allah was made towards the close of the afternoon, the 179th infantry being interested and close spectators of the Divisional artillery action, which drenched the slopes in front with a splendid-looking barrage, which apparently did the 181st Brigade good service. A sigh of relief went round when it became clear that the battle was over, Jerusalem was safe, and the prospect of a return to the city for a rest was opened. Some of the Battalion obtained billets that night in Kulundia, Battalion Headquarters being pitched on a roof. The weather, capricious as ever, and seeing the battle over, now cleared, and, although cold, was fine.

December 30th was spent in Kulundia, the Brigade still being nominally on support duty. The Battalion presented a sorry spectacle, none having washed or shaved for days, and that morning the barren hillside resembled a huge open-air barber's saloon. The expressions of pain upon hundreds of faces as the none-too-sharp razors pulled at the growth of days, assisted by a scanty lather in ice-cold water, were comical. Afterwards they all felt and looked new men. The rumour of a return to the city was confirmed overnight, and at dawn on the last day of the year the Brigade commenced its trek back of some six miles. The men were delighted to find that they had been allotted the same billets; it was like coming home! Relieved from the

THE DEFENCE OF JERUSALEM

stress and struggle of the past week (the worst so far in the Battalion's history), and the occasion being what it was, there was legitimate cause for rejoicing, and everyone who could possibly be spared from actual duty soon crowded into the city, the inhabitants of which enjoyed what must have been their most profitable time in memory. The pleasures to be secured were somewhat scanty, it is true, but the best was made of what there was, and for once it is probable that the festivities of the Englishmen rivalled those of their Scottish colleagues, engaged in their great Hogmanay orgy. It was a fortuitous circumstance that released them on such a night.

From the Divisional troops who had remained in the city the Kensingtons realised for the first time the critical nature of the position during the preceding few days, and learned how preparations had been made for evacuating the city should the necessity arise. To the Division which had the honour of accepting the surrender of Jerusalem had fallen the brunt of the work of defending it against the expected, if delayed, counter-attack. The 53rd Division on the Mount of Olives had done its share of serious fighting during the last three weeks, and had held the British right flank solid, but the main frontal attack had been hurled against the 60th's lines, where the Kensingtons and the Queen's Westminsters had borne the brunt and withstood the spearhead of the attack. Thus ended the defence of Jerusalem. Staking all on the effort, and fighting magnificently over very difficult country, in pouring rain and intense cold, the Turks had failed, and more than failed, for they had now been hurled back a distance of ten miles from the city walls, which they were destined not to see again, save as prisoners.

So ended, too, the first great phase of the British offensive, opened (it seemed now so long ago) on that sultry October night against far-away Beersheba. Fittingly enough, the date was December 31st, 1917. Thus a chapter of history and of time closed together. . . .

THE LAST YEAR

CHAPTER XXV

JEBEL EKTEIF—JERICHO

The expectation of a good rest in Jerusalem was not realised. Before the New Year's festivities were concluded the orderly-room was packing up again, under orders to proceed to a fresh sector of the line at 6 a.m. on January 1st. This was somewhat of a blow, but in the prevailing general cheeriness the news was not taken badly, and to the tune of " Old Soldiers Never Die—They Simply Fade Away," the Battalion tramped out of its comfortable billets on a fine morning, and headed east for the Mount of Olives. Crossing the Jericho–Jerusalem Road and turning south east, a couple of hours' march brought them to the historic village of Bethany, where Headquarters was installed in a monastery. The 2/13th took over from the 4th Royal West Kents, being in brigade support behind El Aisawiyeh; the Battalion was billeted mainly in this village, but A Company (Captain Foster) manned the " Sniper's Post " on the Jericho Road. This post was relieved by each company in turn every second day

No sooner were the troops established in this new line than the weather again broke, and continuous rain fell for three days, rendering conditions miserable. On January 3rd, Major-General Shea presented medals won during the first Jerusalem operations. A quiet period was spent here, broken only by a reconnaissance on the 8th along the Jericho Road to inspect damage reported to have been done to culverts. The next day four Turkish deserters came into the 2/13th lines, followed by two more on the 10th. The Battalion now relieved the 2/15th in the right sub-sector, on Bullock's Ridge, but the situation remained quiet.

There was no Turkish force within appreciable distance, the enemy having withdrawn some five miles, holding the line by a series of strong posts.

The country to the east of Jerusalem was even more difficult than that to which our men had been accustomed during the Jerusalem operations, and completely desolate. The high bare hills were broken by very deep wadis, which rendered movement almost impossible, many of them scarcely affording foothold for goats, and in consequence the usual patrol work between the two opposing lines could not be carried out. From the Mount of Olives (approximately 3,000 feet) the ground dropped away in a succession of rocky hills down to the River Jordan and the Dead Sea (1,200 feet below sea-level), a distance of some sixteen miles as the crow flies. This formidable terrain was to prove the next battleground of the 60th Division.

General Allenby had now decided upon another bold flanking move against the enemy left flank, and once again the rôle fell to the lot of the 60th Division, which was by now becoming accustomed to being " Allenby's Flying Squad." The first move was to clear the enemy out of the difficult country between Jerusalem and Jericho. It was known that the attack would not take place for some weeks, and at this time detailed orders were not issued, but it was decided that as many officers as possible should familiarise themselves with the ground in front, and with this end in view a preliminary reconnaissance was undertaken on January 13th by the Commanding Officer, the Adjutant, the four Company Commanders, and fifteen O.R.s. The ground covered lay over what were known as Kent and Sussex Ridges, in the general direction of El Muntar, which was known to be the Turkish left position. A further reconnaissance was made three days later.

During this fortnight in the line about Abu Dis the Battalion had a very quiet time, generally occupied in making tracks and a few defensive positions. Trench digging was out of the question, owing to the nature of the ground, neither was there any expectation of such defences ever being required. The various specialists carried on with their training, whilst a few deserters continued to straggle into the lines, mostly unkempt-looking Greeks with little stomach for fighting for the Turks. Quite a number of officers and N.C.O.s managed to get back to Jerusalem for baths, on varying pretexts! The Brigade was relieved by the 180th on January 26th, and the Kensingtons again found themselves in Rothschild's Schools in Jerusalem. Here they remained one week—the first real rest for months, although in common with the rest of the Brigade they were called upon to provide a large number of working parties, chiefly engaged in road-making in the precincts of the city.

It was a great treat to enjoy a hot bath again, to which they were marched in large parties. The day after coming again to Jerusalem, the G.O.C. presented further medals won by members of the Battalion. Brig.-General Edwards relinquished command of the 179th Brigade, retiring on account of age, and, as he said, "to make room for a younger man." A tall, spare man, he was a somewhat dour personality and in this respect the very opposite of his Divisional Commander, but he had ever been in the front of things and was regarded by the men as a grand old veteran, and held in great respect. A soldier through and through, he lived to die peacefully some twelve years later. He was temporarily succeeded by Colonel Thompson, C.R.E., afterwards to become Labour's first Air Minister, who perished so terribly in the airship disaster at Beauvais. Colonel Thompson first made the acquaintance of the 2/13th on the last day of January, when he inspected its billets. Shortly afterwards the command of the 179th Brigade was assumed by Brig.-General E. T. Humphreys, D.S.O. (now Lieut.-General, C.B., C.M.G., D.S.O.).

The stay of the Kensingtons in Jerusalem came to an end on February 2nd, when they moved to a camp near El Aisawiyeh. Further large working parties were furnished from here until the 11th, when they relieved the 2/17th in the centre sub-sector, with Headquarters again in Abu

JEBEL EKTEIF—JERICHO

Dis. An officers' reconnaissance was carried out on the 13th towards the Wadi Suwaz and El Madowerah. The usual line routine occupied the Battalion until February 18th when the stage was set for the advance to Jordan.

Once again the 179th Brigade found itself as the right flank of the 60th Division, although this time it was the 2/14th, on the extreme right, who made the first move. The objective was the hill of El Muntar, thought to be strongly held by the Turks. This was to be carried by the 2/14th and the enemy left flank rolled up, preparatory to the main attack on Jebel Ekteif, which lay immediately in front of the Brigade's line of advance. The 2/14th moved off from reserve on February 17th, one day earlier than the rest, and, reaching a position some eight miles from El Muntar, lay in hiding until the night of the 18th. The 2/13th moved forward on the 18th to a concentration point in the Wadi Auwaz, and awaited the result of the 2/14th attack on El Muntar. The latter place proved to be surprisingly lightly held and was captured by the Scottish without much difficulty other than that occasioned by the very awkward nature of the country. On the 19th, therefore, the Battalion moved forward to deploy prior to the assault on Jebel Ekteif.

C Company (Captain Baker) acted as advanced guard, with one platoon of B and one platoon of D Company as right and left flank guards respectively. The night was pitch-dark and the going terribly difficult; the sides of the wadis were precipitous, with here and there a narrow ledge that scarcely justified the name of path. Visibility was restricted to a few yards and the march was carried out entirely by compass bearing. On to Khan el Ahmar, the Battalion was soon on the right flank of the 2/18th Battalion, and at half an hour past midnight the Commanding Officers of the 2/13th and 2/18th met and held a hasty conference. The Kensingtons proceeded along the ancient Pilgrims' Road in an easterly direction to Hudeib, and here C Company took up a covering position. The remaining three companies, with A as advanced guard, entered the deep wadi and progressed slowly. They were under orders to deploy and then advance up the opposite slope by scrambling up the boulder-strewn side, getting what cover was possible. The earlier reconnaissances and aeroplane photographs had revealed the ground as being exceedingly difficult, but had quite failed to gauge the impossible nature of the task which now confronted the Battalion. There was scarcely foothold for a goat on the sides of that forty-feet-deep wadi, and try as they would, the heavily equipped men slipped and fell time and time again. The entire scene was shrouded in impenetrable darkness and Lieut.-Colonel Mackenzie waited anxiously for news of progress.

When the position was reported to him, he ordered an immediate reconnaissance with a view to finding an alternative route, but all attempts to do so failed. There was no sign of the enemy and no shots were fired; an uncanny stillness lay over everything. The dark mass of Jebel Ekteif loomed forbiddingly in front, like the side of an immense house. The first grey streaks that told of approaching dawn began to appear, and there was grave danger of daylight finding the whole Battalion spread over the Wadi Sidr and helplessly exposed to enemy fire. Two companies were accordingly ordered to return to the dead ground southwest of the Pilgrims' Road; the remainder (A and D Companies) tried to reach the position by crossing an adjoining hill and entering other wadis. In the meantime Brigade had been informed of the unfortunate check, and the 2/15th (in support) was ordered to take the place of the 2/13th as one of the assault battalions, and attacked farther to the left. Daylight came, and with it severe fire from machine guns and mountain artillery in position behind Jebel Ekteif. Faced by the impassable barrier presented by the Wadi Sidr, the luckless Kensingtons took no part in the first assault, but A and D Companies were able to supply useful covering fire to the 2/15th, and Headquarters Company was able to have a pot at the enemy. By 8 a.m. Jebel Ekteif was taken, and whilst A Company rejoined B

JEBEL EKTEIF—JERICHO

and C Companies near the Pilgrims' Road, D Company was detailed as support to the 2/15th.

The Turks made no attempt to counter-attack Jebel Ekteif, being in retirement over the whole line of hills. The rest of the day was spent quietly, but as rain was falling the whole time, the troops spent a thoroughly uncomfortable time on those barren hills. Water was short, and the parched men were glad to catch rain-drops from the rocks to cool their tongues. During the morning the three companies temporarily out of action moved down again into the Wadi Sidr and lay at the foot of the captured hill. At midday the Brigadier called a conference, which Lieut.-Colonel Mackenzie attended, on Jebel Ekteif. From the very commencement of the campaign, nature had proved almost as formidable an enemy as the Turks, but this was the first and only occasion when she had succeeded in beating the Kensingtons, and no doubt the chagrin and disappointment at the futility of the night's work was fully expressed. But there was no time for an inquest; the Turks had been dislodged from most formidable positions all along this section of the line, and if they were to be prevented from establishing themselves afresh on the lower hills, immediate action was imperative. The road to Jericho now lay open, and this was the moment to seize it.

Already the Australian mounted troops were working along the broken ground on the extreme right, close to the shores of the Dead Sea, and soon Nebi Musa was to be theirs. The 2/13th was ordered to co-operate with the 2/18th in clearing the flying enemy from the hills. B Company, under Captain Thompson, moved forward to engage in this work, and found the enemy snipers active from the many excellent hiding-places among the hills. The Battalion bivouacked that night in wretched conditions, B and C Companies mounting the outposts.

The following day (the 21st) patrols were sent out, but were not molested, and it became clear that the Turks were evacuating the whole range of hills, without the possession of which Jerusalem could never be menaced from the east.

Smoke rising from the northern extremity of the Dead Sea showed that the enemy had abandoned the store-houses there, and the valuable grain traffic from east of the Dead Sea was from that day closed to him. On the 22nd two companies moved forward to the Wadi Marazah, leaving the outpost companies in position. This was to conclude the activities of the 179th Brigade for the time being, for the following day it was relieved of its normal duties by the 180th, and set out on the difficult march back to Jerusalem, via the Wadi Sidr, Anwaz, El Aziriyeh (Bethany), and the Mount of Olives.

February 24th was spent resting and cleaning up, in preparation for guard duties in Jerusalem, which were to be furnished on the 25th. The stay in the Holy City was again destined to be short, and on the 26th the 2/13th moved north to Er Ram, and on the 27th were in brigade support at Ras el Tawil, the 179th having relieved the 181st. Ordered to fresh support positions at Tel es Suwan the next day, the Battalion remained for ten days, engaged in road-making, preparing camp sites, and other work of a like nature. During this period the entire unit was inoculated, in batches of fifty per day, whilst similar parties were marched back to Jerusalem for baths.

A vast amount of work was put in by the whole Brigade on making a good road across the hills to Jebel Kuruntul facing the Jordan Valley, from which place there was a sheer drop of some 600 feet to the plain. Jebel Kuruntul is situated at the westward extremity of the Wilderness of Sin, and is reputed to be the Mount of Temptation. A move was made to this place on March 10th, and quite a good camp site was found, despite the wild and inhospitable nature of the country. The weather was changeable, but on the whole tolerable; it was certainly warmer here than on the exposed Judean Hills. The ancient city of Jericho lay just below, 1,200 feet below sea-level; and at this season of the year the Jordan Valley was quite comfortable for British troops, but in a couple of months it would be like an oven. The Brigade had not been in its new quarters many days before rumours were afloat of an advance across the River Jordan, and on the 15th (which saw Captain C. E. Brockhurst returned to duty from hospital, and resuming duties as Adjutant), the Commanding Officers and Company Commanders of each unit in the 179th went out on a reconnaissance towards the river. The Turks were holding the whole of the far, or eastern, bank, together with a bridge-head at El Ghoraniyeh, where the only bridge (a wooden structure) across the Jordan existed. From the foot of the hills to the river was a distance of some five or six miles, the ground being uncultivated, but covered with small foothills and scrub, which afforded plenty of cover. For a mile on each side of the river banks the scrub was very thick, the vegetation growing luxuriantly. It could only be penetrated by making use of the few footpaths or by hacking a way through the undergrowth, and deployment on orthodox lines was quite impracticable.

This, however, was not the main obstacle to the passage of the Jordan. It was certain that the Turks would destroy the bridge at Ghoraniyeh and thus force an attacking party to ford the river. Here the season was on their side, for at this time of the year the river was swollen by the winter rains and the melting of the snow on Mount Hermon, and it was certain that it presented a formidable obstacle. Local information regarding this point was vague and unreliable, and before anything could be attempted it was necessary that the river be reconnoitred with a view to discovering any available fords and their condition. This duty fell upon the 2/14th (London Scottish), who sent out a company to discover the Mandesi Ford, said to exist some three miles above the Ghoraniyeh Bridge. It had a hard task getting through the scrub at all, and after spending a day on the work, left a party of an officer, a corporal, and four men in hiding on the western bank of the river, to watch for Turks, in the hope that their movements would yield the secret of the ford. The enemy was not unaware of this activity, and the following night blew up the

Ghoraniyeh Bridge as anticipated. Not only this, but they sent out a large raiding party, who succeeded in working round to the rear of the Scottish party, and after a short action, in which the London Scottish faced overwhelming odds, captured the entire party, with the exception of one man, who escaped to bring back the unwelcome news. The company thereupon rejoined its Battalion and brought back valuable but depressing information. Selecting its strongest swimmers, an attempt to ford the river had been made, but every one of the men was swept off his feet by the swift current, and it was clear that the Mandesi Ford could not be carried whilst the river remained in flood. Yet time was of the utmost importance to the realisation of General Allenby's new plan, and so attention was directed to a point on the river between the Ghoraniyeh Bridge and the Dead Sea.

The new plan, which the 60th Division, in company with the Australian and New Zealand Division, the Imperial Camel Corps, the Light Armoured Car Brigade, and one heavy and one mountain battery of artillery, were to carry out, consisted of a bold and gigantic raid against the Turkish Headquarters and dumps at Amman, in the course of which it was hoped to cause severe damage to the Hedjaz railway, on which Amman was an important junction. The Arab Army, under the Emir Feisal and Colonel Lawrence, had been carrying out demolition work on the Hedjaz line at intervals during the past twelve months, and it was expected to link up with this valuable if unorthodox ally at Amman. It was known that the Turkish forces (the "East of Jordan Group") holding the country between Jordan and Amman were comparatively weak, and bold as the plan was, if the element of surprise could be maintained, there was strong hope of success for the British force. This was placed under the command of Major-General Shea of the 60th, and was officially designated "Shea's Group."

The plan was first to force the passage of the River Jordan (a formidable task), then, advancing swiftly across the intervening plain, to capture the heights commanding

JEBEL EKTEIF—JERICHO

the plain and push ahead to the town of Es Salt; this involved an advance of eighteen miles and a climb of over 3,000 feet. With one brigade of infantry to hold Es Salt, and the 1st Australian Light Horse protecting the left flank, the remainder of the column was to advance on Amman, a further fifteen miles to the east of Es Salt. Operation orders provided for two crossings to be made and pontoon bridges to be thrown across, one at Hajlah for the cavalry and camels, and one at Ghoraniyeh for the infantry (60th Division). The 180th Brigade was ordered to force both crossings.

At 7 p.m. on March 21st, the 179th Brigade concentrated in the Wadi Nueiamah and awaited the outcome of the activities of the 180th Brigade. Earlier in the afternoon it was known that the Turks had reinforced Ghoraniyeh by 600 infantry and had sent two squadrons of cavalry to Hajlah. The Kensingtons were lying in the scrub, and soon heard sounds of rapid rifle fire from the direction of the river. The enemy was thoroughly alarmed. The 2/17th had the unenviable job of swimming the river at Ghoraniyeh, and as hour after hour wore on it became clear that the swift current was proving too much for the swimmers. Brisk firing continued through the night, and when dawn broke the weary men of the 179th Brigade were sprawling on the ground asleep, still awaiting the order to advance. The attempt at Ghoraniyeh failed. Farther down the river, at Hajlah, the 2/19th had been more fortunate, an officer and nine men having succeeded in swimming across unobserved, and at twenty minutes past one on the morning of the 22nd the first raft, with twenty-seven men, was ferried over. The whole of that day the process of ferrying over small parties continued under conditions of great difficulty; the Turks were in a position on a hill 1,000 yards away, from which they were able to enfilade the river, and only by lying flat in the bottom of the rafts and punts could men be got over. Eventually a detachment of the Auckland Mounted Rifles got over and galloped down a number of Turkish detachments, whilst

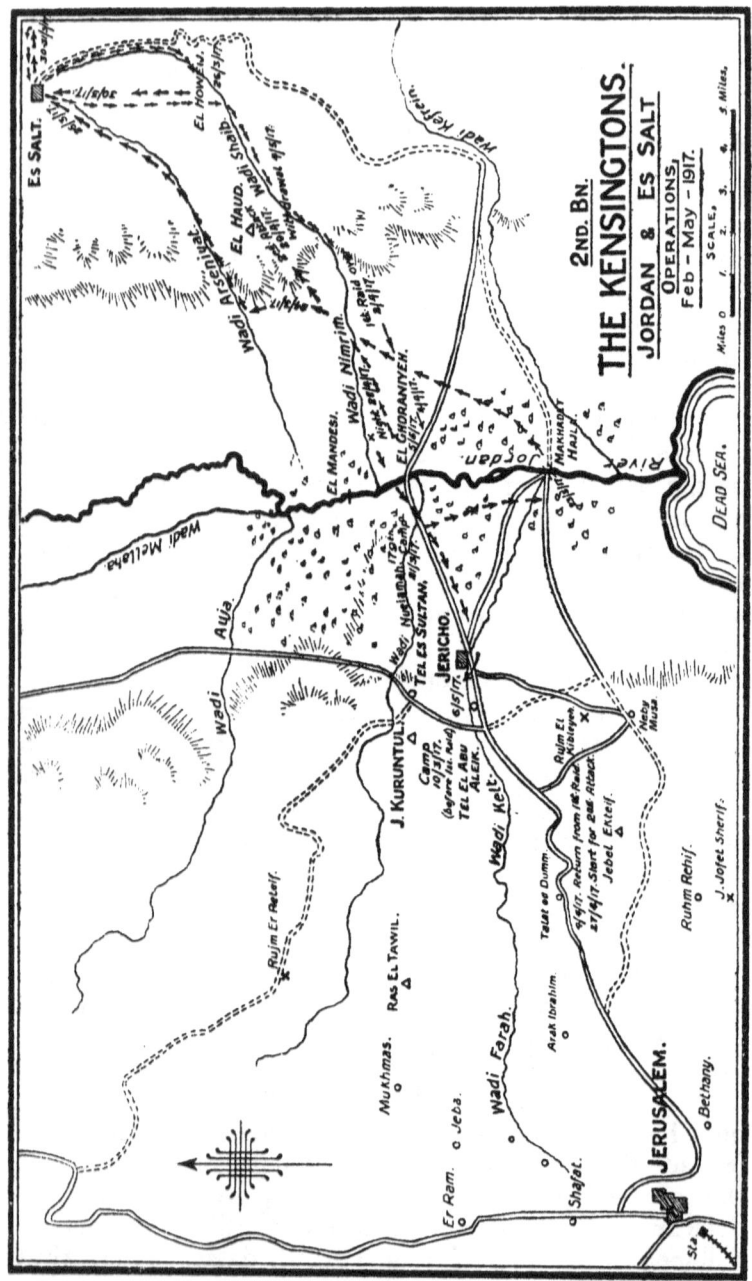

another party crossed the Dead Sea in motor-boats and landed on the Turkish side of the Jordan, and joined up with the units of the 180th Brigade at Hajlah. Meanwhile the Kensingtons still lay concealed west of Ghoraniyeh, and at nightfall the 2/17th again attempted to force a passage there, but without success, and eventually the 179th Brigade was moved down to Hajlah. Here it was held up by the thick undergrowth, and it was not until 11 o'clock on the morning of the 23rd that the 2/13th crossed the Jordan by the pontoon bridge which had by that time been thrown over.

As the 2/13th trudged through a little clearing which had been made in the dense undergrowth, it was astonished to see His Royal Highness the Duke of Connaught and General Allenby standing together watching the crossing. It gave the Kensingtons a thrill to see the aged brother of their own Princess Louise in this far outpost of the Empire's fighting line, and well within range of Turkish fire. As the Battalion went by the Duke handed his packet of sandwiches to Private J. Sharpe, a Headquarters runner; Sharpe was torn between a desire to keep the Royal gift as a memento and the pangs of hunger. The hunger won! To see the G.O.C. was an added pleasure, although his presence well up in the line was not unusual; General Allenby was no arm-chair Commander. Passing through the 180th Brigade, whose magnificent enterprise had alone made the operations possible, the Kensingtons were ordered to extend the Hajlah bridge-head, with the 2/16th on their left. The first stage of the raid was over, but the river had defeated the original idea of a swift surprise.

The following morning saw events develop rapidly. The retreating Turks were in position on El Haud, a projecting hill which commanded the whole of the valley, and before anything else could be done, the 179th Brigade was ordered to capture this hill. The duty fell to the lot of the 2/14th and 2/16th, with the 2/13th in support. At 8.30 a.m. the Brigade concentrated in the Wadi Nimrin, and the attack was launched. The Kensingtons' dispositions were B and C Companies in front, with A Company in support and D Company protecting the left flank of Brigade. The artillery attached to "Shea's Group" had crossed the Jordan overnight, and provided a short, sharp artillery preparation. Up the stony slopes of El Haud went the Scottish and the Queen's Westminsters, and, although troubled for some time by machine-gun nests, were soon everywhere victorious, and by noon El Haud was ours. The 2/13th was not called upon to assist in the attack, other than by its position as support battalion. This success enabled the 181st Brigade to advance in the valley and turn the Turkish right flank; the 2/22nd captured three guns in doing so. The Turks were soon in retreat towards Es Salt, and at 4 o'clock that afternoon the 179th was able to concentrate again in the Wadi Arseniyet, A Company of the 2/13th being called upon to picket the heights, whilst the rest of the men snatched what sleep they could. The following day was a particularly trying one for the whole force, as the weather broke and the continuous rain rendered the only track available a quagmire. Assembling at 7 a.m., the 179th Brigade marched forward to Es Salt in the following order: 2/15th, 2/13th, 2/16th, 2/14th. The route was uphill all the way, and it never stopped raining. The track became worse and worse, and if it took the heavily equipped infantry all their time to find a foothold, the troubles of the transport sections can be imagined. During the day the 2/13th lost four camels with their loads, which slipped over the precipitous sides into the wadi. Seven o'clock in the evening came, and still the weary column staggered on, the language becoming more and more lurid, until there was no breath left even for swearing. Every now and again odd troopers of the Australian Light Horse passed by, and they were loud in their praises of the dogged Londoners, who were fighting the terrible difficulties with all the reserve of will-power they possessed.

It was 11 p.m. when their ordeal for that day ended, a few straggling lights showing that Es Salt had been reached.

JEBEL EKTEIF—JERICHO

It should also be mentioned that early in the morning it had been intended that the 2/13th should provide an outpost line on the heights to the north of the Wadi Arseniyet, to cover the moving column from flank attack, but after two pickets had been posted, these were withdrawn upon information being received that the enemy had retreated too far to permit the possibility of harassing the advancing Brigade. What the privations of the Battalion would have been had it been necessary to maintain the safeguard it is impossible to imagine. It is certain that it would not have reached Es Salt that night. No duties were required of the 2/13th on arrival at Es Salt, and the men sank down in the mud on their bivouac site and endured the pouring rain as best they could. Some summoned up sufficient strength to pitch a bivouac, into which four men would crawl, but many more lay down just as they were and pulled a loose sheet over them. It was nearly midnight, and the transport was still struggling along with the camels (poor beasts!) and there was no prospect of rations or water being issued until the morning.

An alarm was caused during the night by a sudden fusillade of rifle fire, but it turned out to be a little *feu de joie* on the part of the Moabite inhabitants, who were thus expressing their joy at the departure of their traditional enemies.

The following morning (March 26th) it was learnt that no further move was to be made that day, and some attempt was made to establish an orderly bivouac site. The rain of the previous day had vanished, and instead a bright sun gleamed from a blue sky and showed to advantage the white roofs and walls of Es Salt, nestling against the hillside below the height where the Brigade was encamped. The 2/13th was called upon to find various guards in the town, to which access was otherwise rigorously barred. The 2/15th and 2/16th were engaged on outpost duty on the hills to the north, whilst the 2/14th rested. The day passed uneventfully, and such news as came to hand told that the advance upon Amman was proceeding according to plan. Matters were so far satisfactory that on the following day three battalions of the 179th, including the 2/13th, were withdrawn back along the Jericho Road as far as the El Howeij bridge, where there was ample facility for ideal camping. The Wadi Shaib being in flood at the time, all were able to bathe to their hearts' content, the sun continuing to shine brightly. Whilst they were encamped at this point, several wild-looking Arab horsemen came careering down the road, brandishing rifles in the air and shouting hoarsely; it was said that these fellows were part of the Arab forces engaged in operations on the Hedjaz railway, who had seized the opportunity to link up with the British troops, and no doubt were enjoying a little joy ride. During the day a German aeroplane flew over and dropped a few bombs without doing any damage.

Bad news was received that night from Amman. Far from going well, operations were reported to be held up by large enemy reinforcements which had been hurried down by rail, and the cavalry was in dire peril of being cut off altogether. A good deal of demolition work had been carried out to the north and south of the town, but the main objective, the destruction of the tunnel, had not been achieved, whilst Amman itself held out. The whole of the 181st Brigade and two battalions of the 180th had been thrown into the fight to help the cavalry, and the whole force had sustained severe losses. The 179th Brigade was called upon to try to stave off what looked like developing into a disaster. Early on the 28th the London Scottish commenced to march back to Es Salt to reinforce the Civil Service Rifles, who were holding the ground to the north of the town. The Kensingtons and Queen's Westminsters remained at El Howeij awaiting events.

All the following day the Battalion remained standing by, ready to move at short notice, but the call did not come. The rain, however, did, and an uncomfortable night was spent, whilst disquieting rumours continued to float down the line, and large numbers of wounded trickled back. At 10.45 a.m. on the 30th the march back to Es Salt

THE RAID ON AMMAN, MARCH 1918.
Imperial War Museum photograph. Copyright reserved.

commenced; there was a general feeling of uncertainty, and all wondered what was in store. This feeling was enhanced upon arrival at Es Salt, and further news of the Amman operations was received. It was said that the British force had been cut up and was retiring, leaving wounded and stores in the hands of the Turks, who were reported to be in overwhelming strength. Nothing official, however, was issued, and at dusk the order came to march out in the direction of Amman. Strict silence was enjoined, and the column moved along the muddy track in a darkness that could almost be felt. Ghostly strings of camels passed by on either side, bearing their loads of wounded back. The going was exceptionally heavy and progress slow; after some six miles had been covered a motor-cycle despatch rider caught up with the column and delivered a message to the Colonel. Immediately an order was given to about turn and make for Es Salt again. The bewildered troops wondered what was happening, and what was to be the fate of the harassed cavalry and infantry engaged in a fierce rearguard action at Amman.

The situation at Es Salt had become somewhat complicated owing to the arrival of enemy reinforcements, which threatened the left flank of the 179th Brigade. Whilst the 2/13th was plodding its way towards Amman the Turks attacked Es Salt from the direction of Kefr Huda, and this was the reason for the sudden alteration of orders. The enemy was defeated about 11 o'clock that night, the 3rd Australian Light Horse capturing some prisoners and three machine guns. On arriving again at Es Salt, the Kensingtons furnished one company to support the Queen's Westminsters, and the remainder bivouacked where they stood. It now became known that the evacuation of the whole force had been ordered, and this commenced at 7 a.m. on the morning of the 31st. The main body attacking Amman was to withdraw via Es Sir, some way to the south of the Es Salt–Amman Road, the 179th Brigade meanwhile holding Es Salt and covering the retirement. The position of the Brigade during this operation was both exposed and precarious, both flanks being open. At dusk on the 31st A and B Companies under Major Collier took up positions on the high ground covering the junction of the Es Salt-Amman Road and the El Fuhais track. The enemy were actively harassing the retirement of the 181st Brigade, and that night it seemed that the Battalion was almost encircled by rifle fire.

The general retirement continued throughout April 1st and was much impeded by large numbers of natives, who had decided to seek safety across the Jordan, rather than await the return of the Turks who would assuredly punish them heavily for their reception of the British. All day long the road was choked by whole families struggling along with their household possessions on their heads, or loaded upon asses, whose main object in life seemed to be to lie down in the middle of the road. Sounds of firing continued both to the front and rear of the Brigade, but fortunately no attack was launched against Es Salt. Early in the morning A and B Companies were withdrawn to a position astride the main road, taking over posts from the 2/16th. These companies were later relieved by C and D. Early in the evening news was received that the main body retiring from Es Sir had reached safety and the way was now clear for the 179th to evacuate Es Salt.

The Kensingtons were appointed rearguard, reinforced by two armoured cars. Large dumps had been formed of stores which it was not possible to carry away, and at 7 pm. these were fired as the Battalion formed up and marched away down the road which led to the Jordan valley. D Company brought up the extreme rear, with the Scouts as rear-points. The armoured cars proved a nuisance, being continually stuck fast in the thick mud, whilst the mules as usual proved true to their reputation; two of the latter fell over the rocks and had to be abandoned. Otherwise the evacuation was carried through without loss. The weather was good, and the march down the road was carried out much quicker than the march up had been. All the way down parties of unfortunate natives were passed, hurrying along as though possessed, and imploring the " Tommies " to wait for them. The retirement from Es Salt was carried out so successfully that it is certain that the enemy had no idea of what was going on until it was too late to prevent it. It was not until 4.45 a.m. that the Battalion was allowed to halt and enjoy a few hours' rest at Shunet Nimrin.

The march was continued at noon under a blazing sun, and the Jordan was crossed at El Ghoraniyeh without incident, the whole Brigade bivouacking on the plain at 4 o'clock that afternoon. Orders were given for bivouacs to be rendered as inconspicuous as possible among the thick scrub around Jericho, and that there was good reason for this was shown the next day, when " Jerry " sailed over on a bombing expedition. He had a marvellous target, for the whole plain was alive with troops, and a few of his bombs caused some casualties; one fell in the wadi of the 2/13th camp. All day long there was an endless stream of natives crossing the bridge at El Ghoraniyeh, and their sustenance meant additional difficulty for General Allenby. No move was made that day, the whole of the raiding force being in need of rest, but early on April 4th a start was made for Tallat Ed Dumm, the march being via Jericho and maintained for seven hours under a hot sun.

Bivouacs were pitched near the Good Samaritan's Inn, and the next day was spent in resting. The road from Jericho up to Jerusalem presents an exceedingly stiff climb, and would tax the marching powers of any troops, even in the best of condition. After their experiences of the last few days, the troops of " Shea's Group " were anything but at their best, and when again called upon to march under a blazing sun, the spirit of mercy prevailed in high quarters, and orders were given for the men's packs to be transported in motor-lorries up that forbidding hill. The march was therefore resumed lightheartedly on the 6th and a six-hour stretch was accomplished. There were high expectations of a stay in Jerusalem, but these were doomed to disappointment, and the Brigade found itself in a position on the

Nablus Road, near Shafat. Here it made itself as comfortable as circumstances permitted. After a stay of three days, the 60th Division went forward to relieve the 10th (Irish) Division in the line, but the 2/13th was not called upon for line duty, and as things at that time were very quiet, it meant very little difference to its daily routine, which consisted largely of working parties, bathing parades, Lewis-gun training, etc.

During this period there were two important changes on the Headquarters Staff of the 2/13th. Lieut.-Colonel C. M. Mackenzie, D.S.O., relinquished command of the Kensingtons on April 17th, in order to take up fresh duties in England, and was succeeded on April 23rd by Lieut.-Colonel T. E. Bisdee, M.C., of the 2/15th (Civil Service Rifles) London Regt.* Colonel Mackenzie's departure was generally regretted, and he took with him the good wishes of every man in the Battalion, which he had commanded since the concluding days of its training on Salisbury Plain. He was far from being a martinet, but his gentle manner hid an iron resolution, and he was the personification of coolness under fire. The appointment of Captain C. E. Brockhurst to the post of Brigade Major of the 179th left the Adjutancy vacant, and this gap was filled by the appointment of Lieut. (later Captain) E. J. Smith, M.C. Captain Brockhurst had joined the Battalion upon its formation in 1914, and his work as Adjutant had been so conspicuously successful that his appointment came as no surprise.

Beyond occasional desultory shelling and the daily patrolling of enemy aeroplanes, there was little to denote a war on this part of the front, and the Kensingtons were soon awaiting their turn in the line with some interest in order to

---

* Lieut.-Colonel Bisdee was a Regular Army officer (D.C.L.I.), and resumed his Regular Army career after the war. Whilst home on leave from India in 1932, he came down to Kensington one memorable evening and met as many of the 2/13th as could manage to get along. He met a tragic death in 1933, being thrown from his horse shortly after his retirement and return to England.

break the monotony of their existence. About April 21st it became known that they were to move, but general surprise was expressed when it was further known that they were to move to the rear. They seemed to have marched a great way to do very little, but, any change being better than none, they marched away on the 23rd in the direction of Shafat, and again hoping that Jerusalem might be the destination. Once again their hopes were not realised, and there was a sinking of hearts when they espied once more that long, long, dusty trail that led steeply downwards to the Jordan. What was on the boards now?

On April 27th, 1918, the 179th Brigade found itself again at Talaat Ed Dumm.

CHAPTER XXVI

THE SECOND RAID ACROSS THE JORDAN

THE first raid across the Jordan, apart from accomplishing demolition work on the Hedjaz railway, had, it appears, convinced the enemy that Allenby's ultimate advance to Damascus would be by way of Es Salt and Amman. Convinced of this, the Turks retained their Fourth Army east of Jordan, and set to work to strengthen their defences in Gilead, which, so far as Es Salt was concerned, had proved so vulnerable to the small British force a few weeks earlier. It suited General Allenby very well that a Turkish Army should be tied up east of Jordan, and he resolved to strengthen the Turkish conviction of an advance on Damascus via Amman by a second raid. It was also hoped that it would harass and, if possible, cut off the very large concentration of the enemy that had taken place in the neighbourhood of Shunet Nimrin since the first raid. In truth, it seemed a somewhat bold measure, but boldness had succeeded at Beersheba, and the same troops were detailed to carry out the plan—the Desert Mounted Corps and the 60th Division, by now well versed in this type of warfare, which called for great fortitude and dash, together with marching powers of no mean order. When the men knew that the 179th Brigade was once again to attack the identical hill of El Haud, they gasped, but hoped that it would fall as easily as on the first occasion. They were destined to be bitterly disillusioned.

Leaving Talaat Ed Dumm at 6 p.m. on the evening of April 28th, the Kensingtons, with the rest of the 179th Brigade, marched down on to the plain and wound their way through Jericho, bivouacking that night amidst the thick scrub. No fires or smoking were permitted. Operation orders showed that the assault on El Haud was to be

THE SECOND RAID ACROSS THE JORDAN

carried out by the 2/14th and 2/16th, the 2/13th being in brigade reserve. Lying concealed until dusk, the column moved off again on the following evening, the 2/13th following 1,000 yards in the rear of the attacking battalions. Until now the attacking troops had been within the shelter of the strongly wired bridge-head which protected the Ghoraniyeh crossing, held by Indian troops, but now at 6 p.m. they went through the gap in the wire and approached the enemy. The Brigade moved in artillery formation, the 2/13th behind the 2/14th. It was a hot, muggy night, and the dust was stifling, so that the march was a trying one. After a halt in the Wadi Nimrin for rest, the march was resumed about 10 p.m.; there was a bright moon, which threw up the hills in front in bold relief.

Shortly after midnight the place of deployment was reached, and here the pack animals were off-loaded and the beasts sent into the Wadi Nimrin for shelter. As during the approach to Ain Karim, the noise accompanying this work seemed certain to be heard over the clear night air, but no sound came from the enemy in front, who, however, were no doubt well aware of what was going on. The Kensingtons were halted some 1,000 yards in the rear of the Scottish, whose officers were carrying out a reconnaissance before the attack, which was scheduled to take place shortly before 3 a.m. in moonlight. The first sounds of rifle and machine-gun fire were actually heard at 2.22 a.m. and told that the assault had been launched. The Turkish fire assumed a surprising volume, and it was soon known that the attacking battalions were experiencing a very hot time; the enemy were strongly entrenched on El Haud this time, having been engaged in making sangars and such trenches as were possible in the stony soil during the past weeks. The Scottish in front were attacking Spectacle Hill. Our aircraft had reported that the enemy were probably 5,000 strong, and subsequent events proved that this was no low estimate. At 4.30 a.m. flares were seen which told that the 2/14th and 2/16th had gained a footing and were fighting their way up to the main objective. The Kensingtons were ordered to move slowly forward, and came under shell fire.

At 5 a.m. C Company (Captain Thompson) was ordered forward as support to the Scottish, and had to cross 800 yards of open ground under severe machine-gun fire. It was now broad daylight, and orders were given for everyone to seek as much concealment as the ground permitted. At 6.30 a.m. the remainder of the Battalion moved to support the 2/16th, and, having to cross some 1,500 yards of open plain, came under heavy shell fire and sustained numerous casualties; they arrived at a point near the Queen's Westminsters' Headquarters, where it was learned that the issue was very much in doubt. Both the 2/14th and the 2/16th had obtained their first objective, but were precariously placed in more or less exposed positions on the hillside, and it was evident that the Turks were in such strength that further advance for the moment was impossible. Moreover, the 181st Brigade, attacking on the right, had not been so fortunate, so that the line swung back and left the 179th Brigade flank somewhat exposed. A Company (Lieut. Savage) was now ordered to join the 2/14th, and C Company (Captain Thompson) the 2/16th, leaving B and D Companies, under Captains Kisch and Green respectively, with 2/13th Headquarters. So the remainder of that long day passed, thirteen casualties being sustained, including Lieut. (acting Captain) R. P. Shute.

The situation remained unchanged during the following day (May 1st), during which both the Scottish and the Westminsters had a trying time. Both battalions sustained very heavy casualties, owing to their exposed position. The front-line companies were out of touch with their Headquarters, communication only being possible by runners, of whom many deeds of gallantry were recorded that day. Private Cruikshank, of the Scottish, gained the Victoria Cross for great gallantry in endeavouring to carry a vital message, which also earned the D.C.M. for the runner who ultimately got it through. The most ominous rumours were afloat, arising from the fact which was evident to all—

that the present attack had been held up, and that the attacking force was now in such a position that a supreme effort would be necessary either to advance or retire. The two brigades were now grimly holding on to the lower slopes of the massive hill known as El Haud, which was held by the enemy in overwhelming strength in prepared positions. A very different state of affairs from the first attack! Comparatively few casualties occurred on the 1st, among whom was 2nd Lieut. J. T. B. Waller.

The following day the two attacking battalions were withdrawn at dusk in an exhausted condition (the Scottish alone had sustained 48 per cent. casualties), and were relieved by the Kensingtons and the Civil Service Rifles. A summary of the situation as it then existed was issued to Commanding Officers, and it seemed that any further advance on El Haud was impossible. Nevertheless, at 4 a.m. on the 3rd, B and D Companies were ordered to advance up the lower slopes, and were met by a withering machine-gun fire from concealed nests, together with a fusillade of bombs, which were dropped upon any spot which seemed to offer prospect of a foothold. It was quickly realised that to pursue the advance was out of the question, but when the two companies came to withdraw, they found this equally impossible in daylight. They were therefore forced to try to dig themselves in, but little good could be done as they were lying on solid rock, from which the bullets ricochetted in all directions. Here they had perforce to lay for sixteen hours in the intense heat, and without water. The sun had by now attained to great power, and the burning rays came off the rocks like the heat from an open oven. It was a terrible plight for the unfortunate men who were wounded, but nothing could be done for their succour from the rear, the slightest movement on that hillside evoking a stream of bullets from the hidden Turks.

The enemy aircraft were active, flying over the Jordan valley and bombing the transport columns and bridge-head, and searching the foothills on which lay the British force, trying to discover our strength and positions. One

German, flying very low indeed over the 179th position, paid the penalty of his audacity, and fell to a brisk rifle fire in the Kensingtons' line. From where they were lying, the whole of the Jordan valley was plainly visible to the sweating infantry, and, of course, to the Turks as well; the former began to wonder if they would ever have the satisfaction of marching over it again.

Leaving the stalemate on El Haud for a moment, we may learn how the remainder of the operations east of Jordan were faring. When the 60th Division was sent forward to attack the strong Turkish concentration around Shunet Nimrim, the Desert Mounted Corps moved northwards along the plain east of Jordan, with the object of seizing Es Salt from the north-west and thus blocking the only metalled road which offered a retreat to the Turkish force at Shunet Nimrin. An alternative retreat to Amman was offered by the track through Es Sir, which, however, passed through territory inhabited by the Beni Sakir tribe, who had agreed to rise and attack the Turks in the rear as soon as Es Salt had fallen to the Australian Mounted troops. The first objective was gained, and Es Salt was taken before the assault on El Haud commenced, together with a quantity of Turkish transport and troops. The promised rising of the Beni Sakir did not materialise, however (it was afterwards learned that Colonel Lawrence had warned the British that they were a treacherous crowd and not to be depended upon at all), and the Turks being swiftly and very strongly reinforced from Amman, a series of counter-attacks against the Desert Mounted Corps was launched, which extended over three days and ended in the evacuation of Es Salt by the cavalry being ordered on the 3rd. During these actions, the Honourable Artillery Company was forced to abandon eight guns and make its retreat over precipitous country, in which many animals fell over the rocks and were killed.

The treachery of the Beni Sakir left the Es Sir Road open to the Turks, and the Shunet Nimrin force, instead of being an isolated body of troops (which it was hoped would fall

THE SECOND RAID ACROSS THE JORDAN

prisoners to the 60th Division), formed the southern claw of a formidable pair of pincers with which the enemy threatened to cut off the cavalry at Es Salt. The action of the 60th against a vastly superior force in consequence became quite vain, and was only persisted in for sufficient time to elapse to ensure the withdrawal of the Desert Mounted Corps from their precarious and isolated position. Little of this was known to the infantry at the time, beyond the news that the Australians were in Es Salt, which news only seemed to make confusion worse confounded. The Kensingtons had trouble enough of their own, for early on the morning of the 3rd it became known that the Patialas (Indian troops) on their left flank had been forced to withdraw somewhat, owing to enfilade fire. This rendered their position perilous in the extreme, but they hung on throughout that day.

At 8 p.m. they were relieved by the 2/16th and retired a little way down the hill, being in brigade reserve. On May 4th the Turks attempted to assume the initiative by following up their advantage on the left flank, and working round the Patialas. To strengthen the position, C Company was sent up to reinforce the Indians, and this step proved sufficient. C Company remained in the Wadi Arseniyet. Soon afterwards orders were received to evacuate the entire position that evening, and one platoon was detached to assist the 2/16th. Notwithstanding their experiences on El Haud, the men were all loath to withdraw, and as the waiting hours passed slowly by, they sat and gazed with saddened hearts at the plain below. No attempt was made to evacuate the bodies of the fallen and these were buried at the foot of the hills. Many parting messages for Johnny Turk were left, assuring him of a further visit in the future, the words being arranged with stones, accompanied by mock graves enclosing a crescent and so on.

At 9 p.m. the Battalion was gradually concentrated at the foot of the hills, and moved off in the darkness unmolested by the enemy, marching until it reached its former hiding-place in the scrub, inside the wired bridgehead which protected Ghoraniyeh. Very early the following morning the march was resumed and the bridge across the Jordan again crossed, a safe bivouac area being reached after a very trying march under a hot sun. The Kensingtons had again been very fortunate, the total casualties numbering only some fifty killed or wounded, due to the fact that they had not been engaged on the first assault which cost their companion battalions, the 2/14th and 2/16th, so dearly. Nevertheless, the second east of Jordan raid left a nasty taste in the mouth, because at the time it all seemed so futile, but by reason of the fact that it encouraged the enemy to think that General Allenby's ultimate line of advance would be via Amman to Damascus, it caused him to keep the Fourth Army locked up east of Jordan when it might have been opposing the real advance along the coastal sector, so it was adjudged to have been well worth while. It provided food for endless debate in the bivouacs for months to come, and it was always hoped by the Kensingtons that it would be their lot once more to march up the road by the Wadi Shaib and renew their acquaintance with Es Salt, but it was never to be. If only the wily Beni Sakir had played their part, or perhaps if Colonel Lawrence's advice on that important matter had been taken, a different tale might have been told. Who can tell?

Pontoon Bridge across the River Jordan at El Ghoraniyeh.
Imperial War Museum photograph. Copyright reserved.

CHAPTER XXVII

THE SUMMER LULL—1918

WHEN the east of Jordan operations were concluded, there followed a lull (so far as major operations were concerned) along the whole of the Palestine front until the commencement of the great September advance, which was finally to smash the Turks and bring the war in that theatre to a triumphant conclusion. During the whole period from May 4th until September no portion of the British forces was to be seriously engaged, whilst the morale and resources of the enemy were far too low to permit of any initiative on his part. From captured enemy documents it was later known that during the whole of this time their commanders were pressing the High Command for reinforcements, and neglect of their claims even led to the resignation of their commands by the Generals commanding the Fourth and Seventh Armies; the failure of the enemy's spring offensive on the Western Front rendered any substantial reinforcements out of the question, and during these summer months there was a constant state of friction existing between the Turks and their German masters, whom they regarded as "infidels."

Whilst the British forces were relieved from the necessity for taking part in any further attacks during the hot months, the usual line duties had, of course, to be maintained, and, when not engaged in these, the men were continuously at work making roads, at which they could now claim to have become experts.

To return to the Kensingtons, however, on the morning of May 6th they paraded in readiness for the long march ahead, which rumour had it was to terminate somewhere in the region of the Nablus Road, north of Jerusalem. After a short march as far as the ration dump, they were amazed to find a large fleet of A.S.C. lorries waiting to transport them up that awful hill to Bethany; such consideration had not been their lot previously, and as the men excitedly clambered up into the vehicles there were many jokes exchanged as to the probability of a special draft of wet-nurses arriving from " Blighty " in the near future. The A.S.C. drivers became the butt of many shafts of Cockney wit, which they bore good-humouredly. It was a sweltering hot morning, and as the long column of lorries with their heavy loads essayed the tortuous ascent up the well-known road, and swung perilously round the hairpin bends, the radiators commenced to boil. A few lorries were unable to complete the attempt, but the majority made the journey in safety and disgorged their occupants at a point about half a mile south of Shaffat, on the Nablus Road. From here the march was continued for a short distance to the bivouac area allotted to the Battalion. The following day was spent in resting. Then the Battalion marched forward as far as Ram Allah and on May 9th arrived at Ain Arik, where it went into camp for twelve days.

The camp site was pleasantly situated and " a good time was had by all." The days were passed in training, whilst on the 14th Battalion sports were held. It should be mentioned that the 60th Division had now been sent into corps reserve, this being the first time that the Division had been out of active operations since the commencement of the offensive at Beersheba the previous October. For eight months the 60th had undergone an arduous time, and the present relaxation was more than welcome, although it meant a return to intensive training which was not so welcome. However, the extreme heat kept the training programme within a supportable limit. The flies were the chief trouble at this stage, and they were truly awful, giving no one any rest during the hours of daylight, whilst the avidity with which these pests settled upon every morsel of food, even when it was being actually conveyed from hand to mouth, rendered it exceedingly difficult to avoid swallowing flies with every mouthful.

THE SUMMER LULL—1918

On May 21st the Battalion was again on the move, marching to fresh quarters at Umm Suffah, where it remained until June 4th. The camp site was again pleasantly situated in fairly well wooded country; the sun was now moving to its zenith, and each day seemed to be hotter than the last. The fly problem at Umm Suffah was even worse than at Ain Arik. Whilst at Ain Arik, the Battalion's own concert party, the "Percussion Caps," had given their first show to a wildly enthusiastic audience, the performance being repeated at Umm Suffah. The name was derived from the prime mover of the project, Lieut. Capps, who was ably assisted by the second in command, Major Collier, Corporal ("Gippo") Clubley, Private Ritchie Phillips, M.M., and others. Between them they put up a marvellously good performance with the assistance of what few "properties" they had been able to get together during the brief visits on leave to Cairo, and the valuable aid of the Pioneer Sergeant, Fillis, who worked wonders in a short time.

And now came news which, although not entirely unexpected, was sufficiently startling. For some time past rumour had been rife that certain units of the 60th Division were to be withdrawn to the Western Front, where reinforcements were urgently needed after the heavy casualties inflicted by the Germans during their great attempt to break through in March. There had naturally been much speculation on the point, but this was now ended by the news that three battalions of the 179th were earmarked for France, the Kensingtons being the unit left in Palestine. It came as a bombshell, and excited discussion broke out and lasted until late into the night, and long after the last lights were extinguished in the tiny bivouacs. It is useless to debate whether the 2/13th had been honoured in being so singled out; one battalion had to stay to form the nucleus of the new 179th Brigade, the remaining three units of which, it was learned, were to be Indian troops. The reasons which led to the decision were not, of course, known, but the news provoked very mixed feelings.

"THE KENSINGTONS"

Everyone was anxious to take part in the final triumph which, it was clear, lay before General Allenby's command; not a man but knew that the coming of cooler weather in the autumn would see the great advance continued, and visions of mounting guard in Constantinople were entertained—and not perhaps foolishly. On the other hand, events in France were also clearly moving towards a crisis; with the arrival of the Americans, and the feeling that the Germans had played their trump card, and lost, a great Allied offensive was being planned, and the Battalion would have welcomed the chance of taking part in it. It is true that the years had banished the easy optimism which accompanied the singing of the "Watch on the Rhine" in those far-off days of 1914, but the prospect of setting foot on German soil was a tempting one. France, too, almost certainly meant "Blighty" leave, which was a negligible quantity from Palestine, and to men who had been absent from home for two years, pulses quickened at the thought. But, more than anything else, the breaking up of the splendid "Grey Brigade" was a shattering blow. Few brigades in the Army had had the good fortune to be so closely associated as that which contained the Kensingtons, the London Scottish, the Civil Service Rifles, and the Queen's Westminsters. Fine names all! From the winter of '14–15 these four second-line battalions had seldom been separated by more than a mile or two, and the life of one had been the life of all four. A separate existence seemed unreal. But there it was, and on May 28th the three battalions who had been favoured (or otherwise) bade farewell to the Kensingtons and set out on their long trek to the coast, and thence to Kantara and France. Good-bye, Scottish! Good-bye, "Civils"! Good-bye, Westminsters! Good chaps, all; we shall miss you. Farewell, and the best of luck go with you!

Four other battalions of the 60th Division left for France—the 2/17th, 2/20th, 2/23rd, and 2/24th. Indian troops filled the gaps, leaving only one white unit to each brigade. Allenby had acceded to the G.H.Q. request for

THE SUMMER LULL—1918

reinforcements for France with his accustomed boldness, for there was much stern work still ahead, and the Indian units had not yet been severely tested in assault operations. During the last days at Umm Suffah, the 2/13th was engaged in making defence works, and on June 5th moved to Naby Saleh, where it continued with road-making for three weeks. On the first of the month Capt. (Acting Major) R. P. Gladstone was appointed Staff Captain, O.E.T.A. The 2/18th and the 2/21st were disbanded in order to provide drafts to bring the three other units up to strength, the 2/13th receiving a draft of four officers and 117 O.R.s from the 2/21st.

Whilst at Neby Saleh the four companies of the Battalion were dispersed over separate areas to engage in road-making, rejoining Headquarters on June 24th, preparatory to moving to Bireh. Here the everlasting road-making continued, until all ranks were heartily sick of the business. Everyone was therefore tremendously relieved when, on July 19th, orders were received to take over a section of the line at Singil Ridge, held by the 1/6th Royal Welch Fusiliers. Marching via Beitun, the relief was completed on the 20th, the Company Commanders being as follows: A, Captain Shute; B, Captain Baker; C, Captain Thompson; D, Captain Green. The section of the line occupied, as indeed the entire front during these summer months, was very quiet, and there was a considerable stretch of broken ground between the two opposing lines. This demanded a large amount of patrol work, which was usually welcomed as a break from line routine. The weather continued to remain fair, the days being very hot and the nights pleasantly cool and bright. The only relief from monotony was occasioned by a suspected spy, who gave himself up on August 1st, stating that a British aeroplane had come down in the Turkish lines three days previously, and a " demonstration " by one officer and ten O.R.s, which was carried out on the 2nd before Turmus Aya with the object of drawing the enemy's artillery fire. So quiescent had the Turks become (or so short of shells) that our own artillery was seriously in doubt as to the strength of their guns. Even this little performance, however, failed to draw their fire, and it is presumed that the worthy gunners remained in ignorance of the position of the opposing batteries. It may be mentioned that at this point of the line there were ample facilities for camouflage.

On August 3rd the 2/13th was relieved by one of the Indian units of the newly formed 179th Brigade (the 3/151st Battalion) and became the battalion in brigade reserve. The following day was the fourth anniversary of the outbreak of the war and provoked much speculation as to the possibility of there being a fifth; the general opinion was that the coming months would see the conclusion of the Palestine campaign, followed by the transfer of the E.E.F. to France, in readiness for a final break-through in the spring of 1919. So much for speculation, however, and the Battalion supplied working parties to the 2/19th Punjabis, who were in the line, and this work continued during the ensuing week. On August 12th B Company, together with one platoon of C, under the command of Captain L. S. Baker, were detailed to carry out a raid in conjunction with the 2/19th Punjabis. The raid successfully accomplished its object, though the Kensingtons sustained seven casualties (wounded).

Two days later the Battalion returned to the line on the Singil Ridge sector, relieving the 2/19th Punjabis. They remained on duty here for a fortnight, before being in turn relieved by the 3/152nd Indian Infantry. During this period in the line the enemy artillery showed surprising activity and registered daily along our line. The usual patrol work and line routine were carried out without incident. Coming out of the line, the 2/13th marched back a short distance to a camp on " Balua Lake," via the Nablus Road. The " lake " was a dried-up stretch of flat ground, which provided ample facilities for drilling and also for sport, football again becoming a prominent feature of the day's activities. It is probable that too much movement was carried out, and that enemy aircraft noticed this, for on the second day at Balua a long-range gun opened fire with unusual accuracy and planted several shells in the middle of the camp. One particularly successful effort destroyed D Company's dinner! Although falling within the camp area at a time when all the men were assembled for dinner, not a single casualty resulted, many of the shells being " dud." The lesson, however, was quickly learnt, and the tents were removed to a fresh site some 800 yards to the east, whilst orders were issued for precautions to be taken whenever enemy aircraft were about.

The following day produced an unusual excitement, a British aeroplane landing within the Kensingtons' camp on account of engine trouble, departing again for Junction Station after repairs were effected the next day. Captain E. J. Smith, M.C., the Adjutant, went to hospital with sickness during the stay at Balua Lake. Daily training continued, with plenty of physical drill and football to vary the monotony, whilst the concert party continued to enliven the Battalion at intervals. The first intimation that the period of stagnation was nearing the end was a Brigade Church Parade, which was held on September 8th, followed by a march past the G.O.C. 60th Division, Major-General J. S. M. Shea. Such affairs were inevitably the prelude to exciting events, and this proved no exception, for five days later the whole Division had packed up and, turning their faces towards the coast, marched eastwards with expectation high in their hearts. Was this to be the end?

Major Collier was temporarily in command, and behind him swung the marching feet of the old "Thirteenth," once more heading for battle—and it is true to say that every man welcomed the opportunity to write "Finis" to Johnny Turk, as our old friend the enemy was universally known. Beitunia–Ram Allah–Enab Corner–Tottenham Corner–Ludgate Circus—names with old associations and some that were new since the Battalion last trod this ground. On to Surafend on September 15th, via the Wadi Selman and Ramleh, lately G.H.Q. Now there is Rishon le Zion, and the murmur of the breakers on the seashore is almost in their ears. The days are still brilliantly fine and sunny, but the sun has lost much of its power; it is now very like an exceptionally hot English August. The troops are singing lustily " Watcher, me old brown son, how *are* yer ? " And so, on September 16th, they came into the orange groves. The " Summer Lull " was over. . . .

CHAPTER XXVIII

THE SEPTEMBER OFFENSIVE—ARMISTICE

THE way in which the preliminary concentration was carried out and concealed from the enemy was one of the most remarkable achievements of the whole operations. A hostile aeroplane reconnaissance on the 15th reported as follows: " Some regrouping of cavalry units apparently in progress behind the enemy's left flank; otherwise nothing unusual to report." And this at a time when three cavalry Divisions, five infantry Divisions, and the majority of the heavy artillery of the force were concentrating between Ramleh and the front line of the coastal sector, there being no less than 301 guns in place of the normal number of seventy.

Prisoners taken from the coastal sector about this time stated that they had been told that the British would attack on the 18th instant, but they had so often been given the same warning that no notice was paid to this one. Nowhere were enemy troops grouped in reserve who could make an effective counter-attack, a fact which proved that the High Command were in complete ignorance as to which sector of the front was to be attacked. The orange and olive groves completely camouflaged the troops who were concealed in them, and although the ground was literally alive with men, there was no movement permitted by daylight. The Kensingtons found the copious shade afforded by the orange trees a tremendous relief after the glare of the desert, and were only too glad to lie under the trees and pluck the green fruit with which they were weighed down. The orange groves were the work of German and Zionist settlers and were a model of orderliness.

On September 17th the Battalion moved a short distance to a camp site near the seashore, and for two days lay concealed and resting for the strenuous work which lay ahead. On the day that they had left Balua Lake, Captains Foster and Green had received instructions to proceed to Alexandria to await embarkation for leave to England, so that these two officers, who had served with the Battalion throughout its long period of training and service overseas, were unluckily withdrawn just at the moment of final victory. Soon after darkness had fallen on the night of the 18th there were sounds of unusual activity away on the right, where the 53rd Division was engaged in attacking El Mugheir, a Turkish salient, the capture of which was deemed advisable in order to straighten out the British line prior to a general advance. This had now been fixed for dawn on the 19th, and it was a happy augury for success when the 53rd succeeded in gaining its objective and consolidating it.

The work of the first assault had been given to the Indian troops of the 179th Brigade, the Kensingtons lying in close support. Dawn broke clear and fine, promising a hot day. Every precaution had been taken to ensure that the troops could move forward for twenty-four hours without further water or rations, in case of a complete break-through. The men were in fine fettle after their few days' rest and all were on the tip-toe of high expectation. Punctually at 4.15 a.m. the artillery bombardment commenced, and at once it was as though pandemonium had broken loose. Three hundred guns, grouped together in a narrow belt of ground some three miles in extent, roared forth, and the Turkish trenches became a living mass of flame. Nothing like it had ever been seen or heard in that part of the world, and the waiting infantry rejoiced as the shrieking lines of shells passed over their heads. The deafening inferno lasted for only fifteen minutes, and at 4.30 a.m. the Indian infantry " went over." The Kensingtons awaited their turn patiently, whilst the noise of the battle raged just in front. When the order came to advance, instead of having to charge forward to support lines of trenches, they found the enemy had gone! Passing rapidly over the Turkish line, with hardly a moment to look at the terribly efficient work of our guns, they were met by no determined counter-attack, such as had been anticipated, and soon they were over the three lines of trenches, without seeing a Turk other than the casualties and prisoners. The attack had been overwhelmingly successful, and whilst every credit must be paid to the Indian troops who had conducted it with such magnificent dash, there is no doubt that on this occasion the element of surprise had been chiefly responsible for the early Turkish débâcle. A gap had been pierced in the enemy's line, through which the cavalry poured, two hours ahead of their scheduled time.

Some five miles ahead the naval guns from warships off Ain el Yezek were now thundering away, pounding the Turkish heavies and preventing any effective counter-artillery bombardment. A halt was called, and the Battalion stood about in groups, excitedly discussing the stupendous fact that they were standing on what had been Turkish ground only a brief hour previously, and that without sustaining any casualties. It was amazing. Shortly afterwards there was a stir among the crowds of men, which parted to allow the passage of a large open touring car, from the radiator of which flew a small Union Jack. It was the Commander-in-Chief thus early up at the front of affairs, to see for himself how things were going. Those fortunate enough to be close to the car had a clear view of General Allenby, whose features showed no sign of the great triumph he was now so close to achieving. The Commander-in-Chief sat straight upright, looking ahead to where the puffs of smoke showed where our shells were falling among the flying Turks. Shortly after this episode the order was given to fall in, and, facing north, the Brigade set out on one of the most trying, but surely the happiest, marches of its career.

Its job was to march north-east, as fast as it could go, heading for Tul Keram, the Headquarters of the Eighth Turkish Army. The cavalry (4th and 5th Cavalry

Divisions and the Australian Mounted Division) were meanwhile pushing up the coast " road " as hard as they could, turning the Turkish flank. The march was carried out under very trying conditions, the first day being through deep sand and clouds of dust, which meant torture to parched lips, strict orders denying the use of water-bottles without orders. The sun shone from out a clear sky with burning intensity, as the column plodded on at a steady two miles per hour. Reaching the Wadi Nabr el Falik, direction was changed from north to due east, and as dusk was falling a halt was called at Kulunsawah, where the Battalion spent the night. The enemy right flank had now been completely turned and the whole of the coast for some twenty miles northward was in the hands of the cavalry. The 60th Division that night lay facing its objective, the village of Tul Keram. Here the Turks were taken completely by surprise at the rapid advance, and, caught by our cavalry sweeping in from the north and the infantry from the south, put up a very poor resistance. Large numbers of prisoners were taken, but their fate was enviable compared with that of those who tried to escape eastwards towards Nablus, to be caught by our bombing 'planes, which played havoc among the fleeing columns.

Early the next morning (the 20th) the 179th Brigade was again on the move, and, passing through Tul Keram, took the road which led along the Wadi Zeimer, its orders being to take the village of Anebta and secure the tunnel at Bir Asur. Although it was in touch with isolated parties of the enemy all day, very little fighting was experienced, and by nightfall the allotted objectives were easily secured, the important railway tunnel being intact. Few who took part in that march can ever forget the horror of the scenes witnessed as they passed along that road.

The previous evening our bombing 'planes had caught the Turkish column in full flight from Tul Keram, and, flying low, had used their bombs and machine guns to such effect that the road was literally choked with Turkish dead and wounded. On each side of the road, and sprawling

THE SEPTEMBER OFFENSIVE—ARMISTICE

all over the road itself, were heaped corpses of men and animals, upon which the scorching sun had already worked with nauseous effect, distorting the corpses until they looked like awful balloons. The air was simply putrid, and as they threaded their way along that terrible road of desolation, the troops held handkerchiefs to their noses. Everywhere gun limbers and transport vehicles lay heaped in chaos, their animals and drivers sprawling over the wreckage. Never can airmen have had an easier target, and they had reaped an awful harvest. That night the Brigades threw out an outpost line on the surrounding hills, the Kensingtons being the reserve Battalion.

The next day the objective was Messudieh, some five miles north-east of Nablus, where there was an important railway station, and so the march was continued until a position between Ramin and Messudieh was reached. By now the Australian Mounted Division was sweeping down from the north, and before the infantry could get into Messudieh the 5th Australian Horse had ridden into the station and killed or captured the Turkish rearguard. The Kensingtons camped that night on the position they had reached, a barren, rocky hillside commanding the railway. The advance had continued at an amazing speed, and when the news was received that the cavalry was in Nazareth and the 19th Lancers actually on the banks of Lake Tiberias, more than thirty miles to the north, the troops were bewildered at the turn of events, for the Turks were still reported to be holding Nablus in strength, only five miles away to the east. The Kensingtons were very anxious to see Nablus, about which they had heard so much, but it was now a cavalry war, and the Australian Horse captured the town before the following morning. To the infinite regret of the infantry, they were turned back to Anebta on the 22nd. Their part in the war was to all intents and purposes over, and when they turned their backs upon Nablus, they had seen their last action and fired their last shot. This they did not know at the time, and as they wearily retraced their footsteps along that awful road of carnage, they were sustained by visions of Damascus, Beirut, Aleppo—even, perhaps, Constantinople.

The operations of those three days, September 19th, 20th, and 21st, must go down to history as three of the most successful of the war. In that short time two armies were practically wiped out, the captures including over 80,000 prisoners and some 500 guns. The scheme was brilliantly conceived and carried out with rare dash, without a single hitch. The initial credit must go to the organisation which concentrated an army in front of the enemy without its knowledge; for although the Turks and Germans were outnumbered, and the final issue never in real doubt, they had sufficient resources, had they chosen, to put up a vigorous resistance and could have inflicted heavy casualties. So far as the Kensingtons were concerned, it was almost a bloodless victory, whilst the casualties of the entire force were remarkably light. The cavalry naturally had the greatest opportunity, once the line was pierced, and splendid use they made of it.

For four days the 2/13th marched westward, through Tul Keram, Jalkilieh, to Ras el Ain by the Wadi Auja. There it was set to work clearing up the battlefield and making roads. With the exception of one Division (the 7th), which marched steadily northwards up the coastal road, the infantry was now out of active operations, and, in view of the colossal difficulties of supply for the advancing cavalry, was only an impediment in the battle area. Damascus itself had fallen on September 30th to a mixed force of cavalry and the Arab Northern Army (there was a great dispute as to who was really first in the city!) and the beaten remnants of the Turkish Armies were still fleeing northwards, pursued by the 5th Cavalry Division as far as Aleppo, over 300 miles away.

The 2/13th found the necessary work upon which it was engaged very humdrum after the excitement of the preceding days, but the opportunity to bathe in the river here was very welcome. There was an outbreak of malarial fever among the white troops in the area, and on October

THE SEPTEMBER OFFENSIVE—ARMISTICE

2nd it was deemed advisable to move the camp back about a mile, away from the river. On that day Captain E. R. Kisch rejoined the Battalion from leave to England. Six days later the Battalion was relieved from its road-making duties and moved to a camp on the sea coast, just north of Jaffa. Here it was granted twelve days' real holiday and entered upon the most enjoyable time it had experienced since leaving home. Bivouacs were pitched among the dunes in picturesque surroundings, with the sea but a few yards away. Unlimited bathing was permitted and, with no duties other than providing for its needs, the whole Battalion enjoyed a wonderful time. The surf bathing was simply delightful, if somewhat hazardous, and with a warm sun shining overhead, these halcyon days passed all too quickly.

On October 21st the authorities decreed that something must be done to avoid slackness setting in, and so a route march was ordered! There was no doubt a real danger of reaction after the strenuous twelve months the Battalion had passed, but, remembering the marching record of the 2/13th, the idea of route marching for training purposes was not without its humorous side. During the next ten days various forms of training were undertaken, but on the whole this was a very pleasant time. The Battalion welcomed back Captain C. E. Brockhurst on the 16th from Brigade duties, and his place was taken by Captain G. V. Thompson, a well-merited mark of appreciation. November 1st found the 2/13th striking camp and leaving the Jaffa area for the last time. During its stay nearly everyone had gone into the town, which at that time had little to interest them. It was very dirty and had been too recently within the area of hostilities to provide many amenities. Not a few men, however, retained grateful recollections of peaceful church services there.

Leaving camp at 6.15 a.m., the Battalion marched to Yasur, bivouacking for the night, and then marching on to Ludd, where it arrived during the morning of the 2nd. Here it settled down, awaiting further orders, the time being occupied with training. The Turks had asked for, and been granted, an Armistice, and it was now apparent to the Kensingtons that their days in Palestine were numbered. The real question of interest now was whether the Germans could hold out long enough for the Battalion to see further service in France.

There were unlimited quantities of giant, luscious Jaffa oranges at Ludd, and the chief memory of the stay there will probably be the immense number that were consumed. November 11th dawned without giving any indication of the momentous part it was to play in history, and the Battalion was under orders to move back to Egypt. Parade was not ordered until late, and as darkness fell and the camp was being struck and cleaned up, fires were lit, around which the men gathered and sang again and again the songs that had accompanied them throughout the war. The news of the official Armistice was not received early enough to be celebrated in any way, and while the crowds at home were going wild with delight and creating uproarious scenes, the Kensingtons fell in quietly at 11 p.m. and entrained in trucks for the long journey to Kantara. Their own portion of the World War had finished some days earlier and the real Armistice came as something of an anticlimax, the implications of which were not fully realised until they had left Palestine far behind. The sky was lit up by rockets and Verey lights fired in celebration of the Armistice, whilst an anti-aircraft battery in the vicinity fired a final mad salvo of live shells to mark the occasion.

As the long train steamed slowly out of Ludd a few shots were fired in the air as a parting expression of joy, and then everyone became occupied with the impossible task of finding a comfortable position in the jolting trucks in which to spend the long hours ahead. And so the Kensingtons passed quietly out of Palestine, in the darkness of a clear, silent night, their last job of work well and completely finished.

CHAPTER XXIX

FINALE—EPILOGUE

AFTER fifteen hours in the train the Kensingtons sighted Kantara, but would scarcely have recognised it again without being told. When they passed through it seventeen months earlier it was even then a great base-camp and extending daily. Now it was a town, and stretched literally for miles. Here, in this new port on the Suez Canal, lay the true secret of Allenby's final and sweeping success. Here every single requirement of the Army in the field had been foreseen and prepared with monumental patience and unerring accuracy. From here had gone out the means of conquering the desert, that enemy of man and beast, whose power had proved on so many previous occasions more potent than the armed enemy.

Leaping down from the trucks and joyfully stretching their weary limbs, the troops wondered what was going to happen. The mind could scarcely at this early stage take in the great and momentous fact that the war was actually finished; that every gun on every field of battle was this morning silent. The four years and three months of war had seemed an eternity, so much so that it was indeed difficult to recall a time when uniforms were not almost universally worn. But a few days earlier they had been in the very thick and stench of war at its beastliest (the odour of those rotting bodies on the Nablus Road was still in the nostrils), and now, almost overnight it seemed, the prospect of wearing " civvies " and sleeping in a bed had suddenly rushed at them from the far horizon of idle dreams. It was too sudden. The Kensingtons decided to let the matter rest for the moment and turn their attention to what the day was to provide.

For the time being they were to remain in camp at

Kantara, and a week passed with matters taken very easily, the time being taken up with light training and as many games as could be provided with minimum facilities. The weather was now cool, and an occasional grey sky reminded all of England. Speculation was, of course, rife. For a few days they waited anxiously for news that hostilities had again broken out somewhere or other, but as time passed and news and details of the Armistice terms came through, and the war was over beyond all doubt, thoughts of home became firmly fixed in every man's mind. It was hoped that a transport would soon be available to take the Battalion back *en bloc*, and visions of marching gaily through High Street, Kensington, and being disbanded at Headquarters were entertained. The older soldiers scoffed at the idea, and spoke depressingly of " Armies of Occupation." On November 19th the Battalion moved out of Kantara and entrained for Alexandria, where it went into Victoria Camp, which was destined to be its home for nearly four months. Fortunately this was not known at the time!

The first news at Alexandria was of an impending inspection by General Allenby and, after a few days of general training, activities were devoted to preparations for this important event. On November 29th there was a rehearsal of the programme, which actually took place on December 3rd. On that morning the 2/13th paraded as strong as possible and marched to the Sporting Club. The 179th and 180th Brigades lined the road from Sidi Gaber to the entrance to the Club and were there inspected by the G.O.C. Afterwards, the whole of the 60th Division marched past in columns of platoons at ten-pace intervals. It was a proud day for everybody concerned, and chins were well up. It seemed a fitting climax to the operations of the past eighteen months, and in the minds of those present officially ended the war for them. The days that followed seemed stale and in the nature of an anticlimax.

The camp life was very pleasant and, of course, a bed of roses, with no thorns in the shape of forced night marches and unslakable thirst, or the ever-present fear of sudden death or mutilation. But somehow the sting had gone out of life, and although the life was very similar to rest camps behind the line, it was *not* the same, and everybody knew it. The mind of every man was turned towards home and a restlessness took hold of all, so that it was impossible to sit down quietly for five minutes at a time. It was a critical time for the authorities, with so many thousands of men waiting for something to do, and it was decided to ease the tension by instituting a system of educational training. It was announced that classes would at once be formed for instruction in various subjects, including French, shorthand, reading and writing, mathematics, book-keeping, and commercial correspondence.

Large numbers of men handed in their names for inclusion in the various classes, but with all the goodwill in the world, it proved difficult to whip up flagging interest. However, the attempt was made, and the educational instruction carried on until one by one the instructors were withdrawn for demobilisation. A day's holiday was granted on December 17th, which was " Thanksgiving Day," but the real red-letter day came on Christmas Day, when the whole Battalion marched down to the San Stefano Hotel and there enjoyed a splendid dinner, followed by a concert and whist drives. Beer flowed freely, and everyone had a memorable time. All guard duties were undertaken by the Indian troops of the Brigade, and discipline was so far relaxed as to allow a certain lance-corporal, who had dined not wisely but too well, to turn out the guard—and get away with it! He had successfully impersonated the Brigadier. The officers and sergeants officiated as helpers at the Battalion's dinner before adjourning to their respective messes to emulate the other ranks.

A few days afterwards, on December 30th, the entire Battalion marched to Sidi Bishr, where a composite photograph was taken, copies of which are much prized by ex-members to-day. Everything possible was done to make life in camp attractive, and a fine football ground was prepared, whilst leave to Alexandria was granted freely. The town had a good deal to offer, and many happy evenings were spent. The Kensingtons had always been able to field a useful Soccer team (they suffered but one defeat whilst on active service), and they had the great distinction of winning the championship of the E.E.F. The team was sent home to England to represent Egypt in the inter-war zone finals, played at Stamford Bridge, but did not manage to secure the final honour. Meanwhile the educational training proceeded throughout January, with enthusiasm for this instruction rapidly waning. Great excitement was caused by the commencement of demobilisation. It had soon become known that there was no prospect of the Battalion returning to England as a unit, and the men were graded into various classes, according to the nature of their civilian employment. Thus coal miners and railwaymen were high on the list, whilst clerks were correspondingly low. First to go were the "key" men, whose services were urgently needed at home. Then followed the lucky individuals whose jobs had been kept open for them, and whose employers applied for their return. The position in Egypt was governed by the supply of transports available, so that news of a ship berthing always caused excitement and great speculation. Many of the oldest serving members of the Battalion left for England during the latter days of January. On the other hand, Captains Foster and Green returned to duty from home leave, an unlucky circumstance for them, as they had been deemed the luckiest men alive when they left the Battalion in the previous autumn.

On February 12th a Divisional cross-country run took place, an event which the Kensingtons had the honour of winning. Inspections of one sort and another were fairly frequent, two outstanding being that of the Transport Section by Major-General Shea, and of the whole camp by the Corps Commander. March 6th proved eventful for the 2/13th, for on that day the unit was divided into two sections—one for "Home" and the other for "Occupation" duties. The latter consisted of all men who had enlisted after December 31st, 1915, and numbered seventeen officers and 335 O.R.s. This number included certain N.C.O.s who had volunteered to remain. Lieut.-Colonel T. E. Bisdee retained command, with Captain E. J. Smith as Adjutant, and Captain C. T. Foster, M.C., and Captain B. Hull as Company Commanders. Three days later the reorganised Battalion moved down to the docks by special train and embarked on H.M.T. *Ellenga*, leaving the men scheduled for rapid demobilisation behind. This was really the end of the 2/13th Kensingtons as we have known them. There were great leave-takings that day, and many fast friendships of four years' standing were severed. After a few days the remaining men in camp at Victoria were moved to Bulkeley Camp to join other units of the 60th Division, and from there were gradually sent home as facilities permitted. For them it seemed a poor sort of finish to a great adventure, and the remaining days were stale indeed. Then "Blighty" beckoned and all else was forgotten.

The "new" 2/13th enjoyed the trip up the Levant, and made Beirut two days later, going thence to Tripoli and on to Mersina, disembarking at 8 a.m. on March 12th. The Battalion then marched to a camp about one mile east of Mersina and there settled down to await events. On the 15th one company, under Captain Foster, was ordered to Adana, the remainder following on the 24th, being accommodated in old Turkish barracks some two miles northeast of the town. Here it was placed under French command and was employed on police duties until the following August.

So, after just five years of heroic existence, ended the history of the 2/13th. It may, on the whole, be termed a fortunate unit, inasmuch as it was spared the more shattering experiences of the Western Front, and so was able to preserve its own local atmosphere to a far greater extent than most other battalions. And the total casualties were correspondingly smaller. But it can also be said that no finer

EPILOGUE

body of men served throughout the war, and that whatever they were called upon to do, they did it well.

Circumstances called them to serve in three distinct theatres of war, an experience given to few regiments. Their marching record, if not unique, was a very fine one. They really earned the infantry's nick-name of "footsloggers." The fact that they were kept in England for well-nigh two years seems incomprehensible, but when eventually they were put to the test, they proved beyond doubt that they were second to none, and throughout all the varying exigencies of war steadfastly maintained a very high state of morale.

It can be said that the second-line Kensingtons enhanced the proud name they bore—than which they need no prouder boast.

THE END

EPILOGUE

The King's Colour of the Second Battalion was consecrated at the Parish Church of St. Mary Abbots, Kensington, on Sunday, February 27th, 1921, at an impressive service which was addressed by the Chaplain, the Vicar of Kensington. The Colour was hung in a temporary resting-place until such time as it could be removed to the Warriors' (War Memorial) Chapel, which was then being built.

The Colour was " laid up " at a further service on October 30th, 1921, which was attended by a large number of former members of the 2nd Battalion who gathered to watch the passing of the last tangible evidence of the old Battalion. It was carried by Lieut. (afterwards Lieut.-Colonel) W. H. Godfrey, M.M., to a final and fitting resting-place, beneath the shadow of those hallowed walls which have seen so many gatherings of the civilian soldiers of Kensington through the generations. There hangs the Colour to-day —a reminder of a gallant past.

CHAPTER XXX
POST WAR
By COLONEL W. H. GODFREY, M.B.E., M.M.

PREFACE

THIS final chapter of Regimental History—the Post-War—is still being " written," so must needs remain unfinished. Nevertheless, it may not be without interest to record some facts and incidents of the period 1920–35.

Strict limitation of space precludes anything but the sketchiest record; in fact, it has been found necessary to write in diary form, which, although perhaps unworthy of the subject, may give the reader a better idea of changes in personnel, organisation, etc., during these years.

The result seems jerky and more like the headings or synopses of chapters, and for this apologies are tendered, but it was only possible to enlarge on a few of the many interesting incidents.

Readers cannot fail to note how closely H.R.H. Princess Louise has associated herself with her Kensington Regiment. Her constant personal interest and encouragement have been an inspiration to us all.

W. H. G.

"THE KENSINGTONS"

HONORARY COLONELS AND HEADQUARTERS STAFF SINCE REORGANISATION OF THE REGIMENT AFTER THE GREAT WAR

1918. Brig.-General F. G. Lewis, C.B., C.M.G., T.D.
1920. Lieut.-General Sir Francis Lloyd, G.C.V.O., K.C.B., D.S.O.
1926. Lieut.-General Sir John Shea, G.C.B., K.C.M.G., D.S.O., A.D.C.
1929. Colonel Hugh Campbell, D.S.O., O.B.E., T.D.

COMMANDING OFFICERS

1920–4. Lieut.-Colonel Hugh Campbell, D.S.O., O.B.E., T.D.
1924–7. Lieut.-Colonel the Lord Raglan.
1927–31. Lieut.-Colonel Donald Banks, D.S.O., M.C.
1931–5. Lieut.-Colonel W. H. Godfrey, M.B.E., M.M.
1935. Brevet-Colonel W. A. Stone, M.C., T.D.

ADJUTANTS

1920. Major B. M. Kenny.
1921. Major A. J. Harington, M.C.
1924. Captain M. V. Manly, M.C., The Border Regiment.
1925. Captain W. H. E. Gott, M.C., King's Royal Rifle Corps.
1929. Captain H. C. H. Illingwood, M.C., King's Royal Rifle Corps.
1931. Captain H. C. E. Mauduit, M.C., King's Royal Rifle Corps.
1935. Captain H. M. Boyle, M.C., Royal Irish Fusiliers.

QUARTERMASTERS

1920. Captain A. W. Foxwell, T.D.
1921. Captain A. Ridley, M.B.E., late Queen's Bays.
1925. Captain J. Cary, late Queen's Bays.
1934. Lieut. E. D. Knight, M.M., late Grenadier Guards.

REGIMENTAL SERGEANT-MAJORS

1919–21. Regimental Sergeant-Major Goodall, Grenadier Guards.

POST WAR

1921. Regimental Sergeant-Major Stevens, Coldstream Guards.
1925. Regimental Sergeant-Major Hayman, Coldstream Guards.
1929. Regimental Sergeant-Major E. J. Knight, M.M., Grenadier Guards.
1934. Regimental Sergeant-Major Mansell, Grenadier Guards.

ANNUAL SUMMER CAMPS (15 days)

1921. Dibgate.
1922. Aldershot.
1923. East Sandling.
1924. Aldershot.
1925. Swingate (Dover).
1926. Roedean (Brighton).
1927. Colchester.
1928. Bordon.
1929. Seaford.
1930. Aldershot.
1931. Wannock (Eastbourne).
1932. Bordon (Voluntary 8 days).
1933. Myrtle Grove (Worthing).
1934. Colchester.
1935. Myrtle Grove (Worthing).

EASTER TRAININGS

1921. Bordon (Royal Dublin Fusiliers).
1922. Mill Hill (attached Middlesex Regiment) Depôt.
1923. Pirbright (Musketry Camp).
1924. Aldershot (attached The Border Regiment).
1925. Tidworth (attached Welsh Regiment).
1926. Windsor (1st Grenadier Guards).
1927. No training.
1928. Windsor (Coldstream Guards, 3rd Battalion).
1929. Shorncliffe (attached Argyll and Sutherland Highlanders).
1930. Canterbury (attached Buffs Depôt).
1931. Oxford—Oxford and Bucks Light Infantry Depôt.

"THE KENSINGTONS"

1932. No training.
1933. Windsor (attached Welsh Guards).
1934. Aldershot (West Yorks Regiment).
1935. Bordon (Royal Irish Fusiliers).

1920

Regiment re-formed as one Battalion. Lieut.-Colonel Hugh Campbell selected for command. Major B. M. Kenny appointed Adjutant. War-time officers, W.O.s, sergeants, and men from 1st and 2nd Battalions form backbone of new Battalion; much credit due to them for their willingness to " carry on," despite the prevalent revulsion from military service.

Recruiting is slow in consequence, yet the seed is sown and will develop in its own time. The year passes quietly, but the foundations are laid.

The Grey Brigade re-formed, consisting of the Kensington, the London Scottish, the Civil Service Rifles, and Queen's Westminsters (later to be amalgamated) and the Artists' Rifles. Brig.-General F. G. Lewis, C.B., C.M.G., T.D., appointed to command Brigade.

1921

Regiment settling down and looking forward to the first post-war camp. Sudden shock bursts upon its " peaceful " existence. The Coal Strike has spread to other vital industries. Government forms a National Defence Force. By its constitution the Territorial Army cannot be used in a civil disturbance. The Regular Permanent Staff form basis of new Force, and T.A. drill-halls used for recruiting. The Regiment stops training and other activities. Colonel Campbell (the C.O.), and other members of the Regiment volunteer to serve, and become the nucleus of the 13th London Unit of the new Force.

The unit moves to Wimbledon Common to join others of the London Division. Back to 1914 conditions—

crowded tents—primitive cooking—food in mess tins—pole latrines—snow on ground. Majority of men from ranks of unemployed, poorly clothed and shod. Little training possible. Uniform and boots issued later and conditions improve. Men liven up—route march and drill undertaken. Officers in mufti secretly reconnoitre power-stations where guard duties may be necessary—mistaken by police for suspicious persons—and moved on! Weather turns decidedly warm—the 1921 heat wave has commenced. Heat causes many heath fires—fire picquets have busy time!

Drill and appearance now quite good. Great stir caused by suspected presence of Sinn Feiners in the camp—police sent for in fast car—false alarm. An Irishman was " telling the tale " to troops in the canteen—he is " seen off " by police—excitement subsides! Boxing very popular—competitions held in a gravel pit—quite the old-time atmosphere. Seeds of the Regiment's interest and prowess in boxing here sown. Several of the best boxers later join the Regiment and become Brigade and Divisional champions.

Full ceremonial inspection held of whole Wimbledon Common Force—General salute—March Past—all creditably carried out.

Settlement of strike heralds new era of " peace " and demobilisation—three months have slipped by. Altogether a strange adventure!

Letter of thanks received by each officer and man from the Prime Minister (Mr. Lloyd George). Farewells are taken—many men continue their service in the Territorial unit.

May 8th.—Unveiling of the Regimental War Memorial in the drill-hall by H.R.H. The Princess Louise, Duchess of Argyll.

June.—Territorial life recommences.

July.—Voluntary camp is held at Dibgate—war-time hutments. Foundation laid of Kensingtons' post-war reputation for smartness and cleanliness of lines. Brigadier brings other C.O.s through the huts to show how they should be kept!

Drill and simple tactical training carried out. Efforts to rid the mind of trench warfare.

1922

February.—Route march attempted; not a great success. War seems to have damped enthusiasm for parading the streets!

March.—Reduction of annual bounty (at present £5 maximum) to £3 10s. Start of a downward trend. Welcomed by some as a discouragement to the mercenary-minded—others doubt wisdom of this view. They feel that if the T.A. is really needed, its members should receive more encouragement and reward.

April.—Regimental School of Arms re-formed—Boxing Club started, first match held, versus Inns of Court O.T.C., resulting in a draw. In bayonet fencing C Company team gains second place in Divisional competition.

This month sees the last link broken between Brig.-General Lewis and the Kensingtons. He relinquishes command of the " Grey Brigade " and retires. His successor is Brig.-General R. C. A. McCalmont, D.S.O., Irish Guards.

July 22nd.—Inspection by His Majesty the King of the two London Territorial Divisions in Hyde Park. Quite a fine show—the return to H.Q. marred by drenching storm.

July 1st.—Guard of Honour for H.R.H. The Princess Louise mounted at the unveiling of the Kensington Borough War Memorial.

A fifth Company, to be known as H.Q. Wing, added to the establishment, to consist of machine-gun platoon, band, drums, and all that was known as Battalion H.Q.

Camp held at Rushmoor, Aldershot (this area is now known to millions as the venue of the Aldershot Tattoo). Training tightened up, more attention paid to use of ground and section leadership.

November.—Regiment represented at the unveiling of Memorial Tablet to the 1st Battalion in the church at Abbots Langley (the scene of 1914 training) by General Lewis.

POST WAR

1923

January.—The wearing of wound stripes and war service chevrons to be discontinued. The war begins to recede!

March.—First prize-giving since the war held at Headquarters.

April.—Church parade at St. Mary Abbots Church.

May.—Strength now 372. Regiment decides to recruit—Major Prynne adopts modern publicity methods—first time such efforts have been made (later to be copied by other units). He organises a well-conceived scheme. Recruiting depôts opened in Kensington, Fulham, and Hammersmith. Corps of drums march round area. Serving men act as recruiting sergeants. Thousands of leaflets distributed. Result—strength in July, 564.

July.—First march to the Cenotaph by Regiment and O.C.A. as a tribute to the memory of " Fallen Comrades."

November 11th.—Church parade service held in Kensington Palace Field. H.R.H. Princess Louise present. Address by Colonel the Rev. W. R. J. McLean.

1924

January.—First Children's New Year Party held.

January 29th.—Lieut.-Colonel The Lord Raglan (late Grenadier Guards) appointed Commanding Officer.

May.—Regiment enters team for *Daily Telegraph* Cup for first time since the war.

June 21st.—Inspection of 47th (2nd London) Division T.A. in Hyde Park by G.O.C. Major-General Sir William Thwaites.

July.—A second recruiting campaign organised by Major Prynne. Strength raised from 502 to 607. Camp at Aldershot. Strongest Battalion since the war.

1925

March.—A Divisional Sign to be worn on uniform—revival of war-time practice.

"THE KENSINGTONS"

April.—A complete Official List issued of Battle Honours awarded to the Regiment for the Great War. Those selected to be borne on colours or appointments are shown in large type.

"NEUVE CHAPELLE," "AUBERS," "SOMME, 1916, '18," "Albert, 1916, '18," "Guillemont," "Ginchy," "Flers-Courcelette," "Morval," "Le Transloy," "ARRAS, 1917, '18," "Scarpe, 1917, '18," "YPRES, 1917," "Langemarck, 1917," "CAMBRAI, 1917, '18," "Hindenburg Line," "Canal du Nord," "Valenciennes," "Sambre," "France and Flanders, 1914–18," "DOIRAN, 1917," "Macedonia, 1916–17," "GAZA," "El Mughar," "Nebi Samwil," "JERUSALEM," "Jericho," "Jordan," "Megiddo," "SHARON," "Palestine, 1917–18."

June 27th.—Inspection of the two London Divisions, 56th and 47th, in Hyde Park by Director-General of the T.A.

Captain W. H. Godfrey, M.M., appointed a member of the Military Division of the Order of the British Empire in the King's Birthday honours.

October.—Captain W. H. E. Gott, M.C., 60th Rifles, appointed Adjutant.

November.—H.R.H. Princess Louise present at Kensington War Memorial to see Regiment on Cenotaph March—sends letter of congratulation on appearance of troops and O.C.A. Letter also received from General Sir Francis Lloyd, the Honorary Colonel, who paraded with the Regiment.

1926

February.—Boxing—Privates Birnie and Mortimer win Divisional Championships—and reach semi-final in Territorial Army Championships. Bayonet fencing—B Company team are runners-up to Artists' Rifles in Divisional Championship.

April.—Easter training at Windsor attached 1st Grenadier Guards. Living in barracks with them has distinct smartening effect.

POST WAR

May 1st.—General Strike called by Labour Council of Action. Nation becomes startlingly aware of a first-class emergency; all sorts of rumours are rife. Mr. Baldwin calms nation by wireless talks. Government forms Civil Constabulary Reserve; uses Territorial Army organisation as framework as in 1921. T.A. soldiers cannot be used, so Regiment closes down activities, and those officers and men who wish are sworn-in as special constables. Recruiting opens, and the new unit fills its ranks within a few hours—all types join: Brigadiers, Colonels, Oxford Undergraduates, working men and unemployed, a few trade unionists. All walks of life represented. Drill-hall is scene of immense activity and intense excitement. Certain officers become Commanders and Inspectors.

Steel helmets and truncheons issued. Fortunately no occasion to use them in earnest. But many " experiments " carried out to test effect of one upon the other!

Buses ready at the Iverna Garden entrance to transport the force to any troubled area. Many men cannot be persuaded to go home even when " off-duty," so drill-hall becomes a dormitory for several hundred. Canteen does roaring trade—many lively, if somewhat raucous sing-songs held.

A week of tense and trying atmosphere. A move to Agricultural Hall is ordered, the advance party leaves—suddenly the strike collapses. The good old British Public has once again asserted its freedom.

The force is disbanded and the Territorial unit resumes its normal functions.

July—Lieut.-General Sir John Shea, K.C.B., K.C.M.G., D.S.O., A.D.C., appointed Honorary Colonel. Camp at Roedean (near Brighton) memorable for the twenty-four hours spent on the Downs. A very chilly night despite the cocoa dispensed from the cooker touring the outposts. Bn. H.Q. rendered quite picturesque by appearance of C.O. (Lord Raglan) squatting in Arab fashion, wrapped in a coloured blanket!

1927

January.—M.G. Platoon going strong. G.O.C. London District reports, " The results are very satisfactory. The platoon is up to strength, and has the highest average in the Division."

January 29th.—Lieut.-Colonel Donald Banks, D.S.O., M.C., late Service Battalion, Essex Regiment, assumes command.

March.—Private Mortimer again wins Divisional Championship and reaches final of T.A. Championships.

April.—Major-General L. Oldfield, C.B., C.M.G., D.S.O., A.D.C., commanding 47th Division, presents prizes.

July.—Camp at Colchester—many new ideas. Travelling canteen on training, camp-fire concerts, march out to Mersea Island with cookers, bathing and football before return march—a good day. Secretary of State for War—Sir Laming Worthington-Evans, Bt., C.B.E.—inspects the Regiment in camp. Mr. " Jimmy " Forsyth takes film of camp life. *Daily Mail* push-ball creates excitement and much amusement.

October.—Camp film shown to 2,000 members and friends at special Sunday show at Shepherd's Bush Pavilion.

November.—Regiment holds recruiting week at this same cinema, where " The Somme " is being shown. Speeches from the stage by General Oldfield and others. H.R.H. The Princess Louise attends one evening. Guard of Honour mounted.

1928

January.—Regimental cooks win T.A. Cookery Championship Shield at Olympia, open to the whole T.A.

Captain Cary raises a Regimental Military Band from workers at Tate & Lyle's sugar refinery, achieving the seemingly impossible, for so many unsuccessful efforts had been made in the past. The directors of the firm give the project their blessing.

POST WAR

H.R.H. The Princess Louise grants permission for her cipher to be used as a new collar badge to be worn by all ranks. It looks most effective.

Colonel the Hon. H. R. L. Alexander, D.S.O., M.C., Irish Guards, appointed new Brigade Commander.

Easter training at Windsor attached 3rd Battalion Coldstream Guards. The band makes its first appearance.

May 5th.—H.R.H. The Princess Louise presents annual prizes, and displays great interest in Regimental activities.

May 21st.—Regiment has honour of furnishing a Guard of Honour for Their Majesties the King and Queen at the opening of Princess Louise's Kensington Hospital for Children.

The Guard, consisting of 100 all ranks with King's Colour and Regimental Band, under the command of Captain and Brevet-Major W. H. Godfrey, M.B.E., M.M., marched through Kensington and formed up opposite the hospital entrance. Immediately on arrival, His Majesty inspected the Guard, asking many questions, and displaying much interest, particularly in the new collar badge (Princess Louise's cipher). The weather was most threatening, and with his usual consideration the King gave orders that, should it rain, the Guard was not to await his departure. Fortunately the rain held off and enabled a second Royal Salute to be given. The return march, however, was carried out in a regular deluge, and everyone returned to the drill-hall drenched, but happy in the thought that they had had the honour of being members of the only guard to have been furnished by the Regiment for a reigning Sovereign.

The following letter was later received by the C.O.

BUCKINGHAM PALACE,
May 23rd, 1928.

Guard of Honour.

DEAR COLONEL BANKS,

The King desires me to express his satisfaction with the appearance of the Guard of Honour provided by the Battalion under your command on the occasion of the opening of the Princess Louise Kensington Hospital for Children on Monday last, which, in His Majesty's opinion, was most creditable.

    Yours very truly,
      A. H. L. HARDINGE,
        Equerry.

A message of appreciation was also received from H.R.H. The Princess Louise.

Whitsun training held at Pirbright. 60th Rifles fetch detachment in new six-wheel vehicles, and instruct them in Kapok bridging across Basingstoke Canal at Aldershot.

July.—Camp at Bordon. Improved field work. Transport Section wins Brigade Championship. Interesting visit, by fleet of motor-coaches, to Portsmouth where Regiment are the guests of the Royal Navy aboard H.M.S. *Nelson* and are shown all over this " crack " battleship. Mayor and Mayoress of Kensington and other distinguished friends of the Regiment visit the camp and attend special lunch on middle Sunday. Mr. " Jimmy " Forsyth of Gaumont-British takes film of camp life, subsequently shown at Shepherd's Bush Pavilion at Special Regimental " At Home."

Regiment visits H.R.H. Princess Louise at Kensington Palace on return from camp, giving her a Royal Salute and three hearty cheers.

C.O. raises fund from friends of the Regiment and Kensington residents for equipping band and drums in pre-war full-dress uniform. H.R.H. Princess Louise contributes a hundred guineas. Her cipher to be worn on the belt pouches.

October.—Captain H. C. H. Illingworth, M.C., 60th Rifles, appointed Adjutant.

November.—The new Band and Drum uniforms are seen for first time on Cenotaph Parade.

H.R.H. Princess Louise present at Kensington War Memorial.

GUARD OF HONOUR TO HIS MAJESTY THE KING, MAY 21ST, 1928.

HER ROYAL HIGHNESS PRINCESS LOUISE AT THE KENSINGTON WAR MEMORIAL, NOVEMBER 4TH, 1928.

1929

January.—Regiment wins Brigade Boxing Championships.

February.—Cooks are "runners-up" for T.A. Cookery Championship. Private Birnie regains Divisional Championship.

H.R.H. Princess Louise grants permission for Regiment to use the Palace Field as football ground.

April.—Easter training at Shorncliffe attached 1st Battalion the Argyll and Sutherland Highlanders. Regiment marches from station to the skirl of the pipes, and the music of the Highlanders' band. A happy week-end spent. Joint telegram despatched to H.R.H. Princess Louise conveying greetings from all ranks of her two Regiments.

New heating system installed in drill-hall and canteen enlarged.

July.—Camp at Seaford, nearest to the sea of any camp, but mainly rough and windy weather. Interesting combined exercise with the Fleet held. Composite Battalion (company from each regiment of the Brigade), commanded by Major W. H. Godfrey, is to embark in H.M.S. *Iron Duke* (anchored a mile out at sea), from which it will land on the coast after spending the night aboard. The unit leaves camp, only to be sent back after a mile's march, owing to high seas making embarkation inadvisable. Later, they march to Newhaven quay, where launches, whalers, and cutters are alongside to ferry the troops out to the battleship. Band plays suitable nautical music meanwhile. Rear-Admiral Dewar, in command of H.M.S. *Iron Duke*, welcomes the unit, and an enjoyable if somewhat "hammockly-disturbed" night is spent. Destroyer lays smoke screen in the morning, *Iron Duke* fires broadsides, under cover of which troops make a successful landing and advance to connect up with attacking "land" force. The column is heavily "bombed" from the air, but reaches objective. A hundred or so of the Naval landing party march back with Regiment to camp and spend a cheery evening. They march off next day headed by Regimental Band. Quite a naval occasion! Transport Section wins Brigade competition. General Shea inspects Battalion on return from camp in Palace Field, and addresses the troops in his old war-time " gather-round " manner.

December.—Colonel Hugh Campbell, D.S.O., O.B.E., T.D., appointed Honorary Colonel.

1930

January.—Colonel R. V. Pollok, C.B.E., D.S.O., Irish Guards, appointed Brigade Commander. Cooks regain T.A. Championship Shield—Regiment wins Brigade Boxing Championship.

February.—Steel helmets withdrawn, " having no further use for their services "!

March.—Boxing team beats one from the 1st Battalion Argyll and Sutherland Highlanders.

April.—Easter training at Canterbury, attached " The Buffs " Depôt and 3rd Carabineers. Journey made by motor-coach for first time. Officers and N.C.O.s tactical exercise held near Sittingbourne. Colonel Lumley Webb entertains the party at Tunstall. Church parade in Canterbury Cathedral on Easter Sunday.

May.—Colonel Hugh Campbell presents annual prizes.

July.—New-style scarlet-and-grey " Kensington " shoulder patches issued.

Camp held at Aldershot. New scheme tried of attaching personnel of Regular unit to each T.A. unit. Kensingtons have assistance of 2nd Battalion Cheshire Regiment, which is greatly valued. Chief of Imperial General Staff " considers that the close association of Regular and Territorial units has been cemented. Many lessons have been learnt and valuable experience gained."

Large marquee hired from N.A.A.F.I. and used as mess tent for whole Battalion—also useful when " The Roosters " visit the camp to give their war-time show.

1931

January 29th.—Lieut.-Colonel W. H. Godfrey, M.B.E., M.M., assumes command. Captain H. C. E. Mauduit, M.C., 60th Rifles, appointed Adjutant.

Major Prynne returns as second-in-command.

February.—Regiment wins Divisional Boxing Championship Trophy. Private Novell wins T.A. Light Heavyweight Boxing Championship.

Cooks again win T.A. Cooking Championship, accomplishing a remarkable achievement by winning it three years out of four and on the other occasion being runners-up.

Easter at Oxford.—Easter training at Cowley Barracks (Depôt of Oxford and Bucks Light Infantry). Useful officer and N.C.O. training. Captain Gott comes from Staff College to " lend a hand."

May.—Major-General R. F. D. Oldman, C.B., C.M.G., D.S.O., presents annual prizes.

June.—The 253rd Field Battery R.A. (T.A.) bring a mechanised field gun to the drill-hall to give a demonstration; an interesting evening is spent, and afterwards a sing-song in the canteen. The gunners' lorry carries part of the door away with it in backing out. (Probably as a Souvenir!).

August.—Camp at Wannock on the Sussex Downs near Eastbourne, famous for its tea gardens and hills. Someone remarks, " These are more ' ups ' than ' downs '! "

In night operations the Regiment manages to hold " Aerodrome " against all " assaults of our enemies," the Queen's Rifles!

1932

January, February.—Regiment wins Brigade Boxing Championships. Also Divisional for second year in succession.

National economy causes cut in T.A. grants and cancellation of annual camp—a severe blow which has serious repercussions, for the fortnight's camp is the great incentive and reward for Territorial soldiers. All training leads up to camp. The effect upon recruiting and re-engagements is rapid and startling. It will be felt for some years.

March.—A slight respite regarding camp is announced. A week's attachment to regular unit to be arranged for volunteers with reduced pay. This is some compensation, but not the same as our own camp.

Lance-Corporal Finnigan wins Territorial Army Featherweight Boxing Championship, thus crowning a career devoted to the interests of Regimental boxing.

May.—The Regiment asked to stage a war episode at the "Festival of Empire" in Hyde Park on Empire Day, sponsored by the *Daily Express*. Receives War Office permission and calls for volunteers. Mr. Arthur Bryant, the Pageant producer, addresses a meeting and holds two rehearsals. So pleased with results he decides to dispense with any more except the dress rehearsal.

Old Comrades brought in to act the parts of colonial soldiers, and are fitted out by the Wardrobe Mistress!

Regiment episode to be an attack with artillery support (represented by fireworks), the final touch to be a "rush-in" with the bayonet. Most effective, yet quite harmless rubber bayonets issued!

Final rehearsal held in pouring rain. Guards band—Morris dancers—hundreds of amateur performers all soaked through.

To celebrate the occasion and revive damped spirits we let off a "cannon," to the consternation of the Park police, who close in upon us, suspecting the worst. Hurried explanations follow and we are "let off with a caution!"

Everything is set for the much-heralded performance—rations, both solid and liquid, are issued and the detachment marches to Hyde Park headed by the Corps of Drums, the rear brought up by O.C.A. "Colonials."

It is a glorious moonlight night, and many thousands of spectators have assembled. So determined are they to get a good view that the arena is invaded—the small body of police being quite inadequate to get them back to their places —so after many eloquent yet unheeded appeals through the loudspeakers the Festival has to be abandoned with but the overture completed.

Great disappointment is felt by all concerned, but the *Daily Express* keeps its bargain by contributing to Regimental funds and paying the troops for their services.

Sir William Davison, K.B.E., M.P., presents annual prizes.

August.—Voluntary week's training attached to Oxford and Bucks Light Infantry at Bordon, who treat us most hospitably and with whom the Regiment gains a good reputation.

September.—Regimental Lewis-gun team wins the Monro Challenge Cup at London and Middlesex Rifle Association Meeting at Bisley.

November.—Regimental boxing team meets and defeats a team from the Oxford and Bucks Light Infantry.

1933

January.—Divisional Headquarters lays down new form of categorised training. Record card to be kept of each man's progress. Frowned upon by many as being rather " too serious," but much to be said for it. Territorial N.C.O.s get more chance of instructing.

February.—Regiment wins Brigade and Divisional Boxing Championships (this is becoming almost monotonous!).

April.—Easter at Windsor with 1st Battalion Welsh Guards. The detachment privileged to attend ceremonial guard mounting at the Castle, and forms up in the quadrangle under the eyes of the Royal Family. Officers and sergeants conducted round the State Apartments by the King's Equerry, Lord Claud Hamilton.

March.—Private Novell wins T.A. Light Heavyweight Championship, also that of the south-west division of the Amateur Boxing Association.

May.—" At Home " Week held. Drill-hall and Regiment "on show." Demonstrations, etc. The Mayor attends. Result, 30 recruits and keener interest of lady friends in Regiment.

H.R.H. The Princess Louise presents prizes at the drill-hall, making an excellent and splendidly delivered speech. Shows great interest in musical programme and remains until 11.30 p.m.

June.—H.M. The King to hold a review of London Territorials in Hyde Park on June 24th. Rehearsals held, all arrangements made. The day opens threateningly and fears are expressed that a postponement may be made. The rain teems down—but the Regiment parades in Iverna Gardens and commences its march to the Park. The High Street is reached when an officer emerges from car with message for C.O. "Review cancelled—return to your drill-hall." A truly disappointing day!

His Majesty expresses his sorrow at cancellation in a letter to all units.

July.—Regimental team wins Divisional Shooting Match against picked teams of all units.

August.—Camp at Myrtle Grove, near Worthing. Most glorious weather and accessible training ground. Tactical training shows distinct improvement. Civilian clothes are permitted for "walking-out," a concession much appreciated.

November.—Conditions of service altered for men joining T.A. after November 1st. Recruits will have to enlist for General Service. The "pledge" given to a man on enlistment that he shall serve only with his own unit is now abolished.

Winter instruction includes numerous displays of training films, which are quite well produced by the War Office.

1934

February.—Battalion wins Brigade Boxing Championship —this being the eighth year in succession.

Divisional Boxing Championship now won for fourth year in succession. A record that will take some beating!

March.—Battalion cross-country team wins " Novice " Match in London Territorial Meeting.

April.—" At Home " Week repeated—well done and appreciated by large audiences, but recruiting results poor.

Easter at Aldershot attached 2nd Battalion West Yorkshire Regiment. Training includes anti-gas drill. Regimental Corps of Drums plays all Regular units off Church parade. Favourable comments by onlookers on their playing and appearance.

May.—General Sir John Shea, G.C.B., K.C.M.G., D.S.O., presents annual prizes. Captain Cary retires (age limit), his position as Q.M. taken by Lieut. E. D. Knight, M.M. (R.S.M. for last five years).

August.—Camp at Colchester (same site as 1927). Good training. Some fun caused by Kapok bridging the Roman River, having to wait till midnight for " high tide " before this was possible! One senior N.C.O. obliged by " falling-in."

November.—H.R.H. Princess Louise attends Armistice Service in the drill-hall, and takes salute of past and present Kensingtons.

Captain H. M. Boyle, M.C., Royal Irish Fusiliers, appointed Adjutant.

1935

January 1st.—Colonel Donald Banks, C.B., D.S.O., M.C. (now Director-General of the Post Office), appointed a Knight Commander of the Bath in the New Year Honours.

January 29th.—Brevet-Colonel W. A. Stone, M.C., T.D. (late Infantry Battalion Honourable Artillery Company), appointed C.O.

February.—Regiment wins both Brigade and Divisional Boxing Championships (fifth year in succession).

March.—Changes announced in the organisation of the two London T.A. Divisions. Certain infantry battalions are to be converted into anti-aircraft units. " The Kensingtons," however, are to remain an infantry battalion.

"THE KENSINGTONS"

April.—Easter training at Bordon attached Royal Irish Fusiliers.

C.O. obtains permission for a new style of dress cap, dark blue with grey band, to be worn with the S.D. uniform, a privilege only shared by the Brigade of Guards and H.A.C.

May 6th.—King's Silver Jubilee Parade. London T.A. units to line the streets—several rehearsals held. Colonel Stone to command the Brigade—Major E. L. Stacey commands the Battalion. An early start is made—journey by underground to Charing Cross—march up Villiers Street to the Strand, where position is taken up near the Tivoli Cinema on both sides of the street. The Band plays under the portico of Adelphi Theatre and the Corps of Drums marches up and down the centre of the road, their efforts to relieve the monotony of the waiting crowds being greatly appreciated. Royal Salute is given and Colours dipped as the Royal Procession passes. Almost immediately after it has passed the police relax their efforts at keeping back the crowd, which then blocks the road, making forming-up a difficult task—however, eventually it is accomplished, and the Battalion returns to H.Q., proud of having taken its part in the Jubilee Celebrations.

Later in the month the Regimental Band has honour of playing outside the Town Hall for the visit of H.M. The King on his Western London Drive. Regimental children are given position of vantage. Jubilee medals awarded to the Honorary Colonel, the C.O., the Q.M., and three other ranks (C.S.M. A. Simkins, Cpl. P. Green, and Pte. E. Harris).

July.—Camp at Myrtle Grove same site as 1933—glorious weather and good training. Vickers-gun range-takers do well—tieing for first place in the Division.

November 3rd.—H.R.H. Princess Louise present again at H.Q. for the annual Memorial Service. She later takes salute of past and present "Kensingtons" as they leave for the Cenotaph.

December 15th.—New organisation of London T.A.

Division comes into force. There is to be one Division instead of two. The "Grey" Brigade, as such, ceases to exist. "The Kensingtons" now join the 2nd London Infantry Brigade consisting of: The Honourable Artillery Company, the London Rifle Brigade, the Kensingtons and the London Scottish, with the Artists' Rifles attached.

The Regiment is honoured at being selected to form part of such a "crack" Brigade.

Finally, it may be of interest to consider a few of the changes in organisation and training, which post-war military policy and war-lessons have wrought.

Chief amongst these is the increased "fire-power" of an infantry battalion. At present each battalion has a company for supporting fire, consisting of three platoons of Vickers guns (twelve in all), a Mortar platoon with four mortars (a larger edition of the wartime Stokes).

In addition, there is an anti-tank platoon and anti-aircraft section, the remaining three companies each having eight light automatic (Lewis-gun) sections and eight rifle sections. Thus it will be seen how greatly the potential "fire-power" of an infantry battalion has increased since the war. The extreme importance of section and platoon leadership was realised during the latter days of the war, and a great deal of time is now devoted to training leaders by means of courses of instruction, lectures, map-reading classes, and tactical exercises both in the country and on the sand-table.

It is felt that numbers are not as important as well-trained officers and N.C.O.s capable of instructing and leading. Any great national emergency would probably see a "rush to the colours"; the main difficulty would be to train these recruits. It is hoped that the T.A. would be capable of doing so. For this reason mainly, it is now quite definitely the only means of expansion of a National Army and is, in consequence, treated with greater seriousness and respect by the higher military authorities. It behoves all units therefore to maintain their efficiency with well-trained leaders, and men capable of being promoted to leadership, keeping on the strength only those who complete their obligatory training.

The conditions of service since the war have contained an undertaking to serve overseas in case of embodiment.

Sufficient has been written to bring home to readers that the present Regiment is very much alive and training in the same voluntary yet serious spirit, to be of value to King and Country should occasion arise.

CHAPTER XXXI

THE OLD COMRADES' ASSOCIATION

By L. H. T. DREW (SGT.)

THIS book would be incomplete without some reference to the Old Comrades' Association of the Kensingtons. Formed as long ago as March 1914, a fact that will doubtless cause surprise to many of the present members, the Association has grown steadily and reaches its majority in the present year—1935, the publication of this History thus providing a fitting expression of the vigour of its manhood.

Early in 1914 Colonel F. G. Lewis consulted Lieut. and Quartermaster A. Ridley as to what could be done towards stimulating recruiting for the Battalion, which had then fallen in numbers to about six hundred all ranks, the war establishment being approximately one thousand. "Riddles," as he is affectionately known, suggested the immediate formation of an Old Comrades' Association; Colonel Lewis agreed, and having obtained official sanction of the Territorial Force Association, some 1,600 serving and past members of the Battalion were circularised. The results being very satisfactory, a dinner was held at the Clarendon Restaurant, Hammersmith, on June 11th, 1914, in celebration of the formation of the Association. At this dinner, at which Major Stafford presided, owing to the illness of Colonel Lewis, there assembled many old friends of the Regiment, including the Honorary Colonel, Sir Alfred Turner, Major Lumley Webb, and others. Major Lumley Webb became chairman for some years.

The intervention of the war was not allowed to interfere with the development of the newly formed Association, which performed invaluable work during those trying years. Early in 1915 Colonel Lewis granted leave to

Lieut. Ridley to come home from France and address the 2nd and 3rd Battalions, with the result that before the end of that year £1,000 had been collected, the subscription then being two days' pay. Lieut. Ridley returned to France, and Captain Lesser took over the work of the Association. All Old Comrades who served during the war know how well this officer carried on the good work. As officer commanding the Depôt, Captain Lesser had a very difficult task, but no soldier or bereaved relative ever visited Headquarters without being cheered and comforted by this kind and very courteous gentleman, whose sympathy and personal generosity are so well known. The welfare of our unfortunate comrades who had been taken prisoners of war was a task to which he devoted his best energies in spite of innumerable difficulties. Mrs. Lesser too, in company with many other " 13th " ladies, was untiring in her efforts to entertain the mothers, wives, and children of the Kensingtons; indeed, one cannot praise too highly the devotion and self-sacrificing interest displayed by our womenfolk in those most anxious times.

Such is the early history of the Old Comrades' Association. On July 4th, 1919, an All Star Matinée was held at the Royal Court Theatre in aid of the Fund, at which appeared such well-known artistes as Davy Burnaby, José Collins, Will Evans, Peter Gawthorne, Eileen Grace, Mary Grey, Harold Holland & Co., Nelson Keys, Lucy Nuttall, Sybil Thorndyke, Vernon Watson, and others. This matinée resulted in a substantial sum of money being raised. Our good friend Lieut.-Colonel Bisdee had also been successful in getting the accumulated canteen profits of the 2nd Battalion handed over to the Association, which was now able to face the future with a good credit balance in the bank.

The objects of the Association are twofold:

(1) To promote fraternity, good-fellowship, and sympathy among Old Comrades.

(2) To afford assistance to any member in distressed circumstances (as far as funds will allow) after strict investigation by the Committee.

THE OLD COMRADES' ASSOCIATION

The Committee has faithfully carried out its charge, supported by a loyal and generous membership, and it can be said with truth that no old comrade in genuine distress has ever applied in vain.

It is the proud boast of the Association that, in spite of the present period of unemployment and distress, it has not yet had to dispose of any of its securities; grants and loans to needy members having been met out of subscriptions and interest on investments. This, of course, has been made possible only by the consistent support of the members, and the very able financial advice of Captain Lesser. Thus so far matters are satisfactory, but time is passing, and in the years to come, as members grow old and infirm, the Association will have to face much heavier calls on the funds. If this book should be read by any of those who served with the Regiment and have not yet joined the Old Comrades' Association, they are earnestly entreated to do so without delay, for the sake of their less fortunate comrades who have found the peace harder than the war. The annual subscription to-day is only 2s. 6d. (minimum).

The Association also keeps very much alive with regard to the social side, the annual Reunion Dinner being very well attended. In recent years a great gathering has taken place at Headquarters on Armistice night, when a play depicting life in the trenches has usually been put on; written, produced, and acted entirely by members of the O.C.A. and the Regiment. A real sand-bagged trench built on the stage, together with most realistic lighting and effects, has made these shows unique. One London evening paper's description was " better than *Journey's End*."

Two very successful visits to the battlefields have been made, one in 1929, when the party made Arras its headquarters and radiated thence to the various sectors, a special visit being made to the Kensington Cemetery at Laventie, where Colonel H. Campbell, D.S.O., placed a wreath on the memorial. The second pilgrimage was in 1931, when Lille was selected as the centre, and other areas visited. A special trip was made to the splendid

"THE KENSINGTONS"

Ploegsteert Memorial, whereon are inscribed the names of Kensingtons who fell in the attack on Aubers Ridge on May 9th, 1915. Some members of the 2nd Battalion have made the long pilgrimage to Palestine and visited war cemeteries and familiar points in that remote area.

Although the men who went on these tours quite naturally enjoyed themselves and recaptured as far as possible the old spirit of 1914–18, singing the old songs and sampling the French vintages, they did not for one moment forget that they were on a pilgrimage, and as each place of memory was revisited, many were the names recalled of old comrades who had made the supreme sacrifice. Incidents, both tragic and amusing, were remembered, battles refought, and ruin and desolation visualised in place of the bright new houses in the reconditioned villages. In the open country Nature, assisted by an energetic French peasantry, had almost completely effaced the handiwork of war.

A very sporting event is the annual shooting match against the Regiment for a cup. This contest takes place at Pirbright, and the O.C.A. team can still hold its own on the ranges in spite of "anno domini." Good-fellowship prevails, as is usual at such gatherings, in the Guards Sergeants' Mess. The Annual Regimental Dance is a function at which wives, sisters, sweethearts (and also daughters) can thoroughly enjoy themselves. Also, by kind courtesy of the various Commanding Officers since the war, the Sergeants' Mess at Headquarters is thrown open every Friday to all members of the O.C.A. Here they can enjoy all the amenities of a club and spin a yarn with each other.

This chapter would be incomplete without special mention of the work of the secretaries, who, in a purely honorary capacity, have devoted practically the whole of their spare time to the welfare of the Association. During the earlier years Colour-Sergeant W. C. Frapwell and Company Quartermaster-Sergeant H. J. C. Fozard carried out this important work, but for many years now the life and soul of the O.C.A. has been Company Quartermaster-Sergeant J. L. Brown, whose untiring and devoted service has done so much to make the Association the live and successful body it is to-day. During the last two years the duties of the secretary have increased so as to render it practically impossible for one man to carry out the work, and Sergeant S. White has generously come forward, and now holds the position of joint honorary secretary with " Len " Brown.

The Association has always received the utmost assistance from the successive Commanding Officers of the Regiment, and from the Regiment itself, and it is certain that if the latter should ever be called upon to do so, it would faithfully uphold the glorious traditions of which the Old Comrades are so proud. On the subject of ex-service men, it is quite true to say that the men who fought in the Great War are, in many respects, a race apart. This does not mean they are intolerant of youth. In the trenches, when face to face with the stark realities of war, men were shorn of all the affectations of civilian life, and so were enabled to see very deeply into each other's character. Having witnessed the horrors of war, to-day ex-service men seek peace and pursue it, but not in the weak-kneed manner of doctrinaire pacifists, inasmuch as they are still willing to fight for their right to be left in peace.

The wonderful spirit of comradeship engendered in the war is nowhere more apparent than amongst the members of the Kensingtons' Old Comrades' Association. The following very apt lines are taken from Colonel Rorie's book, *A Medico's Luck in the War*:

> As Father Time still marches on,
>   Gone are those days—forever gone.
> And now in peace we sit aloof
>   From shells that tumble on the roof,
> *But linked by bonds we can't deny—*
>   *What soulless wretch would care to try ?*

THE WAR MEMORIAL AT HEADQUARTERS, KENSINGTON.

ROLL OF HONOUR

In compiling this Roll of our Comrades who were killed in action or died of wounds, the utmost care has been taken, after due reference to all official records available, to ensure completeness and accuracy of detail. In the event of any errors or omissions the History Committee tender their sincere regret.

[The Roll does not include the name of any Officer, N.C.O., or man attached from another Unit.]

Lieutenant-Colonel
Shaw, R. E. F., *M.C.*

Majors
Dickens, C. C.
Flower, V. A., *D.S.O.*

Captains
Barnett, H. W.
Herbert, R. B.
Lukis, T. S.
Perry, H. B.
Prismall, A.
Rosevear, A. M.
Rosevear, F. R.
Thompson, G.
Ware, F. H.

Lieutenants
Baker, J. F.
Burn, W. G.
Chant, T. R.
Gates, E. C.

Hart, E. G.
Leigh-Pemberton, T. E. G.
MacGregor, R. M.
Mager, W. G.
Mitchison, M.
Parnell, L. R.
Sewell, N. O.
Sheppard, R. T.
Turner, T. E.

Second Lieutenants
Brooks, G. T.
Bundle, H. N.
Burd, F. B.
Castelli, E. C.
Clifford, G. K.
Davis, M. O. A.
Dawes, R. S.
Druery, D. V.
Ellis, F. W.
Goadby, J. C.
Grosvenor, T. R.
Gruselle, H. E. J.

Jackson, A. G.
Jemmett, G. E.
Kirk, A. C.
Lawrie, N. E.
Lester, A. E., *M.C.*
Lockhart, R. F.
McCallum, E.
MacKenzie, N. O. C.
Matheson, H.
Osborn, W.
Pearce, W. H.
Peters, A. S.
Pilgrim, H. B.
Posnett, W. L.
Ranson, C. S.
Sach, C. B.
Sanders, W. A. T.
Seabury, E. R.
Smith, W. E., *M.C.*
Stern, L. H.
Stockwell, F. R.
Stone, H. R.
Wilson, R. N.

Company Sergeant-Majors
Hockley, H. H.
Howes, T. F.
Moss, J. R.

Sergeants
Aikman, T.
Alsop, W. C. P.
Andrews, H.
Asplin, E.
Baker, W. B.
Ball, R. H.
Beck, E. R.
Belsten, W. H.

Brook, S. J.
Bryant, O.
Burthom, W.
Chamberlain, E. C.
Chennells, J. B.
Choules, J.
Cockett, A. W.
Cope, E. J., *M.M.*
Freestone, H. W.
Fuggles, E. G.
Gill, C. S.
Hanham, S. A.
Heather, J. C.
Heden, A. H.
Holmes, E. G.
Hutchins, H. E.
Innes, R. B., *M.M.*
Jones, L. W.
Kemp, J. H.
King, A.
McCall, W.
Macdonald, E. C.
Mackie, W. J.
McLean, W.
Maplethorpe, C. H. W., *M.M.*
Meacock, T. H.
Meadows, R. W.
Moody, F. C.
Munton, B. F.
Neish, A. N., *M.M.*
Oborn, F. S.
Parkes, E.
Perris, S.
Pocock, F. W.
Salmon, W. F.
Selden, B.
Shelley, A. E.

Sitch, F.
Skipper, S.
Somerville, H.
Southwick, C. T.
Wallace, R. G.
Warrington, T.
Webb, R. H.
Welch, S.
Withey, S. C.
Woodhams, F. G.
Younger, F. C.

Lance-Sergeants
Bentley, H.
Cheshire, F. J.
Cook, R. G.
Hatfield, W.
Jenkins, J. R.
Jones, A. L.
Mills, F. E.
Prior, S. A.
Shepherd, G. H.
Shinn, W. P.
Turtle, P. J.

Corporals
Adams, J. W.
Allcorn, G.
Allcroft, F. C.
Annis, A.
Aston, C.
Barr, D. D.
Bevis, R. E.
Braithwaite, R.
Brookland, E. J.
Carey, F.
Chick, W.
Chilcott, E.

Clifton, A. E.
Crampton, S.
Cudby, A.
Eastment, E. S.
Edwards, J.
Eyles, H. E.
Field, F.
Francis, A.
Francis, W.
Freeman, A. C.
Galt, N.
Giles, C. W.
Goodwin, H. P.
Green, L. J.
Griffiths, J. J.
Gunn, J. H.
Gye, A.
Ham, P. J.
Haslem, J.
Hawken, R. C., *M.M.*
Hawthorn, G. T.
Hutt, F.
Irving, F.
Jenkins, W.
Jones, R. T.
Lawley, R.
Leicester, J. B.
Le Ray, R. J.
Love, S. J.
Marks, W. A.
Maslen, A.
Norman, W. S.
Owen, A.
Palmer, P. J. W.
Parish, T., *M.M.*
Peers, A. M.
Poole, J. E. S., *D.C.M.*
Preston, F.

Prideaux, F.
Ricketts, A. H.
Saffery, S.
Skull, A.
Smith, A. R.
Smith, G. B.
Thompson, R.
Wagner, C.
Watts, C.

Lance-Corporals

Algar, H.
Annis, F. J.
Ashford, R. W.
Baker, E. T.
Battiscombe, C. G.
Beebee, F. A.
Bicheno, J.
Brook, A.
Bryant, C. M.
Bull, W. J. F.
Burden, C. G. E.
Burr, W.
Clarke, H. G.
Coatman, S. W.
Collins, E. R.
Cook, J.
Courtney, H.
Cozens, W. E.
Curtis, G.
Denton, H.
Dobson, S. E.
Duncan, W.
East, F. A.
Egerton, W. W.
Furnival, G. W. J.
Goodwin, J. R., *M.M.*
Green, H.

Hilsden, W. G.
Hoehn, G. C.
Holmes, F. C.
Holttum, A. G.
Humphrey, A. E.
Hunter, R.
Hymans, L. H.
Jarvis, S. H.
Kimpton, F. R. R.
Lander, V. O.
Leaver, T. P.
Little, C. W. B.
Luker, C.
Lye, W.
McGuire, R. A.
Marsden, W. G.
Matthews, E. R.
Melhuish, A. D.
Morgan, D. H.
O'Brien, L.
Ovenden, W.
Palmer, G. R.
Parker, D. J.
Pedder, R. E. A.
Pratt, G. E.
Price, S. N.
Purchase, J.
Richardson, B.
Rickarby, M. C.
Roper, H.
Ross, E.
Rowe, H. B.
Rowsell, J. A.
Savage, A.
Secker, N. H.
Skelton, W., *M.M.*
Skinner, C.
Smith, F. T.

ROLL OF HONOUR

Sydenham, E. S.
Tatam, S. F.
Tavener, R. S.
Thomas, V.
Waldheim, W.
Webb, E. G.
Williams, E.
Woodford, E. W.
Woodley, G. H.

Drummers

Champion, V.
Cole, J.
Field, E. V.
Grant, J.
Hancock, A. R.
Hurst, P. W.
Hyde, H. B.
Mulford, A. W.
Stroud, F. W.

Privates

Abbey, P. C.
Abell, H.
Abraham, H. A.
Adams, J. J. A.
Aland, A. W.
Albin, S. J.
Alcock, P. L.
Aldous, W. R.
Alexander, T. W.
Allen, A.
Allen, F.
Allen, T. W.
Anderson, E. C.
Andrew, F. R.
Andrews, W. F.
Angliss, G. E.

Angus, A. A.
Anstey, J. H.
Appleby, C. H.
Archer, P.
Arnold, W. C.
Ash, E.
Ashberry, B.
Ashenden, G.
Ashley, H.
Ashley, H. E.
Atherton, A. W.
Atkinson, H. C.
Atkinson, H. G.
Atlee, C.
Atterbury, W. R.
Austin, A.
Austin, F.
Austin, W.
Bacon, C. T.
Bacon, H. J.
Baker, A. S.
Baker, V. J.
Baldock, T.
Baldock, W. J.
Baldwin, C.
Ballinger, C.
Balshaw, C. A.
Banks, W.
Barclay, S. W.
Barker, G. J.
Barker, T. H.
Barnes, C. J.
Barnes, G. E.
Barrett, A.
Barrett, F. R.
Bartel, H. C.
Bartlett, R. H.
Bartlett, R. M.

Bartling, F.
Bateman, H.
Bates, A. E.
Batty, G.
Batty, R.
Bayes, C. J.
Beales, S. H.
Bearman, H.
Beauchamp, G.
Bedwell, W. J.
Beer, J. W.
Beeston, E.
Beeston, H. G.
Belcher, G.
Belcher, J.
Belham, W.
Belsten, W. S.
Bennett, B. A.
Bennett, F. C.
Bennett, W.
Bent, F. G.
Berry, W.
Best, G. R. S.
Bevan, T.
Bevis, R. L.
Beynon, A. H.
Biggs, E. C.
Billings, W. T.
Binsted, W. P.
Bixby, W.
Blake, A. A.
Blaker, F.
Bligh, A. V.
Blows, N. W. J.
Blundell, F. C.
Boadle, F. C.
Bolch, H.
Bolding, A. W.

Bowles, W. L.
Bowyer, A. R.
Boyd, F. E.
Braddon, W. C.
Bradford, T. C.
Bradnock, N. C.
Bragg, A. W.
Brand, F. H.
Brandum, H.
Breeden, H. C.
Brind, B. H.
Bristow, W.
Brockington, C.
Brooks, J. R.
Brougham, E. A.
Brown, A.
Brown, F. J.
Brown, H. C.
Brown, J.
Brown, P.
Brown, T. H. (No. 1512)
Brown, T. H. (No. 2200)
Brown, W.
Bryant, H.
Bubb, J.
Bubear, A. G.
Budge, A. G.
Bull, S. G.
Bull, W. F.
Bunney, A. M.
Burgess, E. J.
Burley, H.
Burnage, A. G.
Burns, A. V.
Burns, B.
Burns, W. H.
Burrell, F. L.
Burridge, S. T.

Burton, R. H.
Butler, J.
Butler, W. H.
Butler, W. L.
Butt, A.
Butterworth, W. E.
Byatt, E.
Calf, L. A.
Camp, A. F.
Campbell, G.
Careless, W. R.
Caro, M. S.
Carr, S. J.
Carroll, J.
Carter, C. J.
Carter, J. P. C. B.
Carter, W. J. S.
Castelli, C. C.
Cater, R.
Cattell, R. G.
Chalfen, J.
Champness, B.
Chance, E. J.
Chance, W. T.
Charie, H.
Charles, H.
Cheeld, W. H.
Chell, A. H.
Chevis, E.
Chicken, G. A.
Clare, A. L.
Clark, A. E.
Clark, L. F.
Clark, M. E.
Clarke, A. E.
Clarke, A. F.
Clarke, C. A.
Clarke, F.

Clarke, G. K. B.
Clarke, H.
Clarke, W. A.
Clemens, A. V. C.
Cliburn, G.
Clifton, R.
Clinch, A.
Clinch, G.
Cobb, A. J.
Cobb, E.
Cohen, S.
Cohen, V. E., *D.C.M.*
Coldman, W. A.
Coles, V. J.
Colgate, E. A.
Collins, H.
Collins, J. A.
Collyer, L. C.
Connell, A. S.
Conquest, A.
Cooke, C.
Cooling, S. L.
Coombs, W.
Cooper, C. S.
Cooper, H. W.
Cooper, S.
Coote, A. C.
Corderoy, J. E.
Cork, J. W.
Cornborough, C. C.
Cornwell, A. F.
Corps, R.
Costerton, F. R.
Cotter, V. O. G.
Cotton, R. W.
Cowland, J. T.
Cowles, A.
Cox, R. T.

Cozens, A. J.
Craig, N. E.
Crathern, H. E.
Creighton, R.
Cripps, F.
Cropley, G. R. F.
Crow, W. J.
Crowe, F. J.
Croxford, H. A.
Crush, W. J.
Crutchley, E.
Csako, E. S.
Cue, F.
Currie, O.
Cushings, W. F.
Cussens, W. H.
Daily, E. A.
Daldry, T.
Dallimore, E. C.
Danes, H.
Dark, H.
Davey, W.
David, G. W. K.
Davis, D. K.
Davis, F. M.
Davis, G.
Davis, H.
Davis, S.
Davy, W.
De Beaupré, R. B. A.
Dedman, C.
Delahunt, J. C.
Dennis, T. N.
Dermott, A. W.
Desmond, E. D.
Dimes, F. J.
Dixon, W. C.
Dobson, A. H.

Docker, A. E.
Dodge, G. B.
Donald, A. O.
Dowd, H.
Drake, W.
Draper, F.
Drew, S. H.
Dunn, E. J.
Dunt, C. R.
Dyson, A. S.
Eales, A.
Earl, S. E.
Ebsworth, G.
Eddington, A.
Edgar, J. B.
Edmonds, G.
Edwards, P.
Edwards, P. H.
Edwards, W. H.
Egerton, G.
Elder, D.
Elliston, B. H.
Ells, C. A.
Emms, A. E.
Ernst, W. A.
Evans, A. W.
Evans, D. M.
Evans, F.
Evans, H.
Evans, J.
Evetts, F.
Farmer, H. W.
Faulkner, J. E.
Faulkner, M. H.
Feakes, A. S.
Feetham, F. G.
Ferguson, L. H.
Finch, H. L. W.

Finch, J. B.
Findley, G. E. W.
Finn, J.
Fishenden, T. R.
Fisher, B.
Fisher, F. C.
Fitness, H.
Flatt, W.
Fletcher, F.
Fletcher, T.
Flower, R.
Fobbs, H. S.
Foote, W. J.
Ford, P. S. P.
Fordham, H.
Foreman, D. J.
Foreman, W.
Forrest, C.
Forrester, J. C.
Fowle, T.
Foy, L.
Francis, S. F.
Francis, T. G.
Franks, H.
Fraser, F. J.
French, J. F.
Frencham, F. W.
Funnell, A.
Gale, N. D. M.
Gamble, A. E.
Gammon, A.
Gardiner, W.
Garner, P. A.
Garnett, G. H.
Garrick, J. J.
Gay, B.
Geeson, F. L.
Geeson, W. W.

Geffen, E.
Gibbings, R.
Gibbons, J. H.
Gilbert, R.
Gilham, F. A.
Gilpin, E. J.
Ginsburg, D.
Girling, W. E.
Goddard, A. H.
Goddard, V. F.
Golland, E. E.
Gooderson, A. G.
Goodwin, J.
Goodyear, W. L.
Gray, A. J. B.
Gray, E. J.
Gray, S. C.
Green, C. (No. 4294)
Green, C. (No. 491479)
Green, J.
Green, W.
Green, W. E.
Gubbins, W. C.
Gurney, G. A.
Hackman, C. C.
Haigh, A. H.
Hale, E. W.
Hall, H. (No. 2526)
Hall, H. (No. 6308)
Hallinan, T. H.
Hambrook, A. S.
Handford, E. M.
Hardcastle, H. L.
Hardes, J.
Hardingham, C. H.
Hardwick, A.
Hardy, H. L.
Hardy, R.

Harman, A. T.
Harper, E.
Harper, H. J.
Harris, A. T.
Harris, F. W.
Harris, G.
Harris, J. W.
Harris, W. J. M.
Harvey, F.
Harvey, J. A.
Haswell, A. E.
Hatton, S.
Hawes, H. V.
Hawkes, F. H.
Hawkes, F. J.
Hawkins, G.
Hawkins, M. S.
Hayman, A. E.
Haynes, F. W.
Heal, C. J.
Hearn, H. T.
Heasman, G. T.
Heaver, C. A.
Heaver, G. H.
Hempston, G. F.
Henison, M.
Herbert, P.
Herns, A. A.
Hewitt, C.
Hewitt, J.
Hewson, C. G.
Hext, W. J.
Higgett, F.
Higgins, A. F.
Higgins, L.
Hill, A. R.
Hill, C. R. G.
Hill, F. E.

Hind, M.
Hinde, A. N.
Hinnells, W. H.
Hiscox, E. C.
Hoad, E.
Hoad, J.
Hoddy, A.
Hodges, H.
Hodgkinson, E. V.
Hogg, H. W.
Holder, H. C.
Hollick, W. S.
Holloway, W. A.
Holman, J. A.
Hooker, H.
Horsley, W.
Howell, G.
Hoy, T. G.
Hubbard, R. D.
Hudson, L. S.
Hull, A. J.
Hunt, E. S.
Hunt, G. M.
Hunt, W. H.
Hunter, B. S.
Hunter, R. E. W.
Hurman, A. E.
Hurst, J.
Hurt, F. J.
Hutchinson, C.
Hyde, A. H.
Hyde, G. R.
Hyde, S.
Hytch, H.
Ide, F. E.
Ings, F. H.
Isaacs, I. E.
Isted, H.

Jackson, E.
Jackson, F. C.
Jackson, W. T.
Jacobs, L.
Jagger, A.
James, P. W.
Jarrett, A. S.
Jarvis, C.
Jeffery, F. T.
Jenkins, A. C.
Jiggins, F.
Johnson, H. A.
Johnson, W. A.
Jones, C. J.
Jones, O. J.
Jordan, L. M. H.
Kelleher, J.
Kemp, R.
Kent, C. G.
Kerridge, A.
Ketteridge, C. H.
Kiff, C.
Kinchin, E. H.
King, B.
King, E.
King, W. F.
Kirby, A. W.
Kirby, J. R.
Kyte, R.
Ladbrook, G. B.
Laker, E. H.
Lamb, W. A.
Landrey, S. G.
Lane, C. V.
Lane, J. D.
Lane, L.
Langley, E.
Langley, S. W.

Langton, H.
Law, P. C.
Lawrence, W. H.
Lee, F. J.
Lelliott, C.
Lewis, A. H. L.
Lewis, B.
Lewis, F.
Leyman, F. W.
Licquorish, C. W.
Linken, H. W.
Little, R. D.
Little, W.
Livermore, A. E.
Lloyd, W.
Lock, E.
Lockwood, A.
Lovell, H. A.
Lovely, H. A. H.
Lowe, A.
Lowing, S.
Lye, R. H. F.
Lyon, G.
Macartney, V. J.
McCormick, R. W.
McEntee, H. D.
Macey, H.
McHenry, G. L.
McKenzie, A.
Mackintosh, E. J.
Mackley, G. H.
Macleod, C. G.
McNally, A. E.
McNamara, T.
Macrae, F.
Madden, C. H., *M.M.*
Maggs, E.
Mahoney, J.

Major, H.
Makins, F. A. A.
Malem, W. H.
Mallett, W. P.
Mann, J. H.
Mansfield, A.
Mansfield, A. E.
Maples, J.
Markwell, R. W.
Marlow, F.
Marrin, W.
Marsh, C. G.
Marshall, J. C.
Marshall, T. L.
Martin, C.
Martin, D. W.
Martin, L. N. J.
May, H.
Maydon, A. E.
Mayhew, G. W.
Medus, A.
Mee, P.
Melhuish, S. W.
Mertens, H. G.
Mexson, R.
Michelmore, T. S.
Middell, S. V.
Middleton, A. F. S.
Millington, A. G.
Millington, D. G.
Mills, G. R.
Mills, R. W. A.
Mills, T.
Minter, C.
Mist, J. P.
Mitchell, G. J.
Moat, L. E.
Moate, W. H.

Moller, L. C.
Monk, H. A.
Moorby, V.
Moore, C. W.
Moore, J. H.
Moorey, F. L.
Morey, J.
Morgan, G. H.
Morgan, J.
Morley, G. A.
Morris, S. W.
Mortimer, H. B.
Mott, C. F.
Munday, F.
Mundy, P. D.
Munns, J. H.
Murphy, J.
Myhill, F. L.
Naphtali, H.
Nason, A. M.
Nathan, A.
Neat, W.
Needham, A.
New, C.
Newman, A. M. T.
Newman, A. W.
Newman, F.
Nichols, J. R.
Nichols, J. W.
Nind, W.
Norman, E. C.
Nottingham, E.
Oakey, C. J.
Oliver, G. A.
Oliver, G. W.
O'Mara, J. T.
O'Neill, W. J.
Orange, F. A. J.

Osborn, H.
Oswald, N.
Page, E. C.
Page, P. M.
Pagnoni, G.
Paley, H. L.
Pardoe, F.
Parker, G. F.
Parker, W. C.
Parkyn, S. A.
Parslow, J.
Parsons, A.
Partridge, H.
Patmore, P.
Pattenden, T.
Payne, A. E.
Payne, A. S.
Peach, L. H.
Pearce, E. V.
Pearce, W. F.
Pearse, H.
Pellett, S. H.
Penfold, T. H.
Penhallow, C. S.
Pentland, H. W.
Perrin, H. R.
Perry, H. J.
Petherick, J. E.
Phillips, F.
Phillips, I. C.
Phillpott, W. T.
Philpot, G. A.
Pickard, G. A.
Pickford, S. S.
Pilgrim, E. H.
Pipe, J. B.
Pitter, J.
Pitts, G. F.

Plummer, G. R.
Plummer, W.
Pluthero, P. H.
Pollard, W.
Pollard, W. E.
Pomerance, S.
Poole, B. J.
Pooley, A. J.
Porter, E.
Pownall, E. H.
Pratley, A. E.
Preston, A.
Price, T.
Prime, W.
Prior, R. C.
Prodger, C.
Proughten, T. C.
Pryke, A. G.
Pulley, J.
Purdie, A. J.
Purnell, T. L.
Purser, W.
Quick, C. T. A.
Rabbits, E. G.
Ramsay, W. R.
Ravenhill, W. A.
Raworth, W. A.
Ray, D. T.
Raynard, H.
Read, C. T.
Read, L.
Reader, C.
Reader, E. F.
Reading, W.
Reed, H. A.
Reed, W.
Rees, A. J.
Reeve, G. L.

Reeve, S. A.
Reich, M. W.
Reid, D. G.
Reid, H. J.
Reid, H. W.
Reid, V. B.
Renton, T.
Richards, H. H.
Richardson, A. W.
Richardson, H. J.
Richardson, W.
Riley, T. G.
Rix, T.
Robinson, C. F.
Robinson, G. W.
Robinson, J.
Rogers, G. (No. 4606)
Rogers, G. (No. 4999)
Rogers, H. A.
Root, J. F.
Rose, A. E.
Rowntree, C.
Roylance, H. C.
Ruddock, A. E.
Russell, W. G.
Rust, P.
Ryan, J. W.
Saddington, H. J.
Salter, F. H. L.
Samuels, J.
Sandercock, J. L.
Sargeant, W.
Saunders, H. M.
Saunders, L.
Savory, F.
Sawyer, J.
Schen, R. Z.
Schwaben, C. W.
Scott, R. F.
Scull, P. F.
Searle, F. G.
Sebley, A. A.
Sells, G. V.
Sellwood, J. C. H. D.
Shakes, W.
Sharman, W.
Sharp, C. J.
Sharp, H.
Shea, R.
Shearman, J. G.
Shears, E. N.
Sheldrake, H. A.
Sherwood, G.
Sherwood, S. W.
Shore, B. J.
Shorley, F. G. G.
Shorney, A. C.
Short, G. C.
Shrubsole, F. J.
Shute, A.
Simmons, C. T.
Simmons, W. V.
Sims, F.
Sindall, F.
Skinner, C. M.
Skinner, S.
Slade, R.
Sloman, A. J.
Small, J. D.
Smith, A.
Smith, A. E.
Smith, A. G.
Smith, A. K.
Smith, A. T.
Smith, B.
Smith, C. (No. 1434)

Smith, C. (No. 1994)
Smith, C. G.
Smith, E. C.
Smith, F. R.
Smith, G. W.
Smith, H. B.
Smith, H. C.
Smith, H. J. (No. 1439)
Smith, H. J. (No. 1614)
Smith, H. W.
Smith, J. R.
Smith, S. H.
Smith, S. L.
Smith, W. E.
Smithers, G. V.
Snelling, C. W.
Solomons, M.
Solway, P. G.
Soper, H. A. T.
Sparkes, W.
Sparks, S.
Sparrow, W. C.
Spencer, L. M.
Spencer, R. E.
Spiess, C. H. J.
Spracklan, R. H.
Springett, W. S.
Spurdens, F. W.
Spurr, A. G.
Squire, E. W.
Stagg, T. F.
Stark, F. C.
Steeden, A. H.
Stephens, H. G.
Stephenson, A.
Stevens, P. N.
Stevens, W. S.
Stoatt, C. W.

Stokes, A. A.
Stonestreet, A. J.
Stote, J. C. H.
Stringer, L. J.
Stringer, W.
Style, H. G.
Sullivan, C.
Sully, R. A.
Swan, A. C.
Swan, T.
Swan, T. H.
Sweetman, W.
Swindell, A. W.
Tabraham, W. W.
Tannen, P.
Tanner, C.
Taperell, A.
Tarry, E. H.
Tarver, P. E.
Tattle, B. T.
Taylor, A. W.
Taylor, J.
Taylor, J. G.
Taylor, W. J.
Tegetmeier, A.
Terry, J.
Thaine, A. B.
Thear, A.
Thomas, A. F.
Thomas, E.
Thomas, D. G.
Thompson, E. W.
Thomson, J.
Thorne, C. W.
Thwaites, H.
Tibble, J.
Tidy, W. A.
Timbs, C. A.

Tissington, A.
Tomlins, H. E.
Tooke, A. G.
Trice, F.
Trickey, H.
Trivett, W. C.
Truby, S. W.
Trussell, E. C.
Tuck, C.
Tucker, A.
Tudman, C.
Tulett, M. J.
Turnbull, T. J.
Turner, C. G.
Turner, E. E.
Turner, F. S. P.
Turner, G. P.
Turner, W.
Tussler, T.
Tyler, J. J.
Underhill, R. B.
Underwood, W. R.
Urry, S. F.
Van der Vord, C. J.
Venis, G. F.
Vernon, E. A.
Verrall, J. W.
Vincent, H.
Wain, S.
Wakeman, C. H.
Walden, H.
Walker, H. J.
Walker, S. P.
Waller, J. W.
Walter, A. F. B.
Walton, S. R.
Ward, S.
Wareham, H. S.

Warford, R. G. C.
Warn, H. D.
Warner, J.
Warner, J. V.
Watkins, O. F.
Watling, J.
Watson, W. H. (No. 1968)
Watson, W. H.
  (No. 496469)
Way, C.
Way, W. R. O.
Wayte, F. H.
Weaver, A.
Webb, A. A.
Welch, G. H.
Welch, H.
Wells, A.
Wells, B. J.
Wells, F. V. T.
Wendon, T. H.
Wendt, G. N.
West, C.
West, E.
West, R.
Western, F. A.
Wharton, L. G.
Wheadon, R.
White, W. V.
Whiting, G. H.
Whittingham, H. E.
Whitwell, H. C. C.
Widdicombe, F.
Widginton, G.
Wilcockson, A.
Wilkins, R.
Wilkinson, W. R.
Wilks, T. W.
Willers, E. W.

Willetts, E. J.
Williams, E. C.
Williams, G. E. N.
Williams, H. E.
Willicombe, R.
Willis, J. J.
Wilson, A. P.
Wilson, J. F.
Wilson, L. J.
Wilson, M. J.
Winder, A.
Winter, C. W.
Wittrick, J. P.
Wolfe, L.
Wood, A. I.
Wood, F. J.
Wood, M. J.
Wood, R.
Woodbridge, W. J.
Woodley, J.
Woodman, A. E.
Woodman, W. S.
Woollett, E. N.
Wratten, A.
Wrout, A. E.
Wynne, H.
Yardley, L. A.
Young, J.

LIST OF HONOURS AND AWARDS WON BY THE KENSINGTONS DURING THE WAR

In the absence of an accurate official list the authors were faced with the alternative of complete omission or the publication of a list which painstaking effort and careful research had made as complete as possible. For any unfortunate errors or omissions they offer profound apologies —after a lapse of twenty years the task has been formidable. The Honours and Awards total:

C.M.G.	1	Medaille Militaire	3
C.B.	1	Croix de Guerre (Belgian)	1
C.B.E.	2	Belgian Decoration Militaire	1
D.S.O.	6		
O.B.E.	7		
M.B.E.	4	Italian Bronze Medal for Military Valour	1
M.C.	32		
D.C.M.	16	Chevalier Crown of Roumania	1
M.M.	82		
M.S.M.	14	Mentioned in Despatches	75
Croix de Guerre (avec Palme) (French)	1		

C.M.G., C.B.
Brig.-Gen. F. G. Lewis
(6 mentions)

C.B.E., D.S.O.
Lt.-Col. E. G. Kimber
(2 mentions)

C.B.E.
Colonel W. R. J. McLean

D.S.O., O.B.E.
Lt.-Col. H. Campbell
(1 mention)
Lt.-Col. C. M. Mackenzie
(1 mention)

D.S.O., M.C.
Lt.-Col. T. E. Bisdee
(D.C.L.I. attached)
Major K. E. Hart

D.S.O.
Major V. A. Flower
(2 mentions)

O.B.E., M.C.
Major J. E. L. Higgins

O.B.E.
Lt.-Col. A. C. Hearne
Lt.-Col. P. A. Hopkins
Lt.-Col. G. H. Leigh
Lt.-Col. G. Thompson

M.B.E.
Capt. S. A. Ball
Capt. H. W. Finlay
Major W. A. Phillips
Capt. A. Ridley (2 mentions)

M.C. and Bar
Capt. F. W. Heath

M.C., M.M.
Capt. G. A. Beggs

M.C.
Capt. C. E. Brockhurst
(1 mention)
Capt. A. C. Cattermole
(1 mention).
Major G. W. Collier
(1 mention)
Lt. D. Davies
Capt. L. T. Elvy
2nd Lt. W. V. Foot
(attached)
Capt. C. T. Foster
(1 mention)
2nd Lt. L. C. Gates
2nd Lt. L. F. Handford
Major M. R. Harris
Capt. H. E. Holland
(1 mention)
2nd Lt. W. H. O. Hugh
Lt. A. D. James
Capt. E. R. Kisch
2nd Lt. H. B. Lawson
Major W. W. Leonard
2nd Lt. A. E. Lester
(1 mention)
Major M. A. Prismall
(1 mention)
Capt. H. G. L. Prynne
2nd Lt. W. Read
2nd Lt. J. P. Savage
Lt.-Col. R. E. F. Shaw
(1 mention)
2nd Lt. E. J. Smith
2nd Lt. W. E. Smith
Capt. G. V. Thompson
(2 mentions)
Lt. W. J. West
2nd Lt. E. H. Weston

D.C.M. and Bar
Sgt. F. W. Shepherd

D.C.M.
C.S.M. C. J. Acres
Pte. W. Baker
Pte. V. E. Cohen
Corp. G. E. Cox
C.S.M. J. R. Davies
(1 mention)

LIST OF HONOURS AND AWARDS

Pte. T. E. Emery
Sgt. A. Evans
Pte. I. Hyams
C.S.M. A. E. Kearey
  (1 mention)
L/Sgt. W. Mullins
Sgt. P. R. Pike
Corp. J. E. S. Poole
Sgt. G. W. Squires
L/Corp. R. A. E. Starkey
Pte. J. H. Wood

M.M. and Bar
Italian Bronze Medal for Military Valour

C.S.M. E. Buck

M.M.

L/Corp. L. Arnold
Corp. D. Atlee
Pte. A. A. Attwood
Sgt. F. J. Bardwell
Pte. V. S. Boddy
Pte. A. E. Boorman
Pte. E. Boyde
L/Corp. W. Brazier
Corp. E. Brockhurst
Sgt. F. E. Brownjohn
Corp. G. W. Burberry
Sgt. H. C. Carlile
Pte. P. A. Cole
Pte. F. Coleman
L/Corp. E. J. Cope
Pte. A. O. Cotton
Sgt. S. N. Cowan
  (1 mention)
Sgt. E. Devonshire

Pte. G. M. Douglas
Pte. G. E. Drury
L/Sgt. J. G. Elcombe
Pte. W. G. Flann
Sgt. W. H. Godfrey
Pte. J. R. Goodwin
Corp. R. C. Hawken
Pte. W. E. Hicks-Ussher
Pte. F. W. Holbourn
Pte. W. H. Holden
Corp. J. A. Honey
Corp. F. Hopkins
Pte. G. L. Hopkins
Pte. A. P. House
Sgt. R. R. Innes
Corp. R. C. Jolliffe
Pte. C. R. W. Jones
Sgt. J. Jones
Sgt. R. E. V. Knights
Sgt. S. A. Lane
Sgt. W. Lawless
Pte. J. C. Lawrence
Sgt. H. Legh
Corp. H. Lott
Sgt. C. H. W. Mablethorpe
Pte. A. Mackenzie
L/Corp. J. T. MacOnie
Pte. C. H. Madden
Sgt. A. P. Manzi
Pte. H. F. Maunder
Sgt. G. E. V. Miles
Pte. W. R. Mills
Sgt. A. N. Neish
L/Corp. A. L. Odroft
Corp. T. Parish
Pte. C. Phillips
Pte. R. Phillips
Pte. W. T. Pymm

"THE KENSINGTONS"

Pte. W. F. Regnier
Pte. T. R. Rennett
Sgt. A. E. Robertson
Corp. S. E. J. Rogers
L/Corp. W. R. Rutter
Corp. A. E. Sayer
Sgt. A. H. Saunders
Sgt. G. Sims
L/Corp. W. Skelton
L/Sgt. L. Smeed
L/Corp. F. J. Sowerby
L/Corp. S. F. Sprange
C.S.M. H. W. Stiles
Sgt. W. Symes
Sgt. B. R. Veale (1 mention)
L/Corp. G. F. Warren
Pte. F. West
Pte. C. G. Wigg
Pte. A. J. Williams
Sgt. G. Wills
Sgt. R. D. Wills
Sgt. H. Wilson
Pte. L. J. Wood
Pte. S. Woolvin

M.S.M.

Sgt. W. Anderson
R.Q.M.S. W. Bailey
Pte. E. A. Evis
Corp. A. G. Groom
R.S.M. G. G. Gude
Sgt. P. S. Harman
C.S.M. J. Keleher
Pte. P. J. Mills
R.Q.M.S. H. F. Price
R.S.M. H. J. Semark
C.Q.M.S. A. Skipper

C.Q.M.S. W. J. D. Slatcher
Pte. W. G. Smith
L/Corp. A. Walters

Croix de Guerre (avec Palme) (French)

2nd Lt. A. V. M. Mitzakis (2 mentions)

Medaille Militaire

C.S.M. A. Maggs (1 mention)
Pte. L. Morley
Sgt. H. J. Stafford

Croix de Guerre (Belgian)

C.S.M. P. A. Court (2 mentions)

Belgian Decoration Militaire

Corp. C. H. Closh

Chevalier Crown of Roumania

Capt. C. G. Cavaliar, C.F.

Mentioned in Despatches

Capt. L. F. Baker
Pte. E. J. S. Banks
Lt. G. S. Bladon
Sgt. H. C. Booth
Capt. H. L. Cabuche
L/Corp. A. J. Ching
C.Q.M.S. G. H. Clayton

LIST OF HONOURS AND AWARDS

Capt. C. G. Dickens
Lt. W. N. N. Dunlop
Capt. J. B. Farrer
Pte. W. Forth
Major C. J. Fox
Sgt. W. Geareye
Major R. P. Gladstone
Capt. S. M. Green
L/Corp. P. S. Harmer
Corp. C. W. Hoskin
Capt. C. N. C. Howard
Sgt. E. T. Jones
Lt. H. J. Kadwill
  (2 mentions)
Sgt. E. E. Lingley
Lt. R. M. MacGregor
2nd Lt. R. G. Malby
  (2 mentions)
Lt. E. Mooney
C.S.M. J. R. Moss
2nd Lt. H. B. Perry
Sgt. T. H. J. Raymond
Capt. A. Read (2 mentions)
Pte. A. R. Scott
L/Corp. C. Sexton
Lt. Col. H. J. Stafford
Pte. H. G. B. Stephens
Lt.-Col. E. F. Strange
Pte. R. J. Sullivan
Capt. G. Thompson
  (Connaught Rangers,
  attached)
Lt.-Col. H. L. Webb
Capt. D. H. Whitelaw
  (2 mentions)
R.Q.M.S. F. A. Winfield
2nd Lt. C. M. Wright
  (attached)

INDEX

Abbeville, 17, 82, 83, 237
Abbots Langley, 13, 15, 211, 213, 217, 218
Abeele, 53, 126
Abergavenny, 8
Abu Dis, 331, 332
Abu Ghalyun, 277
Achicourt, 109, 110, 123, 157
Ain Arik, 358, 359
Ain el Yezek, 367
Ain Karim, 308, 309, 313, 314, 316, 317, 318, 320, 321, 351
Aisne front, 108
Aisne, River, 21, 163, 165
Albert, King of the Belgians, 190
Aleppo, 370
Alexandria, 260, 374, 376
Allenby, General, 260, 264, 265, 266, 268, 276, 287, 299, 301, 302, 306, 321, 322, 327, 331, 338, 341, 347, 350, 356, 360, 367, 373, 374
" Allenby's Flying Squad," 331
Amatovo, 250
Ambrines, 64
Amiens, 54, 152, 163, 167
Amman, 338, 339, 343, 344, 345, 346, 350, 354, 356
Anata, 322
Ancre, 226
Anebta, 368, 369
Angle Wood Valley, 92, 93
Angre, 193, 196, 198
Angreau, 193, 196
Antwerp, 204
Anwaz, 336
Anzac Mounted Division, 277, 291, 302, 306
Arleux, 143, 186
Armentières, 158
Armistice, the, 188, 200, 201, 276
Army Council, 9
Arneke, 53
Arques, 129
Arras, 51, 65, 107, 116, 117, 118, 120, 122, 123, 124, 129, 142, 143, 146, 152, 153, 157, 158, 164, 165, 166, 179, 180, 181, 187, 188, 189, 191, 200

Arras front, 108, 112
Artists' Rifles, 14, 57, 59, 221
Aubencheul, 185, 186
Aubers, 192
Aubers Ridge, 31, 43, 44, 50, 180, 217
Aubigny, 231
Aubigny au Bac, 186, 200
Aunelle, River, 191, 193, 196
Australian Light Horse, 286, 342, 345, 369
Australian Mounted Division, 368, 369
Australians, the, 179
Austria sues for peace, 190
Autreppe, 199

Babes in the Wood, pantomime, 202
Bac St. Maur, 40, 42, 44
Bailleul, 53
Bailleul (Oppy Sector), 143
Bailleul aux Cornailles, 164
Baker, Lieut., 314, 316, 322 ; Capt., 333, 361, 362
Balah, 267
Ballincolig, 222
Balua, 363
Balua Lake, 362, 363, 367
Bamber, Lieut., wounded, 40
Bank Copse, 171
" Bantam " Battalion, 68
Barnes, Lieut., 57
Barnett, Capt. H. W., 16, 47
" Barnstormers " Concert Party, 271
Bastion Hill, 252
Bayencourt, 66, 73, 82, 117
Beaulencourt, 100
Beaumetz, 142
Beaumont Hamel, 107
Beaurains, 108, 109, 110, 112, 115, 157, 168
Beersheba, 265, 266, 273, 275, 276, 280, 282, 283, 284, 286, 287, 288, 289, 290, 293, 297, 301, 304, 306, 329, 350, 358
Beggs, 2nd Lieut. G. A., 57, 76; Capt. 200

INDEX

Beirut, 370, 377
Beit Hannina, 321
Beit Jibrin, 302
Beitun, 361
Berneville, 121, 166, 168
Bethany, 330, 336, 358
Bethlehem, 319
Bien Fienvillers, 63
Billericay, 218
Billon Farm, 90, 96
Bir Asur, 368
Bir el Esani, 275, 276
Bireh, 327, 361
Bisdee, Lieut.-Col. T. E., M.C., 348, 377
Black Watch, 7th, 142
Blairville, 169, 171
Blairville cemetery, 172
Blendecques, 17, 21
Bochtagh Mountains, 222
Boesghem, 19
Boiry Becquerelle, 168, 169
Bois de Beaufort, 197, 199
Bois de Biez, 36, 38
Bois de Quesnoy, 185
Bois des Bœufs, 158, 160, 164
Bouleaux Wood, 85, 90, 91, 93, 94
Boulogne, 17
Bourlon Wood, 135
Bow Bells Concert Party, 121, 145, 181, 187
Boyau des Abris, 228, 231
Boyelles, 167, 168, 169, 170, 171, 179, 180
Bray, 228, 230, 231, 235
Brigade of Guards, H.M., 4
British Expeditionary Force, 17, 21, 68, 124
Brockhurst, Capt. C. E., 233, 257, 272, 293, 309, 337 ; Brigade Major, 348, 371
Brownjohn, Sergt. F., awarded M.M., 161
Brunemont, 186
Bulfin, Major-Gen., 259, 265
Bulkeley Camp, 377
Bullecourt, 167, 173, 175, 176, 177, 179
Bullock's Ridge, 330

Caestre, 53
Cabuche, Capt. H. L., 16, 21
Cairo, 261, 262, 271
Calais, 17, 53, 204
Caldbeck, Lieut., 223
Calf, Sergt., 150

Calix, S.S., 204
Cambrai, 120, 157, 179, 186
Cambrai, battle of, 134
Cameron, 2nd Lieut. G. B., wounded, 178
Campbell, Major H., 16, 22, 24, 29, 40, 92, 110
Canadian Mounted Rifles, 153, 181
Canadian Scottish, 236
Canadians, the, 110, 120, 143, 152, 157, 182, 186, 191, 194, 197, 237
Canal du Nord, 179, 180, 181
Canal Reserve Camp, 126
Candas, 63
Cape Town, 5
Capps, Lieut., 359
Cattermole, Lieut., 247
Cavalry Farm, 118, 119
Cavaye, Major-Gen., 9
Cease Fire order, 199
Cellar Farm, 50
Champagne, 108, 124
Chance, Lieut., 7
Château de la Haie, 164, 165
Château Wood, 127
Chemins des Dames, 107, 118
Chetwode, Lieut.-Gen. Sir Philip, Bt., K.C.M.G., C.B., D.S.O., 264, 265
Church of Holy Sepulchre, 320
Cidemli, 252, 256
Citadel, the, 120
Citadel Camp, 83, 84, 95, 96
Citerne, 60, 62, 63
City Imperial Volunteers, 5
Civil Service Rifles, 13, 79, 277, 281, 290, 294, 298, 299, 300, 310, 325, 326, 344, 353, 360
Clarendon Park, 217
Clark, Lieut., 223
Clarke, Capt., 104 ; killed, 112
Coachford, 222
Cohen, Lieut., 37, 57 ; Capt., 64, 86
Cojeul, 180
Collier, Capt., 321, 322 ; Major, 346, 359, 363
Combles, 88, 91, 93, 94, 179
Condonnerie Farm, 46
Connaught, H.R.H. the Duke of, 341
Connaught Rangers, 29
Constantine, King of Greece, 241, 248
Constantinople, 360, 370
Convent of the Sacré Cœur, 43
Corbie, 83
Cork City, 222
Cornwall Camp, 129

INDEX

County of London Territorial Force Association, 7
Courcelette, 93
Croisilles, 152, 172, 173, 180
Croix Barbée, 40, 104
Croix Blanche, 50
Crouch, 2nd Lieut. A. E., 138
Crow Hill, 256
Crucifix Hardicourt, 92
Cruikshank, Private (London Scottish), gains the V.C., 352
Cuesmes, 204
Cuthbert, Col. G. J., C.B., 8

Dache, 253, 256
Dainville, 65, 66, 123, 142, 159
Damascus, fall of, 190; 350, 356, 370
Daours, 83
Davies, Major-Gen., 21, 51
Davison, Sir William, K.B.E., 12, 205
Dead Sea, 331, 335, 336, 338, 341
Deir el Belah, 263, 266, 267, 269
Deir Sineid, 304
Deir Yesin, 316, 318
Delangre Farm, 46, 47, 49
Delville Wood, 130
Demicourt, 135
Demobilisation, 204
Derby Scheme, 82
Desert Mounted Column, 265
Desert Mounted Corps, 266, 276, 286, 291, 299, 303, 307, 350, 354, 355
Desert Mounted Troops, 265
Devil's Jump, 103
Devis, Capt. David, 218, 235
Diah, 304
Dickens, Capt. C. C., 16, 29, 57; Major 73, 77, 78, 90
Doignes, 136
Doiran, 248, 252
Domart, 63
Douai, 190
Douchy, 191
Doullens, 63, 64, 107
Douve, River, 52
Drew, Sergt. L., 160, 161
Drocourt, 180
Dublin, 222
Dudular Camp, 240
Duisans, 157
Dunkerque, 204

East Lancs, 42, 48
Ebblinghem, 53
Edwards, Brig.-Gen., 238, 242, 275, 294, 332

Ecoivres, 157
Ecourt St. Quentin, 181
Ecurie, 142
Egypt, 261, 262, 263, 264, 265
Egyptian Expeditionary Force, 262, 264, 362, 376
Egyptian Labour Corps, 269
El Aisawiyeh, 330
El Arish, 263, 266, 268
El Aziriyeh, 336
El Ferdan, 267
El Fuhais, 346
El Gamli, 270, 275
El Ghoraniyeh, 337, 339, 341, 347, 351, 356
El Girheir, 276
El Haud, 341, 342, 350, 351, 353, 354, 355
El Howeij, 344
El Jib, 306
El Jurah, 310, 313
El Madowerah, 333
El Muntar, 331, 333
El Shauth, 270
Elkington, Brig.-Gen., 200
Ellenga, H.M.T., 377
Emery, Drummer, awarded D.C.M., 30
Emir Feisal, 338
Emperor Napoleon III, 1
Endymion, H.M.S., 243
Er Ram, 327, 336
Erquennes, 199
Es Salt, 339, 342, 343, 344, 345, 346, 347, 350, 354, 355, 356
Es Sir, 345, 346
Estaires, 19, 21, 30, 52, 101
Estreux, 191, 192
Etaples, 53
Eterpigny, 179

Falfemont Farm, 84, 85, 86, 94
Famars, 191
Farrar, Lieut., 112
Farrer, 2nd Lieut., 136
Fauquissart, 102
Ferguson, Lieut.-Gen. Sir Chas., 235
Ferme du Moulin, 192
Ferme du Moulin Ridge, 191, 192, 193
Field, Lieut. E. V., wounded, 29
Fifth Army, 123, 152
First Army, 200
First casualties, 24
First War Christmas, fraternising with enemy troops, 27
Fishguard, 223

INDEX

Flers, 91, 93
Flesquières, 135
Fleurbaix, 42
Flower, Major V. A., D.S.O., 126, 127
Foch, Marshal, 163, 165, 167
Fontaine Croisilles, 173, 180
Fonquevillers, 79, 80
Forêt de Mormal, 190
Formation and Training, 209–224
Foster, Capt. C. T., 272, 315, 321, 322, 330, 376, 377
Fota Park, 222
Fourth Turkish Army, 265, 356, 357
Fremicourt, 130, 134, 135, 142, 179
Fremicourt Camp, 131
French, General Sir John, 27, 42, 51, 223
Fressies, 186
Fromelles, 44, 78, 101
Furnes, 52

Garside, 2nd Lieut. F., 194
Gates, Lieut., killed, 40
Gates, Lieut. L. C., awarded M.C., 287; 296
Gavrelle, 143
Gaza, 264, 266, 268, 276, 286, 299, 304, 307; first battle of, 264
Geudecourt, 93
Ghoraniyeh Bridge, 337, 338
Gilead, 350
Ginchy, 88, 89, 90, 91
Givry, 203
Gladstone, Capt. R. P., 235; Major, 237, 247, 361
Glencorse Wood, 125, 128
Goddard, Capt. F. J., 172
Godewaersvelde, 53
Godfrey, Sergt. W. H., awarded Military Medal, 285; Lieut., 378
Goldies Hill, 256, 257
Gommecourt, 67, 78, 101, 107, 118
Gommecourt Park, 70, 76
Gommecourt Salient, 70, 76, 79
Gommecourt Wood, 66, 67, 70
Gonnelieu, 134
Good Samaritan's Inn, 347
Gordons, the, 228
Gouves, 122
Gouy, 118
Gouy en Artois, 108
Gouy en Ternois, 168
Gouzeaucourt, 140
Grandcourt, 107

Grand Rullecourt, 64, 164
Grande Honnelle, River, 196
Green, Capt. S. M., 272, 279, 293, 352, 361, 376
Gropi Cup, 166
Guards' Camp at Purfleet, 204
Guards' Division, 91, 93, 171
Guèmappe, 115, 118, 120
Guillemont, 85, 88

Haig, Sir Douglas, 68, 93, 100, 124, 136, 237
Hajlah, 339, 341
Haldane, Viscount, 7
Hallencourt, 63
Halloy, 70, 81, 82
Harmignies, 199
Harp, the, 118
Harris, Capt., 57, 64, 77, 78; Major, 127
Hazebrouck, 53
Headquarters moved to Swallow Street, Piccadilly, 3
Heath, Lieut., 57
Heath, Capt. F. W., 133, 151, 161
Hebron, 306
Hebuterne, 66, 68, 70, 78, 80, 81, 117
Hebuterne Mill, 67
Hemsley, Capt. C. M., 186, 187
Hendecourt, 171
Herlies, 31
Hermies, 134
Hermon, Mount, 337
Herne, Capt. A. C., 16
Hertford, 217
Higgins, Capt. J. E. L., 16, 40, 57, 123; Major, 127
Highland Light Infantry (Territorials), 9th, 59
Hill 1070, 281
Hindenburg Line, 107, 112, 117, 131, 134, 135, 136, 137, 138, 140, 141, 173, 175, 180
Holland House, 12, 211, 212
Holland, Lieut., 57, 63
Honourable Artillery Company, 221, 354
Honours and Awards. *See* pp. 425–29
Hooge Château, 128
Hopkins, Col. A. J., V.D., 4, 10
Hopkins, Major P. A., 233; invalided home, 236
Houlle, 123, 126, 129
Howard, Lieut. C. N. C., 42

INDEX

Hudeib, 333
Huj, 301, 304
Hull, Capt. B., 377
Hull, General, 63, 168
Humphries, Brig.-Gen. E. T., D.S.O., 332
Huntriss, Capt. H. E., 42
Hyde Park, 3

Imperial Camel Corps, 288, 338
Imperial Yeomanry, 5
Indian Corps, 31, 36
Inns, Capt. N. J., 137
Inverness Copse, 125
Irish Division, 89
Ismailia, 261, 262, 267
Ivergny, 108

Jaffa, 302, 303, 304, 306, 310, 322, 371, 372
Jalkilieh, 370
James, 2nd Lieut. A. D., awarded M.C., 161
Janis, 258
Jebel Ekteif, 330, 333, 334, 335
Jebel Kuruntul, 336
Jericho, 307, 330, 331, 335, 344, 347, 350
Jerusalem, 148, 303, 304, 305, 306, 307, 308, 309, 310, 313, 316, 317, 318, 321, 322, 323, 324, 326, 327, 328, 329, 330, 331, 332, 335, 336, 347, 349, 357
Joffre, General, 27
Johnson, Major F. S. B., 191
Jones, Lance-Corporal, awarded Military Medal, 35
Jordan, 333, 341, 346, 350, 354
Jordan, River, 331, 337, 338, 342, 356, 357
Jordan Valley, 336, 346, 354
Judea, Hills of, 305, 336
Jurah Hill, 310, 314

Kalinova, 251
Kantara, 263, 265, 267, 360, 372, 373, 374
Karasuli, 250
Karm, 266, 276
Katerina, 243, 245, 246, 247, 248, 249, 259
Kauwukah, 276, 288, 290, 291, 293, 300
Keen, Lieut., 57
Kefr Huda, 345

Kensington Cemetery in the Rue Bacquerot, 52
Kensington Territorials, 9
Kensington Wadi, 279
Kensingtons win Brigade Football Cup, 104
Kh Adaseh, 325, 327
Khan el Ahmar, 333
Khan Yunis, 266
Killingbek, Lieut., 234
Kimber, Capt. E. G., 16, 21; awarded D.S.O., 50
King Edward VII, colours presented by, 9
King, His Majesty the, 9, 26, 223
King, Lieut.-Col. J. C. R., 101, 123
King's Langley, 15
King's Royal Rifles, 60th, 3
Kipling, Rudyard, 18
Kisch, Capt. E. R., 235, 272, 313, 314, 315, 316, 352, 371
Kolokuri, 245, 247, 248
Kulundia, 328
Kulunsawah, 368
Kuryet el Enab, 305

La Bassée, 21, 158
La Fere, 152
La Fosse, 104, 107
La Francas Mill, 32
La Gorgue, 32, 40
La Marguerite, 225
Lagnicourt, 130, 131
Latron, 305
Lattre St. Quentin, 164, 168
Laventee, 22, 25, 30, 42, 101, 102, 104
Lawrence, Col. T. E., 307, 338, 354, 356
Le Bucquière, 136
Le Grand Pacaut, 104
Le Havre, 15, 225
Le Sart, 51
Leatherhead, 216
Leggett, Lieut., 57
Lens, 143, 180
Lesser, Capt., 210, 211
Les Bœufs, 130, 179
Les Bœufs, Morval, 91, 92
Lester, 2nd Lieut. A. E., 149; Lieut., 160, 161
Lestrem, 32, 33
Le Transloy, 96, 97, 100, 129
Leuze Wood, 85, 86, 88, 91, 93, 94, 130
Lewin, Lieut., 57
Lewis, Mrs. A. C., O.B.E., 13

435

INDEX

Lewis, Brig.-Gen. F. G., C.B., C.M.G., T.D., 5, 10, 11, 16, 37, 39, 53, 56, 126
Lewis, Col. Somers, C.B., V.D., 4, 10
Liencourt, 123, 168
Light Armoured Car Brigade, 338
Lignereuil, 64, 66, 123
Lille, 43, 180, 190
Lincolns, 34, 35
Lissack, 2nd Lieut. M. S., wounded, 280
Loch, Brig.-Gen., 66, 147, 157
London Division, 95
London Infantry Brigade, 4th, 11
London Irish, 328
London Regt., 1st, 42
London Rifle Brigade, 53, 56, 153, 156, 173, 185, 187
London Scottish, 13, 14, 73, 74, 76, 77, 78, 86, 90, 94, 97, 112, 114, 115, 116, 119, 132, 136, 137, 138, 139, 140, 141, 156, 158, 169, 173, 175, 176, 177, 185, 193, 194, 196, 197, 198, 201, 218, 243, 246, 248, 249, 251, 253, 277, 281, 282, 283, 290, 298, 299, 300, 310, 313, 314, 320, 327, 337, 338, 342, 351, 352
London Scottish Regimental Gazette, 251
London Volunteer Corps, 2
Londons, 4th, 112, 116, 140, 152, 158, 177
Longpré, 63, 100, 237
Louise, H.R.H. Princess, 8, 9, 12, 14, 15, 146, 205, 341
Louverval Wood, 136, 140
Lowry-Cole, Brig.-Gen. A., C.B., 41, 48
Ludd, 371, 372
Lukis, Lieut., dies of wounds, 40
Lumley-Webb, Major H., 211
Lys, 45, 199
Lys Valley, 66

Mackenzie, Lieut.-Col. C. M., D.S.O., O.B.E., 221, 277, 290, 293, 297, 309, 314, 315, 316, 325, 326, 334, 335, 348
MacLean, Capt., 7; Major, 210, 211; Lieut.-Col., 214, 215, 217, 218, 219, 220
McQueen, 2nd Lieut., 308
Macroom, 222
Mager, 2nd Lieut., killed, 79
Magnicourt sur Canche, 64

Magpie's Nest, 132, 138
Maidstone, 215, 216
Maison Blanche, 228, 231
Malhah, 316
Malta, 238, 239
Maltz Horn Farm, 94, 95
Mandesi Ford, 337, 338
Manitou, 260
Mansell Camp, 99
Marble Arch, 13
Maricourt, 84
Maricourt Wood, 132
Marne, the, 163
Marne, River, 165
Marœil, 146, 235
Marquion, 182, 187, 188
Marseilles, 238
Martinpuich, 93
Mason, 2nd Lieut., 57
Matheran, S.S., 15
Maubeuge, 190, 199
Mavroneri, River, 245, 247, 249
Mersina, 377
Merville, 100, 104, 107
Messudieh, 369
Micmac Camp, 126
Middle Copse, 93
Middlesex, 2nd, 39, 152
Middlesex, 7th, 128
Middlesex, 8th, 66, 78
Middlesex Artillery, 3rd, 1
Middlesex Cavalry, 1, 3
Middlesex Regt., 10th Batt., 7
Middlesex V.R.C. (South), 2nd, 1, 3, 7
Middlesex V.R.C., 4th, 1, 2, 3, 7
Milford Haven, 222
Military Police, 101
Mill Copse, 184
Mill Street, Co. Cork, 222
Millancourt, 82, 83
Milne, Lieut.-Gen. G. F., 250
Minominee, 260
Minster Camp, 8
Moab, Mountains of, 307
Moascar Camp, 261, 267
Moat Park, 215
Mœuvres, 141, 182
Monchy, 115, 160, 164, 181
Mons, 199, 200, 204; battlefield, 200
Mont St. Eloi, 157, 164, 226
Montignies, 199
Monts en Ternois, 123, 226
Moody, 2nd Lieut., 308
Morlancourt, 95
Morlière, 123

INDEX

Morrison, Lieut., 133, 134
Mortlock, 2nd Lieut., 112
Morval, Les Bœufs, 88, 93
Mosque of Omar, 320
Moulle, 123, 126
Muntaret el Beghl, 300

Nablus, 307, 324, 348, 357, 358, 362, 368, 369, 373
Naby Saleh, 361
Naresh, 258
Nazareth, 369
Nebi Musa, 335
Neby Samwil, 307, 308
Neuve Chapelle, 31, 38, 39, 42, 44, 101, 104, 105, 172, 192
Neuve Chapelle cemetery, 36
Neuve Chapelle (British) cemetery, 52
Neuville Mill, 112, 114
Neuville St. Vaast, 226, 227
Neuville Vitasse, 108, 109, 110, 112, 115, 157, 158, 168, 192
Newhaven, 204
Neyland, 221
Nielson, Capt. D. F. C., R.A.M.C., 248
Nivelle, General, 107, 118
Nord Canal, 182
Northumberland Fusiliers, 116, 130
Noyelles sur Seine, 191

Oborn, Sergt., killed, 104
Ogilby, Lieut.-Col., 310, 314, 315
Oisy le Verger, 185
Old Comrades' Association. See pp. 401–405
Olives, Mount of, 319, 322, 329, 330, 331, 336
Olympus, Mount, 243, 248
Oppy, 142, 143, 190, 192
Oppy Wood, 144
Ordnance Corps, 57
Osborn, 2nd Lieut., killed, 194
Ostend, 190
Ouderdom, 126, 129
Ouse Alley, 142

Palestine, 247, 261, 263, 264, 268, 276
Palleul, 185
Parnell, Capt. E. L., 7, 16, 21
Parton, Lieut., 57
Pas, 66
Passchendaele Ridge, 125, 158
Patialas (Indian troops), 355

Pelikas, 249
Pemberton, 2nd Lieut. Leigh, killed, 29
Pembroke Dock, 221
Penn, Lieut., 57, 64, 73
Perry, 2nd Lieut. H.B., 136 ; Capt., 197
Petit Houvin, 123
Petit Vimy, 143
Petra Pass, 243
Phillips, 2nd-Lieut. A. E., wounded, 178
Phillips, Lieut. E. W., 237, 272
Picantin, 24, 27, 43
Pike, 2nd Lieut., 73
Pilgrim's Road, 333, 334, 335
Pinney, General, 49
"Pip" Ridge, 252, 253, 254, 255
Ploegsteert, 52
Plouvain, 179
Poincaré, President, 26
Polygon Wood, 128
Pont Remy, 59, 60
Post-War history. See pp. 379–400
Preseau, 191
Pre-War commanding officers, list of, 10
Prince, Arthur, ventriloquist, 239
Prince of Wales, 26
Princess Mary Gift Box, 27
Prismall, Capt. A., 16, 21, 34, 37, 39, 40
Prismall, Lieut. M. A., 37 ; Major, 162, 172, 200, 204
Prueville, 237

Quadrilateral, the, 71, 72, 89, 92
Queant, 180
Queen Victoria Rifles, 90, 138, 148
Queen's Westminsters, 13, 14, 72, 96, 122, 140, 155, 173, 184, 191, 194, 230, 234, 253, 256, 277, 290, 294, 299, 310, 324, 329, 342, 344, 345, 352, 360
Queenstown Harbour, 222
Quevy le Grand, 203

Racquinghem, 51
Rafa, 266
Ram Allah, 327, 328, 358
Ramleh, 363, 365
Ranelagh, Lord, 1, 3, 10
Rangers, 53, 56, 61, 65, 71, 73, 76, 89, 90, 98, 104, 108, 112, 136, 138, 148

INDEX

Ras el Ain, 370
Ras el Tawil, 310, 324, 336
Ras Hablein, 277
Rashid Bek, 273
Rawlinson, General Sir Henry, 21, 32, 51
Read, Lieut. W., 231; awarded M.C., 233
Red Line, 153, 156, 157
Rheims, 165
Rhine, the, 201
Rhonelle, River, 191
Rhône Valley, 238
Ribemont, 54
Ridley, Lieut. A., 57; Capt., 142
Rieu de Bury, 199, 201
Rifle Brigade, 32, 34, 36
Rimmington, Capt., 323
Riquet, 237
Rishon le Zion, 363
Roberts, Field-Marshal Lord, 18
Robertson, Lieut.-Col. J. Forbes, V.C., D.S.O., V.C., M.C., 185
Robertson, Lieut., 57; Capt., 66
Capt. Robertson (London Scottish), 326
Rochester, 215
Roclincourt, 148, 149, 150
Roclincourt Camp, 146, 147
Roisin, 196
Roll of Honour. *See* pp. 407-423
Rombies, 194, 196
Ronville Caves, 159
"Roosters" Concert Party, 271
Roseveare, Lieut., 57
Roseveare, Capt. F., 172
Rosslare, 223
Rouge Bancs, 48
Rouge Croix, 33
Roumancourt, 181, 184, 185, 187
Royal Air Force, 262, 273
Royal Berkshires, 32, 34, 48
Royal College of Heralds, 9
Royal Engineers, 34, 44, 65, 94, 133, 182, 190, 193, 227, 234, 275, 286, 302
Royal Irish Fusiliers, 7th, 84, 85
Royal Irish Rifles, 27, 32, 34, 48, 99
Royal Naval Division, 51, 198
Royal Navy, 8, 276
Royal Scots Fusiliers, 116, 178
Royal Warwicks, 99
Royal Welch Fusiliers, 256
Rue Tilleloy, 22
Rushdi, 288
Russian débâcle, 148

Sach, 2nd Lieut., killed, 79
Saffron Walden, 217, 218, 219
Sailly au Bois, 66, 70, 71, 78, 81
St. Amand, 168, 169
St. Aubin, 165
St. Laurent Blangy, 181
St. Omer, 16, 17, 18, 51, 52, 53, 55, 57, 58, 59, 123, 129
St. Quentin, 107, 179
St. Requier, 82, 83
St. Rohart Factory, 181
St. Sauveur, 159
St. Sauveur Caves, 158, 159
Salisbury Plain, 11, 210, 219, 221, 294, 348
Salonika, 237, 239, 240, 249, 256, 265
Sambre, River, 191
Sarigol, 258
Sarimaule, 258
Sars le Bruyère, 200
Sauchy Cauchy, 182, 184, 185
Saultain, 191, 192, 193
Savage, Lieut., 352
Sawbridgeworth, 219, 220
Scarpe Valley, 164
Scheldt Canal, 135
Scheldt, River, 191
Schramm Barracks, 116, 120, 189
Scots Guards, 8
Scottish Rifles, 47
Sebourg, 193
Sebourquiaux, 193, 194, 196, 198, 199
Sensee Canal, 180, 182, 185, 186, 190; River, 180; Valley, 175
Serre, 71
Sewell, Lieut., killed, 47
Shafat, 318, 320, 348, 349, 358
Shaw, Lieut. R. E. F., 37, 64, 81; Capt., 101, 127; Lieut.-Col., 133, 136, 145, 146, 147, 162; killed, 171
Shea, Major-Gen. J. S. M., 265, 272, 285, 300, 312, 317, 319, 321, 330, 338, 363, 376
"Shea's Group," 342, 347
Shellal, 266, 269, 272
Shepherd, Lance-Corporal, awarded D.C.M., 30
Sheria, 303
Shunet Nimrin, 347, 350, 354
Shute, Lieut. R. P., 352; Capt., 361
Sicilian, S.S., 204
Sidi Bishr, 375
Sidi Gaber, 374
Simencourt, 118, 121, 142
Sinai Desert, 262, 263, 264, 267

INDEX

Singil Ridge, 361
Skinner, Drum-Major, 70
Smith, Lieut. E. J., M.C., 315, 348; Capt., 363, 377
Smith, 2nd Lieut. W. E., 149, 161; killed, 178
Snowdon, H.M.S., 221
Soba, 306, 307, 310, 312, 319
Somme, 78, 81, 95, 99, 101, 107, 115, 121, 130, 163, 165, 168, 199, 226, 236
Somme battlefield, 84, 101, 152
Somme, battle of, 72, 238
Somme, River, 83
Sorel, 100
Souastre, 66, 71, 72, 73, 80, 121, 168
Souchez, 227
Souchez, River, 153
South Africans, 120
South African War, 4
South London Volunteer Brigade, 4
Southampton, 15
Spectacle Hill, 351
Spencer, Capt., 248
Stafford, Major H. J., T.D., 16, 22, 47, 53, 56; Lieut.-Col., 65, 71
Stafford, Major, promoted Lieut.-Col. and assumes command, 56
Steenbecque, 53
Steenvoorde, 126
Steenwerck, 53
Stewart Camp, 147
Stockwell, 2nd Lieut. F. R., 231, 233
Strand Wadi, 279
Strazeele, 53
Suez Canal, 262, 263, 265, 267, 373
Surafend, 363
Surcamps, 63
Sutherland, 2nd Lieut., killed, 318
Sutton Veney, 220
Symes, Major A. G., 133
Symons, 2nd Lieut., 160

Tadpole Copse, 136, 140, 141
Taggart, Capt. E. O., 37, 73; wounded, 79
Talat Ed Dumm, 347, 349, 350
Tatenghem, 52
Tel el Fara, 269
Tel el Ful, 324, 325, 326
Tel el Nejileh, 302
Tel el Saba, 284, 286
Tel el Sheria, 288, 297
Tel es Suwan, 336
Telegraph Hill, 108, 112, 115, 157
Temptation, Mount of, 336

Territorial Army, 11, 12, 18, 53, 210
Territorial Force formed by Viscount Haldane, 7
Thelus, 228, 235
Thiennes, 51
Third Army, 80, 264
Third Battle of Ypres, 120–30
Thompson, G., Capt. and Adj., killed, 29
Thompson, Lieut., 7; Capt. G., 212; Major, 215, 237
Thompson, Capt. G. V., 279, 316, 327, 352, 361, 371
Thompson, Col. (afterwards Labour's first Air Minister), 332
Tiberias, Lake, 369
Tilbury, 204
Tilloy, 108, 115, 118, 120, 160, 166
Tilloy Wood, 164
Times, The, 40
Tinques, 146
Topsin, 250
Tosland, Capt. A. W., 272, 295, 296
Tournehem, 123
Tower, the, 12, 215
Towy Post, 155
Train, Corpl. (London Scottish), wins the V.C., 316
Transylvania, H.M.T., 238, 239, 254
Tripoli, 377
Truro, Lord, 1, 3, 10
Tul Keram, 367, 368
Tumulus Hill, 310, 314, 315, 316
Turkish attack on Jerusalem, 323
Turkish débâcle, 367
Turks ask for Armistice, 372
Turmus Aya, 361

Uchantur, 258, 259
Umm Suffah, 359, 361

Valenciennes, 191, 200, 201
Valetta, 239
Vardar, 248; Valley, 252
Vauchelles, 237
Vaux en Amienois, 99, 100
Venables, Lieut., 57; Capt., 127
Venizelos, M., 241, 245
Verdun, 68, 69
Victoria, Queen, 3
Vieille Chapelle, 104, 106
Vieux Berquin, 19
Ville, sur Ancre, 99
Villers Bretonneux, 163
Villers Cagnicourt, 187

439

INDEX

Villers sire Nicole, 201
Vimy Ridge, 43, 110, 142, 143, 157, 180, 227
Vincent, Lieut., 57
Vis en Artois, 160, 180, 181
Volunteers from Wimbledon to Bisley, The, 2
Vromeri, 243

Wadi Auwaz, 333
Wadi Arseniyet, 342, 343, 355
Wadi Auja, 306, 322, 370
Wadi el Ghuzze, 266, 269
Wadi es Surar, 310, 313
Wadi Halgon, 279, 281, 285
Wadi Jemmameh, 302
Wadi Khalasa, 277
Wadi Marazah, 336
Wadi Muleihah, 302
Wadi, Nabr el Falik, 368
Wadi, Nimrin, 341, 351
Wadi Nueiamah, 339
Wadi Poplar, 280, 281, 285
Wadi Saba, 284
Wadi Scottish, 281
Wadi Shaib, 356
Wadi Shanag, 272
Wadi Sheria, 298
Wadi Sidr, 334, 335, 336
Wadi Suwaz, 333
Wadi Welfare, 289
Wadi Zeimar, 368
Wakefield Camp, 145
Waller, 2nd Lieut. J. T. B., 353
Wancourt, 108, 114, 115, 123; Tower, 115, 116

Wanel, 100
Wardreques, 51
Ware, 217
Ware, Capt., 57, 73, 76, 77; killed, 79
Warminster, 219, 220, 223, 294
Warriors' (War Memorial) Chapel, 378
Watford, 13, 15, 217
Watten, 129
Wedge Wood, 89, 94
Welch Regt., 6th, 53
West London Rifles, 3, 4, 5, 6, 7
West Riding Regt., 107
Westerham, 217
Westhoek Ridge, 125, 128
White City, 211, 212, 213, 214
Whitty, Capt., 47, 57
Wilde, 2nd Lieut. C. A. G., 175
Wilderness of Sin, 336
Willerval, 143
Williams, Lieut., 57
Wills, Corpl. R. O., awarded Military Medal, 233,
Wills, Capt., 2/15th London Regt., 315
Wilson, 2nd Lieut., 172
Wittes, 51
Wright, 2nd Lieut. C. M., 295
Wright, 2nd Lieut. J. H., wounded, 194

Yasur, 371
Yeomanry Mounted Division, 277
Y.M.C.A., 57, 58, 188
Yorkshires, 7th, 82
Young, Lieut.-Col. W. H., 71, 101
Ypres, 21, 43, 45, 124, 126, 158

www.ingramcontent.com/pod-product-compliance
Lightning Source LLC
Chambersburg PA
CBHW021825220426
43663CB00005B/131